ADVANCED
Project Portfolio Management
and the
PMO
Multiplying ROI at Warp Speed

Gerald I. Kendall, PMP
Steven C. Rollins, PMP

International Institute
for Learning

Copyright ©2003 by J. Ross Publishing, Inc.

ISBN 1-932159-02-9

Printed and bound in the U.S.A. Printed on acid-free paper.
10 9 8 7

Library of Congress Cataloging-in-Publication Data

Kendall, Gerald I.
    Advanced project portfolio management and the PMO : multiplying ROI at warp speed
/ Gerald I. Kendall & Steven C. Rollins.
        p. cm.
    ISBN 1-932159-02-9
    1. Project management. 2. Strategic planning. I. Rollins, Steven C., 1950- II. Title.
HD69.P75 K458 2003
658.4'04--dc21
2002156311

Phone: (561) 869-3900
Fax: (561) 892-0700
Web: www.jrosspub.com

TABLE OF CONTENTS

E-LEARNING MODULE FOR
ADVANCED PROJECT PORTFOLIO MANAGEMENT AND THE PMO

This best-selling title in the PMO space has been transformed into a dynamic e-learning module with multiple learning styles and formats. The online course covers the vital ingredients that make strategic planning, project management and a Project Management Office (PMO) work well together. It examines the PMO and strategic planning in depth, including what is missing from current approaches. The authors show why the current Project Management model must change drastically from focusing on cost and efficiency to focusing on project flow and throughput.

People learn differently, and to date technology-based training has been very static. Powered by iDL Systems, this online course uses a dynamic, state-of-the-art adaptive learning system that analyzes in which style the student learns most effectively and offers the content in that style. The course is designed using highly effective flexible cognitive approaches that create a rich learning environment where you can progress at your own pace. Visit us online at www.jrosspub.com for more information.

Key Features:
- Each registrant who completes the course receives certification as a Project Management Office Professional (PMOP)
- PMPs earn 15 PDUs upon course completion
- Over 400 web pages of instruction with audio and document download
- Course provides a dynamic learning environment by automatically remediating itself based on questions missed on exams

FOREWORD

During the past 10 years, project management has grown from a part-time effort to a profession. Companies that once considered project management as "nice to have" now consider it mandatory and a necessity for the long-term survival of the firm. Today, project management is regarded as a strategic competency for the organization and, as such, can significantly improve the organization's future competitiveness.

Accompanying any strategic initiative or strategic competency is a vast amount of information that is eventually generated and must be absorbed, retained, sorted, restructured, and evaluated such that maximum use of the information is possible. Project management generates enormous quantities of information that can affect not only daily operations of the organization, but the company's future direction as well. This intellectual property must be effectively managed. Therefore, there is the need for the existence of a Project Management Office (PMO).

The physical existence of a PMO is not new. However, using the PMO as a direct input to the strategic planning process of the organization is new. Until now, literature on the effective use of a PMO has been minimal. Published papers covered only small aspects of a PMO, and textbooks on the use of a PMO, for all practical purposes, were non-existent or simply scratched the surface on critical topics.

Today, the marketplace finally has a textbook, *Advanced Project Portfolio Management and the PMO*, by Gerald Kendall and Steven C. Rollins, which is not only the most comprehensive textbook ever published on the subject, but should certainly become the standard for PMO development for years to come. If your organization has a need for developing a PMO, this book should be required reading for all executives.

Being a strong advocate of effective strategic planning, I have found the strength of the textbook to be Part III. This section successfully links the PMO to strategic project selection, prioritization, portfolio management and, ultimately, strategic planning. The abundance of critical information in Part III and throughout the textbook allows the readers to develop their own company-sensitive templates for project selection and portfolio management.

Throughout the text, Kendall and Rollins provide real-world examples of how to make a PMO work effectively. It is always better to learn from the success and failure of others than to learn from your own mistakes. With the importance of the PMO expected to increase significantly over the next decade, this textbook should be in the personal library of all project managers.

Harold Kerzner, Ph.D.
Professor of Business Administration
Baldwin-Wallace College

PREFACE

After decades of improvement initiatives, the majority of project managers still fail to meet their goals. Executives are being fired in record numbers. This book traces the connection between these two facts and provides a mountain of surprising insights. The latest attempt to solve these problems, a center of project management intelligence and coordination called the Project Management Office (PMO), is correct but ill-fated. Without some fundamental change in its focus and approach, the PMO will become another passing fad.

In hindsight, the mistakes that organizations and PMOs make seem obvious. Executives can deliver on their promises if, and only if, they can cause their organization to successfully and swiftly execute the right projects. Activate too many projects, and the system fails miserably. Execute some, but not all, of the right projects, and the results are insufficient to meet the goals. Execute projects sanctioned independently by functional executives, and project managers compete with each other over resources, without clear overall priorities. Some of these projects are "pet projects" of functional areas, without a direct link to overall organization goals.

Project managers try to solve these problems in isolation from the executives whom they support. They focus on methodology, tactical data, and tools without having a breakthrough impact on project cycle time, project flow, and strategic value of projects. Our research shows that over 90% of current PMOs are not connected with their senior management team and have no metrics that matter to senior executives.

Many executives have invested money in project management, but they have not addressed the root problems. Long-standing executive practices are at the root of many project management problems. But without working together, project managers and executives will continue to square off against each other, fighting over project schedules and resources. So time and money are wasted, and executives and project managers alike are very frustrated.

This book provides the insights into why these problems exist. It identifies the root problems and provides a solution for executives, project managers, and the PMO. Complemented by case studies of organizations such as the American Institute of Certified Public Accountants, Babcock and Wilcox, Arlington County, Quintiles, TESSCO, and others, this book describes the missing, vital link between executive strategy and project management.

This book tells executives what they must know to execute flawlessly, using portfolio management as a strategic weapon. Executives must understand the details, at least through Parts I and II of this text, to make project management work in their organization.

To succeed and survive, a PMO must provide meaningful value to the senior management team. This value comes from information (the executive cockpit), recommendations, increasing project management flow, and accelerating durations. If these benefits are not obviously tied to the PMO efforts, we make this recommendation — start putting your resume together. However, before you do so, read this book. It details how to turn your PMO into a value machine. In this book, you will find the metrics, the road map, the processes, and the data to transform your PMO into the executive's and the project manager's best friend.

For project managers and project teams, this book should initiate an important dialogue in your organization. If a handful of project managers or team members begin to question, in a non-threatening way, some of the things that do not make sense, this can become like a snowball rolling down a mountain. Meaningful debate and dialogue can be an important precursor to improving the practice and results of project management in your organization.

In a few hours of reading and learning from the authors' combined 60+ years of experience, you will save years of pain and failure. Learn and succeed.

Gerald I. Kendall
Steven C. Rollins

Free value-added materials available from the Download Resource Center at www.jrosspub.com.

At J. Ross Publishing we are committed to providing today's professional with practical, hands-on tools that enhance the learning experience and give readers an opportunity to apply what they have learned. That is why we offer free ancillary materials available for download on this book and all participating Web Added Value™ publications. These online resources may include interactive versions of material that appear in the book or supplemental templates, worksheets, models, plans, case studies, proposals, spreadsheets and assessment tools, among other things. Whenever you see the WAV™ symbol in any of our publications, it means bonus materials accompany the book and are available from the Web Added Value Download Resource Center at www.jrosspub.com.

Downloads available for *Advanced Project Portfolio Management and the PMO* consist of templates, models, assessment tools and plans, including a detailed plan using Microsoft Project to implement a PMO that covers the first two years of operation and details over 450 tasks.

ACKNOWLEDGMENTS

This book received the help of some outstanding people who care deeply about project management. I am very grateful to Dr. Harold Kerzner, who volunteered a great deal of his personal time to review the manuscript. I had approached Dr. Kerzner when Steve and I began writing the book. At the time, we had not met face to face. Yet he unselfishly mentored me with ideas that have helped to shape the book's format and content. These contributions were more than I ever expected. Yet he did more. After reading the entire manuscript, Dr. Kerzner wrote the foreword to this text, which makes me humbly proud of the effort.

We would not have as rich a text without the voluntary efforts of the case study contributors. To Barney Barnhill and his team at Tessco, thank you for the most comprehensive team response to our questionnaire. Over two dozen leaders at Tessco provided extensive input regarding their journey over the past two years using the 4×4 strategic planning and project management processes. This case study required incredible coordination, which Wendy Sauvlet provided tirelessly. Denise Hart, the Program Management Officer at Arlington County, VA, contributed an outstanding case study on the PMO efforts in this county government. Paul Olinski from Babcock & Wilcox in Cambridge, Ontario provided input on their strategic planning and project management efforts that resulted from using the 4×4 process. Richard B. Lanza, from the American Institute of Certified Public Accountants, shared a very interesting case study about their use of PMO concepts to help many national and regional projects in a challenging environment of 60 teams and 2000 volunteers. Steve Unwin and Douglas Call from Quintiles Transnational responded to our numerous e-mails, providing another view of how a PMO can drive value to a large worldwide organization with many virtual teams. Tina Meier from Oklahoma State University provided great insight into how to transform an organization where everything is a priority into an organization with true priorities. To Marion Segree, EPMO Manager at the City of Kansas City, I owe special thanks. After a week's absence from work, she did the impossible and revised their case study within a day, answering all my questions and making it a compelling read.

I thank Jack Duggal, a PMO expert from Projectize Group, who graciously shared his insights and provided several diagrams for this text. Table 19.1, distinguishing traditional PMOs from the next generation, was adapted from the paper "Building the Next Generation PMO," that Jack presented at the PMI® Symposium in Nashville, TN in November, 2001. These themes are highlighted in the popular seminar series "Building the Next Generation PMO" and the focus of an upcoming book. I also thank Alfonso Bucero from Spain, who provided feedback and great knowledge about his implementation of a PMO at HP.

We gratefully acknowledge the permission we received from the Forrester Group to reproduce a very helpful chart positioning vendors in the enterprise project management tool market.

To my wife and partner, Jackie, for the past 9 years in our Theory of Constraints efforts, thanks for your suggestions, for reviewing the manuscript, and making the presentation of ideas much clearer. I also appreciate the ongoing hours of dialog with our editor, Drew Gierman, and the professional efforts of the J. Ross Publishing staff in putting this work together. It has been a real pleasure to work with Drew over the past 7 years. He keeps things simple.

To my teacher and mentor over the past 9 years, Dr. Eli Goldratt, I can only give a heartfelt thank you. Over the years, he has helped me understand why common sense is not obvious to people. His insights in project management are just beginning to have a global impact. Eli, I hope this book helps to spread the knowledge and returns something of what you so generously gave to me and to the world.

My final acknowledgment is to my co-author, Steve, without whom this book would not have been possible. I know that the only way to describe his effort is "a labor of love." Nothing else could compel someone to make such a sacrifice, to bring our knowledge to print. Steve, you have my deep appreciation, from the bottom of my heart.

Gerald I. Kendall
Navarre, Florida

ACKNOWLEDGMENTS

The creation of this book completes a personal, life-long ambition to document the knowledge gained over my career in helping PMOs bring value to business while I was helping project managers, team members, and others become more successful in project management.

This book was written in record time by most standards. The initial draft of more than 300+ pages was completed in 5+ months. The toughest part of writing this book was not the development of new material but rather how to limit what was written in the planned space. Many times I would write well into an evening only to realize I had written 40 to 60 pages when I should be writing 10 to 15 pages. Passion will get a person into trouble.

Little did I realize that my chance meeting of Gerry Kendall at the 2001 PMI® Symposium in Nashville, TN would actually lead to this personally fulfilling accomplishment. To this, I say "Thank You, Gerry." You have been a wonderful mentor, project manager, and partner in developing this book for PMOs everywhere. Gerry, I am eternally grateful for your involvement in this effort and your guidance throughout the process! You have been wonderful to work with!

Many books on project management exist in the business market today. Very little is written on PMO development, implementation, or maintenance as well as portfolio management — basic, advanced, or otherwise. A book of this nature is long overdue. After all, where do PMOs go today to validate they are on the right path to helping their business grow? Most PMO approaches have been aimed at better tools, better templates. Nowhere are PMOs taught to show people how to better work together for the benefit of reduced project delivery costs and time. The insight to help PMOs apply behavior models to motivate project delivery was learned in the team training I received from the Total Quality Management (TQM) teachings of the late Dr. Edwards Deming and from Florida Power and Light while I was an employee and as a TQM Facilitator at Sprint Corporation in the late 1980s. Additionally, I later added the knowledge learned from applying the Theory of Constraints (TOC) axioms to this mix. To all of this, I am grateful to Dr. Edwards Deming and Dr. Eli Goldratt for the development of their concepts so that others, like me, can leverage these principles into our PMO contributions to business. Without TQM and TOC, this book would not have been written.

I also wish to thank all of those individuals who have contributed case studies about their PMO success stories operating within their business. These folks are truly pioneers and should be recognized for it.

My final acknowledgment is for the Project Management Institute (PMI®). PMI® represents the largest body of project management professionals globally who have come together in association to seek ongoing improvement in project management. My hope is that PMI® will take action to grow PMO conceptual support in helping benefit project managers and team members everywhere become more successful.

After all, if you are like most project managers or team members whose projects fail every year (74% of IT projects fail each year and the number is growing as reported by Standish Group) in their attempt to deliver the objectives, people will tire of the consistent failure and move toward more stable and less career-threatening occupations. We must be better at project delivery for the profession to flourish. Project delivery success rates must significantly improve for business to realize the value of project management. We have miles to go and better methods, better management, and better information are needed to accelerate the pace.

Steve Rollins
Lees Summit, Missouri

THE AUTHORS

 **Gerald I. Kendall,** PMP, is a noted management consultant, strategic planner, public speaker, and project management expert who has been serving clients in Canada, the U.S., and overseas since 1968. His background includes extensive experience as a systems engineering, sales, marketing, and operations executive with an international focus. Recent clients include Babcock & Wilcox, Alcan Aluminum, Tessco Distributors, Brown and Williamson, Agere Systems, Lockheed Martin, and Travelocity.com.

Gerald is certified in the field of Theory of Constraints, and is a graduate and silver medal winner of McGill University. He is a member of PMI. Gerald is the author of *Securing the Future: Strategies for Exponential Growth Using the Theory of Constraints.* He is also the author of a chapter on Critical Chain Project Management in Dr. Harold Kerzner's text, *Project Management, A Systems Approach,* 8th ed. He has had dozens of articles published in magazines and is a frequent speaker at conferences and chapter meetings. He is also the co-author of three recent white papers: "Integrating Critical Chain and the PMBOK®," "Choosing the Right Project Mix," and "How to Get Value from a PMO." Gerald can be reached via e-mail at Gerryikendall@cs.com.

Steven C. Rollins, MBA, PMP, is co-founder of PMOUSA Network. Steve is a well-known national subject matter expert in Enterprise Program/Project Management Office/Project Office startups and improvements. Steve has recently led the deployment of www.PMOUSA.com which was recently launched as a free information source to PMOs in the United States. Steve's background includes extensive experience in financial services, healthcare, human resources, information technology, insurance, and telecommunications. Steve has been a featured speaker at many project management community events, speaking to the "Value Proposition of Project Managers" at PMI chapters and businesses across the United States. Recent clients include American Century Financial Services, Fortis Benefits Insurance Company, Honeywell, HR Block, International Institute for Learning, Jasmine Networks, Kaiser Permanente, Oklahoma State University, Principal Financial Group, Sprint, State of Kansas, and Westell Technologies. Steve is the Knowledge Chair for the PMI Metrics Specific Interest Group and was responsible for leading the framework development and rollout of the first ever comprehensive project management metrics Knowledge Center in 2002 (www.MetSIG.org). Additionally, Steve is the Executive Chair for the Mid America PMO Regional Group that operates as a chapter of the PMI PMO SIG (www.PMI-PMOSIG.org). The Mid America PMO Regional Group has grown from its initial beginning in September 2001 to more than 650 members today and provides information and networking support to PMOs and project management professionals in seven states (Nebraska, Iowa, Kansas, Missouri, Oklahoma, Arkansas, and Texas) plus additional membership around the world. Steve is also co-author of the recent white paper "How to Get Value from PMOs," and the author of white papers "How to Market your PMO" and "Growing the Business, the Value Proposition of Project Managers." Steve can be reached via e-mail at Steve@PMOUSA.com.

INTERNATIONAL INSTITUTE FOR LEARNING, INC.

International Institute for Learning, Inc. is an internationally recognized leader in the field of corporate learning. IIL offers state-of-the-art training and consulting services in Project Management, Theory of Constraints, and Six Sigma to some of the biggest and best-managed companies worldwide. IIL courses and proven solutions have helped make numerous Fortune 500, private companies and government agencies better, more competitive, and more profitable.

IIL's world-class faculty has the real-world experience and expertise to teach you how to progress rapidly and achieve new heights. IIL offers traditional classroom training, web-based "self-paced" training, distance learning via satellite broadcasts, live virtual instructor-led courses, hands-on leadership simulation, CD-ROM programming, and online mentoring. IIL's "virtual" classroom courses are available nearly 24/7 to accommodate the busy professional's needs, budget, and schedule.

IIL is the leading provider of training products and consulting services in project management. IIL's project management curriculum provides a systematic, process-oriented approach that covers every aspect of project management. All of IIL's 40-plus courses are guaranteed to be consistent with the Project Management Institute's PMBOK® Guide, and they are recognized for their proven results.

IIL is committed to helping clients achieve continuous improvement in quality, profitability, and productivity, the hallmarks of business leaders in today's global marketplace. For more information on IIL programs and services or for a copy of their latest course catalog, visit www.iil.com or call 1-800-325-1533 or 212-758-0177.

PART I:
SETTING THE STAGE
FOR A SUCCESSFUL
PMO IMPLEMENTATION

INTRODUCTION — BUILDING A PMO THAT EXECUTIVES EMBRACE

INTRODUCTION

In its ideal form, the Project Management Office (PMO) should represent, for an organization, what air traffic controllers represent to pilots. It should guide projects safely (minimizing the risk) and as quickly as possible to their destination. It should prevent mid-air collisions between projects and resources. It should be the project manager's and the executive's best friend.

In our view, the PMO must do even more. It must drive much higher return on the investment that any organization makes in projects. In this sense, it becomes a value machine. To do so, the PMO must be the arm of senior management. It must help the executives meet their strategic goals by providing them with a single point of knowledge for project management intellectual property, among other things. The PMO must help executives execute.

To date, most of the PMO directors with whom we have spoken describe a very different model of their PMO. In a meeting with over 100 PMO directors in Kansas City in 2002, over 90% told us that they have no direct involvement with or expectations from their executives. They also told us to stop preaching to the converted. They know they need executive involvement and support. This book is intended to help.

Most executives would not agree that a PMO is even necessary, unless they fully understand the problems that project and program managers face today. So that is where this book begins.

3

There are many detailed questions you might have about a PMO. For example, what are the different options for organization structures? Is there a road map that we can follow to successfully implement a PMO? What portfolios of information must a PMO maintain, and what data are included in each portfolio? How do you measure a PMO? What software products are available to support a PMO and how do they compare?

We have included chapters to answer all of these questions and many more. Before exploring the details of the PMO and portfolio management solution, we would like to come to an agreement on what the current problems are in project management common practices. Then the formal definition of the PMO charter, its mission, and deliverables will become much more meaningful.

CURRENT PRACTICES IN PROJECT MANAGEMENT

Some of the practices we see in project management are nothing less than bizarre. By analogy, it is like doctors scheduling surgery in a hospital, regardless of whether or not the operating room is available. Imagine having 10 doctors show up on the same morning, all with prepped patients. No one person "owns" the operating room schedule. The operating room support staff report to different supervisors.

The supervisor decides that she doesn't want to have any surgeon be mad at her, so she instructs the operating room staff to multitask in order to assist all surgeons in the operating room. All surgeons will have access to the precious resource, the operating room table, and the one anesthesiologist and the one surgical assistant, but only for 15 minutes at a time.

Surgeon #1 begins surgery, but must relinquish the table to Surgeon #2 after 15 minutes. Surgeon #2 must relinquish to Surgeon #3 after 15 minutes, etc. Surgeon #1, who could perform his surgery in 1 hour dedicated time, is now stuck for 10 to 15 hours, trying to keep the patient stable. Each time a surgeon is given the precious resource, the operating room table, he struggles to remember how far along he had gotten in his last 15-minute slot, several hours earlier. Fifty percent of the 15-minute time slot is wasted just in getting restarted.

If this already sounds ridiculous, good! We are just scratching the surface of how projects are actually managed in organizations today.

The surgeons cannot afford to waste their time. They are a precious resource. So, in between their 15-minute time slots, they rush out of the operating room to do other important tasks. Sometimes, they become so preoccupied with another task, they do not even make it back to the operating room in time and miss their surgical slot completely. The surgery takes even longer. The surgeons also waste half their time going to and from the operating room, switching tasks.

Senior management of the hospital comes under pressure. They paid a lot of money to build the hospital. The operating rooms are the most precious resource of the hospital. The flow of patients through the hospital, and through the operating rooms, determines how much money will flow through the hospital. And the flow of patients is dreadfully short of what is needed to keep the hospital afloat.

The hospital is being squeezed by insurance companies, HMOs, etc. who are all demanding to pay less money for the same procedure. Senior management cannot hire more surgeons and cannot build more operating rooms.

Reports to senior management make everything seem wonderful, when, in fact, the financial situation is getting worse and worse. The hospital sets up a Surgery Management Office (SMO), to gather information and help patient flow. The first thing the SMO does is demand that everyone fills out detailed time sheets to help ensure full utilization of all resources. Various reports claim that the operating rooms and the surgeons are almost 100% utilized. Yet the revenue flow is decreasing. How can this be? While it is true that the operating rooms are heavily utilized on paper, the truth is that half of the utilization is bad multitasking, moving patients on and off the operating room tables. *This activity generates no revenue.* The SMO reports are not helpful in pointing out this flaw.

To increase revenues, senior management instructs the surgeons to initiate more surgeries per month. Their false belief is that if they initiate more surgeries, they will complete more surgeries. Another false belief is that if all resources are busy doing important work, then the organization's goals will be met.

Faithfully, the surgeons obey and the following month the picture is worse. Fewer surgeries are completed. Rework is increasing. Scrap (a bad word in a hospital) is increasing. The surgeons are complaining constantly that they are having fights with each other over the allocation of the operating room.

Senior management listens but would really like their staff to solve these problems themselves. Aren't they adults? Can't they get along with each other? Why do we, senior management, have to constantly be the referees?

The pressure increases and the executives declare that cost is too high. Procedures are taking too long. Surgeons are allocating too much time to each procedure. Supporting resource time is too high. Much of the focus is on cost and cost reduction. Schedules and budgets are cut across the board.

The following month, the executives are extremely unhappy, but are having great frustration in deciding what action to take. The surgeons *did* drive down the average cost and time per procedure. There was an average 1.5% cost reduction and a 3% time reduction per procedure. Yet the total operating expenses of the hospital did not change one penny. No surgeons or staff quit or were fired. The depreciation expenses of the hospital did not change. The revenues of the hospital did not get any better. In fact, they decreased.

The surgeons used the distortions of cost accounting to make the reports look favorable. Even though the time allocated by surgeons on their time sheets to the actual surgery was decreased, the hospital is still paying them the same salary. So the hospital expenses did not change.

The hospital is now in a crisis. Senior management decides they must take control of the details. They jump in and refocus the SMO to help prioritize surgical schedules, so that the most lucrative surgeries have access to the precious resource — the operating room table — for a full two hours at a time. Finally, some surgical procedures are flowing nicely to completion. The cash flow crunch is over. Senior management breathes a sigh of relief and moves on to "more important tasks." Within a few weeks, the situation has deteriorated again, and senior management must intervene.

The refocusing of the SMO helped to alleviate the symptoms of the problem, but did not get rid of the disease, the root problem. Without executive support and new SMO procedures, the surgeons' behavior reverts back to scheduling surgeries, regardless of the capacity of the system to handle it.

THE CURRENT PARADIGM

We claim that in most organizations, projects are managed this way. New projects are initiated by functional executives, irrespective of the resources available to perform the projects. Senior executives do this because they feel they have no choice. Their project is vital to their success, and, in some cases, to their survival. The project must be initiated. What better time is there to initiate it than right now?

Projects are initiated without collaboration and coordination between functional executives. Where an organization, realistically, has the shared resources to focus on a few initiatives and get them accomplished quickly, we find most organizations focused on dozens of initiatives.

Resources are multitasked between projects in order to please all functional executives. Resource managers also feel that they have no choice. Who are *they* to tell someone several levels more senior to them that they simply do not have the resources available? The resource managers feel obligated to show progress to executives and customers on all projects.

There is far more time spent on reviewing project budgets and focusing on cost aspects of projects than there is on decreasing the cycle time of a project. We claim that this is incorrect. A project is created to bring benefit to an organization. The benefit may come from increasing or creating new revenues (new products or services), by decreasing some existing operating expenses, or by decreasing or improving return on some investment. No matter which of these is true, the benefit is not realized at all until some major milestone of the project or the entire project is complete. The faster the project is completed, the sooner the company realizes the benefit. In many cases, if the project takes too long to implement, there are no benefits (e.g., new product introduction). The competition has already taken the market.

In many projects we have examined, using resources *inefficiently* to complete the project earlier would have delivered more benefit than a focus on efficiency or project budget would deliver. This is particularly true where the revenue or investment benefits that the project brings to the organization are more significant than the project budget.

Project managers and executives are frequently in conflict over deadlines and resources. Project managers and resource managers are frequently in conflict over resources (which ones to allocate to which projects, how many, when they can start a task). Project managers are also frequently fighting with other project managers over resources. *In a matrix organization, with these types of conflicts, it is easy for managers to make resource allocations that are different than the ones the CEO would make.*

No wonder executives are so frustrated with how long it takes to implement a new strategy. No wonder executives are frequently intervening and playing referee, much to their frustration. No wonder project managers are frustrated with executives.

THE PROJECT MANAGEMENT OFFICE INITIATIVE

In our combined 60+ years of experience, we see the current explosion of PMOs as a very significant event, considering project management history of the past 35 years. CIOs, executives, and project and program managers are all looking for better results and a way out of their current problems. Finally, many more organizations are recognizing the need for a more centralized approach.

Briefly, a PMO is a centralized organization dedicated to improving the practice and results of project management. Some PMO initiatives are minimal, involving part-time staff to help out on projects as needed. Other initiatives involve huge infrastructure, with rigid centralized planning, control and methodology.

Are the executives ecstatic about this development? *No!* In fact, our clients and our survey results indicate that there is huge resistance to implementing a PMO and difficulty in maintaining it once it is implemented. Further, many PMOs are not driving breakthroughs (15%+ improvement) in project management results. If they are driving any improvement, it is 1 or 2% on paper. Many PMOs are not even measuring their effect in a way that is meaningful to senior executives.

Most executives we know are very wary about any suggestion that involves an increase in corporate overhead. Executives have ample experience showing that the cost side of any proposition always comes true, while the benefits often do not. At a time when operating "lean" is part of every executive's strategy to keep costs under control, the idea of implementing a PMO is not easy to sell.

We are also witness to many PMOs that initially attract executives with the words "more control." Executives believe that many projects are out of control — in terms of time, budget, scope or all of the above. They are correct, but often attribute these symptoms to the wrong root problem. They believe that there is not enough pressure or centralized control over projects. So when an advocate for a PMO comes to senior management and offers "strict control," the executives' ears perk up.

Unfortunately, all too often "strict control" translates to unacceptable bureaucracy, longer project duration times, resistance and fighting among project managers who believe their independence and creativity are diminished. We believe strongly that the correct answer does not lie in "strict control."

Executives tell us that they are tired of suggestions based on overused buzzwords — improved productivity, better customer satisfaction, improved skills and even improved "quality." Executives need more profits, more stakeholder value, better cash flow, easier ability to get funding, and greater competitiveness. Even if these words are part of a PMO proposal, executives need more. They must see the road map — how the PMO will deliver on these promises.

CHARACTERISTICS OF A PMO
THAT EXECUTIVES WILL EMBRACE

Simply put, executives will perceive value if the PMO helps the executives meet the goals on which they are measured. In order to build a PMO that executives will fully embrace, we claim that it must have the following characteristics:

■   It must drive *more* projects through completion, without correspondingly increasing resources (e.g., 50% more projects).

■ Most projects must be completed in drastically shorter times (e.g., 25% reduction in average cycle times).

■ The impact of the PMO must be clearly felt on both the top and bottom lines of the organization (even in not-for-profit organizations).

■ Executives and managers throughout the organization must feel that they are getting benefit out of the PMO (i.e., they must see what is in it for them).

We are describing results (i.e., 25 to 50% improvement) that imply a significant breakthrough in the practice of project management throughout the organization. To achieve such a breakthrough in results, the ideas presented in this book must make you skeptical or excited or, at least, uncomfortable. Otherwise, they are probably not breakthrough ideas. At the same time, the ideas must not defy common sense. Many radical ideas do not result in improvement for the organization.

Our approach to achieving such a breakthrough is a holistic approach. By *holistic approach*, we mean that we look at the entire collection of an organization's projects (the project mix) and how it is linked to achieving the goals of the entire organization, not just one functional area. *A PMO must be able to help executives with execution of strategy, as determined by the project mix and flow, or the PMO will not achieve sufficient level of value to sustain itself.*

The holistic approach raises the question, "Should all project managers report to the PMO?" Our answer is, not necessarily. To work effectively, there needs to be a strong matrix relationship between the PMO and all project managers. We have seen many examples of effective PMOs without the direct reporting relationship. Results are generally better, longer lasting and happen more quickly when project managers buy in to the goals and efforts of the PMO, rather than being forced into it.

To achieve an organization's goals, the organization must have the *correct* project mix. This means that the projects must balance the needs of the market (the market side) with the need for sufficient internal capability of the organization to supply the market (the supply side). Most organizations we work with have an imbalance — a leaning toward the supply side and weak or insufficient projects addressing the market side.

In Part II of this book, we examine how to choose the right project mix through a new form of strategic planning. This series of chapters suggests how projects should be selected, which projects are selected and how many projects are activated at one time.

Part III describes the PMO in detail. For example, this series of chapters describes how the PMO and the project managers throughout the organization can accelerate projects, how the senior management team can stay involved in project management and how to get all managers working together. It provides PMO metrics, organization structures, roles and responsibilities, the governance model, detailed descriptions of the various portfolios (projects, resources, goals and assets) and their interrelationships.

Part IV provides some advice and the road map to sell the PMO to executives, to implement a PMO and sustain its value. Appendix A provides a PMO maturity model to assess the capability of any PMO and suggest a developmental model to improve the results, no matter where the PMO is starting from.

MARKETING PROJECTS — AN IMBALANCED PORTFOLIO SIGNALS EXECUTIVE TROUBLE

Most organizations have two sides to their business model reflected in their organization chart. This includes a supply side and a market side. Even not-for-profit organizations have a market side — the provision of sufficient services to generate ongoing funding for their organization. Part of the market side in a not-for-profit organization may be the solicitation and justification for funding.

The supply side is defined as that part of the organization responsible for *support and delivery* of the products and services it sells. Typically this includes Information Technology, Research and Development, Engineering and Manufacturing, and Finance and Distribution.

The market side is defined as that part of the organization responsible for sales and marketing. Dr. Eli Goldratt* describes the roles of sales and marketing as follows: Marketing responsibility is bringing the ducks to want the corn in your field, and to sit in your field, preferably with glue on their feet. Sales responsibility is to shoot the sitting ducks. Anyone who thinks it is easy to shoot a sitting duck has never been a salesperson.

Companies that are supply-side driven are more concerned about scarce supply-side resources than customer demand. This is a huge mistake, often costing the company dearly when customer needs change quickly. The focus on the supply side means that many resources are tied up in too many projects that do not represent the biggest leverage for meeting the organization's goals, as determined by the executives.

We often witness project management improvement efforts that are guided solely by supply-side experts. These efforts often fall short of pro-

---

*Dr. Eli Goldratt is the founder of a methodology called "Theory of Constraints," which is used by the authors to meet PMO goals. Dr. Goldratt is the author of several books on the subject, including *Critical Chain* and *The Goal*.

viding exponential delivery gains against strategic objectives. Simply stated, supply-side organizations have a bias toward efficiencies, a focus on cost and are often blind to innovative marketing opportunities.

Companies that are market-side driven are concerned about making good on promised delivery of products/services and capturing market share in changing market conditions within their industry. Marketing functions in many organizations are often driven to focus on the short term, at the expense of the long term. This is a huge mistake, often reflected by marketing departments that function in a sales support role, not in securing the future of their organization.

Many organizations allow their business model and the resulting project portfolio to be driven by the supply side of their company, due to difficulty in completing the work requested. As a result, business decisions on what projects to sanction and in what order, are often based and managed from the supply side (often Information Technology [IT]) instead of the market side.

Therefore, most organizations have a completely imbalanced portfolio of active projects — far too many supply-side projects and far too few market-side projects. Also, the market-side projects are often not strategic, but rather focused on short-term, tactical sales support.

Every organization, during its lifetime, encounters difficulty generating enough market demand to meet its goals, justify its overhead and grow its inherent value. The result is usually drastic cost-cutting measures and re-structuring. *In 2001, more than 1,000,000 people lost their jobs in the United States.*

When an organization faces insufficient market demand, the number of projects in the organization increases. All executives are pressured to find additional ways of meeting their goals. Therefore, the pressure on project managers and resources becomes greater. The result is predictable but not intuitive — *the more projects that are initiated with insufficient resources, the fewer projects are finished and the longer each project takes to complete.*

At this time, the need to deliver *more* goods and services is vital to the health of the enterprise. A key critical success factor is the collective delivery speed and success of project teams, and working on the right projects, especially the right market side projects.

EXECUTIVES MUST SEE THE
PMO EFFECT ON THE BOTTOM LINE

The value of any project management improvement effort can be measured by the ability to improve the bottom line. Therefore, any improvement effort must improve project delivery on both the supply side and the market side in a way that impacts the bottom line.

To be effective, the improvement effort must:

■ connect the goals of the organization to the identified strategies, and the strategies to the project portfolio

■ show whether or not the portfolio is properly balanced between supply-side and market-side projects

■ keep top management involved in the execution of the project portfolio

■ complete projects faster to meet market-side goals of speed to market and competitive advantage and to meet financial goals of reduced cost and better ROI

Therefore, in ensuring that the executive strategies are implemented quickly and that the organization has a healthy project portfolio, any improvement effort must be guided by individuals from a broad functional base. Marketing expertise must be represented in such initiatives.

If the PMO does not properly balance the portfolio of projects, who will? In organizations with such an imbalance, the PMO may do a wonderful job, but still be perceived as a failure because the organization did not address market constraints. The top and bottom line of the organization will fall short of the goals, even though the supply-side projects are successful.

TOO MANY PROJECTS —
ANOTHER ELEMENT OF INCORRECT PROJECT MIX

Most of the organizations that we review have far too many active projects. The number of active projects is completely out of line with the resources available. The result is like the operating room scenario we described above — terrible multitasking with project delays that hurt the organization's bottom line and speed to market.

In one division of Alcan Aluminum, for example, upon understanding the problems caused by too many active projects, the executive cut the number of active projects in half. By having fewer active projects, they were able to complete more projects per year. This is sometimes counter-intuitive. To complete more projects, you must decrease the amount of active projects. It is like watching logs floating down a stream, coming to a narrow spot. If there are too many logs, they will jam and sit in the same spot all day without assistance. However, if you put the logs through so that they are no wider than the narrowest spot, the flow is much faster.

A PMO THAT EXECUTIVES EMBRACED — A TRUE STORY

This real-life example illustrates how a project management improvement effort, motivated as a survival effort, can be done quickly and with huge impact.

Late one year, the Chief Technology Officer (Mike) of a large telecommunications firm paid a visit to one of his department heads (Bob). Mike told Bob that he was not happy with the value received by the company from the work provided by the 40 project managers in Bob's department. Unless Bob could prove the value of the department, Mike was planning to eliminate the department and all of its project managers.

Mike stated that he would be fair and that Bob would have the next fiscal year to prove the value of the department. Mike would measure the department-delivered hard-dollar value by a multiplier of the department's annual expense budget ($7 million). The multiplier Mike used was 3; thus, the target for Bob's department was $21 million of hard-dollar value in delivered work. If the target was not met, jobs would be eliminated.

You can imagine the panic everyone was in. No one in the department had ever been asked to do anything like this before. Many stories surfaced about other groups not surviving the cuts.

Bob pulled together a cross-functional team of project management experts and established a department project management office, the PMO. This group determined that while having this centralized team made everyone nervous, there were several options the PMO could address.

The first option was to take a close look at those assets for which the group provided project management support, such as feature upgrades of software in telecom equipment. The team reviewed vendor contracts on these assets to determine if there was any latitude in the payments to these vendors for the company benefit.

The second option was to review the estimation procedures and how the department won work internally with marketing customers. The effort in this area was to identify the active project portfolio and the fiscal year work plan to see if the team could reduce cycle times and deliver unplanned additional work in the same fiscal year.

The third option was to review the utilization of the department project managers and the quality of the projects on which they worked. Were the project managers working on the right projects in the order the customers needed? Could the team use existing staff that might be underutilized at the time to assist in those projects that were at critical delivery milestones?

The fourth option was to analyze delivery bottlenecks and opportunities to accelerate project delivery and avoid project delivery threats.

The group implemented elements of all four options. The results surpassed all expectations:

■ One of the project teams found a software shortcut that resulted in a $22 million savings for the year.

■ Another project team found old equipment in a company warehouse they could use when a new system became backordered. This adjustment saved 60 delivery days from the schedule and allowed the new system order to be cancelled, thus saving $15 million on the project while delivering significantly ahead of schedule.

■ Several project teams that needed additional manpower (they were waiting on approval for external resources) found staff in the department who could fill the need. This saved another $3 million for the fiscal year.

When it came time for Mike to visit the department again at the end of the fiscal year, the team had its act together. The department PMO had collected project evidence of the savings which demonstrated a hard dollar value of more than $75 million in benefit to the company. The team had beaten the goal of $21 million by more than $54 million. The Christmas bonuses were very good that year.

■ ■ ■

In retrospect, what was the net value of this PMO effort? The PMO value for the year was the excess over $21M that the team delivered to the company, less the PMO investment. The investment to capture this gain turned out to be $0.

The team simply changed its perspective, attitude, way of life, the way they communicated to each other and became more organized through a departmental PMO. They had to. The alternative (layoffs) was not an acceptable option.

SUMMARY —
FOUR ESSENTIAL ELEMENTS TO BUILD A PMO TO LAST

Executives will embrace a PMO that dramatically increases the probability of meeting their goals. Such a PMO will deliver on its promise through four major processes:

■ Choosing the right project mix — a new way of strategic planning

■ Linking the executive team's strategies to current and planned projects

- Managing the project portfolio correctly
- Measuring the PMO to tangibly improve project performance relative to the executives' strategic goals

Further, we claim that if any of these pieces are missing or insufficient, PMO advocates and project managers are put in the untenable position of trying to defend their efforts, budgets and demands for resources. Without all four pieces correctly implemented, the PMO will likely be short-lived.

The correct project mix must ensure a good balance between projects dealing with the supply side of an organization (the organization's internal capacity) and the market side (the marketing and sales areas). Too often, organizations ignore the market side, or focus on short-term sales support tactics. A good balance ensures that the organization rarely faces declining revenues or profits.

In this book, we explain the vital links that are missing between strategic planning processes, measurements, PMO implementations and other project management improvement efforts. We describe how an organization can eliminate, in a few weeks, the internal fights over resources and project priorities that have existed for years. Further, we provide a detailed description of the processes required to fix these problems permanently.

Parts I and II of this book are intended for senior executives and the CEO of every organization, to help you overcome delays and waste in meeting your goals. The entire book is also intended for project and resource managers and project office personnel, as a road map for a holistic approach to managing projects across your organization. Prove to executives how you will help them meet their goals more quickly and effectively, and you will earn their respect and, more importantly, their lasting support.

A COMMENT ON THE CASE STUDIES

One of our objectives in putting this book together was to give readers exposure to a variety of real-life PMO and portfolio management case studies. The case studies illustrate what actual PMOs are doing to bring important value to their executives and their organization. The case studies we gathered represent a variety of industries, as well as for-profit and not-for-profit organizations. We are extremely grateful to the contributors, who volunteered their personal time to make this knowledge and these insights available to our audience. We are also grateful to their organizations for releasing the information.

CASE STUDY — AMERICAN INSTITUTE OF CERTIFIED PUBLIC ACCOUNTANTS

WHO IS THE AICPA?

ISO 9001 Certified

The American Institute of Certified Public Accountants (AICPA) is the national, professional organization for all Certified Public Accountants (CPAs). Its members range from those in industry to those in public practice, government, and education. Its mission is to provide members with the resources, information, and leadership to enable them to provide valuable services in the highest professional manner to benefit the public, as well as employers and clients. More specifically, the AICPA:

■ establishes professional standards; assists members in continually improving their professional conduct, performance and expertise; and monitors such performance to enforce current standards and requirements

■ promotes public awareness and confidence in the integrity, objectivity, competence and professionalism of CPAs and monitors the needs and views of CPAs

■ serves as the national representative of CPAs before governments, regulatory bodies and other organizations in protecting and promoting members' interests

■ seeks the highest possible level of uniform certification and licensing standards and promotes and protects the CPA designation

■ encourages highly qualified individuals to become CPAs and supports the development of outstanding academic programs

WHAT PROJECTS DO THEY WORK ON?

Given the diverse nature of the AICPA, there are close to 60 teams in the organization. Further, there are close to 2000 volunteers who help support and provide guidance on behalf of the various member constituencies. For example, the Business and Industry Executive Committee provides guidance to AICPA activities related to members in industry such as controllers and financial managers. At any given time, there could be hundreds of activities, some being categorized as projects.

The projects generally can be segregated into the following categories:

■ computer systems development to improve the efficiency/effectiveness of operations

- communication initiatives to promote and strengthen the profession's image
- product development to provide members information and education
- standards development for financial statement auditing and other attestations
- services development for members to provide clients

WHY DID THEY ESTABLISH A PMO?

Given the highly fragmented and functional nature of the organization, many times it was difficult to coordinate, let alone be aware of, all the team activities. This led to individual teams identifying and desiring projects related to their segment of the membership but did not allow senior management to properly prioritize the collective Institute's initiatives. Senior management was left to the annual budget process, and associated quarterly update meetings, when each team would come to the table requesting project funds.

The AICPA also appreciated the benefits of project management practices as projects using them would, on average, be more successful. The issue was that they needed these practices spread across the *entire* organization to ensure the predictability of outcomes. Like many organizations, the AICPA project managers were more accidental than those trained in the industry standards.

HOW DID THEY INITIALLY ESTABLISH A PMO?

Given the need for more coordination and predictability of projects, the AICPA's Board of Directors suggested to management that a project office be developed to oversee and report on the activities of all projects. They suggested that such an office be placed close to the CEO's office to provide executive sponsorship.

Although on paper this appeared to be an appropriate strategy, it did not take into account that the AICPA was a complex beast. With over 60 teams and thousands of volunteers providing guidance, a culture shock would ensue if all activities needed to be managed with certain project principles and through one central reporting function. Therefore, it was decided to have the PMO initiate as a consultative rather than oversight body. The mission of the PMO was then set as: "Through consultative engagements with project teams, to sew best practices into the fabric of the AICPA, fostering increased success of the organization."

With a mission in hand, the PMO set out to develop a referential base of internal clients. Teams requesting project management assistance saw the benefits of such practices while also gaining successful closure to their projects. The PMO benefited through an improved reputation, more internal client requests, and, most importantly, an ability to gain access to the underbelly of key projects. Project status information that would never have been provided to an oversight body was now available while the PMO assisted teams. As the PMO became more consultative and operational in nature, it began reporting to the COO instead of the CEO.

HOW DID THE PMO EVOLVE?

With a stable base of internal clients and project teams beginning to utilize industry-standard project management principles, the PMO was in a position to expand its reach. In response, the PMO adopted a project life cycle along with associated training programs.

The project life cycle was sponsored mainly by the COO who, in conjunction with the CFO, provided funding to all projects. Therefore, in order to receive project funding, projects needed to follow the life cycle. Prior to the life cycle, project funding did not have a standard method of being applied. The life cycle defined a project, and the associated steps from inception the establishment of the maintenance programs. Unlike many processes that depend on standard forms, this one provided guidelines. The process was not overly cumbersome and just made plain business sense. Therefore, a business case (one of the process steps) for a project could arguably be written on the back of a napkin, assuming it was an excellent case.

Although teams appreciated the freedom the guidelines provided, most utilized the preferred forms as they increased their efficiency. This was especially true given the forms were provided in an easy-to-use guidebook available on the Institute's intranet. For example, if a project needed to hire a vendor, it was much easier to use a request for proposal and contract template than write one from scratch. The forms were viewed more as tools and, hence, gained more Institute acceptance.

By instituting the life cycle, teams were more willing to identify projects and request assistance from the PMO in following the life cycle. With this, the PMO had the foundation to create a project inventory, as well as track project status on a periodic basis. Again, instead of standard status reports being sent to the PMO, the PMO would periodically meet project teams, discuss project status, and adjust the inventory schedule appropriately.

Currently, the PMO tracks projects bi-weekly for schedule, cost, and risk management status in a simple Excel spreadsheet. The results are entered into a project inventory for analysis and prioritization by senior management. The PMO also provides regular training in the project life cycle and fulfills requests for project management assistance in the areas of:

- business case writing
- vendor selection and contracting
- software development life cycles/standards
- project risk management
- project planning

WHAT BENEFITS RESULTED FROM THE PMO?

In order to manage the performance of the PMO, performance measures were set for a one-year period. See Table 1.1 for specific metrics. All performance measures were met and, in some cases, exceeded. Specifically, the PMO provided "bottom line" savings in the following areas:

- Integrating and, therefore, eliminating duplicative software development projects among teams who had similar objectives

Table 1.1   Performance Measures for 1 Year of the AICPA PMO

Input	Process	Output
Over 50 people trained in project management	Number of days to apply funding to projects that have a business case to receive funding	Positive evaluations (4 out of 5) of the training materials/program though anonymous surveys
Over 20 people trained in project community	Number of projects where all necessary teams were coordinated with prior to the start of the project	Project savings of over $500,000 due to positive evaluations provided by the PMO
Projects planned to finish in 2002	Number of projects occurring outside of the process (this is expected to be kept to a minimum)	Positive impact (qualitative and quantitative) of lessons learned as captured as part of the project budgeting system
	AICPA's software life cycle followed on all technology projects	Positive evaluations (4 out of 5) of the PMO's services though anonymous surveys
		Reduction of a minimum of five projects or $1,000,000 that had no business case or through integrating projects

- Coordinating activities across more than 20 teams for a major AICPA initiative related to reducing fraud in the marketplace
- Improving the business case and planning of initiatives, which led to improved execution and impact for the membership
- Developing a best practice software development documentation standard and associated vendor contract to ensure computer system information assets are properly captured for later use
- Using a parametric tool across practically all software development projects to independently estimate the project's size and aid in the vendor negotiation process
- Capitalizing salary costs (thereby reducing current year expenses) associated with projects that, prior to the project inventory, were not able to be identified

WHERE IS THE PMO GOING FROM HERE?

After two years, the PMO and project management are starting to become an AICPA norm. The PMO is finding a place in independently coordinating activities across multiple teams, as well as assisting managing risk across the entire organization. However, one of the ulterior motives of the PMO when it was established was to disband the function over time. Returning to the mission statement, the PMO exists to "sew best practices into the fabric…". Therefore, as AICPA teams further integrate project management principles into their daily work, there will be less of a need for a PMO, but there will be more successful projects, better prioritization of projects, and an improved coordination of initiatives.

ABOUT THE CONTRIBUTOR OF THIS CASE STUDY — RICHARD B. LANZA, CPA

Rich Lanza currently heads up the PMO at AICPA. Rich has written numerous articles on audit technology for trade publications.

Rich received his undergraduate degree in public accounting from Pace University. He is a past president of the Northern Virginia Chapter of The Institute of Internal Auditors, and is a member of the IIA, AICPA, ISACA, and the AICPA's Information Technology Section.

The author's opinions expressed in this article are his own and do not necessarily represent the policies or positions of AICPA. Official positions by AICPA are determined through certain specific committee procedures, due process, and deliberation.

QUESTIONS

1.1   Discuss two of the major problems with the active project mix that exists in most organizations and how those problems might affect the executive goals.

1.2   What are the four processes that are essential for a strategic project management office to be successful?

1.3   What results or characteristics must the PMO achieve in order to have executives embrace its efforts?

1.4   What are two common project management practices that prevent an organization from meeting its goals?

1.5   What negative effects might an organization experience with a centralized organization such as a PMO exercising more control over projects?

1.6   What are the most compelling reasons for an executive to say "Yes" to a proposal to establish a PMO in his/her organization?

1.7   What are the most compelling reasons for an executive to say "No" to a proposal to establish a PMO in his/her organization?

1.8   What must a PMO do to take a "holistic" approach?

1.9   Why do the authors suggest that the focus on cost or budget, as a top priority, is incorrect? Where should the first focus be?

1.10   How closely related should the cost of a PMO be to its value to the organization?

2

THE RIGHT PEOPLE, THE RIGHT TOOLS, THE RIGHT DATA, THE WRONG RESULT — WHY PMO IMPLEMENTATIONS FAIL

RECOGNIZING THE NEED FOR A PMO

One key difference between successful and unsuccessful executives lies in their ability to execute.* Executives must deliver in two key areas — ongoing operational results and improvement efforts. The PMO is the vehicle to help executives deliver on their improvement effort goals.

Functional managers are continuously evaluated by senior management, their peers, and their subordinates, for their ability to make things happen quickly. "Goodness" is perceived if there is a measurable gain at least quarterly, if not weekly. Anything less implies that a problem exists. Therefore, every leader faces two key project management challenges:

---

*This topic is so vital that a book written on the subject became an overnight *Wall Street Journal* bestseller. See Larry Bossidy and Ram Charan, *Execution, The Discipline of Getting Things Done*, Random House Crown Business, New York, 2001.

- How many of our unit's vital projects can we complete this year?
- How fast can we complete them?

Many projects involve multiple departments and functional areas. Here, we see that management expectations and departmental processes which work well *within* each functional area often do not blend well *between* functional areas. There is often fierce competition for resources. We also frequently hear the complaint of constantly changing priorities, as one manager temporarily wins out over another.

Each organizational unit has its own language, its own standards, its own project management techniques or lack thereof. Often, one unit points fingers at another unit for poor requirements definition, rework and other problems that typically cause projects to be late, over budget and not within the scope envisioned by the end customer. No wonder so many central project management coordination units have sprung up in the last few years to try to resolve these problems. Today, we estimate that there are over 50,000 such organizations in the U.S. alone.

Typically, this coordination is placed with the organizational entity that has the greatest impact on risk management (delivery opportunity and threat) and project spending. Most of the time, we see this coordination fall within the Information Technology (IT) function. Most often we know these entities as Program Management Offices, Project Management Offices, Project Offices, Enterprise Project Offices, Enterprise Program Management Offices, etc. They may not call themselves a PMO, but if they fly like a duck, swim like a duck, and quack like a duck, they must certainly be a PMO.

CONFLICTS BETWEEN PROJECTS

In order to meet its goals, every organization launches multiple projects during a fiscal year. Some projects may have dedicated resources, resources that work on only one project at a time. However, more commonly we see some resource types, such as IT, used across many projects. Moreover, they are often assigned multiple projects at the same time.

Consider, for example, Company A, a large financial services firm with more than 15,000 work force members spread across one dozen business units. In the 2002 fiscal year, there are 15 projects vital to the enterprise. These 15 projects involve multiple business units. All projects must be completed in the fiscal year, in order for each business unit and the overall organization to meet its goals. Each business unit is expected to contribute work force to the effort. Each business unit participating within these "enterprise" projects has limited staff. As a result, resources must work on multiple projects during the fiscal year.

Assume that a central "Project Management Office" does *not* exist for any of the business units or the enterprise. What is the possibility that all of these projects will deliver on time or ahead of schedule?

We claim that the likelihood of finishing most projects on time, on budget and within scope is extremely unlikely. In fact, the Standish Group confirms that only 26% of the projects they surveyed were successful. For IT projects, the figure is only 16%. Why?

Project development work requires process and communication. If you have worked on a project team, you know that often the only constant is change. These changes include changes in requirements, resource availability, and the detailed schedule. These changes can place the best organized project team in dire jeopardy, leaving the team to work in high stress situations that raise the delivery risk even higher.

When change is frequent within a project team, the ability to communicate change rapidly to team members, management and other business units can mean the difference between project delivery success and failure. However, communication is just one of several major challenges.

Change brings about unplanned activity. Therefore, an excellent project plan quickly falls apart when project managers are forced to compete with other project managers over critical resources for which they did not predict a requirement.

Assume you are one of the enterprise project managers responsible for one of the 15 major projects necessary to meet the company goals. Your project involves significant participation from three business units. You feel lucky because your project team has been staffed with some of the very best resources available in the company. Your biggest challenge is that this staff is also working on other concurrent projects.

One month into the project, you find that the assigned work tasks are slipping in all three business units. You determine that this is due in part to the project resources working unplanned activities delegated to them by their business unit management for projects internal to their business unit. This unplanned work is given higher priority than your project work.

You further determine that some of the project team is using different project management methodologies that have different estimating standards, deliverables and work products for essentially the same types of work tasks. You also learn that some of the team members are using spreadsheets to build project tasks lists, whereas others are using project management scheduling so robust that 10% of their time is required to enter and track project work in their areas. You need common data to understand what is going on in the entire project. How do you manage?

THE WRONG RESULT

The push to establish a PMO often comes because of the reasons mentioned above. Often, PMOs are established to bring order to timely project delivery expectations. Sometimes, PMOs are established as "Mentoring PMOs," to facilitate process standardization such as consistent methodologies. In many organizations, the PMO takes on an authoritarian approach as a "Process Cop PMO," to try to force everyone to use common processes. In other organizations, PMOs are established as a "Palace Guarding PMO", to simply protect the organization from out of control and highly visible projects.

Generally speaking, PMOs established with any of these purposes often fail over time. Sure, the PMO initially appears to have an impact. PMO sponsors are usually satisfied early on. However, a strange thing begins to occur. The organization reacts in a hostile manner to bring balance back toward itself as a functional unit, a project team and a resource.

A PMO whose main value is a standard methodology will find its value eroded over time. Today, tools exist to imbed a methodology, including self-learning approaches, across an entire organization. Standard methodology is just one *small* part of the total value proposition of a PMO. Once imbedded, project teams and business unit leaders will question the need for a PMO if no other value drivers are in place.

A PMO that has been established on the supply side of the organization over time may fail to bring enough focus onto the market side (see Chapter 1 for discussion of market side vs. supply side). Every organization, including not-for-profits, experiences market challenges. A PMO that does not have significant marketing and sales skills within the PMO is fated to lose executive interest when the organization loses revenues or market share. PMOs that do not influence the project selection and initiation process for vital projects have a high risk of losing executive support.

PMOs can have the right people, the right data and the right tools but produce the wrong results. If the PMO does not have the correct charter, it will most certainly fail over time.

CHARTERING THE PMO CORRECTLY

PMO value must be measurable to become sustainable. If you cannot measure, you cannot control and if you cannot control, you cannot manage. Thus, the PMO must be aligned with the interests and goals of the organization it serves to sustain itself within the organization year after year.

Our recommendation is for the PMO to focus on portfolio management of:

- Project investments
- Resources

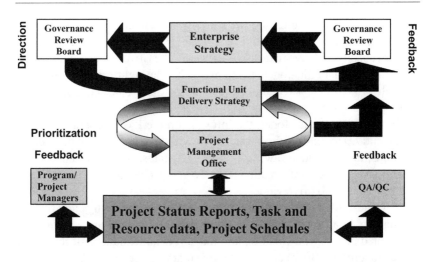

Figure 2.1 PMO Continuous Loop

- Assets
- Strategic objectives

Other PMO efforts should assist organizational entities to meet and/or exceed project delivery commitments. A PMO established in this manner will become recognized as a Return On Investment (ROI) engine for the organization it serves (see Figure 2.1).

PMO VALUE MODEL

Typically, two philosophical approaches for PMOs exist today. One model, which we call the "Cost Containment Model," focuses on containing project costs. The other model, called the "Throughput Model," focuses on meeting organization goals. A Throughput Model is displayed in Figure 2.1.

The model reads counter-clockwise, starting from the top right corner. A value-oriented PMO provides information and recommendations to a *Governance Board* that defines and manages the enterprise project portfolio strategy for the upcoming fiscal year. The Governance Board convenes in a timely fashion to gauge the capability and progress of projects to meet strategic objectives.

The supporting functional areas often use PMOs to help expedite delivery. The PMO provides an excellent vehicle to raise visibility of projects to support the enterprise strategy. Conversely, the Governance Board provides an excellent vehicle to focus the PMO on the priorities, as the Board sees them.

The Governance Board is also responsible for ensuring that the project portfolio is balanced and has sufficient marketing thrust to achieve the fiscal year objectives. Increasing the capacity to deliver without generating equivalent market demand could be a waste. Having market demand without the capacity to deliver can also be a waste. The Governance Board brings all organizational units together to ensure that the right projects, and only the right projects, are active and correctly prioritized to meet organizational goals.

In the Throughput Model, the information the PMO generates is vital for executives to judge if the organization will meet its goals. In most organizations, there is much raw data on project status, project schedules and other relative project information. However, raw data must be transformed into information to drive value.

A value-driven PMO will compile and publish its findings and recommendations to all functional units. In turn, the functional units review the aggregated delivery information and make recommendations of their own to the Governance Board at the same time that they are giving feedback and direction to project teams.

The Governance Board, upon receipt of the aggregated delivery data, reviews the results for compliance to the enterprise strategy. If the results are good (projects are finished, cash flow is being generated, or projects are ahead of schedule), potential exists to schedule additional work. If the results are negative, then the Governance Board must assess if the appropriate actions are in place to address the apparent risk.

Either way (good or bad results), the Governance Board also receives new opportunities that must be evaluated relative to current projects. The Governance Board must answer questions regarding current prioritization of the projects listed in the project portfolio. Should those projects in trouble be stopped, slowed, modified in scope, etc.? As the Governance Board deals with these issues, it has a constant eye on the bottom line and the spending plan forecasted year-to-date. It looks for unused, budgeted project dollars that can be invested elsewhere.

In the Throughput Model, unused budget money can be given to new projects as a means to deliver additional value without having to raise planned fiscal year budget projections. Or it could simply reduce project investment, yielding a better ROI on existing projects. This decision is within the authority of the Governance Board.

As a result of each cycle of reporting to the Governance Board, several things may change:

- Relative priorities of projects
- New projects may be added
- Active projects may be stopped or cancelled
- Decisions may be taken that will affect specific project work plans or investments

One emphasis in this model is to constantly seek to reduce the cycle time of most project work. Thus, throughput acceleration becomes a way of life for the enterprise. PMOs established in this model become ROI engines. Their ability to bring improved rigor and discipline that reduce project duration is a key value of their mission.

A PMO in this model should be able to return to the sponsoring organization a *minimum* of 10% of the total fiscal year project portfolio budget in the first year, either through reduced cost or increased throughput to the organization. This money should be more than sufficient to fund the entire PMO effort within the first two years. We will take a closer look at this and the mechanisms required to make this work in later chapters.

Unlike the Throughput Model, the Cost Containment Model for PMOs does not seek out unspent project budget monies. Instead, it focuses on ensuring that projects are on plan or better regarding spending.

One fallacy with this model is that spending the allocated money is viewed as a positive. Is it really? Cost Containment oriented PMOs practice authoritative delivery methods. A Cost Containment approach creates a "push" behavior environment all the way into the project team. Team members are "pushed" into compliance. The Cost Containment Model operates without a sense of urgency throughout the project, since the value of speed to market and revenue generation is not counted or measured.

The Throughput Model creates a "pull" behavior environment, all the way into the project team. Team members in a Throughput Model are self-motivated by the informal nature of peer pressure and the sense of urgency created to accelerate work delivery while avoiding work delivery delays. In this approach, the project team becomes a learning environment that is safe to work in because everyone is looking for ways to go faster and deliver the project earlier than promised.

In the Throughput Model, cost is *not* ignored. However, the priority of cost is different. Any cost that is not contributing to throughput is considered a waste. Any existing cost (e.g., idle resource) is viewed from the perspective of how can this cost be used to increase throughput.

Which approach would a CEO favor? If the organization is having a cash flow crisis, or has suffered losses due to project overruns, the CEO would probably favor a Cost Containment Model. We stress that, in most cases, this is incorrect for four major reasons:

1. By focusing on throughput as a number one priority, any project costs that are not contributing to throughput are an obvious waste. The cost containment occurs naturally, more quickly and, from our experience to an even greater extent, as common sense rather than through force.

2. There is a limit to cost cutting or cost containment. There is no limit to throughput.
3. Throughput drives projects to completion faster, which usually means less cost incurred, faster ROI and less interest accrued on the project investment until the return is achieved.
4. Cost cutting can kill the value of a project completely when it is done as an end in itself, making no sense to participants. For example, witness the skepticism and poor morale on a $5 million project, with dozens of highly paid people, where key senior team members are not allowed to spend $500 for a project management tool to help them manage the project data.

Please do not interpret this message about the focus on cost the wrong way. We understand that there is always waste in organizations. We accept that managers who are not vigilant about waste eventually are overcome by it. We are simply suggesting that you will actually end up with better results by focusing on throughput as your number one priority. With this focus, *anything* that is not contributing to throughput is an obvious waste.

THE "RIGHT" PEOPLE

Once the business understands what it should expect from the PMO, identifying the PMO staffing requirements becomes much easier. If the PMO value proposition is not established before most of the PMO staff is brought in, the PMO will tend to focus on staffing with people whose first priority is PM methodology, not bottom line results. Executives will lack the buy-in that the PMO needs. The PMO will begin life with one foot in the PMO grave.

The "right" people includes a balance between people from the supply side and people from the market side of the organization. This is equally true in not-for-profit organizations.

A PMO must be able to market its message in order to get the collaboration of people who do not report to the PMO. This requires skills in marketing and communications. Any PMO that does not have these skills and does not use them from Day 1 is in jeopardy of becoming extinct.

Finally, the PMO should cover multiple disciplines. We have witnessed PMOs that are almost 100% IT resourced. This is a huge mistake. Every functional area that is involved in projects should feel that someone in the PMO represents their best interests.

THE "RIGHT" TOOLS

Every PMO searches for ways to optimize project management proficiencies within its service areas. PMOs may purchase Enterprise Project Management (EPM) tools that are top of the line and cost hundreds of thousands of dollars. PMOs may also use tools to improve visibility of real-time project progress data. These are all important items to consider.

The maturity of the organization with respect to project management skills has a large impact on the acceptance by the user community of the EPM tools and processes. Often in organizations with low project management maturity, sophisticated tools meet heavy resistance. This is especially true with functional units that are normally autonomous to the enterprise in how they manage their work.

This resistance is affected by the dynamics of how different functional units compete with one another for shared resources. Almost all organizations have functional units that perform better than others, or are "more favored" by the CEO. This pecking order creates political incentive for those "less favored" units. Thus, the political environment and the CEO or senior management can drive what tools will be accepted and supported across the organization.

If the PMO begins business without a marketing plan to gain strong buy-in on tool usage from most, if not all, functional units, the PMO will have begun its own death march. The KISS (Keep It Simple, Stupid) formula works best at the beginning.

Thus, in a PMO startup, the PMO must understand functional unit behavior characteristics and needs. The PMO must determine what is in it for each functional unit. A PMO that has solid knowledge of the different politics in play and the drivers for each functional unit will be able to establish itself more quickly as the "best friend" of the enterprise. Such a PMO can avoid falling into the trap of becoming a "process cop."

THE "RIGHT" DATA

Today, many functional units are covered in mudslides of data. They are overwhelmed and not able to sift through the data and transform it into information useful to them.

In every type of organization, profit or non-profit, functional units compete with one another every day. The issue is often scarce resources or different views of how and where to change the organization. When it comes to scare resources, functional units often view themselves as stand-alone. To survive, they must compete or risk falling to the last spot and missing their fiscal year objectives.

The challenge for the PMO is to assist these units to be *collectively* better at project delivery. In order to improve, project delivery must be measured. The measurement process is often accomplished through project status reporting from all identified projects that are key to the business.

Most PMOs use some variation of a project status report to help communicate why progress is what it is. Sometimes the news is great and sometimes it is very bad. Everyone wants to report great news. Department heads do not typically rush to the executive suite to communicate bad news. A PMO that takes the position of "Town Crier" in a competitive work environment is a sitting duck.

The PMO must choose carefully what data it presents. As the PMO commences business during startup, the first project the PMO should undertake is winning the trust of the people it will serve. Unbiased reporting and other "even-handed" measurements that paint bad pictures of project managers can go against this trust. Essentially, this is the "Dragnet Reporting" style, "Just the facts, Ma'am, nothing but the facts."

The problem is not in reporting the facts. PMOs lose support when the facts seem to point a finger at a functional unit or a project manager. The role of the PMO is to diagnose system problems in project management and to help solve them. A project that is behind schedule needs more than a factual report.

The PMO can be very effective by making sure that the project management methodology or tool provides timely information. If the PMO can help the project managers to identify problems early, corrective action can be taken in small doses. This provides less stress to the project team and also to the Governance Board. Remember that projects are more likely to be cancelled if the corrective plan requires major changes. Also, the more often this happens, the greater the likelihood that the Governance Board will question what the PMO was doing all this time.

To establish trust, the PMO finger must first be pointed at the system, not at individuals. The PMO should be helping individual functional managers and project managers to find ways to address the problems to present to the Governance Board. In this context, the four portfolios described in Section III of this book (Project, Organization Goals and Objectives, Resources and Assets) and the relationships between them are a great start to quickly building a valuable pool of data.

With this data, the PMO must answer on the following questions:

1. What are the organization's strategic objectives?
2. What projects are active today and how do they link to the strategic objectives? To the organization's strategic assets?
3. What other projects must we complete to achieve each one of those strategic objectives?
4. What resources do we have to complete all current and planned projects, and are those resources sufficient?
5. What are the root causes of project problems? What are the three biggest problems that impact many or most of the projects?

6. How are the projects doing? The focus here should be to gain agreement on a clear and simple (not simplistic) measurement system and some targets, so that PMO value and effectiveness can be shown.
7. How can we move projects to completion more quickly?
8. How can we get more projects done?
9. How can we achieve Deming's* level of predictability in project management for the three major attributes — on time, on budget and within scope?

THE "WRONG" RESULT —
WHY PMO IMPLEMENTATIONS FAIL

1. The PMO did not define its value proposition.

The PMO is in business to help the organization meet its goals. Almost anything else is a waste of effort that will be realized sooner or later. For example, it may take weeks or even months to force project managers and their teams to use a methodology that the PMO is pushing. PMOs should strive to demonstrate tangible value in the first three months in terms of improving project delivery speed. The political pressure to deliver value will increase month by month. At some point, the PMO will run out of time. In the chapters that follow, we present techniques to help the PMO achieve true value in the first 30 to 60 days of operation.

2. The PMO is not perceived as impacting project delivery abilities.

PMOs that are focused primarily as administrative score-keepers, information providers or process developers have a declining value curve (see Figure 2.2). These PMOs start out by fulfilling a critical senior management need for information. The organizational units and project managers, receiving negative press without tangible help from the PMO, resist the PMO. This resistance becomes more serious over time and is often a defensive reaction to the PMO. The organizational units set up defenses, such as collectively discrediting PMO data or pointing out the lack of visible help, so that the PMO cannot hurt them with the regular PMO message. The end result over time is the diminishment of the PMO mission importance. When the combined resistance of a few functional units exceeds the perceived

---

*W. Edwards Deming, the great quality genius of the 20th century, is discussed more extensively in Part II of this book. His statistical methods and overall philosophy provide an approach to bring predictability to any process. With Deming's approach, a system is in control when you achieve the goals of the system more than 95% of the time.

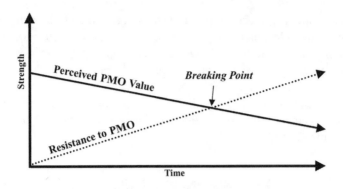

Figure 2.2   PMO Value Curve

value of the PMO, the PMO will cease to exist — it has no tangible value to prove its worth.

3. The PMO is seen as a threat — most often too authoritative.

Many established PMOs operate in this manner. There are some environments where strict adherence to authority works well. For example, businesses that gain revenue through the military or government agencies are often required to follow strict project delivery guidelines such as "Earned Value" techniques.

These businesses are measured and compensated on the Earned Value metrics as a percent of available compensation for a particular project phase. So, if the business achieved 90% of the Earned Value metrics for a project phase, it would receive 90% of the available compensation for that project phase. For some firms operating this way, their survival may depend on the cash flow and the careful tracking and progress associated with it. In cases of survival, authoritarianism works. Authoritarian PMOs operating in these environments can sustain themselves because there is a clear value proposition. However, as we point out in later chapters, these PMOs are leaving a lot of fruit unpicked.

In most organizations, if the PMO becomes too intrusive, managers will come together in an informal posse and hunt down the PMO sponsors. When the PMO sponsors are finally cornered, they will be given a choice — themselves or the PMO. The sponsors' decision is quite easy to make when they think about how to make mortgage payments.

If your PMO has this authoritarian style, check the strength of your sponsor(s). It may not be too late to modify the PMO value proposition and begin turning the corner.

4. The PMO is too low in the management reporting structure.

PMOs that are established in this mode are usually found in the supply side of the business — normally IT. Chief Information Officers (CIOs) often create PMOs to help them gain control over the project management environment. This type of PMO is sometimes established as a defensive measure against pressure from other groups. Often, they are catching the blame for projects failing to meet requested timelines and promised quality levels.

This type of PMO exists near or below "radar detection". This means that the PMO often spends most of its time collecting data on IT project initiatives. The CIO needs the data to survive and certainly wants to improve project management results.

However, establishing a PMO at a low level means that the manager has to swim against the main stream political current of not just those in the market side of the business but all of the IT work force as well. How do you like those odds? You would have to be immortal to escape certain death in this PMO model. If the PMO value proposition is not sponsored correctly by the CIO, with direct links and support from the senior management team, it is likely to fail.

The PMO must be doing things that are on the executive radar screen. In fact, relative to projects, the PMO should be providing the executives with the cockpit information necessary to ensure successful executive execution.

5. The PMO does not have buy-in from the senior functional managers.

PMOs that do not cultivate the buy-in from the senior leadership of their organization or of other organizations that are customers of the senior leadership are making a serious mistake.

We have witnessed many PMOs that take, as their first action, some initiative that rolls out processes, tools, or some other tactical improvement, all of which focuses on the project management community *only*. This initiative requires diverting functional resource and project manager time away from their projects and into providing data and learning methodology and tools.

What about the senior functional managers, the project sponsors, the fiscal year strategic objectives? A PMO that takes an initiative that excludes, or does not explicitly include, the interests of senior managers across functional areas puts the project teams in a cross fire. The project team must now choose priorities between the PMO initiative and the project managers' initiative. Who do you think the project teams will listen to first and last?

For example, as the PMO leader, assume that you have decided to roll out an EPM tool to help project teams become more proficient at executing their work plans and managing risk. Traditionally projects never come in on time or on budget. You have set up training workshops on how to use the new tool and related processes. As the tool workshops roll out, word travels across the organization that the tool is very sophisticated and requires significant project team involvement in conversion activities to achieve any tool benefits.

It is the 3rd quarter in the business cycle and it is now apparent that many of the key projects will not make their original delivery date estimate. The heat is on. The project teams are in trouble and now must make a choice. Business unit leaders are pressing their project teams to deliver and are demanding success or else. The PMO loses every time in this scenario.

6. **Project Management Overhead — the bad PMO acronym.**

Teams may see PMO initiatives as unnecessary overhead. Such PMOs will fail to sustain themselves in most economic conditions. The work community simply cannot see any benefit in using the PMO to help themselves. Project teams must see something in the PMO for themselves if the PMO is to prosper. The baseline measurement must be the PMO value proposition.

7. **The PMO is micromanaging — trying to control every project directly.**

Dr. Harold Kerzner comments, "If the project managers report to the PMO, then the PMO effectively micromanages projects and the result may be a loss of strategic direction for the firm. For strategic efforts, it may be advisable for the project managers to report to the strategic PMO on a part-time basis.

"One problem with having project managers report to a PMO is that the respective line managers will be reluctant to give up their best project managers to a PMO. The line managers view this as a loss of control and a reduction in authority and possibly power.

"The only time I have seen project managers report effectively to a PMO is when it was a customer-focused PMO, where the PMO focuses exclusively on one customer base, such as in the armed forces of a country. Recently I was with a strategic PMO in Mexico that is responsible for strategic decisions such as project selection, prioritization and tracking ROI. They want to see *only* milestone schedules and understand the danger of getting too involved in projects. However, each of their large functional areas (headed up by asset managers) has their own PMO in which the project managers are direct reports. So they have both a strategic PMO and four resource PMOs (all interconnected) at the same time."

Our view is that project managers should have internships within the PMO to understand its purpose, functions and methods. However, the internship, generally speaking, should be in performing a PMO role, not a project management role.

SUMMARY

Simply put, PMOs fail because they do not set out their mission as providing measurable value to their universe of customers. First and foremost, the executive team must see the PMO as providing tangible help towards meeting the organization's goals. Each and every project manager must see the PMO as a trusted group who is helping them to meet their goals. Functional managers at all levels must see the PMO as helping resolve resource conflicts and other crises and getting the project work done faster and better.

PMOs that report too low in the organization or PMOs that have an imbalanced Governance Board often put their focus on time sheets, methodology, and other efforts that fail to drive value within the first 60 days. The PMO Value Model and its full implications are covered throughout the rest of this book. The Value Model focuses on throughput relative to the goals of the organization, rather than on Cost Containment.

Value means completing more projects in less time, year after year, that contribute directly to the organization's goals. Value means continual improvement in predictability for the three parameters — on time, on budget and within scope.

QUESTIONS

2.1 Discuss the major PMO types and how their approaches can lead to their demise.

2.2 What are the differences between a PMO organized with a "Cost Containment" approach vs. a "Throughput" approach?

2.3 What are the four types of portfolios on which a PMO must focus?

2.4 Explain the basic role of a PMO in the throughput model.

2.5 What negative effects might an organization experience with a centralized organization such as a PMO exercising more control over projects?

2.6 What are the most compelling reasons for an executive to say "Yes" to a proposal to establish a PMO in his/her organization?

2.7   What could be compelling reasons for an executive to say "No" to a proposal to establish a PMO in his/her organization?

2.8   Why do the authors suggest that the focus on cost or budget, as a top priority for the PMO, is incorrect? Where should the first focus be?

2.9   List and explain several reasons why PMOs fail.

2.10   Where might authoritative PMOs work best and why?

2.11   Are the authors asking too much of the PMOs? List the pros and cons.

2.12   If your PMO had a $100 million portfolio budget to help deliver, how much should the PMO expect to help save the business in a Throughput Model approach over the fiscal year? In a Cost Containment approach?

2.13   True or False — It is permissible to establish a PMO and hire staff before defining the PMO mission and requirements.

2.14   True or False — In a Throughput Model, the PMO often dictates the priority of projects in a portfolio.

2.15   True or False — There are more than 50,000 PMOs in the United States today.

2.16   True or False — PMO leaders never have to worry about executive buy-in.

3

WHAT IS A PMO AND WHAT SHOULD A HIGH VALUE PMO DO?

WHAT'S IN A NAME? EPMO, EPO, PMO, PO...

There are many different names for a PMO, implying different authority and functionality. A PMO that simply measures project work without providing expertise in how to do the work is often called a "Project Office." The name Project Office is misleading. Many decades ago, the term was used in the construction industry, referring to the main controlling office for a single project. For example, on the site of the construction of the Empire State Building in New York City, you would find the Project Office.

In many companies today, this type of Project Office does not provide support to the project management community. Rather, it seeks data from the project management community relative to status reporting, updated schedules and other related documentation. In this manner, it is easy to see why a Project Office could be seen as a threat to the project manager who is struggling with a difficult assignment. Many people see this kind of reporting as unnecessary overhead. Few people like to report bad news and most people find a way not to.

Before anyone will make a serious additional effort to provide data to another business unit, they must first see what is in it for them. In the case of the Project Office described above, their answer is frequently "nothing" and their effort is synonymous.

To establish project management standards as well as help the delivery community do their best, the PMO concepts described in this book are recommended. In this model, standards and practices are established and voluntarily followed to help improve project delivery.

In large organizations, this unit might be termed "Enterprise-Wide" or Enterprise Project Management Office (EPMO). This signifies that such a PMO has influence beyond one business unit or functional area.

In some cases, the "project" in EPMO is viewed more from a program perspective. A program is a collection of projects that have something in common, usually a product line or business unit emphasis. In this case, EPMOs with "program" as part of their charter name may focus on the project initiatives with the largest budgets, in an effort to provide the best management oversight and support possible.

ORIGINS OF THE PMO WITHIN AN ORGANIZATION

Regardless of what such an organization is called, a PMO is sanctioned and launched to improve the organization's project management *results*. Since everyone within the organization views results from their own unique, local perspective, the PMO can have a very different look and feel from one organization to another.

In today's world, it is very rare to see organizations establish a PMO because they want to. Usually, they have to. They have tried other means to bring their projects under control. The PMO surfaces when senior management is feeling the pain. **Unfortunately, this is often the beginning of bad positioning for a PMO entity**.

There are many possible combinations of the determining factors of a PMO, as outlined below. These factors have implications for the ultimate PMO value to the organization. The success and influence of a PMO depend heavily on from where in the organization the PMO will operate. Should the PMO originate from the market side of the organization or from the supply side? Oftentimes this is determined by the amount of current delivery pain being endured by the sponsoring management team, and where the sponsor for the PMO sits.

The major factors that describe the PMO functions and influence are discussed below and include:

- Reporting structure
- Themes
- Models

REPORTING STRUCTURE

The reporting structure includes the supply side, the market side, and the senior executive(s) with responsibility for both the supply side and the market side.

Most PMOs we encounter report to the CIO or another entity within the supply side of the organization. While the PMO sponsor can come from anywhere in the organization, we see this kind of reporting structure as setting the stage for bad PMO implementation. For the same reasons, a PMO that reports to the market side also will have limited results.

These comments are not intended to infer a negative connotation on the CIO or any other functional unit. Rather, what we see is that the PMO will ultimately fail due to lack of involvement from the most senior of the executive team or negative influence from other organizational units.

The PMO must be able to influence scheduling and decision-making across all projects. Otherwise, some organizational units will see the PMO as their enemy or as a powerless entity. But the role of the PMO is not one of referee. The PMO must have enough influence to solve the constant resource crises and project priority shifts *permanently*.

Therefore, the reporting structure that makes the most sense is to an executive with responsibility for both the supply side and market side of an organization, or what we term the *business unit head*.

CASE STUDY — A HEALTH INSURANCE ORGANIZATION

A recent consulting assignment with a large health insurance organization involved the implementation of a new sales force automation system. The system had to be implemented within 3 months, due to significant legislated changes in this state's health care system. The volume of incoming calls, new proposal generation and insurance policy changes could not be handled with the existing telemarketing staff, sales force and computer systems.

This organization is a weak matrix organization where project managers have no authority and all the responsibility. The EPMO in this case needed commitments and decisions made quickly to meet the deadline. Decisions and firm resource commitments were needed from the vice presidents of sales, IT, marketing and operations. To whom should this EPMO report in order to ensure that all would cooperate by making this their top project?

The answer became obvious when the major reason for delays was analyzed. Everyone on this project team wanted this project to finish on schedule. However, within each functional group, there were conflicting projects. The conflicting projects were also important. Without the CEO becoming quickly aware of the conflicts and making decisions to remove the conflicts, the EPMO would not be able to solve the problem. If this happens more than once, project managers within the organization stop paying attention to the PMO.

THEMES

The two themes, cost containment and throughput improvement, are culturally vastly different. We see most PMOs operating with one of these two themes.

Cost containment is traditional in nature. It focuses on the efficient use of resources and budgetary controls. It assumes that the solution to an organization's project management problems is to enforce strict standards and controls. This approach often leads to a work environment where much PMO effort is spent collecting data, using authority and imposing negative consequences on violators.

The PMO resources are often applied to projects in financial trouble, where the motivation is to stop the bleeding. In addition to the resistance this approach creates across the organization, there is also a limit to the value of the PMO, based on how much cost can be contained. In this type of PMO, it is rare to see any concerted effort at cross-functional portfolio management, one of the important emerging functions of an advanced PMO.

Throughput improvement focuses on driving down project cycle time dramatically, flowing more projects through the organization, and choosing a better project mix to meet the organization's goals. With this theme, any projects that do not contribute to the organization's goals are a waste. Therefore, although cost containment is not the primary mission, there is often better cost containment with the throughput approach. Waste becomes much easier to recognize when the focus is on throughput. There is also no imposed limit on the value with this approach.

The main challenge with the throughput theme is in educating managers across the organization. The PMO must work hard to ensure that expectations are changed among project teams. The throughput theme is discussed more thoroughly in the next chapter.

MODELS

Four value models exist within the two major themes. They are as follows:

1. Project Repository Model (a low or no value model)
2. Coach Model (a tactical model that can provide some value for a short time)
3. Enterprise Model (a strategic model oriented to central control of all major projects)
4. "Deliver Now" Model (a high-value strategic model focused on throughput, delivery acceleration and choosing the right projects)

PROJECT REPOSITORY MODEL

The PMO serves as a source of information on projects, methodology and standards in this model. This PMO assumes that the enterprise has embraced a cohesive set of tools for project design, management and reporting. This model occurs most often in organizations that empower distributed, business-centric project ownership or with weak central governance.

We term this a low or no value model because this PMO lacks accountability for bottom-line results. It assumes that data and methodology have inherent value. Therefore, such an organization does not attempt to drive tangible, measurable value from its efforts.

COACH MODEL

The Coach Model is an extension of the Repository Model. It assumes a willingness to share some project management practices across functions and uses the PMO to coordinate the communication. Best practices are documented and shared and project performance is actively monitored. Results are used to raise enterprise performance and train inefficient or new project managers. In the Coach Model, the PMO acts primarily as trainer, consultant or mentor. It also becomes a source of information on project processes. In this model, the PMO often helps in project setup and post-project reviews.

This PMO, while providing meaningful tactical help, will always be second-guessed by the senior management team, especially during hard times. The executives, always challenged to provide a better bottom line, will constantly ask, "Do we really need this overhead? Sure, it's providing some benefit, but is it worth the expense?" The reason this questioning occurs is that if a project is successful, the project manager, the team, and the functional sponsor grab the credit. The coach is often not awarded the credit. However, if projects are not successful, the coach is given all of the blame.

Without the senior management team becoming primary customers of this type of PMO, our observation is that this organization becomes the top candidate for the next budget cut.

ENTERPRISE MODEL

This model usually implies a much larger investment and, therefore, usually has a stronger mission, charter and support than the previous two models. It enables risk management as projects initiate and mature in the development cycle. It plays a major role in multi-project management by identifying bottlenecks that hamper all projects. Often within this model, there is some gathering of data to build the enterprise project portfolio (information about the major projects that the organization has sanctioned).

The most consolidated version of this organizational model concentrates senior project management expertise and execution within the PMO. Some or all project managers are staffed within the shared service model and consigned to projects as needed. The model assumes a governance process that involves the PMO in most projects, regardless of size.

While this model is heading in the right direction, we observe that most PMOs within this model have no direct link to the CEO or business unit head. There are no immediate bottom-line expectations of the PMO. If you take senior project managers out of a functional area, place them in such a PMO, and then farm them out again as project managers, has the PMO really added significant value to the entire organization?

From what we have seen, there is a large disparity between PMOs using this model. If the senior members of this PMO, outside of their project responsibilities, are able to get together, vet common problems, and implement across-the-board solutions, then the value proposition is much greater. In reality, from the PMOs that we have surveyed, we observe PMO resources either working hard on projects or focused on non-leveraged efforts.

"DELIVER NOW" MODEL

In this model, the emphasis is on delivering measurable value to the executive team within each 6-month period. At initial startup of this PMO, the resources focus on accelerated project deliveries across all major projects.

This model has sponsorship at a very high executive level (CEO or Senior Vice President). Its metrics are tied directly to senior management performance. It seeks to deliver or influence at least some of the following within 6 months:

- Strategic planning (choosing the right projects)
- Project coaching for delivery acceleration opportunities and delivery threat avoidance
- *Integrated* project status reporting and scheduling with the portfolios
- Knowledge transfer to selected resources
- "Project portfolio" including relationship to organization goals and assets, current workload, tactical progress, status and correction plans
- Monthly "operations plan and forecast" that identifies portfolio opportunities and threats, top issues, top risks, projects over/under budget, and portfolio fiscal summary

- Global project prioritization model for all projects, current and proposed
- Governance Board setup and/or modification that enables the force-ranking of the portfolio of projects
- Project management training, coaching and mentoring on projects that are on the executive radar screen

WHAT EVERY PMO SHOULD DO

For a PMO to become a prized organizational unit, it must take on the following functions (once the PMO is created):

1. **Drive project cycle times down** — There is enough low-hanging fruit among all of the active projects for the PMO to make a quick and significant impact. There are also many different aspects of project management that can be attacked to achieve quick results. The biggest leverage usually comes from taking a systems approach, as described in Part II of this book. The systems approach addresses:

   - The multi-project constraints, especially the overloading of resources, the failure to stagger projects appropriately, and the waste that results from constantly changing priorities
   - The single-project constraints by changing project measurements

   However, there are tactical opportunities as well that come from experience. For example:

   - Ensuring that a valid, well-thought-out project plan exists
   - Ensuring that everyone involved is committed to the project plan
   - Communicating expectations, progress and problems regularly
   - Performing a quality control review of the requirements definition to prevent rework
   - Performing risk analysis on the major components of the plan
   - Ensuring rigorous change control procedures are in place and understood

2. **Facilitate choosing the right project mix** — Strategic planning and project management go hand in hand. Since most organizations have far too many active projects on their plate, with an imbalance of projects between the market side and the supply side of the organization, a high-value PMO addresses this problem head on. A PMO can add a lot of value by helping to eliminate and deactivate projects that are not as important to the organization.

3. **Develop and maintain an executive cockpit, through key portfolios** — The PMO must put itself in a position, right from the start, of providing invaluable information to executives, project managers and resource managers. The key portfolios are the Project Portfolio, the Resource Portfolio, the Asset Portfolio and the Strategic Goals Portfolio. See Part III of this book for detailed descriptions and discussion of portfolio management. The cockpit allows executives to see what is going on, from a high level, and to change course in time to avoid collisions with shareholders, customers or competition.

4. **Track and report progress (high level)** — This effort is the detailed work behind function 3 above. The executives need to know if the projects will complete in time and within scope to meet their goals. They also need to know if the financials are good. They must be involved in any major scope decisions that could impact their goals. Project managers, knowing that the PMO is using data for executive reporting, are much more willing to provide data. For projects in trouble, the PMO data must include what action(s) it is taking to correct the problems. Resource managers need accurate, up-to-date reports to do a good job of managing and coaching their resources. The key contribution that a high-value PMO can make is to ensure timely, accurate information in an easy to use form. The earlier project managers can recognize a problem, the better chance they have to fix it without major effort. The PMO has an important role to play by helping to identify and resolve problems and limit the number of crises that are escalated to the Governance Board. This is also necessary for PMO survival.

5. **Mentoring** — The PMO staff are the project management experts who have the scars to prove it. These people must be believable and have the ability to interface tactfully in delicate situations with all levels of the workforce. They are forward observers and will typically be seen as the PMO center of excellence.

6. **Tools** — The PMO houses the project management tools technical experts, who also often staff the Help Desk.

7. **Help Desk** — Response time is critical to the value model of the PMO. Fast, knowledgeable response means good value.

8. **Methodology** — How-to methods are needed in every organization for project management. This PMO function should be to provide expertise, marketing and encouragement without bureaucracy or a police force. The focus should be on how to use the minimum necessary methodology to ensure predictable results.

9. **Corrective action** — The PMO must seek to eliminate any measurements that cause people to prolong project cycle times. The PMO must use the reporting and the Pareto Principle to find the biggest causes of project delays, rework and other negative effects. The PMO focus on corrective action is not on a per project basis. Rather, the view is enterprise-wide.

10. **Facilitate the Governance Board** — Every project portfolio needs management oversight to establish the order of work. It is not the PMO itself that sets project priorities. However, the PMO is responsible for helping senior management define the process and exercise it. The senior management is in charge of ensuring that the strategic objectives of the business are met. The PMO should, however, ensure that the Governance Board is represented by a balance of market- and supply-side executives. The PMO must ensure that Governance Board meetings are convened regularly and that decisions are made, recorded and communicated formally. The PMO is responsible for communicating decisions of the Governance Board to all concerned, and for helping to implement those decisions.

11. **Prioritization of the project portfolio** — A business unit understands its own project inventory and priorities. However, in most organizations, there are no predefined prioritization schemes. Nor is there typically a commonly accepted rationale for sorting out priorities between business units, other than having the CEO or Senior Vice President referee. Common language is required. The various approaches to project prioritization are discussed in a later chapter.

12. **Help projects in trouble** — While PMOs can provide some important help for projects in trouble, at least part of the PMO's mission is prevention. Every troubled project should be analyzed to determine root causes for the trouble. If it is a skills issue, then training or skills development must be provided to prevent it in the future. If policies or measurements caused the problem, these must be changed to avoid wasting time and also to avoid making the PMO become nothing more than a search and rescue unit.

13. **Project management training** — The PMO should play a major role in developing a standard, high-quality training strategy for the organization. The most successful programs we have seen are ones that offer participants many choices, as well as some mandatory programs to build the common language. Also, because many project managers view their work as a profession, the PMO should have a professional development approach and career track that makes training significant to highly motivated project managers.

14. **Marketing and communication** — A high-value PMO is one that communicates regularly and meaningfully with all of its customers. The communication takes many forms. Information, customized to each customer, must be available online. Web-based live communications are becoming more common, especially for projects with global resources. With executives, the PMO should never underestimate the importance and the power of simple, face-to-face communications, well planned to minimize the executives' time. Marketing implies that the PMO needs to continually sell its value, and bring its internal customers to use the service more.

15. **Archives** — There are several reasons why it makes sense to have all project archives in one place. For example, this is a great place to keep "lessons learned." A smart person learns from his or her mistakes. But a wise person learns from other people's mistakes. Archives are also useful in case of legal repercussions from any past project work. Also, records of individual accomplishments and work performed can be helpful when recruiting for future projects.

WHO ARE THE CUSTOMERS?

For the PMO, almost everyone in the organization is a customer. Here are the key groups:

Project Sponsor — This is one of the most forgotten customers in the organization. It is incumbent upon the PMO to understand the sponsor's needs.

Project Teams — When project teams are in trouble, where do they go for help in their organization? A PMO or Project Office that presents itself as a valuable support aid will develop a valuable source of informal information about active projects, team morale and other issues. This is critical to the PMO because it enables an early warning system and a validation of the data being provided to the PMO.

Governance Board — This is a formal team comprised of executive leaders (or their delegates) from across the organization. Their mission is to direct the organization strategically, using projects as a way to meet organization goals. The key services provided by the PMO are information, analysis and recommendations.

Functional Units — Functional units typically compete with each other for use of common resources, assets, etc. There is always an informal pecking order among the functional units. Any PMO that ignores this has a death wish. The PMO should establish and maintain excellent communications and support with the head of each functional unit.

Project Managers — Prior to the PMO, when project managers were encountering trouble with completing project delivery, to whom did they turn? The PMO helps project managers get their voices heard at a level high enough to solve some of their major problems. PMOs are not silver bullets, but the project manager is not the Lone Ranger. The major difference that the PMO should make to these customers is the reduction of pressure from resource conflicts and the positive guidance based on experience.

Resource Managers — The PMO has a valuable interface with all of the organization's resource managers. Prior to the PMO, resource managers were either victims of constant priority changes or they made their own decisions on where to allocate resources. In this case, they often were abused by the project managers and sponsors who found themselves on the short end of the resource stick. With the PMO resolving major resource contention, resource managers can use reports provided by the PMO to allocate resources with confidence. In turn, the resource managers can help guide the PMO in terms of understanding where the weaknesses are, suggestions for training programs, etc.

THE ADVANCED PMO TWO-YEAR PLAN*

THE FIRST SIX MONTHS

As in any new situation, there is a need to build powerful communication and understanding between the customers and the PMO.

General: The objective of the first 6 months is to help everyone understand the bottlenecks that block or hurt project delivery. When the PMO customers can improve their cognitive skills to recognize opportunities and threats to project delivery, results will normally follow.

Project Sponsors: They worry too much about the PMO and how it is portraying the status of their project. They will continue to see the PMO as a threat until the PMO demonstrates that it is committed to helping sponsors meet their needs. Frequent communication is essential.

Governance Board: The PMO needs some breathing room to get itself established and develop the portfolios. Until the PMO has reliable information, the Governance Board will not have the data and information upon which they are expected to make key decisions. It is helpful if the PMO can facilitate a strategic planning process toward the end of the first 6 months, with the entire senior management team. The second 6 months will be more important for the Governance Board.

---

*Note that this topic is discussed in detail in Chapter 28, providing the road map for implementing a PMO.

Project Managers: As projects are reviewed among all project managers, expect some storming. Remember that the PMO is new and it is very likely that project estimates will begin to receive some question. Also, project managers may see the PMO as another "flavor of the month" initiative by senior management, and hope it will disappear.

Project Teams: Team members learn that the PMO is a friend. Earn their trust and respect one team member at a time. During the first 6 months, the PMO must ensure that it does not ignore team members who have valuable information to share. We have seen dramatic progress here when the PMO offers to facilitate problems without trying to impose its will on the project manager or team members.

Functional Units: The PMO must not place the project managers and their teams in a position where they must choose who to listen to regarding project delivery — their functional unit management or the PMO. If the PMO starts a war, the functional unit will likely win.

THE SECOND SIX MONTHS

In the second 6 months, it is important to cement into place the ownership of the portfolios by the Governance Board. This may take the entire 6 months, but that is acceptable. By giving the Governance Board ownership of the portfolios, it is as it should be. They fund the work. They should direct the priorities and choices of active projects.

General: Ask all customer groups to support expediting project delivery.

Project Sponsors: This is an opportunity to sell project sponsorship training — how to be a project sponsor. Pilot the concept first on several of the more receptive sponsors. Focus training on what sponsors can do to help project managers accelerate decision-making and overcome roadblocks. Sponsors also need help with quantifying the value of their projects and providing data necessary for prioritization.

Governance Board: In this time frame, the Governance Board process should begin to mature. The project prioritization process should be implemented and it should be smoothed out. Getting ready for the next fiscal year through this process combined with strategic planning is the next challenge for the PMO.

Project Managers: By now, project managers should be viewing the PMO as a friend. Work behind the scenes with those who do not share this view. New methods of delivery acceleration should become standard and well understood by all project managers. Some project managers may use the PMO on a confidential basis because the PMO has a broad, cross-functional view and remains functionally independent.

Project Teams: The PMO can be the catalyst for an attitude of "Learning Teams." The PMO provides the focus on the biggest leverage factor for accelerating delivery and quality. Project teams grow their own value through partnering in training programs with the PMO. As team members apply their new training, expect to have to reinforce the training multiple times, in different ways, until the attitudes and new skills become a habit.

Functional Units: Remember the pecking order? The PMO may be causing this order to change somewhat. In the second 6 months, with demonstrated bottom-line value, the PMO has earned some influence. Navigate your way carefully. Use the Governance Board as the way to vet and resolve conflicts, and also to enforce important decisions on project workload, prioritization and staggering of projects according to resource availability.

THE THIRD SIX MONTHS

The PMO is entering its second year. The value proposition should have been measurable and clearly achieved for the first year. If not, the focus must be on correcting the problems and stabilizing the PMO to predictably achieve its targets.

If the PMO was successful, the challenge in the second year is to be better. The first step is to identify the current constraint. Where is the biggest leverage point today in improving project management results? Remember that the improvement is according to the goals of the organization, not according to the quality of project management practice.

The Pareto Principle and Root Cause Analysis should have helped determine the areas of focus. Regardless of what those areas are, remember that to make a permanent and meaningful improvement, you must change human behavior. Focus on the behavior of the culture you want to support and that is expected of the PMO. The behavior involves all of the customers of the PMO. Whenever you complete a major improvement, the behavior model has changed and the constraint will be something new.

General: Remember the Deming Principle — Plan, Do, Control, Act. Apply this concept to all processes implemented in the first year.

Project Sponsors: Educate the sponsors on the collective impact of projects, and the relationship of their project to the overall goals of the company. Let them know what you are doing to help them. Know which sponsors are doing well and who needs hand-holding.

Governance Board: Maintenance mode. Focus on portfolio balance. The Governance Board may upgrade the prioritization model for projects.

Project Managers: If the PMO has implemented the high-value model, project managers will look to the PMO for help in accelerating and ensuring project results. The PMO's work with project managers typically expands with the explosion of trust and resulting requests in the second year. If so, the PMO may need to bring on more mentors.

Project Teams: "Learning Teams" are working hard to deliver. Project teams are finding it easier to bond, thus making it more difficult for the naysayers to survive as team members. The PMO continues with training that helps team members improve their job value in a project team.

Functional Units: Go back to the business units and ask them how the PMO can do better for them. Do so very informally. Let the Governance Board select some items that will provide the biggest leverage of PMO resources.

THE FOURTH SIX MONTHS

Revisit your value proposition and identify value opportunities that will help your customers perform better. Check out the quantitative value provided year to date. Are you on plan, behind or ahead? You have 6 months left. You should plan on a major senior management review at this time, and determine the charter for the next 2 years.

General: The PMO is established, and senior management is entrenched in the PMO philosophy. Now is a good time to examine the PMO maturity model in Appendix A, and determine where to focus on maturing to bring the biggest value to the bottom line over the next two years.

Project Sponsors: With a focus on choosing the right project mix, you should begin to see project sponsors taking a more global view of projects. Project sponsors should be attuned to the idea that the organization has a few strategic resources, and that they have a responsibility to not waste those precious resources with "pet projects".

Governance Board: The new strategic objectives for the next fiscal year are being determined, with PMO facilitation. Try to get a quicker start on the impact the new objectives will have on project prioritization, critical resources and other major resource demands.

Project Managers: Has the PMO achieved 100% buy-in from this community? What is missing? Plan, Do, Control, Act. How can mentors be better for the project managers?

Project Teams: Training and support must continue to emphasize immediate value to team members, both in delivery acceleration and risk management skills, and in communications.

Functional Units: Who is not on board? Why not? Keep at it.

SUMMARY — DETERMINING WHAT YOUR PMO SHOULD REALLY DO

A correctly implemented PMO should begin to show tangible results in its first 6 months of existence. To do so, the PMO must help executives to directly link their strategic planning process to project management across the organization.

A PMO will provide value if its customers are constantly seeking project delivery acceleration. This requires developing project team cognitive skills to recognize delivery opportunities and threats as they uncover them. These skills are vital to the competitive advantage of the enterprise.

Some of the great value of a PMO is provided by causing the organization to complete more projects than were planned for the fiscal year with the same resources, and to get projects completed sooner. In some companies, speed-to-market is the difference between a huge profit and a marginal profit or even a loss.

Where does your PMO stand in your organization? How do you describe the value proposition of your PMO? Look at the PMO Maturity Table in Appendix A to determine how your organization's PMO fits into a PMO that is providing value. If the answer is unknown or unclear, then hopefully you can begin by helping your PMO and yourself find the PMO value from the insights thus far and from those presented later in this book. Of course, you could continue your current course. What do you have to lose? As you reflect on this last question, think about the millions of people who lost their jobs since January 2001.

QUESTIONS

3.1   Who should the PMO report to and why?

3.2   What are the major differences between a PMO organized with a "Cost Containment" approach vs. a "Throughput" approach?

3.3   What are the four types of portfolios a PMO must focus on?

3.4   Explain the basic role of a PMO in the Throughput Model.

3.5   What negative effects might an organization experience from a PMO exercising more inspection over projects?

3.6   Discuss how closely related the cost of a PMO should be to its value to the organization. Where can the PMO locate opportunities to be better?

3.7   List and explain several types of PMOs.

3.8   If your PMO had a $100 million portfolio budget to help deliver, what is the minimum amount that the PMO should help save the business in a Throughput Model approach over the first fiscal year?

3.9   True or False — It is important to define the PMO requirements before establishing a PMO.

3.10   True or False — In a Throughput Model, the PMO often dictates the order of projects in a portfolio.

3.11   True or False — PMO leaders never have to worry about organizational buy-in.

4

MOVING PROJECT MANAGEMENT FROM THE COST MODEL TO THE THROUGHPUT MODEL

LOCKED IN A PARADIGM

There are two models for the focus of a PMO — the Cost Model and the Throughput Model. These models are so opposed that they cannot realistically coexist within an organization. Some organizations have a PMO in existence solely to plan and manage large cost-reduction efforts. Our view is that this may be necessary and correct for the survival and short-term health of an organization. For long-term health, the organization must execute projects that will build revenue, replace old products and services, overcome the competition and satisfy the customers and the markets now and in the future. Therefore, to begin strategic project management, we advise our clients to change their model — how they view the value of a PMO to their organization.

In the Cost Model, the paradigm is to look for the most efficient way to perform tasks. Look carefully at Table 4.1. It shows the impact on cost and time for having one, two, three, or four people working on a task simultaneously.

Table 4.1   Duration and Cost Options to Perform a Project Task

Number of Resources	Time per Resource (weeks)	Total Time (weeks)	Total Project Cost ($1000 per week)
1	100	100	$100,000
2	45	90	$ 90,000
3	40	120	$120,000
4	35	140	$140,000

For example, the first option has only one person working on the task. It would require 100 elapsed weeks of one person's time and would cost $100,000.

The second option proposes two people working on the task simultaneously. In this option, some efficiency is gained in the work, reducing overall cost to $90,000. That is because even though you are paying two people instead of one person, they can complete the entire job in 45 weeks. It would be like having a load of lumber (say 4 × 4s, each piece 10 feet long) moved from the front yard to the back yard. If one person does the work alone, they are dragging the lumber on the ground, burning all their energy to fight the friction with the ground as they move the wood. With two people, they can pick up each piece of wood and carry it much faster.

The third and fourth options add people, but now the effort is losing efficiency. Total resource effort is increasing every time we add people. Probably more time is being spent communicating with each other, so it takes more effort to get the same work done. Cost has gone up, even though the elapsed time has gone down (from 100 weeks, to 45, to 40 and finally to 35 weeks).

Which option would a typical project manager choose? In a presentation given to 200 project managers at a national conference, the attendees were asked this question and over 95% chose option 2 — the least cost option.

WHAT IS WRONG WITH FOCUS ON COST AS THE NUMBER ONE ISSUE?

Consider if this example is from an industry where being first to market with a new product or service makes a huge difference in profitability. For example, in the industry designing new integrated circuits or chips for computers, cell phones, cable devices, etc. on a popular chip, being first to market could be worth *$1 million per week*.

In this industry, what is the difference between a project that takes 45 weeks (option 2) and a project that takes 35 weeks (option 4)? The difference is $10 million. Of course, subtract the additional $50,000 in extra cost from the inefficiency, and you are still left with $9.95 million.

Consider another example, taken from a real-life case study. You are a project company that modifies wide body aircraft (747s, DC10s, etc.). Each aircraft that is modified (e.g., from a passenger aircraft to a cargo aircraft) is unique in terms of the specifications of the owner. Therefore, each such modification is a project.

The average time in this industry to do this type of work is three months, anywhere in the world. Imagine you are the owner of such an aircraft, and that you charter (rent) the aircraft to customers who pay you tens of thousands of dollars per day in charter fees. If you wanted to modify your aircraft, and every day that your aircraft is parked in a hangar you are earning $0 per day, what would determine where you have the work done?

Assuming that you found two companies that could do the work with equal quality to your satisfaction, one very important factor would be how long it takes each company to do the work. Suppose that most companies require three months, but that you found a company that could do the same quality work in two weeks. The value to you is that instead of being out of pocket for 90 days, you can charter your aircraft for another 75 days, giving you tens of thousands of dollars per day in charter revenue. Would you be willing to pay an extra $50,000 in modification fees, to be able to earn over a million dollars in additional charter fees?

In the real-life situation, the answer was a resounding *yes*. Israeli Aircraft Maintenance Division's backlog of work increased from two months to one year when it improved its cycle time to complete these types of projects. In other words, customers were willing to book this company's services one year ahead of time.

THE COST MODEL OF PROJECT MANAGEMENT

Most of the organizations that we visit operate in the Cost Model of project management. This model has several characteristics:

- First priority in any improvement effort is on reducing cost or increasing efficiency.
- Reducing the cost of a project is considered valuable, regardless of the impact on project cycle time.
- Cost numbers and labor utilization are "fudged" to show good reports, especially when the effect is bad for the organization as a whole.
- "Cost" or "efficiency" is a topic at project meetings much more often than "throughput," "competition," "revenues," or "flow."
- Improvements in project management, if there are any, that actually affect the bottom line in a tangible way are slow and painful. Most PMOs discuss their benefits in intangible ways.

- Each element of cost of a project is viewed by its weight, which is the equivalent proportion of the overall project budget that the cost consumes. In this model, each dollar of cost is viewed equal to every other dollar of cost, regardless of where the cost is being invested or cut.
- The figures used in cost–benefit analysis (if any) are often a fantasy. No one in the organization is held accountable for the achievement of the benefits. However, the project manager *is* held accountable for the project budget.
- Resources are multitasked, which most executives consider good, because it provides a very high utilization (efficiency) of expensive, precious staff resource.

On the surface, this Cost Model of how to manage the collection of an organization's projects seems valid, or at least to have some good points. The project manager typically comes from one discipline (often an IT, engineering or production discipline). This person does not and cannot control how much revenue will come from a new or enhanced product, or from any other aspect of a sales or marketing effort. Nor do they typically control each functional area's budget. Further, many managers have seen revenue projections from new products or services to be so exaggerated as to be totally lacking in any credibility.

Therefore, on the surface, what can you hold a project manager accountable for? The obvious answer is "the project budget and schedule". At the same time, there is one CEO of a medical products company who said that everyone accused him of resisting change and being reluctant to invest in technology and infrastructure in the business. He complained that almost every project was completed over budget and schedule in the previous five years, and had not achieved the benefits claimed when the project was started. There was always a good excuse, but the Cost Model obviously was not working for them.

At one Fortune 100 company, the CEO was so upset with this phenomenon of not achieving project benefits that in one quarter he implemented a new accountability model. His new procedure required the company budget to change at the end of the project, reflecting the proposed benefits of the project. For example, if the project was going to deliver a new product, and the justification was increased sales, the projected sales were added to the sales quota and sales budget. If the project was to deliver a savings in operating expenses, the operating budget of the department was reduced at the end of the project.

This forced accountability, and at least made people think more carefully about what benefits they were willing to be held accountable for. However, it did not solve the problem entirely.

Take another look at the list of characteristics of the Cost Model. If your company's key constraint is not having enough market demand for your products and services, then it may help to approach projects inefficiently (in terms of labor utilization) in order to get speed to market with new product development or engineering efforts. For example, if subcontractors can help speed up the development effort, even though they would cost more than in-house staff, even though their quality is not as good, even though they don't have as much experience, it might make sense to use them anyway.

THE COST MODEL DOES NOT WORK TO THE ORGANIZATION'S BENEFIT

We are suggesting that the key criterion to making decisions on project resources and budgets is if the net impact on the organization's overall goal is positive or negative. We are also suggesting that the Cost Model often does not provide the correct answer in terms of what is best for the organization as a whole. It does not help to clearly distinguish project choices, to decide which projects are the top priorities.

We saw another sure sign in a real-life company that the Cost Model does not work. In a project company (one where the company earns its revenues by delivering projects), the company has every employee completing weekly time sheets. People who are not billable to projects risk being laid off. The company audited the time sheets and found that 30% of all entries for the previous quarter were made to projects that had already been completed. A computer glitch allowed people to still log time against projects that were closed. The Cost Model, combined with the efficiency syndrome, drives behavior that is not good for the company as a whole. In this company, employees who were measured on being billable made certain that they met this measurement by tricking the system.

THE THROUGHPUT MODEL

We have worked with many organizations. We have not seen one organization yet whose purpose in life is to minimize cost. The owners of a for-profit organization expect that organization to make more money, now and in the future. In public companies, the satisfaction of the owners (shareholders) is often directly correlated with the value of the shares.

Most companies have found that they cannot cost-cut their way to dramatic, sustained share value growth. Examples include companies such as Apple Computers, Lucent Technologies, Nortel Communications, and all of the North American automobile manufacturers. For share value to grow substantially over time, the company must grow both revenue and profit.

The same concept is true in not-for-profit organizations. For example, if a hospital expects to thrive, it must find a way to increase its services to its customers over time — to flow more patients and more types of services through its doors. Charitable organizations must generate funding, which comes from being successful in how they provide services.

The element of cost control that everyone wants to achieve is to not waste funding or investment. However, the first test of whether or not any investment is a waste is the predicted effect on the organization's goal. This is why the Throughput Model offers a better approach.

The Throughput Model suggests that the number one focus of any organization should be throughput, which is essential for long-term health. We use a definition of throughput based on Dr. Eli Goldratt's Theory of Constraints Model. In a for-profit organization, throughput is the money collected from customers minus the money paid to external vendors to produce products or services. Note that throughput is not recognized until money is collected from the customers. Therefore, throughput is not a fantasy benefit of a project, but rather real money generated by a project.

By focusing on throughput as a top priority, any expenditure that does not help to generate throughput in the organization is a waste. This provides a means to identify and cut waste from a system.

THREE PRIMARY MEASUREMENTS FOR ANY PROJECT

There are three primary measurements of the value of any project to the organization as a whole:

- Throughput
- Investment
- Operating expense

Unless the project exists to meet a legal or other mandatory requirement, the project should have an impact on one or more of the above global measurements. In most organizations that we visit, we seldom encounter anyone who knows what the value of the project is to the organization in these basic terms.

If a project is to have a positive effect on an organization's goals, it must do one of the following:

- Increase throughput
- Reduce investment
- Reduce operating expense
- Have the combined effect in the three measurements that results in an obviously positive effect on the bottom line now and in the future (e.g., increase investment, but provide a dramatic resulting increase in throughput, such that the investment is recovered within two years or less)

A project that can affect two of these simultaneously is even better. A project that impacts three is even better. The formal definitions are as follows:

Throughput (T) — The value of the products and services you deliver to customers minus the direct cost of goods or services sold or paid to outside vendors. In a for-profit company, this is how much money is left in the bank account after payment has been received from customers and outside vendors and subcontractors have been paid for parts, materials and services. In a not-for-profit organization, the value of the products and services is still required, but it is often expressed in a non-monetary form. For an example, see Kendall's book *Securing the Future.**

Investment (I) — All capital investment and investment in inventories at all levels (raw materials and parts, work in progress, and finished goods throughout the supply chain). This includes all investments that must be written off over more than the fiscal year.

Operating Expense (OE) — All of the money that the organization spends to turn its investment into throughput. This includes all annual expenses. It also includes all labor costs, depreciation expense, and supplies consumed during the year.

Note that by using these definitions, we avoid the distortions of cost allocations inherent in most accounting systems. More information on the throughput approach is available through the Institute of Management Accountants publication 4HH and through the book *Throughput Accounting.***

If we do not know the value of a project in terms of its projected impact on T, I, and OE, how can we realistically judge the relative priorities of projects? If we do not hold projects accountable to their impact on T, I, and OE, how can we expect a company to be successful in meeting its strategic goals?

---

*Gerald I. Kendall, *Securing the Future, Strategies for Exponential Growth Using the Theory of Constraints,* St. Lucie Press, Boca Raton, FL, 1997, p. 211, Scarborough Public Utilities Case Study.

**Institute of Management Accountants and Arthur Andersen, *Theory of Constraints (TOC) Management System Fundamentals Statement Number 4HH,* Institute of Management Accountants, 1999. Thomas Corbett, *Throughput Accounting,* North River Press, Great Barrington, MA, 1998.

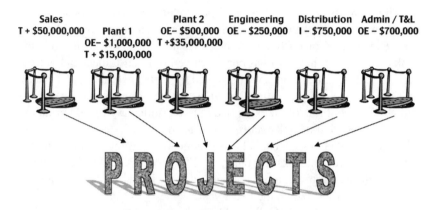

Total Company Goals – Sales ↑$300,000,000
Profit ↑$ 25,000,000

Region A

Sales		Plant 2	Engineering	Distribution	Admin / T&L
T + $50,000,000	Plant 1	OE– $500,000	OE – $250,000	I – $750,000	OE – $700,000
	OE– $1,000,000	T +$35,000,000			
	T + $15,000,000				

Figure 4.1   The Silo Cost Model Approach to Projects

PROJECT PORTFOLIOS —
COST VS. THROUGHPUT MODELS

Examine the collection of your organization's projects. If there is any relationship established between the projects and the organization's goals, it is often through a silo allocation of sub-goals to each functional area. For example, see Figure 4.1. The problem with this approach is that one silo can achieve its goal but at the same time do significant damage to other silos. For example, if engineering cuts back its staff, it might achieve a great cost reduction. But what happened to those new products that the sales force needed this year to achieve its goals?

The Throughput Model implies the understanding that in order to meet the organization's goals, the combined cooperation of all functional areas is needed. The entire concept that some parts of the organization generate cost while others have the exclusive right to claim revenues is eradicated. Instead, there is recognition that projects must collectively be released to meet the organization's goals. The picture changes to look like Figure 4.2. Note that this does *not* do away with accountability. It simply reflects that each part is held accountable for doing what is good for the system as a whole, not what is good for a silo.

An approach to managing the entire collection of an organization's projects to drive value to the organization is illustrated in Figure 4.2. In this simplified example, the organization's goal of increasing profit by $25 million is achieved through the implementation of an integrated collection of ideas.

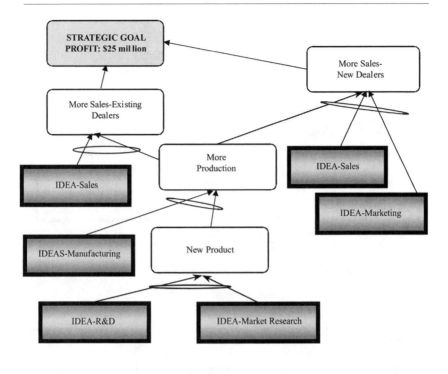

Figure 4.2   The Throughput Model for Projects

The strategy begins with the implementation of market research to determine the market's needs. From that, the R&D area develops a new product. In order to produce the new product in quantity, the manufacturing area must implement improvements. The result is more production capacity — enough to satisfy existing dealers and new dealers. However, in order to generate sales of a new product to existing dealers, the sales force must implement some promotion. In order to generate sales to new dealers, marketing and sales must put their heads together to identify a way to generate and close leads from new customers and perhaps even from new markets.

If and only if all of these ideas work together like clockwork, then the company's target will be achieved. If one idea fails, the results will be less than needed. These effects are discussed extensively in the book *Execution* by Bossidy and Charan. The former executive of Honeywell cites cases where executives were unrealistic with their goals, since the actual initiatives were not sufficient to achieve them.

Each of these ideas is translated into one or more projects, but now the difference is that each project is inextricably linked to the organization's goal. This is illustrated in Figure 4.3.

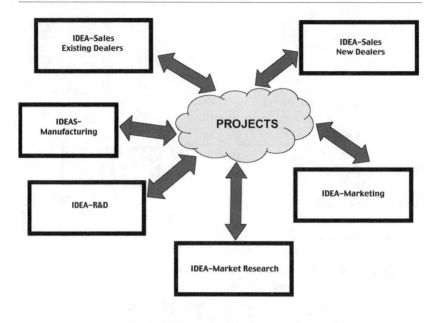

Figure 4.3   Strategy Driving Projects

One big difference between the Throughput Model and the Cost Model is in understanding the dependencies that exist between elements of cost and throughput.

In the Cost Model, a project manager looks at eliminating elements of project cost as inherently good. The impact on throughput is not visualized. Each element of cost is not considered in light of its dependency or relationship to throughput.

In the Throughput Model, the relationship between T, I, and OE is constantly visualized. For example, in Figure 4.2, in the Throughput Model, if product development cost can be reduced in the R&D idea, but it will not deliver according to the needs identified in the market research or it will not deliver in time for sales to meet its goals, then the cost reduction may have a negative impact on the organization's goals.

The Throughput Model has been tested in numerous organizations. A book published in 2000 details documented results in hundreds of articles, books, Web sites and videos.* The model works as long as the top executive buys in.

---

*See Victoria Mabin and Steven Balderstone, *The World of the Theory of Constraints*, St. Lucie Press, Boca Raton, FL, 2000.

SUMMARY

There are two major philosophies to improving project management using a PMO or corporate project management expertise:

1. Focus the PMO on ways to reduce the cost and increase the efficiency of project management. The focus here is usually on tools and techniques to solve problems, increase efficiencies and decrease project expenditures and budgets. The PMO role is viewed primarily as training and consulting or, in the extreme cases, as a police force. The emphasis is to bring errant projects under control, reduce project budgets, squeeze more out of resources, use resources more efficiently, and enforce rigid methodologies to reduce rework. This is the Cost Model.

2. Use the PMO as the main strategic vehicle to drive company-wide improvement by helping the company to select the right projects, and by using the PMO as a vehicle to drive bottom-line value from the company-wide project management effort. This is the Throughput Model.

We do not claim that the first approach is irrelevant. It may be necessary where the company has huge project overruns and no one is following any standards.

We believe that the second approach, the Throughput Model, will have much greater executive and senior management appeal. There is a role for standards and efficiencies within a PMO, but it falls secondary to the overall goal and comes only after the constraint of the organization is recognized.

In fact, our experience with PMO failures shows that people who focus on cost rather than bottom-line value as their top priority end up with their executives abandoning the PMO effort. With the Throughput Model, every project is evaluated according to its impact on T, I, and OE, the three global measurements of any organization. This provides a link between overall organizational strategy, specific strategies of each functional unit and the projects these strategies drive.

The Throughput Model ensures that the organization chooses a project mix that is balanced, with sufficient projects to meet the organization's goals.

QUESTIONS

4.1   Name three characteristics of the Cost Model of project management.

4.2   Which characteristics of the Cost Model might result in a "silo" approach to initiating projects?

4.3   Most functional executives believe that the "silo" approach is good for them. It allows them to have autonomy over which projects they approve and initiate. Using Figure 4.3, explain to a vice president of manufacturing why the "silo" approach may not work well for the organization.

4.4   How does the Throughput Model propose to connect projects to an organization's overall goals?

4.5   Define the three global measurements used in the Throughput Model.

4.6   If an organization was to invest $1 million in building a new product, and the product was expected to yield $5 million throughput in its first year with absolutely no increase in operating expense, would this be a good investment for the company? Who should be held accountable for the $5 million increase in throughput, and why?

4-7.   A not-for-profit public electric utility has limited funding for new projects. It is considering two new projects. One project involves an investment of $1 million toward building power generating stations. With this project, the utility would not have to purchase as much power from external sources. Its wholesale cost of electricity would be reduced by $500,000 per year. Another project would also use a $1 million investment to reduce outages, making the power more reliable for its customers. This has been a major problem in the past few years, resulting in tangible losses for its customers of $2.5 million per year. How might the concept of throughput be used to determine which project is a better investment? Why?

4-8.   In what way might an accounting system and cost allocations distort the benefits projected for a new product? How do the T, I, and OE measurements avoid these distortions?

PART II: STRATEGIC PLANNING — CHOOSING THE RIGHT PROJECT MIX

5

STRATEGIC PLANNING — THE NUMBER ONE REASON FOR PROJECT MANAGER STRESS

INTRODUCTION

Many PMOs begin life with the mission of improving the practice of project management throughout their organization. From an executive point of view, this is not a meaningful mission. Executives do not go to shareholder meetings and cocktail parties to brag about what a professional group of project managers their organization has. Their mission is to make more money (or in a not-for-profit organization, to achieve the goal). If an executive is told that the reason for poor project performance is poor skills, many executives will accept the premise. However, to an executive, this is not the end but simply the means to the end.

The statistics seem to support this phenomenon. While project management success is improving, executives are being replaced in record numbers.* This is not to say that the improvements in project management processes are irrelevant. However, it implies that they are insufficient to help executives to keep their jobs.

To accomplish their goal, executives need the correct projects to finish faster. They need to drive more projects through their organization without adding resources. If a PMO improves project management practice, but the company has a lousy strategy, what good will this do for the organization? If a PMO imposes a formal life cycle approach on all projects and many senior managers complain to their boss about unnecessary bureaucracy, how long will the PMO continue to get executive support?

Below are some strategic planning examples that spotlight a huge problem common to all organizations.

The CEO of a public water and electric utility, serving over 300,000 residents and several thousand commercial customers, performed annual strategic planning with his executive team. They would go to a retreat each year and develop a list of 75 major initiatives to be accomplished. When they reviewed their performance the following year, they found that very few of the 75 items had been accomplished. Each year, they added to the list, even though it was futile.

The president of a $250 million communications distributor complained for two years that the strategies in his "Focus Book" were not being implemented. When we completed strategic planning with his top teams, the first step was to identify the existing projects in the company. Several hundred projects were identified, of which only about 50 were sanctioned by the senior management team. The company had the capacity to handle about 25 active projects. No wonder the president's ideas were never implemented.

The third company is a division of a worldwide aluminum manufacturer, representing 4300 employees and 19 manufacturing plants. Figure 5.1 describes all of the initiatives bubbling up from all of the different divisions.

In this aluminum company, the executive had to deactivate 50% of the active projects in order to achieve his strategic plan. In a co-presentation with one of the authors, the vice president said that he did not deactivate enough projects.

We cite these stories because they are representative of most environments we consult in today. What is happening here?

---

*See Jim Johnson, Turning Chaos into Success, *Software Magazine*, December 1999. The Standish Group reported the results of a study of 23,000 projects and claimed that in 1999 project management success rates were improving. The figures had improved over 50% (from 16% of projects finishing on time, on budget, and within scope in 1994 to 26% by 1998). However, witness the statistic that 163 of the Fortune 500 CEOs were fired between 1992 and 1996, according to *USA Today*, April, 1997, Page B1. In an article on April 8, 2002, *USA Today* quoted a study by outplacement firm Drake, Beam, Morin stating that 57% of the 367 large corporations surveyed have replaced their CEOs in the past three years.

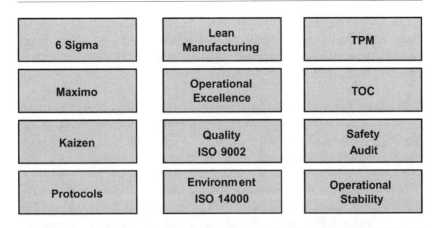

Figure 5.1 Operational Initiatives Driving Projects of an Aluminum Manufacturer

THE MULTI-PROJECT RESOURCE CONFLICT

By definition, project managers live with uncertainty in every project they manage. Since a project is a collection of tasks that have not been done exactly in the same way before, project managers expect some things to go wrong.

The problem is that project managers believe they are being given an impossible task to begin with. They know, right from the outset of a project, that they will have to fight hard for resources, and that there is no assurance they will be able to keep their resources as long as they need them. We call the current practice of strategic planning the number one problem causing project manager stress. This is because most strategic planning processes are flawed when they create, sustain and exacerbate the resource conflicts across the organization.

The problem begins with each functional executive being measured on achieving his or her functional goals. For example, the vice president of sales is targeted with sales volume and sometimes with gross profit targets. The manufacturing executive has operating budget targets, production targets and efficiency targets. The purchasing executive is held accountable for the purchasing budget, cost of materials, vendor performance, etc.

Pressure is put on executives from outside their function. Sometimes it comes from the CEO or the board of directors or shareholders. At other times, customers pressure to get a better deal. Competitors can put the heat on a company to change faster. Often, one functional area pressures another by finger-pointing or through logical arguments about how they cannot meet their targets because they are dependent on another functional area that is not performing. Sometimes even vendors selling goods and services to a company can apply pressure. Sometimes the pressure can come from below, from the organization's own employees or a union.

In order to respond to these pressures, the executive must change something, and every change initiative implies at least one project. Since an organization has limited resources, almost any new project demands resources that are already busy doing other work.

The logical response of the resource managers would be to hold off initiating new projects until resources become available. But this is not acceptable to the functional executive who is being held accountable for results this quarter and this year. The functional executive responds to pressure by exerting pressure to move resources to his or her project.

Of course, if resources are limited, there is also pressure not to move the resources. So begin the meetings where the CEO or a senior executive becomes the referee. Resources are sometimes moved, but these conflicts are not permanently resolved. They simply resurface at the next senior management meeting.

Another solution that resource managers employ, with devastating consequences, is either bad multitasking or splitting of resource pools.

BAD MULTITASKING

Multitasking occurs when we ask a resource to perform more than one task at a time. For example, in the same month, an IT software engineer splits his or her time between several projects. By itself, multitasking is not bad. Many executives view multitasking as good because it keeps resources busy, utilizing expensive resources more. Multitasking becomes bad when the combined duration of all projects increases as a direct result of the multitasking.

For example, in one medical products company with which we worked, the CEO delegated strategic planning to a process improvement team, the direct reports to the vice presidents. Each direct report had a full-time job and several other projects they were juggling. It was 6 months before the strategic plan was even developed and approved, and another 6 months after that before the first idea was implemented. During that time period, the company changed from being a publicly held company to de-listing on the NASDAQ exchange. It had acquired two new companies, sold a third company, and one third of the process improvement team had quit. Of its revenues, 50% were from a product that was being hit hard by manufacturers in the Far East. The strategies it had identified the year before were obsolete long before they were implemented.

Without bad multitasking, the strategy would have been developed and approved within 8 days. It would have been implemented in full within a 5-month period.

SPLITTING RESOURCE POOLS

Some companies claim to have dedicated resources on most of their projects. However, when you examine the resource allocation, you find that they have taken a pool of, for example, six people and split them among multiple projects. If it were feasible to apply all six people to one project, what would have happened to the cycle time (duration) of that project? The answer is simple. The project would have been completed much sooner.

Splitting a resource pool to satisfy multiple masters (multiple executives demanding to see progress on their projects) has the same negative effects as bad multitasking. It prolongs the duration of multiple projects.

SYMPTOMS OF DEFECTIVE STRATEGIC PLANNING

In an organization that has an unpredictable strategic planning process, some or all of the following symptoms can be seen:

- Project and resource managers often fight over resources. The organization's arteries are clogged with too much work.
- Priorities of projects frequently change, with resources reassigned.
- Senior managers have the authority to unilaterally approve and release projects.
- Projects are released as soon as approved by a senior manager, irrespective of the availability of the resources to do the work.
- Senior management frequently complains about how long it takes to implement change.
- Even when a strategic idea is implemented, the company sometimes does not achieve major or expected improvement.
- There is no comprehensive document or portfolio that links all of the organization's projects to the goals and the strategic plan.
- There is significant turnover at the senior management level, right up through the president.*
- The strategic plan is presented as a list of ideas or initiatives. There is no attempt to validate if those initiatives are sufficient by themselves to meet the organization's goals. The cause–effect logic tying those ideas and the resulting effects to the goals of the organization is absent.
- The list of ideas in the strategic plan is not sequenced. Therefore, each executive assumes that he or she must try to implement all ideas simultaneously, and that his or her functional initiative must be the top priority.

---

*See previous statistics showing that 33% of Fortune 500 executives were fired between 1992 and 1996, while 54% were replaced in the past three years.

PROJECT MANAGER STRESS FROM
LIMITED HUMAN CAPITAL

In dozens of workshops when we ask project managers to identify what makes it so difficult for them to deliver their projects on time, on budget and within scope, we hear the above symptoms over and over again. Today's project managers face huge problems in resource conflicts, project delays and commitment of team members. The topic of a 2002 speech to a Toronto, Canada audience of over 1000 project managers sums it up: "This Is Crazy! How to Get Your Life Back: Transcending the Madness of Today's Projects."

We claim that this stress is the direct result of the executive team either choosing the wrong projects or releasing these projects without regard to the organization's capacity to perform the projects. By analogy, this approach is as absurd as allowing any executive to expend capital at any time, irrespective of the amount of money the organization has in its bank account. Human capital must be managed at least as well as financial capital.

THE MISSING LINK BETWEEN STRATEGIC
PLANNING AND PROJECT MANAGEMENT

In any given time period, an organization can identify that its biggest problem in meeting its goals is either internal or external. An internal problem implies that the market is making demands beyond the internal capability of the organization. This is usually an excellent situation to be in because this ensures that the employees' jobs are secure. The organization needs everyone to work full out to try to meet market demand.

We use the term "usually an excellent situation" rather than "always" because sometimes the organization has made promises to the external world beyond its ability to deliver. In this case, the organization's reputation suffers and customers will look elsewhere the next time to fulfill their demand. Consider the AOL fiasco several years ago, where customers spent hours frustrated trying to connect to the Internet.

If the organization has an external constraint (implying that it has internal capacity beyond the current demand), the constraint could be in several places in the supply chain. For example:

- Suppliers to your organization might not have enough parts or materials
- The market is not demanding enough of your products or services
- The distribution channel has difficulty with the logistics of getting the right products to the right places in time to meet customer demand

■ Retailers or resellers are not effectively marketing or selling your products or services

A healthy organization is one that is consistently able to keep its constraint internal without making impossible commitments to customers. In other words, it is able to drive up demand for its products and services and manage its suppliers to keep its internal resources operating to capacity. If the organization increases capacity, it will also work simultaneously to increase demand for its products and services. If customer tastes change, the organization is ahead of the curve by having discovered these changes early on. It is also ahead by having segmented its markets so that it can shift existing resources to other segments when some markets decline.

Given this brief overview, the strategy of an organization must identify where its constraint is (internal or external). If it is internal, detailed strategies must be put in place to increase flow of products and services. If it is external, detailed strategies must be put in place to increase either demand or work on the front end of the supply chain, if that is where the problem is located, or work on distribution logistics.

These strategies must then be linked explicitly to projects. The symptoms of defective strategic planning, described above, indicate that this is not the case. Instead, we often identify many projects within organizations that do not recognize where the constraint of the organization is located. Often, there are no or few projects that are dealing effectively with the constraint.

THE ROOT PROBLEMS OF STRATEGIC PLANNING PROCESSES

The previous discussion points out that strategic planning efforts lack sufficient team play, especially when it comes to enterprise-wide project management. In Part II of this book, we analyze and provide a solution to the core problems of strategic planning. They are outlined below:

■ Executives do not speak the same language. This implies that executives tend to view their organization through the eyes of their experience and their silo — the functional area they feel most attached to. They do not have a sufficiently deep, common understanding of the organization as a whole.

■ The organization has measurements and policies that are oriented to each silo, which are often in conflict with each other and in conflict with the overall goal. These measurements cause functional executives to push projects into the system, irrespective of the capacity of all resources to do the work.

■ Executives lack the skill to build a strategy that has the commitment of the entire senior management team, meets the goals of the organization, and can be implemented with current or planned resources.

■ Strategies ignore internal systems that are out of control. When executives attempt to improve something before bringing it under control, they often throw the entire system into chaos.

The problem that we have seen with many PMO efforts is that the PMO executive views these problems as beyond his or her control. If these problems are ignored, then the PMO staff is forced to deal with symptoms of problems that result from the root problems discussed above. Dealing with symptoms of a problem within project management is about as effective as in medicine. The symptoms recur and, eventually, the patient (in this case, the PMO) becomes very ill or may even die. The disease must be eradicated, or it will kill the PMO at the very least, and eventually the entire organization.

The PMO has an excellent chance to change some bad practices that have been ongoing for many years. In fact, it must do so in order to show enough of an impact to its organization to keep executive attention. A top priority of any PMO should be to help executives do a better job on the project portfolio, which will have a huge impact on the overall organization.

SUMMARY

If an organization has a bad strategy, much of the efforts of the PMO could turn out to be a waste. Poor strategies implemented well are still poor strategies.

To provide value to the organization, the PMO must help its organization choose the right project portfolio (the project mix that will drive positive effects that are necessary and sufficient to meet the organization's goals). In addition, the PMO must quickly and dramatically fix the resource conflicts. To do this, it must convince executives to stop pushing new projects into the organization, irrespective of the resource capacity to perform those projects.

These two missions of the PMO require educating the executive team, creating a common language to view the organization holistically, providing new skills in strategic planning, and having the executives simplify and remove conflicting policies and measurements. This is no small task. Part II of this book is devoted to showing you how to accomplish this task.

QUESTIONS

5.1 Why is the current practice of strategic planning the number one reason for project manager stress?

5.2 What do bad multitasking and splitting resource pools have in common?

5.3 What is the connection between strategic planning and bad multitasking?

5.4 What problems does bad multitasking create for a project manager? For a resource manager?

5.5 What might tell an executive that he or she has a flawed strategic planning process?

5.6 How do you permanently overcome a flawed strategic planning process?

6

APPLYING DEMING, GOLDRATT, AND SIX SIGMA TO SYSTEMS THINKING

HOLISTIC THINKING

When conducting strategic planning, why make the same huge mistakes others have made? A smart person learns from his mistakes. A wise person learns from other people's mistakes. There are two great geniuses of modern times who have a great deal to teach about strategic planning and holistic thinking. W. Edwards Deming and Eliyahu M. Goldratt, working with many organizations and industries, discovered, firsthand, the underlying root problems causing so much customer dissatisfaction. They analyzed problems, verified the root causes and invented solutions that brought companies to be first in their industry worldwide. Today, their knowledge can be readily combined with other powerful holistic approaches, such as Six Sigma, to exponentially move an organization toward its goals.

Our point in including some of the work of these great, holistic thinkers in our text is that organizations today are burdened with far too many of the wrong projects, and not enough of the right projects. The combined thinking of Deming and Goldratt provides a remedy for this problem. Their holistic approach provides excellent clues that help us understand why some projects will be a complete waste of time and why others will make the situation worse, not better.

There are two common problems with many geniuses. The first problem is that no one can understand them. This is where the genius of Deming and Goldratt is different. They were both able to take their concepts and put them into terms that average people can understand.

The other problem with geniuses is that no one listens to them. Goldratt claims that out of everyone who tells him his analysis of situations is correct, only approximately 1% actually implement his proposed solutions. Why? Often, the answer lies in resistance to change. To the individual or group proposing a solution, the solution is so obvious that, in their minds, you would have to be stupid not to understand it. To another individual or group looking at the exact same situation, there is nothing obvious about it. In fact, the only thing obvious to the other individual is how dangerous or stupid the proposed solution is (for a variety of reasons).

Some of Goldratt's genius in the past few years has revolved around his work on buy-in and overcoming the layers of resistance to change. He realized that we only solve part of a problem when we correctly analyze it and come up with a solution. A major part of solving any problem is to communicate its characteristics in a way that gets buy-in — buy-in to the problem and buy-in to the solution.

SIX SIGMA

This methodology traces its origins to Motorola in the 1970s. Unlike the methodologies of Deming and Goldratt, Six Sigma has been popularized by Wall Street, with the comments of former GE CEO Jack Welch, and books and presentations by many others.

Six Sigma offers a way to achieve a quality breakthrough, in terms of reducing errors to parts per million. It does so by asking the right questions, measuring the correct values, and changing processes to prevent errors from occurring. Correctly applied, it is focused on what matters to a customer much more so than what matters internally.

BLENDING METHODOLOGIES

Sadly, we see people in organizations constantly fighting with each other over which methodology to use. Our message is that each of these methodologies, and others such as Lean, offers different angles toward a complete solution to project management problems. Combine the thinking of all of them, and an organization will begin to move towards its goals at warp speed. What has been missing in the approach to date is the umbrella under which various methodologies can operate in harmony. We believe that the Theory of Constraints is such an umbrella.

In this chapter, we take a brief look at how the works of Deming and Goldratt converge in the project management arena. Each one contributed greatly to the problem analysis and solutions described below. We also offer our insights into where Six Sigma fits into this picture.

PROJECT MANAGEMENT —
A SYSTEM OUT OF CONTROL

Consider any task estimate provided for a project task. A project is, by definition, a one-time effort — something that an organization has not performed before in exactly the same way.

For example, one of the large U.S. telephone companies has an IT group that implements and upgrades local area networks in each location in which the company operates. On the surface, this work might look like repetitive operational work rather than project work. But take a closer look. The following attributes of each local area network are very unique:

- Physical characteristics of each location, which impact ease of laying cable, electrical interference, etc.
- Expertise of people within the location, which impacts how long it will take to turn over local control, amount of training required, and acceptance of the new environment.
- Culture and expertise of the local workforce. For example, some new implementations are a result of a takeover, where the local workforce already had a perfectly good network. Imposing a different network means that the implementation team must overcome huge resistance to change.
- Responsiveness of local suppliers.
- Volume and transaction mix of local work.
- Specific software portfolio used.

Given these characteristics, some network implementations may require 3 days until the new environment is working to the complete satisfaction of the local management, while others may require several weeks.

If the manager of network services gives an estimate for implementing a new network, or for any one of the tasks involved in implementing a new network, we can predict one thing with almost 100% certainty. The estimate will be wrong. It may be too high or too low, but it will almost certainly vary.

In spite of all this uncertainty, in this organization each employee is held accountable for each task estimate he or she provides. Project managers manage employees to finish their tasks on time, according to their estimates.

Dr. W. Edwards Deming, the great quality guru of the 20th century, would probably be appalled at this practice. Dr. Deming described that there are two states for any system — *in control* and *out of control*. **Out of control equates to unpredictable, while in control equates to predictable better than 95% of the time.**

Dr. Deming recognized that any system will move from one state to the other. Management's job is to keep the system in control. In order to have a system that is predictable better than 95% of the time, Deming taught managers to design processes that could distinguish between two types of "Murphy", or in his term, variation — common cause and special cause variation.

Common cause variation is an inherent part of any system. For example, in project work, common cause variation includes individual tasks taking longer to complete than the estimates. *Therefore, it is totally ludicrous to hold someone accountable for something that is unpredictable.*

Deming taught managers to not blame employees for common cause variation. He showed managers that when they interfere with common cause variation, they can easily throw the entire system into chaos. Managers must only intervene when they are dealing with special cause variation. *According to this philosophy, managers should say nothing when one task, by itself, takes longer to complete than its estimate (unless the variation itself is determined to be within the realm of special cause variation).*

Therefore, one vital skill of any manager is to be able to design a system where common cause variation can occur and the system can still meet its goals. A second essential management skill is to be able to distinguish between common and special cause variation in any system.

Deming's work was largely in the area of repetitive processes, such as those found in mass production. However, his thinking was extended by Dr. Goldratt and applied to the non-repetitive processes inherent in a project.

What is common and special cause variation in project management? What is common and special cause variation in strategic planning? We will provide some examples shortly. First, we will introduce a process that bridges Deming's and Goldratt's thinking.

DEMING AND GOLDRATT ON
PROJECT MANAGEMENT — STEP 1

Every holistic approach has some common elements. A follower of Deming, Domenico Lepore, and a partner of Goldratt, Oded Cohen, got together and wrote a book defining and explaining 10 steps to any improvement effort.* Step 1, the starting point for improving any system, is that there is a clearly stated and understood system's goal, with holistic measurements.

A system, by definition, consists of interdependent events. Therefore, the measurements of any system must be holistic in nature. The measurements must drive every individual to do what's best for the system as a whole, and not just for his or her local department or function. In our consulting work in strategic planning, often the most important project (and one that is almost always non-existent) is to align the measurement systems across the organization and eliminate all of the de-motivating measurements.

An individual project can be viewed as a system (or a subsystem within the entire collection of all projects of an organization). Goldratt suggests that the goal of a project is to deliver some tangible benefit to an organization. For most projects, the entire project or a major part of it must be completed in order to realize the benefit. Also, for most projects, the sooner the project is complete, the sooner the organization realizes the benefit.

Therefore, for most individual projects, the goal is the fastest successful execution of the project. Unfortunately, the measurements that exist often do not help this goal at all. For example, there are two measurements that often run counter to this goal:

- Finish tasks on time
- Cost reduction

In his book *Critical Chain*,** Goldratt describes how the common practice to hold people accountable to finish individual tasks according to their estimate leads people to inflate estimates or provide totally confusing estimates, masked by bad multi-tasking. In turn, these estimates lead to behaviors such as "Student Syndrome" and "Parkinson's Law," which guarantee that tasks and, therefore, projects will take longer to complete.

Task time estimates are just that — estimates. They are not deterministic (predetermined, exact) numbers. Therefore, Goldratt insists that "it is not important if any individual task finishes on time. The only thing that is important is that the project finishes on time (or early)."

A measurement focused on reducing project cost or budget, without considering the impact on the cycle time of the project, is not holistic. The

---

*See Oded Cohen and Domenico Lepore, *Deming and Goldratt, The Theory of Constraints and the System of Profound Knowledge*, The North River Press, Great Barrington, MA, 1999.

**Eliyahu M. Goldratt, *Critical Chain*, The North River Press, Great Barrington, MA, 1997.

fact that many project managers do focus so much effort on project cost can often be traced back to poor project definition, especially in identifying the benefits of the project. If many benefits are left as intangible, no wonder so many times project managers are rewarded primarily for meeting or beating their project budgets.

Every organization we visit has a collection of projects, often with common resources that work on more than one project at a time. We call this environment the multi-project environment. The goal of the multi-project environment is to satisfy the goals of the overall organization. This means that the collection of projects must be:

- the correct projects overall to meet the organization's strategic objectives
- implemented quickly — in time to meet competitive threats, real customer needs and shareholder expectations

There is one other important implication. The more projects an organization can flow to completion in a given time period with the same resources, the more successful they will become, assuming that these projects are the correct projects. By correct, we mean having a positive effect on the organization's goals.

In the multi-project environment, we also see measurements and practices that run counter to the goal of this bigger system. The measurements and practices we see include:

- Release new projects as soon as they are authorized, without regard to the capacity of the organization's strategic resources to do the projects. This measurement drives horrible multitasking of resources, increased cycle times of projects and logjams in the work.
- Keep everyone as busy as possible (bad multi-tasking).
- Frequently change priorities as crises occur or executives scream.

Deming would definitely call this a system that is out of control. We can tell because most organizations have less than 50% of the projects finishing on time, on budget and within scope.

DEMING AND GOLDRATT ON PROJECT MANAGEMENT — STEP 2

Once a system's goals are stated and the holistic measurements are in place, Deming claims that there must be a deep understanding of the system before you begin any improvement process. This is what Lepore and Cohen refer to as Step 2 in any improvement process.

We are witnesses to many PMOs that try to drive standardized project management methodology throughout their organizations. They often experience huge resistance from project managers, which may already be a sign that they have not achieved the deep understanding that comes from this step. Or, if they have such an understanding, they may not have agreement on the problem from the groups they are serving.

Goldratt suggests that the first layer of resistance to change is that people do not agree with you on the problem. This implies that people see the system and the interactions in the system differently. Goldratt further suggests that if we cannot communicate our intuition, then the only thing we can communicate is our own confusion.

To understand the project management system and the root problems, we must examine how projects are initiated. In many organizations, there is a formal system and an informal system. In many organizations, projects exist through the informal system. The informal system dramatically interferes with the work coming from the formal system.

Further, how are projects released into the system? How are resources allocated and how are resource conflicts dealt with? How are individual team members managed? Is there one system or many systems? Do executives link their strategic plan to all of the projects active within the organization? Are project benefits formally tracked and managers held accountable? How is reporting done? What other measurements and practices exist within each project team? Do team members also have some full time responsibilities? How do they prioritize their own work? Do project and resource managers always agree on priorities? If not, how are conflicts resolved?

The answers to these questions are the beginning of a deeper understanding of project management within any one organization. Only after we understand what drives human behavior on projects and how the dependencies within and between projects are handled, can we be successful in moving on to Step 3.

DEMING AND GOLDRATT ON
PROJECT MANAGEMENT — STEP 3

Step 3 in the process of improving project management is to "make the system stable." This implies having a system in the first place, identifying how the system will distinguish between common and special cause variation, and getting the system to meet its goals more than 95% of the time. For projects, this means delivering on time, on budget and within scope more than 95% of the time.

Deming taught managers to recognize special cause variation through trends. He also taught managers that one statistic alone can be misleading. We find relatively few managers using Deming's concept of Statistical Process Control. Organizations that have implemented Critical Chain have seen that trend reports work beautifully as a predictive tool to give early warning to projects moving out of control.

In project management, there is a set of clearly identified processes. The Project Management Institute (PMI®) offers these processes and knowledge areas in a professional guide called the *Project Management Body of Knowledge (PMBOK®)*. This is an excellent start.

Some processes that are missing or only vaguely defined are the multi-project coordination and strategic processes, as outlined in this book. For example, the portfolio management, governance and prioritization processes must exist formally in any organization in order for project management to improve dramatically.

For project management, Goldratt offers a solution that is complementary to the PMBOK®.* This solution incorporates the principles of following trends to distinguish between common and special cause variation, but without the burden of becoming a statistician. He calls it *buffer management*. While buffer management is a later step in the process of ongoing improvement, the system must be set up in the first place to allow stability.

In making a system stable, Goldratt has the following advice: "When you find yourself in a hole, the first thing to do is to stop digging." In project management, this means stop measuring people in ways that drive behavior that is detrimental to the system's goal.

Statistical fluctuations and Murphy are a normal part of any task execution on a project. The main advice, at the outset of making a project management system stable, is that the system must allow for individual tasks to exceed estimates without causing the project deadline to be blown. One example of special cause variation might be when three or more tasks in a row exceed estimates by a large amount.

The complete system Goldratt suggests is described in Chapter 17. There is an excellent reference for understanding Deming's approach to variation and how to manage it.** This book should be required reading for every project manager.

---

*Gerald Kendall, George Pitagorsky, and David Hulett, *Integrating Critical Chain and the PMBOK®* white paper, www.iil.com, 2000.

**Donald J. Wheeler, *Understanding Variation – The Key to Managing Chaos*, SPC Press, Knoxville, TN, 2000, with thanks to Mr. Yvon D'Anjou from Alcan for recommending this book.

DEMING AND GOLDRATT ON
PROJECT MANAGEMENT — STEP 4

Goldratt defined a system for project management called *Critical Chain*. It has two sides — one that addresses an individual project and the other that solves the problems in the multi-project environment.

We will summarize by stating that within the single project environment, Goldratt describes the root problem as the common practice of holding people accountable to finish their task according to their estimate. Through cause–effect logic, he describes how this measurement drives project cycle times longer and almost guarantees unpredictability in results. The solution is a new measurement that we call "the relay runner work ethic" combined with a system of buffers and buffer management.

Within the multi-project environment, the root problem is the practice of pushing new projects into the system, without regard to the capacity of the strategic resources to do the work. The solution is a pull system that is simple enough to implement in any organization of any size or complexity. Strategic resources are the ones that are involved in most projects, and determine, more than any other resources, how long the combination of projects will take. We discuss this further in Chapter 17.

DEMING AND GOLDRATT ON STRATEGIC PLANNING

If you ask people across an organization what they think of their executives' strategic plan, we encounter many individuals who roll their eyeballs and ask, "What strategic plan?"

Deming's principles apply as much to strategic planning as they apply to any other process. However, in strategic planning, the stakes are much higher. We must build greater predictability into a strategic plan. The book *Execution* (see Bibliography) points out how lame some strategic planning processes are.

One of the major obstacles that Goldratt encountered in trying to implement change across an organization is that people (executives) on the inside do not see their organization holistically or through common eyes. Rather, each executive sees their silo and a partial picture of the other business units. Further, the measurements and practices throughout most organizations are counter to each other and sometimes threaten the goal. This has been borne out by organizations that have implemented the Theory of Constraints methodology. When they attempt to resolve conflicting measurements, it often takes them the better part of a year, and they find themselves going through department by department just to *find* the measurements that are the primary drivers.

Therefore, before we go about improving an organization, we must develop a deep common understanding and put in place holistic measurements. Only then can the strategic planning become predictable.

Goldratt developed a process called the 4×4 to address these issues of strategic planning. He called one of the authors when the process was new and asked him, "Did you hear about the 4×4 process for strategic planning?" The author (Kendall) responded, "Is that where you hit someone over the head with a big stick?"

Goldratt responded, "No, that's the 2×4!" Goldratt described the process and Kendall tried it for the first time in 1999. The results were promising, and he repeated the process with several major clients. The companies that have implemented have done very well, as the case studies show.

Kendall, however, was not completely satisfied. While organizations publicly proclaimed that their strategic plan was allowing them to meet all of their goals, there was still an element missing to help ensure predictability.

Most organizations do not govern their multi-project environment with a sense of order and predictability. When the executives develop a new strategic plan, the tendency is to shove a bunch of additional projects into the system, creating chaos. Many organizations do not have a central group skilled in advanced project management. Many organizations do not have a project portfolio, meaning that they really have no idea how many projects are currently active, what those projects are, relative priorities, etc.

The PMO, in combination with the 4×4 process described later, provides an approach to strategic planning that finally has a chance to meet Deming's criteria for predictability. Perhaps with this predictability, we will see a lot less than 54% of CEOs replaced within a three-year period (see footnote in Chapter 5).

SIX SIGMA — WHERE DOES IT FIT IN PROJECT MANAGEMENT?

Six Sigma talks about reducing defects to parts per million. Another way to view Six Sigma is that it will increase predictability of the results your customers expect. Already this implies that we are dealing with a repetitive process (e.g., manufacturing parts or handling service calls, making pizzas, taking mortgage applications, etc.).

While each project is unique in some way, there are some processes that are repeated across all projects. For example, every project involves planning, scheduling and executing. Every project has a requirements definition. Every project has work broken down into tasks, assigned to individuals.

The Critical Chain approach, described earlier, is designed to bring the project management system into control, according to Deming's criteria. The Buffer Management can then be used to recognize where the system needs to improve. This is one obvious place where Six Sigma thinking can play an important role.

In many projects, for example, we hear complaints about poor requirements definitions and the impact on rework. Imagine the impact of reducing this rework in half. We will assume, just for illustration, that 80% of all project complications (measured by buffer penetration in Critical Chain) is due to rework of requirements.

The approach that we have seen some project managers take is to demand detailed, cast in concrete requirements of the end user or customer. The penalty, if requirements change, is that the project manager can either refuse to do the change, or will force the change through some change control board, demanding more time or more money to accomplish the change.

The end customer is therefore understandably reluctant, if not completely paranoid, about allowing requirements to be cast in concrete. This is not a helpful answer to deal with the issue.

In project management, the Six Sigma approach begins with the definition that there are three states we are seeking for requirements definition. (1) We want the requirements to be free of defects (which we would need to define, as not all rework is a result of defects). (2) We want the requirements to be delivered on time. (3) We want the requirements to be delivered at the lowest possible cost.

Five key steps in the Six Sigma methodology are abbreviated as DMAIC:

1. **Define** — Define the processes used in requirements definition which contribute to the problems. What formal steps should be taken?
2. **Measure** — Measure the current performance of these processes. Once the performance factors are known, performance can be charted. One factor might be the number of days of unplanned rework, as a percentage of requirements definition effort.
3. **Analyze** — Analyze the data to assess prevalent patterns and trends (look for the root causes). Is there a correlation, for example, between the amount of rework and the duration of a project? Is there a correlation between the amount of rework and the length of time between definition and implementation?
4. **Improve** — Improve the key product/service characteristics created by the key processes. This might be the statistic highlighted in Step 2 above, or some other service characteristic.
5. **Control** — Control the process variables that exert undue influence. For example, if a key variable turned out to be the skill of the end

customer doing the requirements review, the PMO might choose to perform requirements definition training for end customers. Or it might choose to have the service providers perform prototype (simulation) reviews in order for the end customer to gain some hands-on experience before freezing requirements.

There is obviously much more to Six Sigma than what we have summarized here and many other aspects of projects that Six Sigma can and should contribute to. We are merely suggesting that there is an important place for this methodology in every project management effort. It can be used both to improve the organization and to improve the project management performance. For further information, we recommend reading one of the many books on Six Sigma, such as the one by Harry and Schroeder.*

SUMMARY

Deming and Goldratt provide an integrated systems approach to delivering projects on time, on budget, and within scope. When Deming's philosophy is applied to project management, and Goldratt's Critical Chain and 4×4 strategic planning methodology is implemented, organizations have a better chance of meeting their goals. Further, these powerful holistic approaches blend well with Six Sigma, a way to reduce errors and provide dramatically increased customer satisfaction.

The basic principles are:

- Every system must have a clearly defined goal and holistic measurements.
- Management must have a deep understanding of the system, the dependencies within the system relative to the goal and the cause–effect relationships within the system.
- There must be a way to make the system stable. Within project management, this implies a way to get 95% or more of the projects to meet their goals. Within strategic planning, it means the strategic plan meets or exceeds targets 95% of the time or more.

We are witnesses to many PMOs using approaches that are not driving measurable value for executives. The Deming, Goldratt, and Six Sigma approaches provide a focus for the PMO, better quality of life throughout the organization, and much needed executive support for the PMO staff and effort.

---

*Mikel Harry and Richard Schroeder, *Six Sigma, The Breakthrough Management Strategy Revolutionizing the World's Top Corporations*, Doubleday, New York, 2000.

QUESTIONS

6.1   Why is it important for management to distinguish between common cause and special cause variation in a project?

6.2   Why is variation from a project task time estimate considered to be common cause variation?

6.3   In their book, Lepore and Cohen describe the 10 steps to any improvement effort. Why should the first step be to define the goal(s) of the system and the measurements?

6.4   What are the goals of the single project environment and the multi-project environment?

6.5   What does "make the system stable" imply for project management?

6.6   What is the biggest problem Goldratt encountered in implementing cross-functional change over the past 20 years?

6.7   How do executives unknowingly contribute to the problems of managing multiple projects?

6.8   Before offering a solution to executives for managing projects holistically, what must you do to overcome the first layer of resistance to change?

7

THE EIGHT MAJOR SUBSYSTEMS THAT STRATEGIC PLANNING AND PROJECT MANAGEMENT MUST ADDRESS

THE MAJOR COMPONENTS OF ANY ORGANIZATION

Every organization has interdependent functional departments that are necessary to meet the organization's goals. Sales must be able to effectively sell the product or service. Operations must be able to get the order entered and processed through all the departments. Purchasing must ensure that the raw materials are ordered and delivered. Engineering has to design the product and manufacturing has to produce the product in time to meet the customer need. If any one of the functional areas fails, the flow of products/services is disrupted.

These functional areas use interdependent processes to bring money into the bank account. Projects should improve the company, which means they should bring more money into the bank account (or achieve other tangible aspects of the goals of the organization).

In most organizations, project management conflicts originate due to each functional area attempting to achieve its own specific objectives and optima. While each functional area believes that it is doing what is best for the organization as a whole, in reality there is a huge conflict between optimizing locally and optimizing globally.

Through discussion and examples, this chapter illustrates the beginning of the common understanding necessary to make project management work holistically.

The components we examine include:

- **Operations** — controlling the flow of goods and services, including purchasing
- **Finance and Measurements** — the scorekeepers
- **Project Management/Engineering** — the way change, including new and improved products and services, is implemented across the organization
- **Distribution and Supply Chain** — all the links between vendors, internal operations and the end user
- **Marketing** — "Bring the ducks to want to sit and eat the corn in your field, preferably with glue on their feet"*
- **Sales** — "Shoot the sitting ducks. Anyone who thinks it is easy to shoot a sitting duck has never been a salesperson"*
- **Managing People** — Driving enough commitment, respect and mutual understanding throughout the organization to achieve the organization's goals
- **Information Technology** — Using the new bureaucracy to enforce better rules

Hopefully, we are not insulting people who work in other parts of an organization, such as Accounts Payable or Payroll. These are necessary to any successful organization. However, we rarely see major problems in these departments and that is why we are not addressing them as part of generic strategic planning. Mostly, these organizations are part of operations or finance.

The major components above cover the market side of the supply chain and the internal or supply side.

SUBSYSTEM 1: OPERATIONS — THE UNIVERSAL CORE PROBLEM

Have you heard about companies where some managers spend a lot of time trying to control costs and prevent unnecessary overtime, while at the same

---

*Dr. Eliyahu M. Goldratt, from the Goldratt Satellite Program broadcast live in March–May, 1999.

time other managers are spending excessive money to expedite products to angry customers? Or have you heard about companies where, all during the quarter, the finance people are screaming, "absolutely no overtime." Yet at the end of the quarter, just before the financial results will be calculated, the same executives are screaming, "I don't care how much overtime you have to pay. Get the product shipped before the end of the quarter!" These conflicting messages are very common in the lifeblood of every organization — operations.

"Operations" is a term that has several different meanings in business. We describe operations as including those functional areas responsible for the logistics of producing a product or service and delivering it to the next link in the supply chain. For example, in a manufacturing company, operations includes the scheduling and production activities in the plant — all of the logistics required to produce and ship products. In a hospital, operations includes the scheduling and conducting of surgery and patient care (pre- and post-operative). In a bank, operations includes all of the services provided to customers, including those conducted in the bank and those provided through Web sites and mail.

Functions associated with operations are looked on as "cost centers." Therefore, many "improvement" projects in these areas are designed to reduce costs and increase efficiency. The philosophy that often guides managers of these areas is that the more products you can produce with the same fixed overhead, the lower will be the cost per product. This philosophy falls apart when the product or service is available but the customer does not want it. It also falls apart when product cost is calculated based on predicted volume, and the predicted volume does not occur.

For cost centers that produce or provide products or services, we often encounter metrics such as "performance to budget" or "efficiencies." For example, in a manufacturing environment, parts produced per hour per work center or machine is a common measurement. In a consulting firm, utilization of the consultant's hours is a common measurement.

EFFICIENCY MEASUREMENTS — EXAMPLE

These types of efficiency measurements are often in conflict with achieving flow (getting just the right products out to customers on time). This places the operations function in direct and constant conflict with sales, engineering and finance. For example, in one medical products company we worked with, there was a division that assembles medical kits for surgical procedures. The efficiency measurement in this plant is the number of kits the assembly teams can put together per shift.

In order to assemble kits for any one procedure, each item (sometimes numbering in the dozens) must be staged so that the assemblers can pick the items and place them appropriately in the surgical tray. This requires some time to set up for each different kit. Some kits have long set up times and are short runs (small quantities being ordered). Other kits have shorter set up times with larger quantities.

If you were the foreman of one of these teams, being measured on how many kits per shift you could assemble, would you want to set up for 3 hours and be able to assemble only for 1 hour? Of course not! You would look for orders with the shortest set up times and largest quantities ordered. Typically, supervisors in this situation will look beyond firm orders and add quantities for "future orders." This increases the amount of production they can achieve with the same set up time.

With such a measurement, you can imagine that some kits (the ones with long set up times and small quantities ordered) end up being backordered for long periods of time, while other kits are in an oversupply situation. While this phenomenon looks wonderful on the efficiency reports, the organization's bottom line is suffering in two ways — missed sales for some kits and excessive inventory carrying costs for other kits. This situation is real, not imagined.

If the typical hospital orders a variety of kits, and finds that some kits are backordered for long periods of time, they may find another supplier, not just for the backordered kits, but for all their surgical kits.

Eventually, when the customer or the salesperson screams loudly enough, the plant will expedite the "inefficient" production of the low volume kits, only to go through the same conflict repeatedly every few days or weeks.

CHRONIC CONFLICT BETWEEN EFFICIENCY AND FLOW

Goldratt suggests that the existence of a chronic conflict such as this (produce for efficiency vs. produce to meet customer demand) is a sign that the system is broken. In operations, the reason for this chronic conflict is the efficiency measurement(s) and associated practices trying to squeeze every resource to its fullest.

This philosophy is often counter to achieving good flow of products and services. In operations, we often see managers focus on idle resources, assuming that any resource standing idle is a waste. In reality, managers do more harm to their organization when they try to utilize every resource 100%.

OPERATIONS — THE SOLUTION

An organization can actually achieve much better results by having protective capacity and flexibility — some resources deliberately standing idle, but available to protect other more critical resources. For example, in NASCAR races, while the driver is the critical resource, his or her mechanics will stand idle for most of the race, ready to act if and when needed to help the driver win the race.

In order for operations people to work as a team with the rest of the organization, they must accept that the primary purpose of their organization is not to be efficient. Of course, if too much waste exists in the system, then the products are often priced out of the market by competition. At the same time, the rest of the organization needs to understand that constant disruption to operations can hurt flow.

What operations needs is a system that allows it to meet two different operations goals — minimize waste and good flow. The system must be predictable, according to Deming's standards. This means that the product or service must be delivered consistently on time to customers, meeting quality and other expectations, better than 95% of the time.

For the PMO, the significance of having a predictable operation is in the number of projects required. The more predictable the operation, the fewer the projects required to make the system work.

Goldratt invented such a system that applies widely to many types of operations. The system typically simplifies operations and implements the relay runner approach. It is called Drum, Buffer, Rope*, and it assumes that Murphy exists in operations. It provides a method of distinguishing easily between common and special cause variation, and tells managers when to investigate problems and when to ignore them. The system also lends itself to ongoing improvement and integration with other techniques such as TQM, Lean Manufacturing, and Six Sigma.

By having executives understand how efficiency measurements hurt them, and by seeing one example of an operations system with predictability, executives are prepared to discuss their own environment, the inherent measurements, the behaviors of people, and to what extent they have a system with predictable results. This lays the groundwork for good strategy.

SUBSYSTEM 2 — FINANCE AND MEASUREMENTS

Why does it take so long for executive strategies to be implemented? The answer we have found in most organizations is that there are simply too many active projects in the system. The meaning of "too many" is that there are more projects than there are resources available to work on those projects.

---

*For further information, see the Bibliography references to *Theory of Constraints Self-Paced Learning Program on Operations.*

In these circumstances, each active project blocks the progress of other projects. It is like having the organization's arteries clogged. The lifeblood of change, projects, cannot flow very quickly or sometimes cannot flow at all.

Who put all those projects into the system? In many cases, the answer is the executives. If the executives created the problem, why can't they simply solve it by removing some active projects? We believe the answer lies in measurement systems within each organization that drive executives to continually activate new projects.

Goldratt suggests, "Tell me how you measure me, and I will tell you how I will behave. If my measurements are unclear, then no one can predict how I will behave, not even me!"

In most organizations, executives cannot keep their jobs for long if they do not meet their specifically designated goals. Since CEOs hold each executive accountable for their local contribution to the corporate goal, each functional executive is left with no choice but to initiate projects to meet their functional goal. In operations, the goal is often couched in terms of reducing costs or increasing efficiencies. In sales, it is increasing revenues. In engineering, it may be in terms of reducing scrap, increasing quality or producing more specifications with the same resources.

Goldratt suggests that "The purpose of measurements is to motivate the parts to do what is good for the system as a whole."* When we analyze the measurements within each functional area of an organization, we typically find dozens of measurements, many conflicting with each other. Conflicting measurements pit people against each other, even when they have common goals.

For example, consider measurements on inventory. In Figure 7.1, we see that the sales organization wants to increase inventory to be able to satisfy more customers on the spot. It is very frustrating for salespeople to make a sale, only to find that the company cannot meet the customer's required date due to lack of available inventory. Production, on the other hand, is trying to decrease inventory to meet its goal of cost cutting. Since it is charged with inventory carrying costs, Production appears to be in conflict with Sales. A third player enters the picture and has yet a different goal. The Finance Department wants to maintain inventory where it is. It has to meet banking covenants and shareholder expectations. If inventory is reduced too much too quickly, it causes the cost of goods sold to increase, showing reduced profit for the firm. Inventory is also viewed as an asset by the bank, and is considered to be collateral for lines of credit and loans.

---

*For further information, see the Bibliography references to *Theory of Constraints Self-Paced Learning Program on Finance and Measurements.*

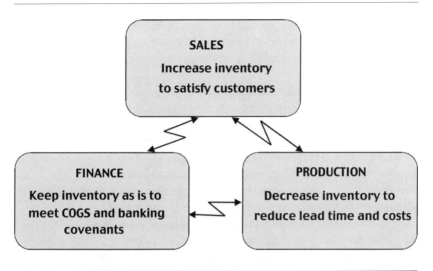

Figure 7.1 Conflicts Between Functional Measurements

THREE GLOBAL MEASUREMENTS FOR ANY ORGANIZATION

Organizations often initiate projects according to their local measurements. But will the project really be good for the organization as a whole? The Theory of Constraints identifies three global parameters of any improvement effort — a useful measurement system to be able to compare project priorities with a common view. While outlined in Chapter 4, we repeat these definitions here for convenience.

Throughput (T) measures the goal units (typically money) generated by the system. In for profit organizations, this is calculated as the money received from customers minus the money paid to external vendors for raw materials and other external costs that are incurred per product sale. Simply put, it is the money left in your organization's bank account after you have paid the external vendors for raw materials and parts.

Investment (I) is the money tied up inside the company in capital investment and inventories at all levels.

Operating expense (OE) represents all the expenses incurred within one year to turn the investment into throughput. Any operating expense that does not help generate throughput is a waste and should be eliminated.

These three measurements have various derivatives, such as net profit (T – OE) and return on investment (net profit divided by investment). These measurements and their derivatives can easily determine the net present value of any project (future cash flows from a project translated to today's dollars assuming an interest rate).

Most organizations we visit do not have these three measurements identified on all projects. Without these measurements, project priorities are subjective and changed frequently, creating chaos for project and resource managers.

Without these measurements, we also witness distortions of cost accounting systems that can make any project look justified, even when it does not have a meaningful positive impact on the bottom line. Note that with the three measurements, there are no cost allocations.

These measurements help an organization determine which projects to deactivate, in order to permanently fix clogged arteries. Since an organization's resources are so limited, the measurements should focus the organization's resources on its biggest leverage point.

If an organization has excess capacity, the measurements should be leading the organization to implement projects involving sales and marketing. If the organization's capacity is less than market demand, the measurements should lead the organization into projects to manage the highly constrained resource, to squeeze everything it can out of it.

HOLISTIC MEASUREMENTS AND THE FIVE FOCUSING STEPS

There is an attribute of metrics that we find missing from most organizations — the team attribute. In a successful football team, the receiver is designated and the play is designed so that every member of the team is working to help the quarterback throw the ball and help the receiver get free to catch the ball. There is an old Indian proverb that suggests a tree would never be so foolish as to let its branches fight with each other.

In organizations, the metrics and practices often do not lend themselves to having everyone subordinate themselves to the constrained area. Organizations need more of the metrics to cause team play.

Goldratt defines five focusing steps to promote team play. The steps are as follows:

1. **Identify the system's constraint.** In this step, everyone in the organization is made aware of what and where the constraint is. By "system," we mean the organization or the supply chain, not a computer.
2. **Decide how to exploit the constraint.** This causes people to squeeze everything they can out of it. Don't waste any part of a constrained resource.
3. **Subordinate everything else to the decision to exploit the constraint.** This means that every part of the organization is now a team player, whose purpose is to help the organization achieve the goal by doing everything possible to help squeeze flow out of the constraint.

4. **Elevate the constraint.** This usually means spending capital or hiring more people, which implies more projects. In many organizations, the improvement effort unnecessarily starts here. Often, a constraint can be brought under control simply by following Steps 1 through 3. We always find active projects at this stage, when the previous steps have not been taken. When the previous steps are imbedded in everyone's thinking and processes, some new projects are not necessary.

5. **If in the previous steps, a constraint has been broken, go back to Step 1.** This becomes a process of ongoing improvement.

The combination of correct metrics, as described above, with the five focusing steps, creates a team from of a bunch of seemingly independent silos. *Without* the correct metrics and the five focusing steps, project management becomes and remains a battlefield between functional areas.

SUBSYSTEM 3 —
PROJECT MANAGEMENT/ENGINEERING

If the airline industry had the same record as we have in project management (74% failure), there would be thousands of crashes in the U.S. every day. Using another comparison, for almost 4 days out of every week, our car would break down before getting us to our destination. Or three quarters of hospital patients would not get out alive!

While project management goes beyond just the engineering function, most engineering involves extensive project work. The core problem of engineering in many organizations is identical to the core problem of project management across an organization. Most engineering departments are in a multi-project environment (multiple projects using common resources).

Every individual project is made up of multiple tasks. By definition, projects are unique and have elements of surprise. Some projects are more unpredictable than others. Within every project, some tasks are more unpredictable than others.

If we want projects to behave as predictably as airline flights, cars, or surgeries, we must approach a project holistically. The problem begins when we treat individual tasks as if we can make them predictable. We often see project managers holding individuals accountable to their task estimate. The assumption they are working with is that if each task is delivered on time, then the project will be delivered on time.

In trying to get each task to be performed according to its estimate, the project manager is defying the basic laws of statistics. Statistics can work in our favor over a collection of tasks. At the individual task level, Murphy can easily wipe us out. Individual task times are mostly unpredictable. Therefore, if an individual task takes twice as long to perform as estimated, it is quite possibly within the realm of common cause variation.

In many organizations today, team members are measured on finishing their tasks on time or on the accuracy of their estimate. The more people are held accountable for individual task estimates, the more they will fight for bigger estimates. If this practice was working, we could predict that the majority of projects would finish on time today. But this is far from true.

Often, estimates are given not as a level of effort in a task, but as a due date. The reason for this practice is that many, if not most people in organizations today are multitasking. They are working on more than just one project. Most people we survey claim to be juggling several projects plus a full time job assignment.

With multitasking, people have the ability to quote and justify a due date that is way beyond the level of effort. For example, ask a computer support person who is supporting dozens or hundreds of users when a particular problem will be solved. If the problem is complex or involves a dependence on someone other than the computer support person, the response may be several days to several weeks. Does that mean that the person will be working on the problem for days or weeks? No. His or her effort on a particular problem might be minutes or hours.

If today is Monday and the computer support person told you to expect a resolution by Friday, what action does he or she take? Does he or she begin working on your problem immediately? Often, the behavior we observe is that the computer support person believes he or she has time before he or she needs to start working on the problem. He or she has more "urgent" problems on his or her desk — promises made a week or two ago that are due today. The Theory of Constraints calls this behavior "Student Syndrome." It mirrors the behavior of students studying for an exam the night before, even when the professor gives them two weeks' notice of a test.

There are other negative behaviors caused by measuring people on finishing their individual tasks on time. These behaviors are described in the book *Critical Chain*.*

The answer to achieve predictability and shorter cycle times on individual projects is simple. Forget about trying to protect individual tasks. We do not care if individual tasks finish on time or not. We do care if the project finishes on time.

Follow the five focusing steps described above. Identify the constraint. In an individual project, the constraint is called the Critical Chain — the

---

*Eliyahu M. Goldratt, *Critical Chain*, North River Press, Great Barrington, MA, 1996.

longest chain of dependent events, where the dependencies are either task or resource related.

Protect the entire project by placing protective buffers in strategic places. Allow individual tasks to take longer than expected. But measure people in a way that encourages them to finish their task as quickly as possible and pass it on to the next resource as soon as possible.

Then manage according to Deming's rules, ignoring common cause variation (individual tasks taking longer than expected) and reacting correctly to special cause variation. The rules are easy to follow by monitoring buffers and trends. In Critical Chain, trends mostly determine the type of variation with which you deal.

While these rules work very successfully within individual projects, they do not address the constraint of the multi-project environment. When looking at a collection of projects, we must address the behaviors that push too many projects into the system, without regard to the capacity of resources to do the work.

In the multi-project environment, the constraint is the strategic resource — the resource that, more than any other resource, impacts the cycle time of the collection of projects. It might be the resource that is most heavily loaded across most of the projects. It might be the resource that people fight over the most.

Functional executives exacerbate the problem by pushing their new projects into the system, even when this strategic resource is already overloaded. There are now sufficient case studies documenting examples of Critical Chain application in the multi-project environment to prove its validity.*

The combination of single and multi-project Critical Chain has transformed predictability from the 0 to 25% range to the high 90 to 100% range within one year, in some organizations. When combined with top-down implementation and senior executive involvement, the results are more assured.

SUBSYSTEM 4 — DISTRIBUTION

Some organizations produce a product or service without dependence on materials suppliers, and deliver directly to the end user, without intermediaries. If your organization fits this profile, you may skip this section.

---

*Harold Kerzner, *Project Management: A Systems Approach to Planning, Scheduling and Controlling*, *Eighth Edition*, John Wiley & Sons, New York, 2002.

Most organizations, including governments, have significant distribution challenges. We describe the distribution challenge as one of getting just enough of the right products to the markets in time to meet and match consumer demand. The classic distribution problem is having too much of some items in one geographic location and not enough of the same items in other geographic locations.

Why does this happen? We often find the answer in the measurement systems that drive distribution across a supply chain. For example, plant production is recognized and rewarded when a plant ships its products. Distribution centers are rewarded when they ship their products, keeping inventory to a minimum and inventory turns at a maximum.

This scenario causes each link in a supply chain to push its products onto the next link as hard as possible. In some supply chains, we have seen manufacturers threaten their distributors and retailers for not being willing to accept more inventory, even when it is obvious that they do not need the inventory.

The question that many organizations do not deal with effectively is why the results are so unpredictable. To answer this question, put yourself in the shoes of the person who must forecast the consumption of specific products during a time period. We will use the example of a new line of shoes in an international chain over the next month.

If you had to forecast how many shoes of each size would be needed in one store in Toronto, Canada, how accurate would your forecast be? The correct answer would be "very inaccurate.".

If you had to forecast how many shoes of each size would be needed in one region of Canada, would your forecast be more or less accurate? The correct answer is "more accurate." One store is impossible to predict accurately. However, statistical fluctuations begin to average out over several stores.

If you had to forecast for the entire country, the accuracy increases even further. Based on the accuracy of the forecast, where should you keep most of the inventory of shoes? The correct answer is, in a national warehouse, ready to ship to individual regions as needed. The next highest level of inventory would be at the regional warehouses, so that they can quickly replenish individual stores according to the unpredictable fluctuations in demand at each store. If the regional warehouses have enough inventory to cover these fluctuations during the time it takes to replenish their inventory, and they have the transportation methods worked out to bring their stock quickly enough to each store, the problem of predictability is largely solved.

The problem in many organizations today is that there are measurements that encourage the opposite of this behavior. For example, we often see divisions of the same company selling product to each other at transfer prices. In this case, each division is motivated to push their inventory to the next link in the supply chain as fast as it can, and to seek as high an internal transfer price as possible to make it look like it is profitable.

These kinds of measurements are not conducive to keeping the inventory where it makes sense. Goldratt suggests a philosophy that every link in the supply chain should adopt. "As long as the end consumer has not bought, we have not sold."* With this philosophy, each link in the supply chain is acting like a team player, seeking an approach that makes sense not just for it, but for everyone. The correct measurements will also reduce conflicts between manufacturers and their resellers. Today, we often see these entities competing with each other.

When distribution is unpredictable, organizations flood their people with projects that deal with the symptoms of distribution, rather than with the core problems of measurements and policies. For example, there may be projects attempting to improve the accuracy of forecasting, implementing a complex new forecasting system. Other projects may deal with inter-company or inter-warehouse transfers. Inventory reduction programs within regional warehouses often dominate.

When the root problem is addressed, the distribution paradigm is changed from a push system to a pull system. A central inventory pool is created, with replenishment geared to match consumer demand a much greater percentage of the time. In this paradigm, it is not unusual to witness inventory reduction in the total system of 30% or more, with fulfillment rates increasing into the mid- to high 90s.

SUBSYSTEM 5 — MARKETING

Goldratt's analogy for marketing and sales begins to identify the core problem of many marketing efforts. He claims that "Marketing's function is to bring the ducks to want to sit in your field, preferably with glue on their feet. The role of sales is to shoot the sitting ducks."**

When we listen to many vice presidents of marketing describe their projects, we hear a great deal about data analysis and sales support. We find many people within marketing functions who rarely visit clients or prospects. Good marketing people ask their customers and prospects a completely different set of questions than the salespeople would ask.

---

*For further information, see the Bibliography references to *Theory of Constraints Self-Paced Learning Program on Distribution.*

**For further information, see the Bibliography references to the *Theory of Constraints Self-Paced Learning Program on Marketing.*

In order for any organization to stay healthy, an organization must satisfy its markets better than the competition, at least in some aspects. The more important customer problems it can satisfy, the better the chances of retaining and expanding the customer base.

Therefore, there is a very important question that a marketing function must ask, analyze, and address. This question should become the meat of projects in marketing. The question for both customers and prospects is "What problems do you have that no one in our industry is addressing?" In other words, marketing must discover what problems it can solve in the industry that no competitors have yet solved. Salespeople, on the other hand, ask, "Did you have any problem with our company in your last order"? This is an excellent question for a salesperson who wants to retain a customer's business. It is not meaningful for a marketing person who wants to gain market share or own a given segment.

The problem with asking the marketing question as phrased above is that most customers are not intuitive enough to answer such a question directly. To understand what the marketing opportunity is to gain a huge competitive advantage, a marketing person must be able to access senior customer management and ask them to tell him or her about their business.

For example, the president of a furniture manufacturing company called on prospects and asked them what made it so hard to run a furniture retail store. He heard comments such as, "You see this huge inventory in the store. Most of it has been sitting here for 6 months or more, and I'm paying the bank huge interest charges to finance all of this inventory. And at the same time, I have customers who walk into the store and can only find a partial living room or bedroom set, or the color that they want is not in stock."

The president of the manufacturing company asked the owner of the retail store why he had so much inventory. The owner, looking at the president as if he were nuts, said, "Are you kidding? It's you guys that force furniture dealers to take so much inventory!"

"How so?" asked the president.

"First, it takes you 8 to 12 weeks to fill an order. So we have to hold large quantities of inventory to last for at least several months. Second, if we don't buy large quantities, we don't get a decent discount and then we can't compete with other furniture dealers down the street. And finally, if we don't buy at least half a truckload of furniture, we get killed on freight charges."

With this information, it became clear how the furniture manufacturer could create a compelling marketing offer and beat the competition. He launched a marketing program with transportation logistics that offered new dealers three major advantages:*

- No minimum order quantities — no penalties for freight.
- Volume discounts would be based over time, not on a per order basis.
- Guaranteed replenishment every two weeks.

With these promises, the dealer could satisfy more customers with less inventory, and substantially reduce carrying costs. With fewer stock-outs, their sales would increase. Also, they could respond more quickly to changes in consumer taste, by carrying a smaller inventory and turning it more often. They could also carry a greater variety of products. A byproduct for the dealers was that their administrative time to configure an order was drastically reduced. For the most part, they were on a replenishment system, just replacing what they sold in the previous two weeks.

Note that the implications for project management are significant. The furniture manufacturer did not need huge pots of data and custom, complex analysis and reporting. He did not need to implement complex co-op advertising programs to attract new dealers. He did not require complex sales analysis to track different discount structures for different dealers.

In most cases, the companies are not changing their products. Rather, they are changing their policies — policies that have become imbedded in their industry by all suppliers. These are policies that drive customers crazy. We have seen policies like this in every industry in which we have worked.

For example, in the airline and car rental industries, there are frequent user programs that give awards. However, there are often restrictions (dates of use, the ability to upgrade, etc.) attached to the awards that prevent the customer from fully enjoying the award.

Hospital buying groups (called GPOs — General Purchasing Organizations) drive hospitals crazy with policies restricting them from going outside the agreed upon products.

Some restaurant fast-food chains drove customers to the competition by making it hard for them to order a customized product. These concepts even apply in smokestack industries (e.g., steel and aluminum) that are 100 years old.

To apply these concepts successfully, marketing must understand how to increase the customers' perception of value for their products, working from an external view of the problems that the market has with most or all

---

*Gerald I. Kendall, *Securing the Future, Strategies for Exponential Growth Using the Theory of Constraints*, St. Lucie Press, Boca Raton, FL, 1997.

suppliers. You do not work from an internal view of the product itself and its features.

To accomplish a huge impact on a market, marketing must analyze the customers' problems in more depth than has typically been done in the past. This requires some skills that we often find lacking.

Another important aspect of marketing strategy is to segment markets, not resources. The idea is to operate in independent market segments such that, while some segments may be moving down, others are simultaneously moving up. This protects the organization's revenues and stability, as well as insulating its employees from market turmoil. Segmentation is done in many different ways. You know that you have achieved good segmentation when the price and quantity of a product sold in one market is not impacted by the price and quantity sold in another market.

One example of segmentation is having different geographic markets that are isolated from each other. Another example is in the airline industry, where the same seat can attract different pricing, depending on how far in advance the seat is booked and what cancellation privileges are desired.

The companies who apply the two methodologies (compelling marketing offer and segmentation) achieve a competitive advantage typically lasting 2 to 5 years without a roller coaster ride in revenues and profits. It puts the company in a position of being able to create more demand than it has capacity to fulfill, letting it pick and choose its customers. This gives the company enough predictability to ensure employee security and satisfaction and avoid the deadly spiral of ongoing downsizing.

SUBSYSTEM 6 — SALES

There are two types of sales that impact any organization — internal and external. Internal sales, or buy-in, are necessary to drive commitment to any project. This is not easy in light of competing projects and many people's experience that change does not always bring improvement.

Regardless of which type of sale we are referring to, we claim that the core problem in both cases is a missing skill. If the missing skill is not addressed, project management is negatively impacted in several ways. For example, if someone is advocating a project that would have a positive impact on the organization, but cannot sell it effectively, the organization loses the potential benefits of the project, and the individual becomes discouraged. People can become so discouraged that they either leave the organization or stop thinking about how to improve the organization, becoming apathetic since they believe no one will listen to them.

For external sales, if the missing skill is not addressed, we see projects constantly revolving around sales campaigns, reorganizing the sales force, mergers and acquisitions that never capitalize on the value of the new resources acquired, and trade shows and other sales activities that are often a partial or complete waste.

The best analysis on sales skills that we have seen is in a book by Neil Rackham.* In a 12-year, $1 million research program that studied over 35,000 sales calls, Rackham identified the key differences between successful and unsuccessful salespeople. Unsuccessful salespeople tend to jump, too quickly, into selling the solution (the features of their product or service) before they fully understand the customer's problem.

In internal sales, the same problem occurs. Someone inside a company has an idea — a solution to a difficult problem that they have thought about for a long time. When they approach other people inside their organization to present their solution, they are not greeted with open arms. Rather, they are greeted with resistance to change. The greater the resistance, the harder they push their idea.

To increase predictability in any selling or buy-in process, the Theory of Constraints suggests that you overcome the layers of resistance to change in sequence:

1. Agree that there is a problem.
2. Agree on what the root problem is and that it causes some undesirable effects for others.
3. Discover the different possible solutions to the problem that the buyer is thinking about and explain clearly and logically why one possible solution is a better direction to move in. Or explain clearly and logically why there is no conflict between the direction you want to take and the direction the buyer is thinking about.
4. Agree that the solution will overcome the problem and its resulting undesirable effects. Prove that your solution has a good chance of succeeding.
5. Rigorously document any concerns the buyer has that the solution will lead to some unacceptable negative side effects. Show how to overcome these negatives.
6. Rigorously document any obstacles the buyer may encounter when implementing the solution. Help the buyer overcome those obstacles in any way you can.

For example, in the case of the furniture manufacturer described in the marketing section above, the steps would flow as follows:

1. Confirm with the dealer that he is not happy with the amount of inventory he has to carry, missed sales, complex ordering proce-

---

*Neil Rackham, *SPIN Selling*, McGraw-Hill, New York, 1988.

dures and having to order huge quantities to avoid excessive freight charges and get discounts.

2. Show the dealer how manufacturer policies and practices lead to these problems. The manufacturer policies include per order discounting, infrequent shipments, minimum order quantities and minimum freight charges. When this was done in real life, it was not hard to convince dealers that the manufacturers were to blame for their problems. In fact, it astounded them that a manufacturer would admit it.

3. Show the dealer how any attempt to deal with these problems on his own is futile. Without the manufacturer being willing to change its policies and practices, the dealer simply will not be able to solve the problem.

4. Show the dealer the solution and how it overcomes his or her problems. In this case, the solution proved how the manufacturer could ship every two weeks, how the ordering would be greatly simplified, how the dealer's inventory would decrease and sales would increase. The new system of no minimum order quantity, proportional freight charges with no minimums and quantity discounts over time was imbedded in a straightforward contract.

5. Once the program was worked out, it was rare for a dealer to identify negative consequences. In fact, the offer was so good, some dealers were worried that the manufacturer was hiding something from them. It looked too good to be true.

6. By the time dealers started to identify obstacles to implementing the program, they were already sold. The obstacles were documented and dealt with. For example, the dealer might be required to have a computer system to link to the manufacturer. The dealer's buyers would need to be trained in the new procedures. There were also some seasonal considerations where buying habits changed and orders would need to be customized.

The key changes required to reduce unnecessary or ineffective projects in sales are to train people in the missing skill. We have seen executives try to overcome resistance to change with brute force, and it seldom works. People do not like to have solutions shoved down their throats. The whole organization suffers badly from indigestion. There is a better way — learning how to overcome the layers of resistance to change systematically.

SUBSYSTEM 7 —MANAGING PEOPLE

To be successful in implementing new strategy, a company must change the behavior of people. To implement projects effectively, project managers must be able to manage people to resolve conflicts, drive the correct behaviors and gain buy-in and commitment to implement the changes quickly and correctly.

It seems strange that leaders throughout an organization are constantly participating in training courses on how to manage people, yet we see very little accountability to apply the training on the job. As a result, we often witness managers taking actions that de-motivate people.

We often hear people call this kind of training "soft skills." Yet if we want an organization to achieve high levels of predictability with its people, the organization's leaders must learn how to deal with issues in a way that drives strong commitment from all participants. "Soft skills" has an implication that dealing with people is an art and that you cannot follow procedures. We disagree.

In a 5-year study of the attributes of companies that have moved from "good" to "great" conducted by one of the authors of *Built to Last*, Jim Collins* describes how great companies do not go out of their way to motivate people. However, they do go out of their way to remove policies, practices and people that de-motivate others.

For example, during the course of any project or any formulation and implementation of new strategy, we are witness to many conflicts. In the Theory of Constraints, Conflict Resolution consists of a series of well-defined steps performed in sequence. Understanding the conflict and communicating the conflict are distinct processes, each requiring separate formal steps. If we want to predict that 95% of the time or more we will resolve conflicts in a win-win way, it is necessary to follow a process, at least in one's head if not on paper.

The most success we have seen in addressing people issues is when the top executives are the first ones to go through and learn the techniques. They set the example by using the techniques themselves and insist on the techniques being used throughout the organization. They hold their direct reports accountable for using the techniques. In several companies, we have seen the CEO or vice presidents demand that their direct reports bring conflict diagrams to present at each weekly meeting. We also see these executives using conflict diagrams in presentations and emails.

Resolving conflicts is just one skill. Another mandatory people skill is the ability to construct a plan to implement change with complete consensus of the team responsible for the implementation. Too often we see the concerns of team members ignored or overruled, resulting in predictable loss of commitment.

---

*See James C. Collins, *Good to Great: Why Some Companies Make the Leap... and others don't*, HarperCollins, New York, 2001.

The message in the previous examples is that respect drives commitment and rapid resolution of issues. Respect means using procedures and techniques that consider other people's needs and points of view, and seeking win-win resolutions. The problem that we are witness to time and again is that many managers "shoot from the hip" and often end up shooting themselves in the foot or shooting their team members in the head.

To achieve win–win requires thinking logically with respect for other people's needs. There are some excellent examples in the book *It's Not Luck.**

SUBSYSTEM 8 — INFORMATION TECHNOLOGY

Information Technology is necessary, but not sufficient, to improve an organization. IT groups suffer from the same syndrome as engineering groups — too many projects for the resources available, bad multitasking, constantly changing priorities, projects that are cancelled before completion, etc. Certainly, the previous discussion on project management applies completely to IT. However, there is another issue that is also very important.

IT groups often have to replace legacy (old) systems with new systems. For example, in the past five years, ERP (Enterprise Resource Planning) systems have become very popular, especially with the Y2K threat. Fortune 500 companies have spent several hundred million dollars each implementing such systems, only to find that the results are questionable or non-existent.

The problem is not with the ERP systems. If the organization does not dramatically change some rules of how it does business, then the software will have little or no impact. This specific problem with ERP systems is just the tip of the iceberg. The problem exists with much of the work that IT is called upon to perform. The problem is elegantly described in Goldratt's latest book.**

Computers have the tremendous capability to enforce rules, to become the new bureaucracy of an organization. In order to harness this bureaucracy to make organizations more successful, the executive team must understand how it wants the rules to be changed and why this will improve the organization's results. If a company is changing software and hardware, but not changing the rules and measurements that drive human behavior, we claim that the effort will likely be a waste of time.

---

*Eliyahu M. Goldratt, *It's Not Luck*, North River Press, Great Barrington, MA, 1994.

**Eliyahu M. Goldratt, *Necessary But Not Sufficient*, North River Press, Great Barrington, MA, 2000.

IT departments need to develop a much deeper understanding of the business and be able to wear a business hat when conducting their work. This is difficult when the technology is so complex and changes so rapidly. It is a challenge for many IT departments to keep up with the technical demands of the profession, increasing user demands, and changing and unreliable vendors. However, this is often a question of priorities, and we suggest that IT needs to put a priority on understanding the business over understanding the technology.

The biggest improvement we have witnessed in IT contribution to an organization came when IT was included in the strategic planning of the entire organization. They saw their role change from "get rid of the old legacy systems" to "help the company increase throughput."

Without this, technology just makes the obsolete systems faster. Today, IT has more of a direct impact on customers than ever before. IT often owns a significant portion of an organization's projects. To move from 16% predictability to 95% in projects, IT must be part of the solution.

To bring IT on side, the IT staff must:

- Be educated on the business
- Participate fully in strategic planning
- Learn and practice new methods of project management to eliminate many active projects and drive projects through much faster

The first 4 days of the 4 × 4 process, described in the next chapter, provide such an opportunity to learn the business.

SUMMARY: STRATEGIC PLANNING — TYING THE PIECES TOGETHER

Strategic planning should also become a predictable process to any organization. With all that an organization has to accomplish just to keep up with change, the last thing people want to do is to execute a strategy and find that their efforts did not bear fruit.

Therefore, strategies also must use some of Deming's and Goldratt's principles to succeed now and in the future. The steps suggested in the 4 × 4 process, described in the next chapter, utilize the concepts we described in this and previous chapters. These steps include:

1. Have all leaders throughout the organization develop a deep, common understanding of the system. At a minimum, the organization must address operations, finance and measurements, engineering/project management, distribution, marketing, sales, managing people and IT. This implies understanding the major processes, the flow of

work, the measurements and the cause–effect relationships and dependencies throughout the system.

2. Make each of the eight subsystems stable and predictable.
3. Bring the constraint inside the company, with a control valve and knowledge to grow the company by simultaneously growing the markets and alleviating the constraint. To do this requires a compelling marketing offer — one that addresses customer issues better than competitors. It also requires a system to control and grow internal capacity correctly. The Theory of Constraints provides one alternative to such systems.
4. Segment your markets, not your resources, so that you can move resources into rising segments when other segments are falling.
5. Develop a strategy to put your organization on the road to ongoing improvement. Part of that strategy should make your organization the 2000 pound gorilla in the market, by identifying one factor in which you can consistently beat your competitors by a mile.
6. Put your organization on a process of ongoing improvement, by consistently going through the five focusing steps:

   a)   Identify the systems constraint.
   b)   Decide how to exploit the constraint.
   c)   Subordinate everything else to the decision to exploit the constraint.
   d)   Elevate the constraint.
   e)   Go back to Step a.

QUESTIONS

7.1   What impact does predictability have on project management throughout an organization?

7.2   What impact does finance have on all of the subsystems of an organization?

7.3   Why are the eight subsystems discussed in this chapter vital to any strategic plan?

7.4   If the constraint of a company is in the market (not enough demand for its products and services), which of the five focusing steps applies to the production department? To engineering? To IT? Why?

7.5   What role is suggested for executives in managing people?

7.6   What should executives do to ensure the success of any wide-spread leadership-training program?

7.7   Describe the two key elements to any strategic marketing effort.

7.8   Why would people selling an idea internally have the same root problem as salespeople selling a product to a customer?

7.9   Why might it be better to have predictable systems inside an organization before attempting a dramatic market growth?

8

THE 4 × 4 APPROACH TO STRATEGIC PLANNING

There are several major obstacles which block executives from defining and implementing a good strategic plan:

1. Executives do not speak the same language. Executives are usually experts or very experienced in a few, but not all, functional areas. They often see themselves being challenged with problems caused by other functional areas. Therefore, executives view the company through the eyes of their functional responsibilities and with a narrow understanding and empathy for other functional areas.

2. CEOs often hold individual functional areas accountable by allocating pieces of overall goals to each functional area. For example, we have heard this type of conversation in a multi-billion dollar company board room:

    CEO: Why are we 10% under budget this quarter in sales and gross profit?

    VP Sales: We would have made our targets if manufacturing did their job.

    VP Manufacturing: I know we were supposed to reduce operating expenses by 10%, but how can we do it if Sales keeps giving us last minute emergencies. Most of our overtime expenses this quarter were either because of sales emergencies or due to a lousy sales forecast.

And engineering specs are so tight, no wonder our scrap level is going through the roof. No one could manufacture to those specs!

VP Engineering: We were told to reduce customer defects — that is what is causing a lot of problems in sales. So we had no choice. We had to make the specs tighter.

These individual functional goals often ignore the cause–effect relationships (dependencies) that exist between functional areas and processes. One missing element is the deep, common understanding of the entire organization. Rather than promoting team play, which CEOs generally prefer, the allocation of goals creates an environment of competition or finger-pointing between the silos.

3. There are too many active projects already in the system. Many resources are suffering from bad multitasking.

4. The project portfolio is not correct or balanced. Most often the project mix is slanted toward the supply side of the organization, and away from the market side. Too many projects have, as their mission, to improve internal functions, systems or product design, and not enough are geared to addressing the real needs of the markets and securing long-term competitive advantage.

5. Marketing skills are lacking. Most organizations' marketing efforts are focused on sales support and product enhancement. One major element that is missing is a deeper understanding and analysis of the problems that the markets have, not just with your organization, but with every organization in your industry. Another symptom of missing skills is the difficulty that most organizations display in translating an individual customer request into a generic need of the entire market.

How do you know when your organization needs a different approach to strategic planning? Here are just a few thoughts:

1. One example is when your organization does not consistently meet its goals (i.e., overall goals are not met or exceeded more than 95% of the time). "Consistently" means looking at the past five years, for example.

2. Some of the subsystems are not performing predictably (i.e., better than 95% of the time). For example, project management does not deliver 95% of projects on time, on budget and within scope. Operations does not deliver what the customer wants on time more than 95% of the time. Sales does not generate the desired sales volume at the desired margins better than 95% of the time.

3. The constraint of the organization is in the market or in some other part of the supply chain, not internal to the company.

4. You have downsized more than once in the past five years.
5. The jobs of some executives are in jeopardy.

4 × 4 PROCESS — OVERVIEW

The 4 × 4 process was developed to overcome these obstacles and help executives deliver consistent, sustainable results, now and in the future. A correct strategy should enable an organization to keep their constraint inside the company, and therefore under its control. The term "4 × 4" stands for two parts, each one of which takes approximately 4 days.

The first 4 days (usually split into four 1-day segments) is designed to develop the common understanding and language by all senior management. This part of the process is also very useful to help other groups gain a common, holistic understanding of the business. Therefore, this same process is often replicated downwards throughout the management of the entire organization, and sometimes even to all employees. One executive described it as "drinking from a fire hose for four days". In spite of his 20+ years of experience in the distribution industry, he declared this process a major development in his education and knowledge of how his company was being run in each silo.

The process includes 8 segments, each of which looks at the organization from a different angle (see Chapter 7 for a description of these areas):

- Operations
- Finance and Measurements
- Engineering/Project Management
- Distribution
- Marketing
- Sales
- Managing People
- Strategy

At a project management conference* in May 2002, we surveyed attendees to determine how many of them claimed to have a deep understanding of each of these major processes in their organization. We also asked them how they thought their executives would answer this question. Table 8.1 shows these results.

---

*Bloomington, Illinois, Project Management Institute Regional Conference, May 9-10, 2002.

Table 8.1   Percentage of Those Surveyed (Total 43) Claiming a Deep Understanding of Their Organization's Processes

Process	You	Executives
Operations	32	58
Engineering	32	16
Marketing	16	47
IT	79	21
Distribution	26	44
Finance	21	65
Sales	12	65
H.R.	26	49
Project management	88	16
Procurement	35	33
Overall strategy	35	67

Note: The last column describes how they believe their executives would answer.

The participants in this survey were all members of the Project Management Institute. No wonder the majority of them felt they had a deep understanding of project management. Also, the majority of attendees came from the IT function, where most project management responsibility seems to reside. This is also reflected in the results. Most of this group was from the insurance and banking industries, which were performing extremely well relative to the rest of the economy.

However, note the claim that there is little deep understanding in most functional areas. While most attendees claimed that a higher percentage of their executives would say they had a deep understanding of their processes, the figures are not encouraging.

Also note that project managers typically experience more cross-functional exposure than other individuals (e.g., plant supervisors or managers, purchasing, finance, administration).

THE FIRST 4 DAYS — APPROACH

We define a "deep understanding" as having knowledge of the supply chain which includes the following:

■   The major processes and their interdependencies. For example, everyone should have the same understanding of how customer needs and requests are translated into orders, how customer orders result in work for engineering, manufacturing, purchasing, finance, etc.

This understanding should track processes from suppliers through to end customers. A 1- or 2-page summary is better than a book.
- Measurements that drive each functional area.
- Where the various elements of throughput, investment and operating expense enter the system.
- Cause–effect relationships between entities within the supply chain. There is a significant focus here on the relationship between problems that exist across functional areas and a root problem that is related to policies, measurements or skills (the three major types of root problems that drive human behavior within organizations).
- Understanding the difference between marketing and sales. The deep understanding comes from having management apply the concepts to evaluate their own organization. Also, many organizations do not have predictability in their revenue streams over the longer term. To gain the deeper understanding of why this occurs, we convey knowledge of one approach to achieve short- and long-term competitive advantage. This knowledge often highlights a gap between what most organizations call marketing (sales support) and what marketing actually should be.
- How to manage people in an environment involving change.
- The real meaning of "strategy." Strategy should promote team play, tying the functional areas together like players in a football game. Sometimes having one area operate inefficiently leads to the best results for the team. Also, the strategy should give the organization a predictable, lasting, multi-year competitive advantage. Since most strategies we have seen are not achieving this goal, the knowledge shared in strategic planning also highlights the gap and deepens the understanding of why an organization is not there yet.

With this in mind, we use the 8 presentations described above to deepen the understanding of all functional executives. Each presentation is enhanced with questions and discussion to translate the generic presentation uniquely to each organization. For example, in the operations segment, we discuss what primary operational measurements exist in each area that drives operations. We examine what system the operations group uses to achieve predictable results, and to what extent the operation is achieving those results. We document the symptoms of problems in operations, and to what extent they mirror those discussed in the presentation.

By the end of the eighth session on strategy, the executives have spent about 20 hours being educated and 10 hours in intensive, facilitated discussion on their environment. We observe a transition during this time. Often, people enter into the first session feeling quite skeptical about what value they expect to receive. By the eighth session, we witness most, if not all, executives enthusiastic about applying what they have heard and learned to their own organization's strategy.

We also witness another important change. Executives are thinking differently about what they believe is necessary to improve their organization. They are thinking beyond their own silo. They are doing a much better job of evaluating their ideas to understand the implications beyond their silo.

Deming suggests, and we agree, that this kind of deeper understanding is a necessary prerequisite for improving a system. From our experience with this technique to date, 4 days has proven to be enough time to generate a strategy that makes a dramatic difference to an organization's performance.

4 × 4 — THE SECOND 4 DAYS

The two biggest problems we must overcome in order to have a successful strategic plan are:

1. Getting the executives to recognize the futility of dealing with symptoms of problems. They must recognize and be willing to attack the root problems that have plagued the organization's performance for years.
2. Getting the executives to really commit to implementing their strategies. From our experience, we see plans the executives agree to implement at a strategic planning meeting, but in reality they only pay lip service to them.

To overcome these problems, Goldratt included several safety checks and intermediate objectives in the process.

The strategic plan is a project. Therefore, before the end of the session, there is a project plan to implement the strategy with specific commitments from each participant to time frames and sequence of implementation.

We allow 4 days for the strategic planning approach, with specific goals for each day. The fourth day is a "buffer," allowing for variation in timing of the previous 3 days.

Each day's work is documented, and each executive receives ongoing updates of not only their work, but the work of the entire team as well.

DAY 1 — STRATEGIC PLANNING

Before the session, the top executive (CEO or Business Unit Director) clearly defines the goals of the organization (quantitative and qualitative). Each executive is asked to bring their biggest problem blocking them from achieving the goals of the organization. With the statement of their biggest problem, the executives are asked to quantify what the impact of overcoming the problem will be on throughput, investment, and operating expense.

Therefore, from the beginning of this session, everyone knows whether or not the combination of problems represents enough to achieve the goals of the whole organization. If not, the executives must dig deeper.

Some examples are:

- The distribution center finds it difficult to manage large, quick shifts in customer demand.
- The sales organization is unable to grow the number of buyers by 10% per quarter.
- There are unsatisfactory levels of inventory.

Every problem that an executive brings to the table is typically not something brand new. It has been around for awhile and there are no firm plans to deal with the problem. Otherwise, by definition, it would not be part of this strategic planning session. The Theory of Constraints views these kinds of issues as conflicts.

In other words, to explain why a problem exists over a period of time, the Theory of Constraints assumes that there is some huge conflict blocking its resolution.

For example, consider the problem described above wherein the distribution center finds it difficult to manage large, quick shifts in customer demand (see Figure 8.1). If the center could hire and maintain extra staff at all times, this would meet their requirement to react to large, quick shifts. But that would blow their operating budget. Presumably, the overtime required to handle these shifts does this as well. So the conflict occurs between adding or reducing staff.

Each executive is taught to express his or her biggest problem as a conflict diagram, in the form illustrated in Figure 8.1. Typically, it takes about 30 minutes to instruct the executives and about 1 hour for the executives to draw their conflict diagram. The diagram, if correct, presents a compelling reason for the existence of the problem. Every time you move in one direction on the conflict arrow, you jeopardize the need on the other side.

For example, in the distribution center case, every time you move to cut staff or overtime to meet operating budgets, you reduce the flexibility of the distribution center to respond to large, quick shifts in customer demand. If you add staff, you kill your ability to meet operating budgets. Since distribution organizations typically operate on very slim margins, there is always huge pressure to watch every penny, especially in labor and overtime costs.

While this exercise brings some insights from the executive who faces this dilemma every day, it has an even greater value. Each executive presents his or her conflict diagram to the other executives in the room. Suddenly, everyone can understand clearly why their peer has such a difficult time managing his area. But they also see a connection to their own prob-

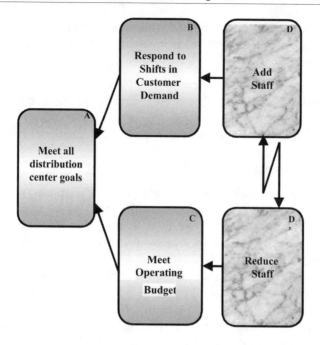

Figure 8.1 Example of Long-Standing Executive Conflict

lems. These conflicts interact between functions, compounding the challenge to get the whole system to perform.

Once every executive has had the chance to present his or her conflict diagram, the group examines the commonality in these problems. Each problem is connected, somehow, to the organization's goal. Therefore, there is a common dilemma underlying all of these problems. The executives are taught how to derive a generic conflict from a group of conflicts. Their job, for the remainder of the day, is to derive the root problem of the entire organization, by finding the generic conflict from the ones presented. In addition, they find a solution to this core conflict.

Every organization has such an underlying conflict. For example, in the distribution company, the conflict lay between being selective or being diverse in pursuing opportunities. Often, when the company was selective, it missed some major opportunities that threatened its stability, revenue, and profit targets. When it was diverse, it ended up with too much on its plate, not enough marketing and sales staff to capitalize on opportunities, excess inventories, excess labor in the distribution center, etc. This underlying conflict related to every single problem that every executive in the company had brought to the 4 × 4 session.

DAY 2 — STRATEGIC PLANNING

The ideas to overcome the core problem of the organization (from Day 1) are a great start to overcoming each executive's biggest problem. For some executives, these ideas will completely eliminate their problem. In most cases, however, these ideas are not sufficient.

Therefore, the goal of Day 2 is to identify all additional ideas required to overcome all problems identified. During this day, using the instruction from the previous day, each executive works on his or her problem. When the executive believes he or she has a solution, he or she presents his or her ideas to the team for scrutiny.

The process allows all executives to understand their peer's problem in more depth, and to gain support for their solution. This support is critical because solutions to conflicts often require participation from more than the functional owner.

There is another aspect to the process occurring on Day 2. During the first 4 days, the executive team was exposed to problems that drive systems out of control. It was also exposed to solutions that bring predictability to all aspects of an organization. Some of the solutions are already well-thought-out approaches to problems of logistics, project management, finance and measurements, distribution, marketing, etc.

The executives often find, in some disciplines, that they do not have to reinvent the wheel. The Theory of Constraints solutions will overcome their biggest problem.

By the end of Day 2, the executives have a set of ideas that, if implemented correctly, have a high probability of meeting the goals of the organization.

DAY 3 — STRATEGIC PLANNING

The ideas must now be turned into a high-level project plan. This requires more detail, sequencing, assignment of responsibilities and estimated duration.

The executives first examine the collection of ideas. They identify all major obstacles to implementing this collection of ideas. *In all organizations, one standard obstacle is that there are already too many active projects.* Therefore, in all organizations, the executive team must deactivate some projects to make sure that this strategic plan is implemented quickly.

Deactivating projects is typically a project in itself. The reason is that most organizations do not have an organizational portfolio of projects. So the first step is for the executives to gather the portfolios in their respective areas. One executive is typically assigned the task of collecting all the data and presenting it back to the executive team (or a subset of the team). From this master list, deactivation can begin.

Typically, executives discover that there are many existing projects that are either not sanctioned by the executive team, or projects that will not make a major contribution to the organization's goals. In many organizations, we see 50% or more of the current projects deactivated. Once this step is taken, the provision to flow the strategic plan more quickly is achieved.

All of the ideas, and their obstacles, are sequenced into a plan using the understanding of the team members and the logic of what must come first, what must come second, etc. Typically, there are between 50 and 100 items that are sequenced in such a plan.

As items are sequenced, the owner of each item (typically the executive who invented the idea) estimates duration and is assigned responsibility. This executive is the one responsible for project managing the implementation of that idea and for reporting back to the executive team.

At the end of Day 3, the project plan is in place. Each executive needs to go back to his or her respective area and flesh out the plan. The CEO or his or her appointee becomes the overall project manager. This is the most important project of the entire organization. To succeed, it must be monitored regularly (weekly or biweekly) with status updates from all active participants.

DAY 4 — STRATEGIC PLANNING

As mentioned earlier, Day 4 is a buffer. It is used if any of the previous three days' activities take longer than planned. In most 4 × 4s, Day 4 is usually utilized.

THE OVERALL 4 × 4 PROCESS

Most organizations with which we work have some functional areas that lack predictability. For example, most organizations do not complete 95% or more of their projects on time, on budget and within scope. Many organizations lack operational predictability, or do not have sufficient marketing strategies to keep them at a two-year competitive advantage.

The 4 × 4 process teaches executives how to achieve better predictability to meet the standards that Deming and Goldratt had in mind. So, the first focus of the 4 × 4 is to help executives ensure that they have the built-in flexibility and control in their organization to be able to grow rapidly without losing control.

The next priority is to bring in the marketing methodology to provide a two-year minimum competitive advantage. The TOC approach is to do a thorough analysis of the problems (undesirable effects) of the market(s) and to identify opportunities for the compelling marketing offer and for segmentation.

Market segmentation is one key to organizational stability and security. If an organization is operating in enough *different* segments simultaneously, the theory holds that as some segments are declining (the organization is losing market share), others are increasing. This gives the organization the ability to shift resources between segments to keep revenues flowing.

Once these ideas are implemented, the organization is ready to begin the biggest challenge of all — to identify how to achieve a 10+-year competitive advantage. We claim that the organization is ready mentally because of its success in achieving the previous ideas of compelling marketing offers and segmentation.

To achieve a 10-year advantage requires identifying the possible factors of importance to the markets, and becoming exponentially (by a factor of 5 to 10 times) better than the competition in one factor. For example, if you were in the airline industry, it would allow you to bring customers from point A to point B in 1 hour, when your competitors are taking 5 hours to do the same thing. This usually requires changes in technology, policies, production methods and distribution approaches.

SUMMARY

The problems of constant battles over project resources and constantly changing project priorities are deeply rooted in the approach to strategic planning used by many organizations today. The first part of the answer lies in building a deep understanding of the entire supply chain among the entire executive team. Then, the executives must build a deep understanding among their peers of their biggest problem. The use of a simple diagram technique helps each functional executive get buy-in from the team into his or her problem and how it blocks organizational goals. Each executive develops the solution to overcome his or her problem. The combination of initiatives overcomes the collection of problems. This process, using a new approach called the 4 × 4, solidifies executive commitment and has been successfully applied to achieving dramatic improvement in both project management and total organization results.

The important first step in implementing any strategic plan is to address the problem that we see in every organization —too many active projects. By deactivating a significant percentage of projects, according to the organization's true resource capacity, the strategic plan can be implemented more quickly and effectively.

BABCOCK & WILCOX CANADA — CASE STUDY

Babcock & Wilcox Canada (BWC) is a Canadian operating unit of McDermott International, Inc., a leading worldwide energy services company. Babcock & Wilcox boilers supply more than 270,000 megawatts of installed capacity in over 90 countries around the world.

Babcock & Wilcox Canada

a McDermott company

In the past six years, BWC has attained approximately 30% of the world market for replacement nuclear steam generators, and leads the replacement market in the United States. These complex products are built as unique projects for each client, spanning several years of design, engineering, fabrication and construction.

BWC has manufactured 50% of all of the process recovery boilers in operation at pulp and paper mills in North America. Worldwide, approximately 20% of the process recovery boilers in operation are BWC boilers.

In support of its worldwide clients, BWC also performs boiler erection, boiler repair, alteration, plant improvement and operations maintenance services, with diverse mechanical and construction capabilities. BWC also designs and delivers environmental emission control systems. With a major manufacturing facility in Cambridge, Ontario, BWC relies on shared resources and a combined project portfolio from its varied divisions to achieve its annual goals.

THE SITUATION PRIOR TO THE 4 × 4 STRATEGIC PLANNING PROCESS

BWC undertook the 4 × 4 Strategic Planning Process starting in January 2000. During the previous three years, the company had excellent financial performance. The motivation to strengthen the process improvement effort was driven by two major needs: (1) the need for greater shareholder value and growth, and (2) the need to meet increasing external pressures of competitor consolidations

Major emphasis in the previous year had been on meeting the Y2K deadline to install a new business system. The new system was expected to deliver cost savings and process improvements. However, due to the intensity required to implement the software with so many Y2K efforts, the software was implemented but few associated process improvements were made. This left the organization with the daunting task and increased pressure to make process improvements after the business system "going live."

Senior staff started in earnest in May 1999 to focus on process improvement. They quickly learned that to improve what matters most is hard to identify. Every senior executive had projects identified that he or she wanted delivered. However, with scarce resources to actually carry through the process improvement projects and more projects than resources, BWC needed to take a different approach. The Theory of Constraints offered the possibility of a methodology for focus. Because of this, the Senior Staff agreed to pursue the Theory of Constraints even before they became aware of the 4 × 4 process.

LESSONS FOR ESTABLISHING A PMO

Before the 4 × 4 process was initiated, BWC determined that the cultural factors of accountability and responsibility needed to be tuned up in order to move the organization forward. The Senior Staff developed action plans to prepare the culture for process improvement by working on the training process, management commitment, and accountability.

The Senior Staff established an Executive Steering Committee for Process Improvement consisting of the President and half of the executive team to ensure high priority, demonstrate commitment, and communicate expectations.

The Senior Staff also established an 11-member Process Improvement Team to drive continuous process improvement. The team charter was:

- To be cross-functional
- Receive appropriate training
- Identify process improvement opportunities with good payback, ranging from smaller to larger and complex
- Sanction owner teams to proceed with implementation

The direct link between the Process Improvement Team and the Executive Steering Committee is an excellent model for a PMO reporting structure. It allowed the BWC executive team to perform the governance functions, while the PI team focused on managing the details of the process improvement projects.

WHY BWC CHOSE THE THEORY OF CONSTRAINTS 4 × 4 PROCESS

In 1999, the facilitator of the Process Improvement Team and Manager of Training and Development was introduced to the Theory of Constraints at a public workshop. He invited Gerald and Jacquelyn Kendall, the 4 × 4 experts, to present the process to BWC's Senior Staff.

Some Senior Staff were concerned that the process would not enable them to address their most important issues. Others were concerned that the Theory of Constraints would force them to focus on only one issue. However, once the process was thoroughly explained, the Senior Staff were willing to proceed.

The 4 × 4 process provided three important attributes that the senior staff saw as vital for success:

1. A methodology that was focused on overall, global goals, but would also generate actions with early benefits. BWC wanted more than the use of the methodology. They also wanted to learn the methodology. Therefore, BWC adopted an approach involving intensive training and education on the Theory of Constraints.
2. A focus for applying resources where the greatest results were possible
3. A method for Senior Staff and the PI team to build a common language, with consensus on a common improvement strategy consistent with the strategic direction of BWC

BUILDING A COMMON LANGUAGE

The 4 × 4 process was very effective in providing an analysis of the whole organization for the PI team working with the executives. The PI team believed it had identified the right areas to work on for improvement through nine priorities contained in the PI Strategic Plan.

To secure help with the implementation of the PI Strategic Plan, the PI team used the extensive training provided in the 4 × 4 for 20% of the organization's managers, supervisors, project managers, and union leadership at all of its locations across Canada. BWC also developed and delivered a shorter, customized version of the training for its shop supervision. The training provided a common language for company-wide improvement.

This company-wide approach was reinforced further when cross-functional teams were set up to redo BWC measurements and increase marketing actions. The marketing team was very effective in setting strategies for many short-term needs.

Because of its importance to the division, the original marketing team was led by the president of the company at the time of the 4 × 4 process. He has recently retired and the new company president has further emphasized the importance of marketing by restructuring the various marketing activities in a common area. The establishment of global measurements for the division using a small Measurement Team and extensive collaboration with all departments further reinforced the value of the organization working toward common improvement goals. Marketing and measurement alignment was the top priority in the PI Plan.

BUILDING A UNIFIED STRATEGY, FOCUS AND SET OF STRATEGIC PROJECTS

Prior to the 4 × 4 process, improvement projects were identified individually by departments in addition to those identified through a centralized business planning process. However, the priorities for the company as a whole were not always as apparent as they could have been. Projects were often in competition with each other for scarce project management and other resources.

The 4 × 4 did identify more clearly the priorities for projects. As a result, the high priority projects received better focus through the PI team. Because of the number of improvements required using IT, a separate Steering Committee was set up to prioritize and review the progress of IT projects.

Since implementing the 4 × 4 process, improvement projects are becoming even more tightly tied to BWC's strategic goals. Implementing process improvement projects with an emphasis on results has become a strategic goal in itself.

LESSONS LEARNED

The 4 × 4 process jumpstarts improvement. This has both good and bad implications. The good implication is that the 4 × 4 clearly focuses on where to start. However, the creation of such a comprehensive strategy leaves a senior team with a collection of major projects to define in detail, integrate with current projects, and implement.

Without a PMO infrastructure in place to develop specific project plans and monitor their implementation, the PI team at BWC had to perform a lot of the functions of a PMO in order to execute the improvement plan.

As a result, the new leadership at BWC is in agreement that more accurate, detailed project plans and up-front quantification of expected results are key requirements for the PI team in future.

CONCLUSIONS — SOME LASTING RESULTS

The development of the common language and measurement system at BWC has permanently changed the thinking of BWC employees across the country. There is a much stronger marketing emphasis, with direct focus by the president. For example, one of BWC's business unit managers says that PI thinking helped BWC to structure an unusual agreement with a customer to use BWC technical resources.

These direct and measurable impacts on individuals performing the day-to-day business of BWC add up to a powerful, holistic impact on the entire organization.

BWC has made excellent progress in eliminating the measurements that put departments in repeated conflicts with each other. BWC has maintained its leadership position in the worldwide nuclear and fossil fuel steam generating business. The processes described in this case study and, more importantly, their application and enhancement by the PI team, have contributed to this success.

QUESTIONS

8.1   Explain the five major obstacles to having an effective strategic plan. How is each of these obstacles overcome using the 4 × 4 approach?

8.2   What is the purpose of the first four days of the 4 × 4 approach to strategic planning?

8.3   Describe the definition of "deep understanding" as it is used in the 4 × 4 process.

8.4   How does the 4 × 4 approach accomplish its purpose of the first 4 days?

8.5   If Goldratt's satellite series on the eight supply chain topics was not available, how else might you accomplish the objective of the first four days?

8.6   Why would an executive be committed to implementing the strategic plan developed during the second four days?

8.7   What preparation must the CEO or head of the business unit do for the 4 × 4?

8.8   What value does it have to the owner of a problem to translate a problem into a conflict diagram? What value does it have to the executive team members?

8.9   Describe, in bullet form, the objectives of each of the last 4 days of the 4 × 4 process.

8.10   What is the risk of not producing a project plan, with duration, assigned responsibilities and dates, at the end of the 4 × 4 session?

8.11   Who has the ultimate responsibility for implementing the strategic plan?

8.12   What should a CEO do if one of his or her executives does not participate in the 4 × 4 session?

8.13   How actively should the CEO and the executive team participate in the implementation of the strategic plan?

8.14   What are some symptoms that infer the need for a new method of strategic planning? Why?

9

THE RIGHT MARKETING PROJECTS

THE PROJECT BIAS OF MOST ORGANIZATIONS

When we look at the project portfolios of most companies, we witness a strong bias toward projects that address the internals of the organization as opposed to the rest of the supply chain. It is as if the attitude of many executives is "Improve everywhere!" The problem is that organizations do not have unlimited resources.

We call this a bias because for many organizations their constraint is in the market, not in internal capacity. Further, many of the internal improvement projects will have little or no impact on addressing the market constraint. In other words, for many projects, the customers could not care less about what the organization is doing to improve its internal performance.

For other organizations where the constraint is inside the organization, we also witness many projects in areas not related to the internal constraint. In other words, the silo mentality reigns supreme. There is no recognition of how precious the human capital is. The push is to improve everywhere, rather than focusing on the biggest leverage points for the entire organization.

DEFINITIONS

We define the supply side as that part of the organization responsible for support and delivery of the products and services it sells. Typically this includes IT, Research and Development, and Engineering and Manufacturing, supported by Finance, Administration, Procurement and Distribution.

We define the market side as that part of the organization responsible for sales and marketing.

IMPLICATIONS

Companies that are supply-side driven are more concerned about scarce supply-side resources than customer demand. This is a huge mistake, often costing the company dearly when customer needs change quickly. This identical concept is valid for governments and not-for-profit organizations, which lose votes and funding when they ignore the needs of their constituents and donors.

Companies that are market-side driven are concerned about making good on promised delivery of products/services and/or capturing market share in changing market conditions within their industry and in new markets.

Marketing functions in many organizations are often driven to focus on the short term, at the expense of the long term. This is also a huge mistake, reflected by marketing departments that function in a sales support role, rather than in securing the future of their organization.

Most projects today are managed by non-marketing resources. In fact, from our survey results, the majority of today's PMOs originate from IT and report to CIOs. In some industries, where the PMO is engineering-driven (e.g., the auto industry), we know of PMOs reporting to engineering. Even when other functions are heading up a PMO, it is rare to find marketing as the driving force or even represented. As a result, business decisions on what projects to sanction and in what order are often based and managed from the supply side instead of the market side.

Therefore, most organizations we visit have a completely unbalanced portfolio of active projects — too many supply-side projects and too few market-side projects.

Every organization, during its lifetime, encounters difficulty generating enough market demand to meet its goals, justify its overhead and grow its inherent value. The result is usually drastic cost-cutting measures and "right-sizing" (see Figure 9.1).

When an organization faces insufficient market demand, and incurs lay-offs, the number of projects in the organization often goes up, not down. Every executive is pressured to find additional ways to meet his or her goals. Therefore, the pressure on project managers and resources becomes even more unbearable.

At this time, the need to deliver *more* goods and services is vital to the health of the enterprise. A key critical success factor is the collective delivery speed and success of project teams working on the right projects, and especially the right marketing projects.

Figure 9.1   In 2001, More Than 1,000,000 People Lost Their Jobs in the United States

THE RIGHT MARKETING PROJECTS

We propose that the right marketing projects must focus on three elements to drive lasting competitive advantage and security for the short and long term. These elements deliberately ignore inherent product features. Many of the highly successful companies in a given industry do not have the best mousetrap. But they do have excellent marketing. These are the critical elements:

- ■ A compelling marketing offer that will provide a 2 to 5 year competitive advantage, usually without inherent changes to the products or services being offered. This offer addresses important client needs — needs that go beyond the strict product capabilities. In fact, the marketing offer changes policies that are rooted in the industry, making the offer look revolutionary to customers and impossible to competitors. For one detailed example, see Kendall's book, *Securing the Future*.* We also further discuss examples.

---

*Gerald I. Kendall, *Securing the Future, Strategies for Exponential Growth Using the Theory of Constraints,* St. Lucie Press, Boca Raton, FL, 1997, Orman Grubb Case Study, pp. 237-247.

- ■ Market segmentation that removes the risk of economic downturns, geographically oriented or industry-oriented economic cycles. Additionally, this segmentation stresses using the same employees in different segments, providing lasting security and satisfaction to employees. This is critical, not simply for the sake of making employees happy, but to ensure that there are no demotivators to creativity and that there are constant improvement efforts.
- ■ Focus on gaining order of magnitude improvement in one factor, which will make the organization 500% better than its closest competitor is a factor of importance to its markets. This subject is discussed in the next chapter.

COMPELLING MARKETING OFFER

Many organizations go through huge efforts trying to add features to their products and services. This is especially true in organizations that are involved in manufacturing sophisticated or technology driven products. It is also true of organizations producing products with a lot of engineering behind them. The more features they add and redesigns they do, the more they are turning their organizations inside out to produce and support these more and more complex products and services. Also, this approach drives the number of projects up.

One excellent example comes from the high technology industry, specifically those companies producing Enterprise Resource Planning (ERP) integrated software solutions. Over the years, these products have become so feature-rich that two major negative effects have resulted. First, customers are now arguing that they should not have to pay the huge price tag for this software because they use only approximately 5 to 10% of its capability. Second, the complexity of maintaining software that has become so convoluted over time has increased. These problems are brilliantly described in Goldratt's book, *Necessary But Not Sufficient.**

Ask the simple question, "What do my customers complain about?" and the answer invariably comes back to problems customers have with your organization. This information is often not useful to developing a compelling marketing offer. The question an organization must answer is, "What rooted industry policies bother the markets in which we operate?"

By rooted industry policies, we imply that customers would complain not just about your organization, but about every company in your industry.

---

*Eliyahu M. Goldratt, *Necessary But Not Sufficient,* North River Press, Great Barrington, MA, 2000.

For example, there is no shortage of these issues in the passenger airline industry today. Some examples of policies and practices that drive airline customers crazy are:

- Inability to use frequent flyer miles during blackout periods
- Charges or lack of flexibility to change reservations (now upwards of $100 per ticket per change)
- Extensive use of hub airports, putting masses of passengers into crowded terminals with poor food choices and long lines at the airline service counters
- Canceling flights when an equipment problem occurs
- Misleading information about flight delays

Goldratt assumed that if an organization could change one or more deeply rooted industry policies, policies that hurt customers, two things would occur. First, it would be difficult for competitors to copy, because policies (especially ones that have been standard in an industry for years) are hard to change. Second, it would enable that organization to easily capture more customers and gain a two-year competitive advantage. This would happen because that organization would be unique in rejecting rooted industry policies and also because competitors will not follow suit.

In the case studies we have read and the studies in which we have been personally involved, we have seen a 5-year competitive advantage. Here are some examples:

1. Furniture Manufacturing — Common industry practices include quantity discounts on a per order basis, forcing retailers to order large quantities (e.g., 3- to 6-month supply from each supplier) without knowing what consumer demand will be during that time. It also forces retailers to incur large carrying costs for excessive inventory, among other complications explained in Kendall's book, *Securing the Future*. Another practice is minimum freight charges, also forcing retailers to delay replenishing partial sets of furniture, leading to lost sales.
2. Medical Laboratories — Giving information to doctors about laboratory tests in a standard format, rather than customized to the way that suits individual doctor preference. Refusing to consolidate information in a computer system from different laboratories into a standard format.
3. Steam Generator Manufacturer — Selling steam generating equipment to factories rather than the use of the steam, forcing customers to deal with all of the maintenance issues and complexities of the equipment.

4. Glass Manufacturer Selling Glass Components to Other Factories — Standard policies include providing a shipment of various glass components in a random sequence and replacing broken glass components on standard manufacturing lead-time schedules.

5. Retail Banking — Standard policy includes extensive written applications and waiting periods for loans and mortgages.

6. Printers — They hide their most precious resource, the graphic artists, in the back room to ensure that they are not "bothered" by customers during the initial design stage. By doing so, they encounter endless rework and aggravation from customers.

7. Medical Products for Hospitals — Hospitals have combined their purchasing power into GPOs: purchasing organizations that negotiate great deals with suppliers based on the buying power of several hospitals in a given region. Unfortunately, the resultant GPO policies have some negative side effects to the hospitals. It takes a lot of effort for a hospital to justify a new or a "non-standard" product (i.e., a product for which the GPO does not have a negotiated deal).

Each offer is unique. Even within the same industry, there could be multiple offers that are unique.

The problem we see with many marketing approaches is that the ideas are too easy for the competitors to copy. For example, lowering a price is typically the easiest thing for any competitor to copy. It takes minutes or hours for competitors to not only emulate, but exercise one-upmanship as well.

Many other marketing programs are tactical, rather than strategic, in nature. For example, when we visit marketing departments, we see a lot of effort going into things such as sales campaigns, appearances at trade shows, advertising, catalogs and brochures, packaging, etc. Many marketing departments cannot recall the last time they visited one of their existing clients or clients of competitors.

To develop and drive significant business increase from the compelling marketing offer, an organization must take the following steps:

1. Research and document the complaints that the markets have, not with your organization, but with the entire industry. To do this requires visits to some existing customers as well as to some prospective customers. The customers sometimes do not reveal these issues through simple questions. The information you want to get out of a customer is what makes it hard for them to do business with your industry. You are more likely to obtain this kind of information from an executive of the customer or from the purchasing vice president than from a procurement agent.

2. Do a rigorous analysis that ties at least one of those complaints to a common practice or policy in your industry. Use this analysis in sales presentations to customers, showing how that policy leads to negative effects that hurt customers.
3. Determine how you can change the standard practice in a way that will make a noticeable difference in the market.
4. Test your proposed changes within your own organization, to document and eliminate any concerns before you roll out the change.
5. Pilot the change by visiting selected prospects and seeing if the proposed change excites the customers enough to do (more) business with your organization.
6. Train the sales force in how to sell this compelling marketing offer.

Goldratt refers to this process as the "Mafia Offer," meaning that the organization is putting together an offer too good to refuse. We prefer to use the more conservative term, "Compelling Marketing Offer." We thank Babcock and Wilcox for this suggestion. Further examples are documented in the Goldratt Satellite Program Modules on Marketing and Sales.*

MARKET SEGMENTATION

Often, an organization's policies and pricing strategy force people inside the organization to treat all customers the same, when, in fact, the markets are naturally segmented. Goldratt defines a segmented market as one in which the prices and quantities of products sold in that market are totally independent of the prices and quantities of the same product sold in any other market.

For example, the price and quantities of M&M candies sold in a shop at the airport would have no impact on the price and quantities of M&M candies sold in non-airport shops. Note that this does not mean that you can sell goods at the airport for any price, despite what some vendors think.

There is a major strategic advantage to segmentation when an organization can operate in 15 to 20 segments for the same products or services that are independent of each other's economic cycles. The advantage is multiplied when the organization can use the same staff resources to service the different segments.

This is a huge advantage because as some segments are encountering a down cycle (for whatever reason — economy, competitors, government regulation, etc.), the organization can shift its resources to the more lucra-

---

*See Bibliography for information on the Theory of Constraints Self Paced Learning Program (also known as the Goldratt Satellite Program).

tive segments, maintaining sales, profits, shareholder value and job security simultaneously.

Often, organizations do not segment at all or nearly as effectively as they could for one very simple reason. They believe there is a fair minimum price for their goods or services which covers all of their overhead and gives their organization a "fair" profit. This leads organizations to deadly cost allocation practices for goods and services, distorting what is ultimately good for them and for the different market segments.

For example, what is the value of a tool, such as an electric saw, to a homeowner who may use the tool only a few times a year? Perhaps it is worth $35 to $50. What is the same saw worth to a craftsman, who will use the tool every day, if the saw is sold with an "industrial strength trademark and 5-year warranty?" The answer, in reality, is $125 for a product that is exactly the same.

We know of a truck spring manufacturing company that applied the segmentation strategy beautifully. It used to produce truck springs only for brand new North American trucks. Of course, when economic conditions hit a down cycle, it had to lay off workers and, at one point, almost shut down an entire plant.

This company first explored the aftermarket, selling truck springs as repair parts. As the economic cycle would go into a tailspin for new trucks, the demand for repair parts soared. This is the perfect paradigm for good segmentation. It further segmented by capturing some of the European market.

Segmentation further secures the business as long as an organization is careful to segment its markets and not its resources. Being in two segments rather than one is more secure. However, to have statistical protection and predictability, according to Deming's criteria, organizations should look towards a segmentation strategy with 15 to 20 segments.

Examples of segmentation include:

1. Airline industry, where, for example, the same seat is worth $500 to a traveler who booked it the night before and $175 to someone who booked 2 months in advance.
2. Car rental companies, which have different prices for business travelers and occasional renters.
3. Hotels and motels, which increase their occupancy rates by having special pricing for last minute deals or for Internet bookings.
4. Computer chip manufacturers that sell the same chip for up to three times as much if the order lead time is less than a week as opposed to one month.
5. Cable TV companies, which sell exactly the same wiring and converter for prices ranging from $10 per month to $100 per month, depending on what stations the customer wants to watch.

6. Restaurants that offer half-price deals to people who are willing to arrive early.

SUMMARY

Most organizations we visit have a mix of projects that are heavily biased towards internal improvements (supply side) rather than dealing with issues in their markets (market side). Further, many internal improvements have little or no impact on dealing with the organization's current constraints, and therefore do not improve the organization's profits or help it meet its goals.

In marketing, we often witness projects addressing tactics rather than strategy. Marketing strategy should clearly provide both a short- and long-term competitive advantage. To do so, the organization must do more than build a better mousetrap. Marketing must identify problems customers have with the industry as a whole, not just product features. By overcoming one or more of these, especially if these complaints hurt customers in their pocketbooks, your organization can gain a lasting advantage of typically 2 to 5 years.

Further, market segmentation offers another way to insulate the organization from shifts in market tastes and economic cycles. The key to market segmentation is to strive to enter into 15 to 20 different market segments that are insulated from each other or, even better, go up and down at opposite times. Organizations that segment successfully are careful to segment their markets, not their staff. This ensures that they have the flexibility to shift staff to more lucrative segments as opportunities change.

QUESTIONS

9.1   True or False: Sales and marketing functions should always report to the same vice president because they have the same goal.

9.2   What are three aspects of marketing that the authors claim are rare in most organizations?

9.3   What types of questions would you have to ask customers and prospective customers in order to analyze a market and put together a compelling marketing offer?

9.4   Why is a compelling marketing offer so difficult for competitors to copy?

9.5   How long should it take to analyze a market and put a compelling marketing offer into practice? How long should it take before the organization sees tangible results?

9.6   What are some common practices (rooted industry policies) that you have seen in two industries not listed in this book? How might a company change those policies to capture a competitive advantage?

9.7   How should the definition of segmentation cause an organization to reexamine the way it does business with existing customers?

9.8   What are some other examples of segmentation besides those included in this book?

9.9   What can you predict, with near certainty, about the fate of an organization that does not have compelling marketing offers and does not practice market segmentation strategy? Why?

9.10   Who, within an organization, needs to be involved in putting together and finalizing the types of marketing strategies outlined in this chapter?

10

SECURING THE FUTURE — THE 10-YEAR ADVANTAGE VIA THEORY OF CONSTRAINTS

Moving from a good, stable, predictable organization to one that is the top performer in its industry requires more than what we have described thus far. Some of the characteristics of leadership required to build a top-performing company are brilliantly described in the research done by Jim Collins, co-author of *Built to Last*, and outlined in his recent bestseller, *Good to Great.**

Companies that achieve the long-term advantage outperform their competitors in several ways:

- For publicly traded companies, their stock values grow at a factor of several times their industry average, sustained over 10 years or more.
- They focus on one or two factors in which they are superior to their competition by a factor of several hundred percent.
- They have the control valves in place internally to grow without losing control. One of the most important control valves, according to the research of Jim Collins, is expanding with the right people in place. This is also confirmed in the book *Execution*, referenced previously.

---

*James C. Collins, *Good to Great: Why Some Companies Make the Leap... and others don't*, HarperCollins, New York, 2001.

This part of an organization's strategy requires the identification of the factor(s) that will form the basis of the long-term advantage. It also requires the precise and professional coordination of dozens of projects impacting different areas, to bring the dream to reality.

Here are some examples of factors and their implications in the industry:

- **Automobile** — The factor in the 1970s and 1980s was quality. The implications were that the quality factors that impacted the end consumer were changed by several hundred percent. For example, failure rates on parts moved from parts per thousand to parts per million. The number of parts in an automobile was reduced by several times. Consumers could drive a car for a year without any special maintenance. The Japanese took this factor and achieved an advantage for more than 15 years.

- **Banking** — Mortgage loans are approved in minutes (or worst case — days) instead of weeks. Web-based mortgage loans have achieved this already.

- **General store** — Imagine one store where you are several times more likely to find what you need than in any other general store (clothing, hardware, groceries, gardening, CDs, greeting cards, etc.). Imagine in the same store, the prices are typically lower than any competitor, and guaranteed to match. WalMart has surpassed its competitors by a factor of several times in revenues and earnings. However, WalMart's consistency in achieving results year after year is even more impressive.

- **Gambling** — Provide jackpots that are several times larger than competitors. The super lottery games provided by groups of states sell many more tickets than individual state lotteries.

- **Fast food** — Offer several times as many low calorie options as your competitors. Combine this with other factors (a weight-loss hero, more varieties of healthy food, advertising) to portray an image that appears much more health-conscious than the competition. There is a reason why *Entrepreneur Magazine* ranked Subway® as number one of the top 500 franchises.

- **Internet service providers** — The difference between dial-up and high-speed-based Internet users in the mid- to late 1990s who would consider paying $50 per month for such a service. Today, that number is large and growing.

- **Cable and satellite TV services** — How many channels are enough? In the early 1990s, cable TV services offered a handful of channels. The satellite services entered the market and upped the ante by a factor of several times. The next factor became digital service — the ability to get movie theater quality picture. Today, these are no longer factors because the competitors have all caught up to the initial provider. What will the next factor be? Perhaps the ability to select the movie of your choice from a library of hundreds or thousands accessed randomly and viewed at your convenience.

IDENTIFYING THE FACTOR
FOR EXPONENTIAL IMPROVEMENT

In every industry, there are a variety of factors that influence customer demand. Today, many or most of the customers in the various markets base their choice of product or service on several key factors. In order to compete effectively, your organization is already at least average in these key factors. Therefore, there is a very important implication. *The factor that an organization will pick to excel with is often one that is not a key factor today, but has the potential to become a key factor.* This is a factor that may be important to less than 10% of your current market, but will be the number one factor to a much greater percentage of the market in the future.

When you analyze the importance of various factors to existing customers, such a factor barely shows up on a chart. Goldratt describes it as a tail on a distribution curve showing the relative importance. However, as Goldratt claims, "where there is a tail, there is usually a dog!"*

For example, surveys conducted in the 1970s on the importance of quality to automobile buyers found that it was in the top ten, but not close to number one for the majority of buyers. The Japanese changed the paradigm by doing an order of magnitude improvement in quality. Another example relates to watches in the 1960s. At that time, quality was an important factor, and many people bought Swiss watches, which had a high quality image. In the 1980s, the factor became features that were associated with electronics and the new digital era. People looked for digital displays, alarms, multiple times, hourly beeps, etc. How many of those watches were made by Swiss companies?

In any given product or service, there are a multitude of factors. These factors can include variables such as speed of delivery, customization (colors, styles, options), speed of service, quality of product, quality of service, variety of products offered/displayed, geographic locations/proximity, cleanliness, speed and depth of the learning curve, packaging, lead time, on-time performance, staff training, etc. Once chosen, the factor becomes the basis for the company becoming the best in the world in its industry.

---

*See the Bibliography references to the Theory of Constraints Self Paced Learning Program Module 8, Strategy.

ONE EXAMPLE OF A FACTOR AND THE PROJECTS IT DRIVES

We will use the example of a fast food chain, with several thousand franchisees, that picks the factor of "healthy food choice" as the one with which it will gain an order of magnitude improvement. Before choosing this factor, the chain would probably consider factors such as:

- **Price** — This is difficult to sustain any long-term advantage with, especially when the competition already has cheaper alternatives.
- **Appeal to children** — The difficulty with this factor is that all of the franchisees are in relatively small locations, without the flexibility to easily add children's structures.
- **Variety of choice** — This factor has some merit, but is a challenge given the simple equipment that exists in most locations. However, when considered in conjunction with "healthy food choice", it definitely becomes part of the overall plan.
- **Décor** — While important in some sit-down fancy chains, décor does not hold much potential, especially given consumer research in the fast food industry.
- **Cleanliness** — Many fast food chains have deteriorated in the past 10 years. This factor has an association with customer perception of "healthy food choice". However, it may be hard for customers to perceive a factor of several hundred percent difference.
- **Speed of service** — The franchises already have a record of 4 minutes customer service time, on average. To make this a factor implies a target service time of 1 minute or less — worth considering but the logistics would be very challenging.

In going with the factor of "healthy food choice," the organization decides they will have several times as many low calorie choices as their biggest competitors, with several times the combinations when you consider buns and toppings. The following projects are identified to implement these changes across the thousands of franchisees:

1. Development of products (sandwiches, buns and toppings).
2. Development of comparisons between their new products and their competitors in calories and fat content.
3. Market research to prove the new concepts and pricing strategy.
4. Pilot the new concept in select locations.
5. Revision and printing of new menus.
6. Development of new oven technology and procedures for baking a larger variety of buns with varied content and flavoring.
7. Recruiting a "hero" or role model to represent the new image.

8. Design of an advertising campaign.
9. Negotiation with advertising media (print, TV, etc.).
10. Gaining buy-in and understanding of all existing franchisees.
11. Ordering new equipment.
12. Development of the training and roll-out strategy worldwide.
13. Revision of the point-of-sale systems to accommodate new products.
14. Various marketing projects to track results, stay on top of the competition, ensure positive consumer reaction, etc.

These are not all of the projects. However, an organization with a PMO and the right focus can make this happen quickly and professionally. Without a PMO, the projects would still be launched, but the lack of coordination and focus would mean a lead-time of many years instead of 1 to 2 years.

WHY THE 10-YEAR ADVANTAGE MUST FOLLOW OTHER STRATEGIES

When an organization picks one factor and drives an improvement of several times, it usually implies turning a company inside out. There are changes required throughout the organization, which must be perfectly coordinated. A misstep in one functional area and the entire idea could fail or be disastrous.

Before beginning on this journey, it is important for people inside the organization to have confidence and believe that it is possible to achieve such a major improvement. Also, the systems inside the company must be stable enough to allow for an increase in sales of several hundred percent over a short period of time, without blowing out the brains of the organization. This means that it must already have predictable systems in all areas and know where the control valves are to adjust capacity with increases in market demand. The reverse is also true. The company must also be able to adjust market demand in stages that match internal capacity increases.

These prerequisites imply that the organization must first implement the ideas discussed in previous chapters. The senior management team must have a single, holistic view of their organization. Their measurements must be set up to drive team behavior. The senior management team must have experience in subordinating themselves and their functions to the organization's constraints. These experiences build the capability and confidence in the organization that result in the attitude of "we can do anything we want to do!"

Further, we see many senior management teams comprised of many A-type personalities. These personalities are also called "drivers." These are people who are very aggressive, forceful, and who won't take "no" for an answer. While some of these characteristics can help implement change, there is often a negative side effect. These personalities also seem to take unilateral action, without considering the implications to other functions.

As Collins alluded to in his book, *Good to Great*, CEOs must evaluate their teams and get people who are not able to take a holistic approach "off the bus."

ROLE OF THE PMO IN THE LONG-TERM STRATEGY

The PMO must play an active role in the implementation of the organization's strategic plan, both short and long term. If not the PMO, then this mammoth work is often delegated as part-time assignments to senior managers or their direct reports. The result is that the work rarely gets done, or takes many, many years.

However, there is a significant obstacle preventing the PMO from undertaking such an initiative today. Based on our current knowledge of PMO staff, most PMO teams must first undergo some intensive training in strategic planning.

We have witnessed a huge difference between teams that have such training and teams that do not. We do not know of a better process than the first four days of the 4 × 4 to complete such training. Fortunately, Goldratt has done an outstanding job of creating the series of eight modules and making them available as valuable knowledge without demanding a prohibitive investment. There are no prerequisites to viewing the satellite series, although the series is well supplemented by some 20 books by various authors on the subjects covered in the series.

The alternative to such a series would be to purchase and read a collection of books in each area of the supply chain. The problem with this approach is that it is more time-consuming and may also cost just as much. Also, the books would not integrate into an approach to strategic planning that would make sense.

The stages of moving an organization from good to great can be orchestrated using the 4 × 4 approach. The PMO team would ensure that the sequence of change would proceed using the following general approach:

1. Put the holistic measurements and understanding of the systems in place to drive holistic behavior. Implicit in this step is eliminating conflicting and erroneous measurements throughout the organization. Take away the demotivators.

2. Make the systems stable (especially operations, project management, and distribution)
3. Create a compelling marketing offer to drive the constraint inside the organization, and to create a 2-year competitive advantage
4. Create multiple segmentations (preferably 15 to 20) to increase stability, ensuring that the same people resources are used, as much as possible, in different segments and in new markets
5. Identify the factor that will provide an improvement of several times over the competition, and make it the basis of a 10-year competitive advantage. Identify the project plans in all functional areas, and the sequence to implement such a factor.

This role for the PMO is not something that comes naturally. However, if an organization wants to derive value from a PMO, it must recognize that the PMO must focus on organization strategies, and move quickly away from a focus on trivialities.

SUMMARY

Moving an organization from being good to being number one in its industry requires more than a compelling marketing offer. The organization must identify the factors that will drive it to become the best in the world. Usually, it is only necessary to find one such factor, but this implies a mammoth change to the organization. Within the one factor, the team seeks an improvement of several hundred percent.

This usually requires extensive change throughout an organization, with many projects that must be perfectly coordinated across functional areas to achieve the end goal. Such an effort usually requires a multi-year project and a great deal of stamina from the executive team.

Therefore, before commencing such an effort, the senior management team must ensure that it has implemented strategies to make its internal systems stable and to have tried at least one compelling marketing offer to build the confidence of employees in all areas. Further, the PMO must also be stable and able to achieve project management goals (on time, on budget, and within scope) more than 95% of the time.

The PMO is the logical choice for coordinating such an effort. Provided they are educated in strategic planning, the PMO team will have the 30,000-foot view of the organization's projects — a necessary condition to make such an effort successful.

QUESTIONS

10.1 Pick an industry and describe one factor that could be improved by several hundred percent. Describe the changes required inside the company. Describe why such an improvement would provide a long-term competitive advantage.

10.2 What are some examples of factors that might impact retail book selling?

10.3 Why would the senior management team want to have the PMO controlling the implementation of such a strategy?

10.4 What negative effects might happen if an organization were to pursue the 10-year advantage before implementing a compelling marketing offer? Before stabilizing its systems?

10.5 True or False: The strategy to focus on one factor to provide a 10-year advantage is almost the same as the compelling marketing offer.

10.6 Suppose that an organization has identified a factor that will give it the 10-year advantage. Also assume that the organization has some senior management team members who are A-type personalities and not strong team players. The CEO has decided to replace those senior managers. What should be done first — replace the senior managers or move forward with the projects to gain the 10-year advantage?

10.7 Why aren't PMOs typically involved in this kind of major strategic planning work today?

PART III:
THE PMO IN DETAIL

11

THE GOVERNANCE BOARD AND PRIORITIZATION MANAGEMENT

DOING PROJECTS WITHOUT A PROJECT MANAGEMENT OFFICE

What is wrong with operating without a PMO and without a Governance Board? Some skeptics claim that not much has changed in project management since the time of the construction of the pyramids, except for one glaring improvement — we no longer kill people for not completing their work on time. We are much more civilized — we just fire them!

Organizations track projects in several different ways. Project costs are tracked through the finance department, but often not by project. Resources are tracked separately through the human resources department. However, human resources and finance do not typically track by project. Their orientation is to track according to the organization chart or financial chart of accounts, by department, unless you are part of a company whose business is projects (e.g., a construction company, a shipbuilding company, etc.).

The finance department and the human resources department are not typically integrating project data tied to strategic goals. Nor do they typically have the time or expertise to monitor projects closely or intervene on a timely basis. This is not intended as a criticism of these functions. Rather, it simply reflects that they do not perform multi-project governance, nor do they typically provide the information to govern the project portfolio successfully. As a result, money is lost. These losses are not recognized on a P&L statement as something related to project management. Therefore, it is an important challenge to educate executives on the value of project governance. Let us first look at how the loss happens.

PERFORMANCE TO BUDGET — LEAVING MONEY ON THE TABLE

In most organizations, each functional area has a finance-approved budget and a human resources-approved headcount. One primary measurement of the functional areas is performance to budget within the headcount plan.

Often, project resources come from various functional areas. If a project needs more dedicated resources to deliver (e.g., a new product in time to meet a competitive threat), the functional areas usually resist. After all, they have a headcount plan that is difficult to change. Further, a functional executive often favors projects that they have sponsored. They want to keep headcount working on their projects, not other initiatives.

HR and Finance are usually very resistant to exceeding planned cost or headcount. Therefore, we often see vital projects either being delayed, or significant game playing. "I'll give you more resources but only if you give me more budget/headcount."

At the same time, since the functional areas often fight long and hard battles over budgets and headcount, another type of game playing occurs. If business slows down in one area, the functions impacted do not want to lose budget or headcount. Often, these areas initiate local projects to keep their resources busy, and to ensure that they will spend the full budget dollars.

Without a PMO, it becomes every function for itself, with the CEO trying to referee. However, most CEOs do not have the time, patience or project management skills to track all of the organization's projects against the organization's goals. Time and again, when we work with organizations that create their initial project portfolio, we witness surprise from the senior executives over how many active projects are in the works. The worst shock of all from senior executives is to find out how many active projects are not directly tied to any of the organization's strategic goals. This is just one part of "leaving money on the table."

WHERE TO NOW? THE NEED TO COORDINATE AND OPTIMIZE

Tracking compliance to the strategic plan requires awareness of how projects are proceeding at the various levels of the organization. This effort need not be massive. Projects or programs performed across functional units require coordination. Coordination is very important because the organization will likely not meet its revenue, expense, investment and ROI goals without it. Therefore, the cost and the risk of rework or work failure need to be managed well.

These concepts are explained in Chapter 4. See Figures 4.2 and 4.3 as an example of how strategies and projects must be linked.

As the strategic plan is translated into projects (see Figure 4.3), the Governance Board is interested in seeing the progress toward achieving their strategic objectives. To do so meaningfully requires standardization across all functional units in terms of work plans and progress against plan. Without a PMO to provide simple, effective standards and coordination, many organizations find this to be a daunting task.

Individual work methods often vary widely, even within a functional area. This, by itself, is not a problem. However, there must be a common language and common understanding of work plans, tasks and progress to achieve something meaningful.

For example, one functional area might be using an Earned Value approach to determine how much of a project is complete. In calculating schedule achievement, earned value treats all work the same. Therefore, you could see an earned value report that portrays a project as 50% complete, when only 10% of the critical path work has been completed. Another functional area might be using Critical Path, and yet another might be using Critical Chain. A PMO will not have a realistic overall picture until the reporting is standardized.

As work plans and progress measures are standardized, the workforce needs to take action to accelerate their work delivery and/or avoid work delivery threat. The PMO, with the complete support of the senior management team, can effectively collect and communicate critical information back to the workforce to help these goals.

THE GOVERNANCE BOARD

Governance Board membership comes from the senior management team of the business unit or enterprise. The role of the Governance Board is to steer and to decide. After the startup phase is over, the Governance Board typically meets once a month.

Most organizations have new requests to consider at least monthly, plus decisions to make relative to key project review information. In highly volatile businesses, some Governance Boards meet weekly. This is also true where customers drive project demand. The turnover activity and urgency of new project requests will often determine the pressure to meet. We know of other Governance Boards that meet quarterly. From our perspective, this is a red flag. It could mean that the Board may react too slowly to changes in market, economic, and internal conditions to meet an external threat.

The purpose of the Governance Board is to review and direct the prioritization of the project portfolio. This process enables the project managers and their work teams to calibrate their work schedules according to the priorities set by senior management. This information is vital to reducing time and effort in working out resource and project conflicts. It is also a key factor to gaining delivery speed in accomplishing the strategic plan.

We call this process a "force ranking," meaning that all projects and programs are given a separate priority, with no duplication of priorities (i.e., we do not allow ten different projects to all be a number one priority).

Specifically, at each Governance Board meeting, the following are expected outcomes:

- Approval or denial of new project submissions
- Activation of approved projects (Activation is formally starting a project. This is different from approval, which is putting the project into the queue.)
- Deactivation of active projects
- Termination of projects (Termination is the polite way of saying that the Governance Board is killing the project.)
- Official prioritization decision
- Request for further analysis (Usually, this is for new project submissions that either lack sufficient information to make a decision, or where there is a significant issue that is not fully understood.)
- Resource reallocations based on priorities
- Strategic resource decisions
- Communications of decisions, based on a predefined communications plan

GETTING STARTED

In most organizations that do not have a well-organized Governance Board, the project prioritization decisions seem to fall to the supply-side functional executives (often the CIO). This result is largely ineffective because these leaders already have resource conflicts with other functional executives. If the CIO, for example, is trying to do this function, he or she cannot say "no" to other executives without some sort of business, political or social repercussion. Thus, moving the decision-making process to the Governance Board helps the organization execute projects more smoothly, with drastically improved relationships.

The first meeting of the Governance Board will set the priorities of all recognized active and proposed major projects. All functional executives and the CEO or head of the business unit should attend.

If the purpose and significance of this meeting is properly communicated, and the CEO or top unit leader is supportive, all executives will go out of their way to be part of this process. See Chapter 26 for further commentary on selling the PMO concept to executives to build the enthusiasm.

Sadly, many PMOs do not set up their Governance Board properly from the outset, and a great deal of conflict results. This calls to mind a recent engagement where this very event occurred. The CIO of a mid-sized insurance company could not step out of his office without being accosted by one of the many functional executives he served. The CIO was concerned with their constant attack on him for not meeting delivery deadlines. He felt certain that much of the fault lay with them and not IT. Things were so bad that when we began consulting with this company, we could hear whispers in the hallways that he was a "goner".

As part of our effort to implement their PMO, we met with the CIO about setting up the Governance Board. We explained how the plan to establish the Governance Board should work and what tasks the CIO should perform.

The CIO invited the business leaders to form a Governance Board and initially they declined. So he did his own prioritization of projects, unilaterally, and sent out his prioritization of projects in the portfolio to the functional leaders for their information. You can imagine the type of response he received. The CIO was losing more ground.

We recommended that the CIO explain the purpose of the Governance Board in terms that showed what was in it for the business leaders. Then, he should ask the business leaders again to come together to form the Governance Board. This time they did. However, they were very hostile early on in the first meeting.

More than 25 functional leaders attended the first meeting. The PMO manager didn't get three words out of his mouth when an agitated senior manager said, "I want to know if I can leave. I have a lot of work to do and besides I really do not want to be here. Why can't the CIO just do this anyway?" The CIO looked like he had been shot in the head as he turned to us to answer the question.

We responded on the CIO's behalf, "You are welcome to leave. We are sorry you cannot stay. But before you go, we need one commitment from you for the work we will do here today. Tell us whom you are giving your proxy to vote on your behalf. That way, when we vote on prioritizing all projects, including yours, that person can vote for your projects as if that person were you."

Most of the people in the room were already competing over resources. As he surveyed the room, he could not identify anyone he would give his proxy to. Finally he stated, "I will stay for a while. Let's get on with this."

Thus, the shift from the supply-side business unit leader (the CIO) making the prioritization decisions to the Governance Board (represented by supply-side and market-side leaders) was completed. The group made its first force rank list that day.

Now the CIO could focus on positioning his department to support the entire organization without fear of working on the wrong project. What a change for the CIO as his professional life was now on the upswing (he was soon promoted to the Corporate Parent).

NORMAL PROCESS OF THE GOVERNANCE BOARD

The force ranking is accomplished through the authority and consensus of functional unit leaders or their delegates. The Governance Board determines the order of programs and project work based on interdependencies and also how that order best serves the overall strategic objectives for that fiscal year.

The portfolio manager or the person in the PMO responsible for this function should submit status and recommendations before the meeting to all Governance Board members, and to other senior managers who might be affected by Governance Board decisions. This allows for dissenting opinions to be heard by the Governance Board. The pre-meeting submission should include:

- Summary status of active projects in the portfolio, with links to the organization goals
- Proposed changes — additions, activations, deactivations, and terminations, with assumptions and justification
- What-if analysis — projected impact of various changes and related assumptions
- Recommendations from the PMO or portfolio manager
- Dissenting opinions and assumptions that are different than the PMO's
- Back up documentation (e.g., opportunity and risk templates, project financial and schedule information)

The PMO provides administrative and facilitative support for the Governance Board by performing the following duties and providing associated deliverables:

1. Manage the collection of progress reports and other related documents for the Governance Board and the organization. Part of this management is sifting through the details to provide the major highlights that require Governance Board steering and decisions.

2. Manage the data repository of project-related information correlated to the fiscal year strategic plan.
3. Prepare what-if analysis for new proposed projects.
4. Facilitate the Governance Board meetings including scheduling logistics, report preparation and distribution, and meeting agenda.
5. Prepare, publish, and distribute in advance of the Governance Board meetings the operations plan status and forecast reporting.
6. Administratively manage the prioritization model on behalf of the Governance Board.

PRIORITIZATION MANAGEMENT

The key to effective prioritization is to keep the approach simple and easy to understand by all managers across the organization. There are two distinct parts to managing prioritization. One is to establish a prioritization model that all functional leaders buy in to. The second is to ensure that work is released to functional areas according to the priorities, resolving major resource conflicts and improving project flow throughout the organization.

Any executive should have the right to bring proposed changes in project priorities to the executive team at the regular Governance Board meetings. However, it is crucial that the portfolio manager, in cooperation with the executive, has done his or her homework. The executive team must understand the impact of a proposed project or change in priority on the company's goals. Which existing project priorities would have to change? How would that impact the existing projects, relative to the goals of the company?

The following is an example of a simple project prioritization scheme. There are two major elements. Under the major elements, each individual item could be rated 0 to 5, where 0 is no impact and 5 is maximum impact:

1. Opportunity
   a. Impact on organization goals: 25%
   b. Internal Rate of Return: 25%
   c. Fit with long term strategy: 25%
   d. Throughput per strategic resource unit: 25%
2. Risk
   a. Technical: 20%
   b. Market: 20%
   c. Feasibility: 20%
   d. Legal: 20%
   e. Financial: 20%

This conceptual model recognizes that an organization typically has both financial and non-financial goals. The internal rate of return recognizes the financial goals. The impact portion recognizes the non-financial goals. However, it can also recognize that a project with a lower rate of return may have a bigger impact on company goals just because of the magnitude of the project.

The item "Fit with long term strategy" recognizes the concept imbedded in Collins' book, *Good to Great.* Becoming the best in the world at something is not an overnight occurrence. Most organizations never get there simply because they change direction frequently or simply try to tackle every opportunity rather than being selective.

"Throughput per strategic resource unit" recognizes that the organization has relatively few strategic resources that will determine how many projects they can complete in a year. For example, in one organization we worked with, the place where most projects got stuck was within the Technology Services group. This group is responsible for all internal systems and the company's Web site, as well as customer interfaces for order entry.

The strategic resource (in this example the Technology Services group) determines, more than any other resource group in the organization, how many projects can be completed and how much change can be accomplished. For example, a project that will generate $10,000,000 in additional revenue, but will consume 50% of the organization's strategic resource for a full year may not be as beneficial as a project that will generate $5,000,000 but only consumes 10% of the strategic resource. The implication is that we could only do two of the first type of project per year, yielding a total of $20,000,000. But we could do 10 of the second type of project per year, yielding $50,000,000.

The risk factor is a modifier. Even though a project may look very attractive from the opportunity point of view, it becomes less attractive as the risk increases.

One of the risk factors is technical. Risk can increase if the project depends on new, untried technology. Complex or geographically dispersed technology also increases risk. If a successful project requires a major upgrade in people's technical knowledge, that can be a risk. Other technical risks include the alignment of technology on this project with current technology in the company. There can also be technical risks with data. For example, if the project depends on extensive new data being gathered from multiple sites, this is more risky than using existing data.

Another risk factor is the market. This applies to new or changed products or services, where market acceptance is an unknown. Product failure is also a risk, especially in consumer or high public profile situations.

A third type of risk is the feasibility of executing the project to completion. Is this a type of project the organization has done before? If the project requires you to add a brand new organizational unit, or change the organizational responsibilities significantly, this increases the risk. Similarly, if you have a brand new business process, risk increases. If you have a combination of the above factors, it is even more risky.

Legal risk is increasing in importance, at least in the North American market. The cost of fighting legal battles has forced companies into receivership. Also, some jury awards are seemingly outrageous.

Financial risk might reflect the proportion of an organization's capital that might be required to get the project off the ground, and the amount of additional investment that might be required to make it work or to abandon the project if things do not work out.

Each organization can customize these prioritization ideas to its issues. However, it should be kept simple and understandable to all business leaders. In the Portfolio Management chapter, these prioritization approaches are combined with other issues to make strategic portfolio decisions.

STEPS TO ESTABLISH THE PRIORITIZATION PROCESS IN YOUR BUSINESS

CREATING THE PRIORITIZATION PROCESS

1. Collect the strategic objectives for the current or coming business year.
2. Define a "straw man" prioritization template or spreadsheet, with a fill-in-the-blanks approach.
   2.1. First determine what opportunity factors should be considered; that is, what makes one project a better opportunity for the company than another project. See Table 11.1 for an example of opportunity factors.
   2.2. Next determine what risk factors should be considered. See Table 11.2 for an example of risk factors.
   2.3. Then determine the relative importance of the different factors. Allocate a relative percentage to each grouping and to each factor. Make sure that the sum of the weighting percentages totals 100%. Table 11.1 shows relative importance of factors according to the opportunity. Table 11.2 shows relative importance of factors according to the risk. Note that some of the factors that apply in one industry will be different in another industry.
3. Fill in the opportunity and risk templates for each project. (Note that before you have final agreement on the template parameters, you can fill in a few examples and circulate them to give senior management a feel for how it will work).

Table 11.1 Opportunity Scoring Template

Priority Assessment for Project : Develop a laptop Web RF access	Weight	Score
Factor	Weight	Score
For each Business Goal score 1-5:		
5 Directly aligned with strategic priority		
1 Indirectly contributes to strategic priority		
0 Not aligned with strategic priority		
Business Goals	25%	11%
• Improve market share or develop new market	5%	5
• Cross-sell across divisions	5%	0
• Increase revenues	5%	5
• Lower costs	5%	1
• Decrease Investment	5%	0
Impact	50%	40%
Customer Impact	25%	
5 Resolves significant problems and issues affecting many customers		
4 Fulfills commitment/promises made to many important clients		4
3 Improves customer service quality perceptions		
2 Resolves significant problems and issues affecting a few customers		
1 Fulfills commitments/promises made to a few clients		
0 No or negative customer impact		
Strategic Potential	25%	
5 Clear opportunity to lead the industry with significant payback through business growth		
4 Potential to grow market share and improve competitive posture		4
3 Could turn into a significant opportunity in the future		
2 Consistent with development trends of the industry		
1 Something interesting to have		
0 Unlikely to provide strategic advantage		
Competitive Urgency	25%	23%
Advantage we can realize by acting quickly	20%	
5 Urgent - first entry market leader by acting now		5
3 We can use project to leapfrog the competition		
1 We will attain par with competition		
Window of Opportunity	5%	
5 The window of opportunity aligns exactly with the project schedule		
3 The opportunity will remain valid six months from now		3
1 The opportunity will remain valid one year from now		
0 The opportunity will always remain valid		
Total Opportunity	100%	74

4. Determine the following additional data and enter on a spreadsheet or template (see Table 11.3):
   4.1. Total financial impact (net present value [NPV] projected or range of projection and investment)
   4.2. Utilization of organization's strategic resource
   4.3. Calculation of throughput per strategic resource unit
   4.4. Cash flow implications by year — first 2 years
   4.5. Suggested ranking (based on formula or intuition)
5. Provide instructions to complete the template.

APPLYING THE PRIORITIZATION PROCESS — IMPLEMENTATION

1. Gain permission from the Governance Board to distribute the prioritization template to all program and project managers
2. Require all program and project managers to obtain signature approval from the vice presidents responsible for revenues, costs and investments before returning the completed prioritization template.
3. Load the data by project into your project portfolio software or spreadsheet.
4. Determine several different rankings, using different assumptions. For example, rank as if the following were top priority:
   a. Cash flow
   b. Risk score
   c. NPV per strategic resource week invested
   d. Opportunity score
   e. Strategic asset ranking
5. Sort the portfolio in order of the most important program or project first, for each of the different priority rankings used in Step 4 above
6. Determine prioritization recommendation, based on consideration of all factors

Table 11.2   Risk Scoring Template

Risk for Project: Develop a Digital Access RF IC	Weight	Score
Product / Service Risk	40%	30%
Potential Financial Damage to Customer on Product Failure	30%	
5 Greater than $1,000,000		5
3 $250k to $1,000,000		
1 Less than $250k		
Compliance to State and Federal Regulations	5%	
5 Unclear		
3 Non-compliance is known but is being addressed		
0 No known issues		0
Public Impact (Catastrophe)	5%	
5 Potential to create a major, catastrophic headline		
0 Project cannot possibly cause negative press		0
Technical	30%	21%
Degree of "newness"	10%	
5 Technology is new to us and unproven in the marketplace		
3 The technology is widely available, but new to us		3
1 The technology involves a functional upgrade to technology in use		
0 The technology is routinely used		
Architectural Alignment	5%	
5 Strategic building block with enterprise wide value		
3 Potential to be strategic building block		3
0 Not applicable		
Data Access	15%	
5 Direct mainframe access required		
4 Requires alteration of existing interfaces to existing data sources		4
0 No data involved		
Feasibility	30%	11%
Regulatory Barriers	10%	
5 Requires external regulatory approvals never applied for by our company		
3 Requires external regulatory routine approvals		
0 No requirements for legal review		0
Organizational and Operational Barriers	15%	
5 Requires new business processes, organizational re-design, and non-existent operational resources		
4 Requires two of the above		
2 Requires one of the above		2
0 Requires none of the above		
Resources	5%	
5 More than 1 project manager and multiple functional areas		5
3 One Project manager, multiple functional areas		
0 One project manager or small project with reliable resources		
Total Risk	100%	62

7. Distribute to members of the Governance Board, with an explanation of the different possible rankings. Point out the different priority rankings based on the different criteria.

These steps will make a big difference in having a productive first Governance meeting.

PORTFOLIO MANAGEMENT

See Figure 11.1 for the overall flow. This is a process to collect data, assess and report on how progress of the projects and programs within the portfolio are performing compared to the strategic plan. This process is managed by the PMO on a day-to-day or week-to-week frequency, receiving status reports and updated delivery schedules to use for publishing portfolio reports.

All initiatives that are deemed "Mission Critical" are normally included in the project portfolio. The project portfolio illustrates all work within the fiscal year and sometimes beyond. It includes all open and active projects, all pending projects waiting to start, and all closed, completed or cancelled projects.

The project portfolio reflects information on how each project is performing according to the strategic plan and how projects may be dependent on or predecessors of other key projects.

The Governance Board reviews the project portfolio for certain key information. It wants to know, for example:

1. How is it doing in comparison to its peers?
2. Is there any chance for it to move up in force rank order?
3. Is there any money available for it to activate more of its work or to help existing projects?

Table 11.3   Key Project Portfolio Information

Project	Opportunity Score (%)	Risk Score (%)	NPV (mm)	Investment (mm)	Strategic Resource Utilization (weeks)	NPV $ per Strategic Week Invested	Cash Flow 1st Year (mm)	Cash Flow 2nd Year (mm)	Sugg. Rank
				Project Cost/Benefit Analysis					
Develop a laptop web RF access	76	62	$35.00	$15.0	507	69,034	-$15.0	$5.0	2
Develop a handheld web RF access	65	51	$7.00	$2.0	320	21,875	$1.0	$3.0	3
Implement XYZ Financial Software	30	10	$1.50	$8.0	100	15,000	-$8.0	$0.5	5
Upgrade Web with new cart, config., etc.	89	30	$22.00	$2.5	32	687,500	$5.0	$15.0	1
Armed Forces encrypted web RF access	68	75	$125.00	$17.5	675	185,185	-$8.8	-$8.8	4

Total Portfolio Management

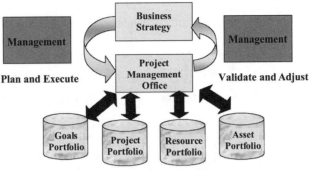

Figure 11.1 The Portfolio Management Process

OPERATIONS STATUS REPORTING AND FORECASTING

The PMO provides the Governance Board with regular reports that describe what has happened and how those events compare to what was promised. Also, delivery assessments are made for the next 30, 60, and 90 calendar days regarding delivery acceleration opportunities and delivery threats.

Publishing this report requires the assimilation of project data and trends, performed cyclically. These data and trends identify projects over budget, under budget, late, early, in-trouble, etc. Bottleneck identification and improving and degrading trend lines in projects in these reports show whether the situation is deteriorating or improving.

FINDING ELEMENTS OF THE VALUE PROPOSITION

As the organization leaders learn how to use the information provided by the PMO, it becomes easier to take early advantage of different opportunities. Typical opportunities identified are:

1. Accelerating projects that are dependent on projects that have accelerated.
2. Canceling projects that are no longer appropriate.
3. Re-ranking projects because they have changed in importance.

4. Re-establishing the order of importance of the strategic objectives when the business environment changes (for example, September 11, 2001).
5. Reassigning the most important resources to the most important projects.
6. Finding project delays that no one was aware of and finding remedies to reduce those delays.

Typical delivery delays often seen in the operations status reporting and forecasting report:

1. Projects waiting on other projects that have stalled.
2. Projects significantly under-spending. Many managers from the supply side are much more cost-oriented than throughput-oriented. A PMO with a correct understanding of the portfolio will see the opportunity to apply some unspent money from cancelled or accelerated projects on other work.
3. Project managers not able to provide delivery status on mission critical projects.

A PMO that helps its organization in this manner becomes an "ROI Engine." Such a PMO should return a *minimum* of 10% of the total project portfolio investment in any year from these simple processes.

SUMMARY

Linking the strategic objectives of an organization with projects, and doing work to accelerate progress are critical components to helping the business achieve all of its goals. Finance and human resources departments are typically oriented to functional organization structures, not to project structures. The PMO, therefore, can easily become a key contributing support element to this success.

Many PMOs begin life from a supply-side function — the function responsible for most of the projects and most of the project resources. In many organizations, this is the CIO. It is vital for the PMO to transfer governance of the project portfolio to the senior executive team. To do so, the PMO must provide vital data that will help the Governance Board make informed decisions about project prioritization and sequencing.

Prioritization involves first gathering some key information, such as opportunity and risk rating, cash flow and utilization of the organization's strategic resource. Once the prioritization scheme is accepted and the rankings of all projects by the Governance Board is complete, the PMO must communicate, track, and help to ensure that the project portfolio is managed correctly. This gives PMO team members a focus on accelerating high priority projects, preventing delays and communicating back to the Governance Board and other stakeholders to ensure that everyone is on the same page.

OKLAHOMA STATE UNIVERSITY CASE STUDY

Computing & Information Services (CIS) at Oklahoma State University (OSU) is responsible for providing information technology and customer support for OSU and eight other institutions. This unit comprises 170 full time employees and 100 student employees. In 1996, OSU decided to undertake the deployment of Lotus Notes for the entire campus. At that time, CIS had very hierarchical and functionally independent groups. With the introduction of the Lotus Notes deployment project, there was a need to involve many of these groups and coordinate their activities. The project became a turning point in cross-functional project management in CIS.

Over time, there was further need for more cross-functional coordination of projects. However, each group had the responsibility for its own projects and managing resources. Each group performed its portion of the project, but communication did not always go well. In some projects, different activities were forgotten or missed, which caused conflict between CIS and its end users.

Since each group was responsible for its own projects, several projects were active simultaneously and resources were spread thin across them. It was not unusual for one person to be working on 6 to 10 projects at a time. At one point, several weeks were spent surveying upper management to outline all open projects. At the end of this exercise, it was determined that there were 14 pages (Excel landscape) of projects being worked on by the organization. The organization tried to prioritize these projects and work on several projects, all designated as number one priorities. However, this still caused resource issues.

One of the difficulties in trying to have one set of priorities was that each functional area thought of its projects as being top priority for the CIS group. Often, the priorities were set based on who had the most influence or push to make it happen. There was no formal approach because anyone in the entire organization could start a project with no agreed-to procedures or processes to follow. With the resulting conflicting priorities, some projects were completed behind schedule or simply not completed at all.

In September 2000, after reviewing information provided by the Gartner Group, CIS established a PMO tailored to its needs. The goals were to:

- Manage critical, strategic, cross-functional projects
- Be a role model to the organization for project management
- Establish project management techniques

This PMO started with some internal, small projects to get some early "wins." This helped the PMO develop best practices and further document good processes and procedures. Today, all of the authorized projects managed by the PMO support CIS organizational goals. Further, all PMO managed projects follow processes in a consistent manner.

Management also looked at its prioritizing techniques. It decided to have only one number one project and manage the highest prioritized projects (no more than five) at a level higher than the rest. This does not prevent internal projects from being initiated. However, the organization has decided that the highest prioritized projects will receive the resources needed to complete these projects at the risk of delaying or postponing internal projects.

While project management is not used throughout the organization, almost everyone has been exposed to it through a PMO-managed project. The PMO has established objectives and is working toward these objectives. To date, the PMO has worked on establishing a methodology (which includes a flowchart, step-by-step walkthrough, templates and checklists), roles with responsibilities, training, a repository (to house reference materials and best practices) and reporting. There are many other activities being planned by the PMO to fulfill these objectives.

While working on these internal operations, the PMO has successfully managed 32 projects with a staff of 3. Strategic projects are all being completed, with greatly improved communications throughout the project and within the user community.

QUESTIONS

11.1 Discuss the need to know the value proposition of the PMO before establishing PMO requirements. How might this affect the operation of a Governance Board?

11.2 How might a Governance Board make a positive difference in detecting and overcoming negative events on projects? What would likely occur if there were no Governance Board?

11.3 Identify typical "for-profit" and "not-for-profit" strategic objectives. Do non-profit organizations need to manage their delivery work?

11.4 Why do organizations need project Governance Boards?

11.5 Define force-ranking.

11.6 Discuss who should perform the force-ranking and why it is a benefit.

11.7 Discuss the PMO role with the Governance Board.

11.8 Explain how to implement an organization-wide prioritization process.

11.9 What should the Governance Board members normally look for in the operations status reporting and forecasting report?

11.10 Are we asking too much of Governance Boards? Discuss.

11.11 Explain how PMOs can help the organization's executives by linking the strategic objectives with tactical progress.

11.12 Discuss the effect that raising project progress visibility to the Governance Board might have on the project team member, project manager, project sponsor, and business unit leader.

11.13 What negative effects might an organization experience with a Governance Board? How might you avoid these in the initial setup of the board?

11.14 What is the main reason that an executive would be willing to give up some autonomy in initiating projects to a Governance Board?

12

LINKING PROJECT PROGRESS TO STRATEGIC OBJECTIVES — THE EXECUTIVE RADAR SCREEN

A RECIPE FOR DISASTER

Of the PMOs we surveyed, 97% cited a lack of executive involvement with or connection to the PMO. How can the PMO possibly be effective without this direct and regular involvement? Our answer is, "It is not possible." The survival of a PMO is premised on improving project management. Improvement means directly and significantly impacting the goals of the organization. The executives are responsible for the goals. If the executives do not perceive either enough value from the PMO or enough importance relative to their goals to stay involved, this is a huge red flag. It signals that the PMO will eventually be disassembled or, worse, fated into oblivion as another failed bureaucracy.

GRABBING EXECUTIVE ATTENTION

There is a simple way for a PMO to immediately provide value to executives and, consequently, gain their undivided attention. Link the organization's strategic objectives with projects, also showing the functional area where sponsorship exists. We illustrate this concept with a simple example. The example also illustrates the connection to the Deming and Goldratt approach discussed earlier.

Consider a manufacturing company that has a 75% on-time order fulfillment rate. It delivers late 25% of the time, and customers find other suppliers. The company believes it has an internal capacity problem. At the same time, it believes it has excess cash invested in inventory of some products and work-in-process because some product inventories turn less than three times per year.

The company offers products in the communications industry. The average product life is 9 months, and distributors and dealers are not very loyal to any brand. Therefore, the company knows that it must invent new products. At the same time, while demand for current products in existing markets is shrinking, demand for these products in other geographic areas (overseas and in the rest of the Americas) is increasing. The problem is that this company does not have a strong distribution channel in other geographic areas.

The company sets its strategic objectives as follows:

- Improve on-time order fulfillment to 95%
- Increase manufacturing capacity to add two major new product lines, without increasing the manufacturing budget
- Develop two new products that the market wants
- Reduce inventory by at least $10 million
- Increase net profit by at least $5 million
- Increase sales by at least $50 million

The first step is to link ideas to results that will accomplish the strategic objectives. See Figures 4.2 and 4.3 for an example.

Figure 4.2 shows the concept of linking strategic ideas with results that we believe will lead to meeting the objectives of the organization. The importance of this format is that it allows the entire executive team to scrutinize the cause–effect logic and determine if the overall plan makes sense. Will we really reach our goal with these changes?

Figure 4.2 shows the interdependencies between projects. This clearly shows that one silo (R&D, Marketing, Manufacturing, Sales) by itself cannot hope to achieve the corporate objectives. Not only is cooperation essential, but if cooperation fails to achieve the strategic results at each step, the company will not meet its total objectives.

The next step is to link projects to these ideas. Which projects are in place to achieve these ideas, and what percentage of the overall objectives will those projects accomplish? This process, performed by the PMO, ensures that the company is working on the right projects at all levels, and that the totality of all projects is sufficient to meet overall goals.

Using a table such as Table 12.1 can easily accomplish this goal. The table grabs executive attention on several fronts. The first is to clearly understand which projects are going to help each functional executive achieve his or her portion of the corporate goals. Second, the sponsor is clearly identified. Third, it tells all executives if the current set of ideas and corresponding projects are sufficient to accomplish the overall objectives.

PMO EXECUTIVE PROJECT PROGRESS REPORTING

Table 12.1 sets the stage for linking to project progress. Here the executives are interested in finding out the following:

1. Is the project on target (schedule, budget, scope)?
2. If the project is in trouble, what is the project manager doing about it?
3. Are decisions required to bring the project back on track?
4. Should priorities change?

The graph shown in Figure 12.1 provides several important hints about executive reporting. A picture is worth a thousand words. Executives easily tire of long, drawn out explanations. The question "Is the project on target?" is really three questions. Two of the three questions are answered, in a summary form, in Figure 12.1.

There is a cost line, showing variation from budget by reporting period. There is a scheduling line, showing critical path or critical chain work relative to how much work should have been done in that period. (Critical Chain, a Theory of Constraints scheduling method, is discussed in a later chapter. The reporting terminology used for scheduling is unique).

Note that the chart shows trends over time, which is absolutely crucial in order for executives to make sound decisions. One isolated figure, in one time period, does not tell an executive if he or she is dealing with common or special cause variation, and therefore whether or not intervention is required.

The third part of the "on target" question relates to scope. This question need only be addressed if there is a major scope issue requiring executive attention.

If the project is in trouble, the project manager should be able to state, very clearly, which tasks are currently in trouble and what action has been taken or what help is required from the executives to bring the project back on track.

Thus far, this type of executive project review can be done very quickly. Typically, from our experience, all major projects can be reviewed, using

Table 12.1   Executive Portfolio Summary Status

Objective	Idea and Sponsor	% of Objective	Project	Original and Current Due Date	Status
Fulfillment ↑ 95%	Implement Theory of Constraints Drum Buffer Rope Sponsor—Manufacturing	100%	Training & implementation decisions completed	5/2003	Green
			New reports and tracking systems	6/2003	Green
			Buffer management in place	7/2003 8/2003	Orange
Inventory ↓ $10 mm	Reduce WIP— See above	50%	See above	See above	Green
	Increase sales/turns Sponsor— Sales	50%	Reduced cycle time from Drum, Buffer, Rope implementation (see above)	See above	Green

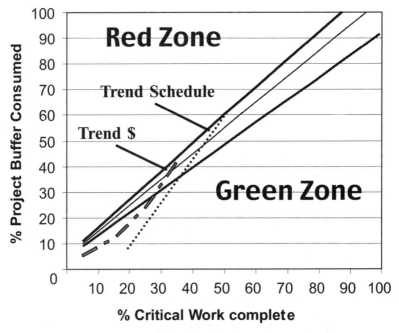

Figure 12.1   Project Trend Analysis (Cost and Schedule)

this format, in less than two hours. For most organizations, once per week or once every two weeks, at the executive level is sufficient.

WHAT ELSE DOES AN EXECUTIVE NEED TO KNOW ABOUT PROJECT PROGRESS?

The PMO should strive very hard to keep executive team project review meetings to a strict, short, regular timetable. The governance meeting is about decision-making and direction, not management (detailed analysis and control). If the discussion goes into areas that are of great interest to one or two executives but not to the others, the PMO can quickly lose control.

Individual executives may want to get into great detail on a given project for many valid reasons. The project may significantly impact a key customer. The project may be the critical component of a major corporate initiative. The project may be in trouble. However, such detailed reviews should be done outside of the executive team group project review.

Therefore, the example project progress status of "Green, Orange or Red", as shown in Table 12.1, is enough to indicate if the project is worth some executive time. Green implies no current problem and no need for further investigation. Orange implies a warning flag is raised, and further investigation and contingency plans are required. Red indicates a current serious problem that must be addressed or the project, and therefore the executive goal, will be impacted. We are not implying that this is the only way to categorize projects. Rather, we are simply illustrating one way to make the process quick and useful for executives.

For Red projects, the PMO should indicate if executive decisions are required, and what their recommendations are. For example, a recommendation on a Red project could be to allocate more resources, to kill the project, to subcontract some of the work, etc. By having the full analysis of options performed before the meeting, and by including proper supporting documentation, the PMO is providing a valuable support function to the Governance Board.

IMPACT OF EXECUTIVE REVIEWS ON TEAMS

Executives should also be aware that these regular reviews are incentives to project teams. For one thing, when team members know that project progress is being reviewed regularly at a high level, they go out of their way to report accurately. This is especially true if a project is not on target. Further, team members are motivated simply by knowing that the executives are interested in how the project is progressing and in which tasks are causing problems. No one wants to be in a Red project, so team members go out of their way to find solutions before the executive review.

SHOULD PRIORITIES CHANGE

As outlined in Collins' book, *Good to Great,* the research points out that great companies rarely need to change basic strategies in consideration of events. If a company is constantly changing project priorities, this is a red flag that the entire strategic planning process is out of control. In Collins' terms, it would imply that the company has not correctly answered the three basic questions:

1. What are we very passionate about?
2. What drives our economic engine?
3. What can we be the best at in the world?*

---

*James C. Collins, *Good to Great: Why Some Companies Make the Leap... and others don't,* HarperCollins, New York, 2001. See Chapter 5, The Hedgehog Concept.

If the PMO has done its homework on projects, ensuring that the needed information is in the project charter before a project is approved, and the strategic planning process follows the approach outlined in Part II of this book, then priority setting and changing is relatively easy.

A great deal of the priority shifting goes away by stopping the fighting over resources between functions. The strategic planning process eliminates part of this by letting the executives holistically see the company and the strategy. The holistic approach replaces the silo approach. However, this, by itself, is not enough to eliminate priority fights.

The second part of the solution is to stagger projects according to the organization's most critical resource. This approach is described later in Chapter 17. After this, there will still be discussions over priorities, but they should be much less frequent and much easier to conclude.

SUMMARY

If the PMO concept is sold correctly to the executive team, the executives will be excited about doing weekly or bi-weekly project reviews. This review gives them vital information tied directly to the goals of the company and to their responsibilities relative to those goals.

When the information is provided in a graphical, trend format, the executives clearly see if they need to get involved in a problem. Their interest is in both the projects they are sponsoring and the other projects that tie together with their own to determine overall corporate outcomes.

A correctly planned and executed review meeting will answer four key questions about the entire collection of projects, within 1 to 2 hours. These questions are:

1. Is the project on target (schedule, budget, scope)?
2. If the project is in trouble, what is the project manager doing about it?
3. Are decisions required now to bring the project back on track?
4. Should priorities change?

This linking of organization objectives to projects is vital to keep the teams motivated and the data up to date. When people know that the project they are working on is being reviewed by the top executives, there is an extra effort to report accurately and to show meaningful progress.

Finally, such regular meetings are key to considering priority changes. If the executive team and PMO have followed the strategic planning approach outlined in Part II, and the Critical Chain approach outlined later in Part III, priority changes should be infrequent.

CASE STUDY — TESSCO TECHNOLOGIES, INC.

TESSCO Technologies, Inc. is a leading supplier of integrated product plus supply chain solutions for the wireless industry. Headquartered in Hunt Valley, Maryland, TESSCO provides solutions to the profes-  sionals who design, build, run, maintain, and use wireless voice, data, messaging, location tracking, and Internet systems.

TESSCO began operations in 1982, and completed its public offering (NASDAQ: TESS) in 1994. Today, TESSCO operates 24 hours a day, 7 days a week, under ISO 9001:2000 registration. TESSCO's Global Logistics Centers in Hunt Valley, Maryland and Reno, Nevada configure orders for complete, on-time and error-free delivery throughout the world. Its product offerings consist of over 34,000 items from over 400 manufacturers. TESSCO currently serves approximately 15,000 business customers and 48,000 consumers per quarter.

The key to TESSCO's success and value add to its customers is its operational platform. This computer-driven capability streamlines the supply chain process and lowers customers' total inventories and costs by providing complete, on-time delivery to the point of use. This fact implies that a large number of the customer initiatives that TESSCO must deliver during a year create demands on the internal Technology Development and Services group that supports and enhances this platform. This Technology Development and Services group is also involved in many of the internal improvement projects at TESSCO.

BEFORE THE 4 × 4

In the fall of 2000, after several years of significant growth, TESSCO's CEO, Robert B. Barnhill, Jr., sought a way to ensure future consistent growth and productivity improvements. At that time, the company engaged in a process that identified key issues for the senior management team to address. On a weekly basis, the issues were reviewed. Each unit/team was asked to undertake projects to address the issues.

While this process spelled out many of the issues and the projects needed to address them, it was departmental in nature. Therefore, the issues were compartmentalized and the focus tended to be local rather than global (i.e., what can I do in my functional area, rather than what must we do across all functions to permanently eliminate the issue). As a result, the issues rolled over, week after week, without permanent resolution. As Wendy Sauvlet, Executive Assistant to Robert Barnhill, stated, "What worked when TESSCO was a smaller company was not working any longer."

Another problem also blocked the ability to make progress. Jeff Kaufman, of the Quality and Project Management Team, describes it as follows. "The number of projects running on and below the radar was extensive, with no one person or group tracking all the initiatives." Carolyn Kehl of the Marketing Operations and Support Team, adds, "There was no formal priority system, and when priorities were set, they were often changed."

Nick Salatino, Vice President of Retail and Consumer Markets, sums up the impact on project management this way: "One of TESSCO's opportunity areas was project management. As a result of not having anyone focused on this important activity, many projects were informally initiated in many ways. As a result, many were never completed, probably never should have been started and, as a result, the important projects were delayed or impacted. This resulted in less than stellar overall financial results."

At the time, Barnhill had read *The Goal* by Eli Goldratt,* and wondered if the principles went further to address the problems of strategy and project management for an entire company. Barnhill met with Gerald Kendall and decided to try the new 4 × 4 approach to strategic planning.

The process was presented to all senior managers and team leaders (a group of approximately 40) in January and February 2001. Barnhill translated some of the generic concepts of operations, distribution, finance, and measurements to TESSCO's world.

THE 4 × 4 PROCESS AND RESULTS

Barnhill comments, "The total system must be fully defined and understood before 'projects' can be defined. Few people totally understood the 'system' that is to be optimized. This definition and understanding is the most important benefit to-date of the 4 × 4 process!" Note that in this context, "system" refers to the entire organization and all its functional areas and interdependencies. Doug Rein, Senior Vice President, Fulfillment and Operations, concurs. Says Rein, "I think the 4 × 4 helped to break down the functional barriers and provide more constructive understanding of the global issues. The process helped to separate the issues from the people, making it easier to focus on the issue and not force blame on the people."

Barnhill adds, "It is easier to do than to think." Before the 4 × 4 process, taking immediate and unilateral action was considered to be a sign of strong leadership. In fact, "Make it Happen" leaders still resist attempts at more formal project management and the thinking behind it. They see it as bureaucracy or additional layers of management.

---

*Eliyahu M. Goldratt, *The Goal*, North River Press, Great Barrington, MA, 1984. This was Goldratt's first book, focused largely on manufacturing and sales.

At the time, TESSCO was ready for a change in the project management approach. As Bob Singer, CFO and Senior Vice President, Finance and Treasury, states, "We needed organizational focus. We had no formal tracking for many of our 200+ projects. After the 4 × 4, we created a project initiation and approval process and a formal resource allocation and tracking system."

The 4 × 4 and new project management processes at TESSCO are creating a major change in this "act now, think later" paradigm. For example, there is now a critical thinking process in place. Leaders using the project initiation forms described above must invest in rigorous analysis of the entire system in order to view the project holistically. The Theory of Constraints focusing steps are required to ensure that no proposal for capital spending is made before exploiting and subordinating to existing capacity. One challenge, in completing the rigorous analysis, is for the initiator to do his or her own thinking, with input from others, rather than having the Technology Group experts do all of the analysis.

Once the initiator has moved through the critical thinking process and exercises, he or she then prepares an in-depth analysis and summary for management review. This summary invokes continued critical thought by requiring the initiator to outline objectives, specifications, projections, risk, company fit, general strategy, and deliverables. As a result, Scott Jasion, Vice President, Marketing Operations, observes, "We [now] put more realistic dates/expectations in projects." Only after these steps are complete does the project move forward for senior management consideration.

At the highest level review, senior management may challenge the thinking behind the project request, reshape the project scope, approve it to move forward, or reject it. Only after this approval may it move forward for allocation of resources. Lynn Schwartz, Senior Vice President, Administration, notes that after the 4 × 4, "We prioritize projects based on their expected results in terms of throughput, investment and operating expense at the global level. Now there is more cross-functional involvement. This has been a very big improvement and has built more collaboration and consideration for the holistic impact of big decisions." While Barnhill is still finding that he must reinforce the need for the process repeatedly, the culture is beginning to change.

The 4 × 4 was intended to help leaders understand that a "project" is a plan to exploit an identified leverage point and eliminate a constraint to maximize the output of the total system. Steven Lehukey, Vice President of Customer Support, describes the benefits of the 4 × 4 as "Project management with established timelines; reduction of projects to 'what matters most'." This understanding is key and requires better acceptance by the organization. To some people the word "project" means an assignment —

something that keeps you away from getting your everyday job done. The 4×4 process and the system definition identified the Technology Development and Services Group as one of the most extensively utilized resources, and often a constraint.

EXPLOITING THE STRATEGIC RESOURCE — THE TECHNOLOGY DEVELOPMENT AND SERVICES GROUP

TESSCO projects have been classified into two areas: (1) Marketing Innovation and New Business Generation and (2) Operational Excellence and Process Improvement

Naturally, the "New Business" opportunities tend to be opportunistic and very perishable (i.e., if not acted upon when the opportunity presents itself, it will be lost). This reality creates a major conflict. Do we want new business or do we want an improved system? TESSCO's strategic resources are typically required for both.

Sometimes, the conflict exists because the organization's most precious resource is wasted. The reality is that TESSCO has built many systems based on the knowledge and control of a few key resources. This unwittingly made the Technology Group the gatekeepers of critical information and the needed source of such information. The tendency, therefore, has been for everyone at TESSCO to engage the Technical Group without doing the upfront, critical thinking.

However, there is a strong force compelling the organization to change, coming right from the CEO's office. As Barnhill comments, "Defining projects through rigorous thinking and collaborative reiteration has been extraordinarily difficult. However, this is a prerequisite to success. For example, today someone might define a project as 'Paint the Building'. Before the project is approved, we need this person to determine if it should be painted, or if the surface should just be covered. What color and type of paint will meet the user requirements? And we must do this, to the greatest extent possible, before deploying the strategic resource."

The up front, rigorous requirements definition is key to protecting and exploiting TESSCO's strategic resource. In fact, Barnhill believes that this is so important that he has invested significant time to facilitate all senior managers and team leaders in discussions on current behavior and how to better exploit and subordinate to the organization's most precious project resource. Jim Gaarder, Vice President, Development, of the Technology Development and Services Group, states, "There is far greater scrutiny of major projects and how they relate to the organization's goals and constraints. We are using project management software far, far more than we have in the past."

Rigorous requirements definition is necessary to accomplish two of Goldratt's recommended steps in the five focusing steps (see Chapter 7 for a complete explanation). One of Goldratt's steps is Exploit the Constraint. In TESSCO's example, this means do not waste the Technology Group's time working on poor requirements definition or rework because of poor up-front specifications. Goldratt's other step — subordinating to the constraint — is not fully understood or implemented yet. However, Barnhill adds, "While people do not like to be subordinated to a constraint, by using more disciplined thinking in requirements definition before involving the Technology Group, it is much better than it used to be. Everyone is beginning to understand the impact on Throughput, Investment, and Operating Expense of each decision. The collaboration today is much stronger than it was two years ago."

There has been a noticeable paradigm shift by leaders in the area of major and new initiatives who now view the Technology Group as a constraint. They actively look for ways to exploit and subordinate. Rick Guipe, Senior Vice President, Market Development and Sales, sums it up by stating, "[The 4 × 4 and strategic project management] has helped us manage the strategic resource. Projects do finish faster and in a more organized manner. Project visibility has improved. Prioritization of projects from a holistic standpoint is much better."

Vigilance is constantly required. There is still a constant stream of minor requests stemming from day-to-day activities, which are not sufficiently filtered with the exploit/subordinate mindset. The key 4 × 4 principle here is that it is not always correct to have a task performed by the most efficient resource. TESSCO's senior leaders are still working to have the rank-and-file buy into this. When this effort is complete, everyone will get information and explanations, perform basic PC tasks and solve other technical problems without involving the Technology Group, even if it takes more of their time and effort to accomplish. And there is the side benefit of the more someone does himself, the more he learns.

MAJOR SOFTWARE TOOL

TESSCO decided to use the Critical Chain multi-project approach for accelerating project delivery and managing the strategic resource. After a two-day Critical Chain workshop and investigation into available software, TESSCO chose the Oracle-based Concerto multi-project planning and tracking software, from Speed to Market.

At the time, TESSCO had very little in-house expertise in project management software. The concept of having a formal project plan, showing the dependencies and resource allocations, was a challenge for many. Concerto is a tool that uses Microsoft Project as a front and back end, with an

Oracle database to hold key information. This was (and still is) a serious challenge. "Load Concerto" became the mantra, rather than "define and build an effective project plan." It has, however, forced thinking as to resource definition and a better understanding of "critical chain."

Doug Rein adds, "Today we are formally tracking our critical projects in Concerto and doing so with much more focused attention and collaboration cross-functionally."

AFTER THE 4 × 4 — WHAT ELSE IS REQUIRED?

The transition to a mature project management organization has been successful thus far, and continues. Barnhill states that "subordination to the organization's strategic resource and collaboration are essential for global project management to work."

Today at TESSCO, with the credo of "Project Management," everyday performance expectations and strategic projects blur and compete. "What do you want me to do, run the business or work on this project?" or "I can't get this done until I develop a project plan!" Organizational paralysis sometimes develops until the "conformance" of getting an "approved" project occurs.

This spells out a need for a PMO/portfolio management skill set to help managers do the necessary homework to present a project opportunity to the CEO. As Stan Sack, Consultant, Leadership Development and Sales Training, explains, "We need a rigorous PMO to manage pipeline projects and stop non-holistic thinking. This will help us maintain fanatical alignment, coherence and consistency." At TESSCO, the formal PMO/portfolio management structure is not fully set up. Therefore, at weekly review meetings, when the homework is not done by team leaders, the CEO role changes from decision-making and direction-setting to management.

Barnhill points out that the concept of a stage gate process, where projects can be killed or deactivated, is important. "What ifs" and "re-plan" based upon "learning(s)/new information" is difficult; people want to proceed with a project plan, even if it drives the bus over the hill, or is no longer needed. Killing and deactivating projects are essential to reduce the impact of the conflicts discussed above.

TESSCO needs to learn and implement the concepts of Project Portfolio Management. To prioritize correctly, it needs to improve its ability to perform analysis with the "what ifs" and "what I know now" considerations. Negative side effects of new ideas need to be anticipated. This will help overcome the current tendency for team leaders and managers to get their project into the pipeline right away, so they can get priority, even when the plan is poorly defined. Adds Bob Singer, "We as an organization must continue to focus on resource constraints and make the trade-off and tough decisions."

RESULTS OF BETTER PROJECT MIX COMBINED WITH BETTER PROJECT MANAGEMENT

> "TESSCO had a good quarter with earnings per share growing to $0.25 from $0.06 for the same quarter last year. Revenue growth was a solid 15% over the same quarter last year and 12% over last quarter. Operations generated over $5 million in cash flow used to pay down virtually all short-term debt as of the end of the quarter. TESSCO is navigating well through turbulent market conditions."

These comments are from the latest quarterly report. While the processes described in this case study cannot claim all the credit, CEO Barnhill states, "Current performance has been greatly aided by the process. Today, we are focused on only 15 top priority projects, with complete cross-functional input and requirements definition." Doug Rein states, "We realized significant financial improvements from our Freight Optimization project efforts, and also drove significant productive change throughout our Distribution Center operations with our Flexible Capacity project."

TESSCO has traveled a long way down the Project Management and Global Thinking road in less than 2 years, and the results are very tangible.

QUESTIONS

12.1 Why must projects be linked to the goals of the organization?

12.2 Can there be active projects that are not linked to any explicit goal of the organization? If yes, do these need to be reviewed by the entire executive team?

12.3 Why don't most executive teams conduct project reviews?

12.4 How can the PMO get executive teams to be willing to participate in project reviews?

12.5 If a project is not on target, what does the executive team need to know?

12.6 How far off target should a project be before the executive team discusses the problem?

12.7 How do executive reviews drive good behavior of project teams? Could executive reviews drive bad behavior? If yes, what could you do ahead of time to prevent the bad behavior?

12.8 True or False: If the organization is in control, project priorities should rarely be changed.

13

DELIVERY MANAGEMENT AND ACCELERATION

DEVELOPING TEAM MEMBER COGNITIVE SKILLS TO ACCELERATE PROJECT DELIVERY

How a project team deals with Murphy during the execution of a project plan is a critical success factor to its ability to finish on time, on budget and within scope. Being able to follow a plan implies both skill and permission to execute without interference.

Standish Group recently reported that 84% of all IT projects fail. What dynamics occur within project teams that apparently lead them to failure? Is it the tools used by the project team? Is it the requirements? Is it the quality of the project data that is leading the team astray? Team members, when questioned about the reasons for failure, often talk about the lack of agreement among their peers, or the lack of resources, time, material, etc. It always appears to be someone else's fault.

Project failures are one of the most compelling reasons organizations seek to bring about common rigor and discipline through project management in their workplace. Our first challenge is to standardize the expectations among team members. By narrowing the differences in work expectations, miscommunication can be significantly reduced and anticipation and predictability of the next step can be reinforced continuously.

MINIMUM EXPECTATIONS ARE
USUALLY GOOD ENOUGH

Standardizing expectations among team members is often one of the most misunderstood functions performed by project managers. Simply handing out assignments is not sufficient. Holding team members accountable is important, but is also not sufficient. Look at the processes that the team members will use to complete their assignments. The point here is to ensure that the processes are manageable, controllable, and measurable. It is said that, "To be able to manage, you must be able to control, and to be able to control, you must be able to measure. Thus, if you cannot measure, you cannot control and if you cannot control you cannot manage." Managing the processes performed by the project team members will provide a strong starting point for the project to be successful. Still, this is not sufficient.

How does the project team perform its work? Is it in a recipe fashion where to bake a cake, a person simply follows instructions and waits 20 minutes for the cake to bake? Is it such that your project team practices an approach that is "every man, woman or child for himself," or do we allow our team members to simply sit in their offices and do their assignments without checking on them? If this is occurring for your project team, you are leaving money, time, and project success on the table.

Many project teams perform their work along the lines of an accepted methodology. Methodologies are project road maps meant to bring about discipline and common understanding regarding how work deliverables are to be completed and how the project should navigate its way to successful completion. In many instances, team members who lack the necessary experience and/or skill to complete a particular deliverable in the project fall back on these methodologies and simply follow the recipe for successfully completing the deliverable or work product. This is accepted practice by many project managers.

Project managers seemingly expect all deliverables to be completed and delivered within 100% compliance of standard expectations. Why? Have you ever witnessed a product, a software application, anything that has ever been implemented that was 100% of what the entire world expected? So why do we expect this of our project team members? Is 80% sufficient? The answer lies within what the project manager defines as acceptable. The team member must not make this decision in isolation. That is part of what causes major delays in projects today.

In his book *Critical Chain*, Dr. Eli Goldratt describes this behavior as Parkinson's Law — work expands to fill the time available. Often, in projects, this means unnecessary effort to add bells and whistles beyond what the minimum specifications call for.

If the minimum specification is acceptable in completing a particular deliverable, then the workflow can be accelerated. Thus, the team member should complete work with only the processes and steps necessary to complete a sufficient deliverable and execute care to select only those process steps that lead to timely completion of the deliverable.

Are we still performing project management? You bet! Only now we have changed the project management theme to be more aware of what is really necessary and sufficient and away from blindly creating all of the deliverables and work products specified by the methodology.

This is what we call *"Delivery Management."* We manage project completeness based on the tolerance we have to acceptable risk (positive and negative) as that risk helps or hinders us toward our goal of completing the project. Essentially, we are very careful with how we spend our time. Only enough time is expended to complete the work and nothing more.

OTHER APPLICATIONS OF DELIVERY MANAGEMENT

As projects start out in the development life cycle, everyone seems busy with their assignments. People are typically working hard, working their 8 hours more or less, and project team life is as most of us expect. Team members are applying the methodologies and standards required by the business to complete the work. Each team member works in his or her silo waiting for the necessary input to do certain aspects of his or her work assignments. Why are we waiting? On tasks that determine the project duration (i.e., Critical Path or Critical Chain), we should not tolerate unnecessary waiting — ever.

What can we do to eliminate the wait? Team members must be on the hunt, all the time, for potential work delays that will impede them in completing their critical path or critical chain work on time. Even if the team members do not eliminate the entire wait, reducing some wait is a far better result than reducing none at all.

We often encounter project wait time in work tasks that are inter-dependent with other work tasks performed by other team members, often from other functional areas. As the receiving team member of the work product or deliverable from another team member, we do not find out that the input to our work is unacceptable until we attempt to use the input in our process. Rework becomes necessary to improve the input item to sufficient quality levels necessary to complete your work task. Everyone suffers as more pressure is placed on the due date.

Team members must develop the necessary cognitive skills to avoid delivery delays while seeking delivery acceleration opportunities to com-

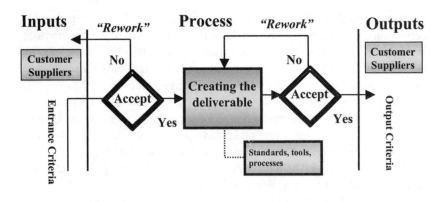

Figure 13.1 The Deming Workbench

plete their work. One way for team members to develop these skills is through a process tool known as the "Deming Workbench" (see Figure 13.1).

THE DEMING WORKBENCH

Dr. W. Edwards Deming, inventor of the Total Quality Management movement, developed the "Deming Workbench." The Deming Workbench has many uses, but in the context of our message we are interested in how it helps team members find ways to reduce work task time while enabling them to perform their work assignments right the very first time.

The Deming Workbench breaks down into three key components. The first component consists of the input necessary to perform the process. Acceptance of the input by the process owner (work task) is dependent upon "entrance criteria." These criteria define what is minimally acceptable. The meaning of "minimally acceptable" is anything less than these criteria will affect the process (work task) that utilizes the input.

The second component is the process application. This is where the work is actually performed. Initially the input is validated and once it has been accepted for processing, work is performed using the process guidelines and associated tools.

Upon completion of the process work, the third component, output, is produced. The produced output is validated against expected exit criteria much in the same way that input criteria were employed to protect the process effort from rework. Thus, exit criteria protect and ensure the quality of the produced output in concurrence with current process expectations and with the next process step to receive the produced output in mind.

When process owners do not recognize the changing entrance or exit criteria requirements, rework often results. Rework is a leading cause of wasted work time in project teams.

How do we prevent rework in our work assignments? This requires sufficient awareness of project-related events that occur outside the peripheral silo of the team members that might indirectly impact their work and place their delivery schedule in jeopardy and possibly the project as well.

There are three compelling points to learn.

1. The team must break down all barriers and look at the project completion on time and within scope as its product, not its task completion. This focuses the team on the second point.
2. To meet the end completion date on time, the handoff of work from one team member to another must be as smooth and error-free as possible. This means that at the formation of every team, the team members should be asked to rigorously define the entrance and exit criteria for each handoff.
3. The team should be measured on the successful completion of the project, as a team, and not on each individual finishing a task on time. It is not important to bottom line results if an individual finishes a task on time. In fact, it is perfectly normal for many tasks to take longer than estimated.

Team members have to extend themselves outside their own silo to look for process influences of which they need to be aware.

HOW THE PMO CAN HELP PROJECT TEAMS

The PMO can provide vital support services to help the project team members deliver a quality project faster by assisting in project "kick-off" meetings. For example, the PMO can educate team members on the concepts of the Deming Workbench (or other tools to reduce rework). In addition, the PMO can proactively solicit the known obstacles to achieving the project goal and deadline, and create a plan to overcome those obstacles; start building team communications; help define the entrance and exit criteria.

The PMO must continually raise the bar of progress visibility for project teams. The improved awareness and coaching from PMO experts will directly lead to development of improved cognitive skills on the part of each project team member when he or she is party to the project work under scrutiny. This visibility can come from many different sources:

1. Project portfolio management
2. Resource utilization
3. Project schedules and progress — online, Web-based, up-to-date information

4. Project status meetings
5. Project management mentoring
6. Governance Board guidance
7. Project management community peer pressure
8. Project work estimates

1. **Project portfolio management** — Published information should make the project priorities crystal clear. Project progress data will also highlight opportunities for acceleration. For example, if the organization's strategic resource will complete a project earlier than expected, this information can be used by the next project to accelerate the work and take advantage of the early finish.

Projects that are in trouble stick out like a sore thumb. The project manager with the troubled project feels the spotlight on him or her to perform and to correct the situation. The spotlight is even brighter if dependencies exist from his or her project to others. However, the spotlight should make the project manager and the team more open to receive help from outside the team. This is where the PMO, as a source of both expertise and coordination, can drive acceleration.

The continuing progress reporting becomes a source of validation that the problem is either corrected or remains a problem. Most project managers believe that the longer a project is under scrutiny, the less likely they are to be successful in their assignment. As a result, from the increasing demand to correct the situation, the project manager will begin looking for ways to reduce effort within the project team that will help bring the delivery expectation back in line. The problem is, if the project manager does not have the skills to find these improvements in normal situations, what is it about the crisis that makes anyone believe the project manager will now make it happen? This is the reality of the fear of project managers who fall into this inspection process. The PMO coaching must be done to help develop these skills.

2. **Resource utilization** — There is one certainty about project resource plans. Some tasks will take longer than expected. Some will take less. Few will finish exactly according to the estimate. In this environment of uncertainty, there are several ways that PMO tracking of resources can bring about delivery acceleration opportunities.

If resources are unexpectedly available, the PMO is the one-stop shop to identify where the opportunities exist, within the project portfolio, to use those resources to speed up the highest priority project. Also, the PMO ensures that resources are working on the right projects at the right time.

PMOs can provide valuable information by tracking resource planned and actual work loads by resource pools over a period of time. This tracking should be done in a way that reflects all planned work by month and by project. If this information is available to resource managers and project teams waiting for resources in order to proceed, then this common awareness will allow everyone to pursue the acceleration opportunities. Also, the fact that key stakeholders have access to resource work plans for the foreseeable future is motivating for the particular resource to meet or exceed those estimates in a positive manner.

3. **Project schedules** — Task assignments should always be open for review to all team members. In this manner, with coaching, team members can learn cognitive skills to discover developing trends emerging from completed project work. These cognitive skills improve current ability to predict when things are moving out of control (unpredictable). Further, they help teams learn how to overcome negative situations. Raising the visibility of the work schedule of all team members helps the team understand its interdependencies. No one enjoys being on the critical path all the time. However, this visibility makes it much easier for people on the critical path to obtain the support they need from their fellow team members, including the delivery of non-critical work on time and with a quality that does not negatively impact the critical path.

4. **Project status meetings** — This is a simple, but key, project management tool to raise work status visibility among team members. In your next project team status meeting, ask all contributing team members to be ready to talk about the following:

- What have they accomplished in the reporting period?
- What are they planning to accomplish in the next reporting period?
- What issues are they having with which they might need help?
- What work acceleration opportunities do they see in their work and others around them that would help the project team?
- What work delivery threats do they see in their work and in others around them that would hurt the project team?

Keep each team member status report presentation to 2 to 4 minutes. Encourage them to use facts linked directly to the project schedule, so everyone can hear and relate to what is said. You can be guaranteed that with each passing status meeting, people will ensure that what they have to say is reflective of the team expectations or they will have pre-empted the bad news so as not to suffer further embarrassment. This is exactly what the project manager wants to happen. People become proactive in finding ways to report good and bad news instead of being reactive and waiting to be asked. An added benefit will be that project status meetings should end on time or sooner.

5. **Project management mentoring from the PMO** — PMO mentors have the accountability and responsibility to always be on the lookout for unreported risk within project teams. Normally, mentors will attend project

team status meetings and observe for project risk. The mentor can add significant value to how progress visibility is communicated. Savvy project managers will see the mentor as a friend and will find ways to use recent progress knowledge to their benefit. The project management community should see the mentor as a project management doctor whose purpose is to help the project manager, project sponsor, and team member stay healthy.

6. **Governance Board guidance** — Knowing that the senior management team is reviewing projects is great for motivating the teams to push harder to keep their projects in control. Further, when a PM knows that he or she could be under the unwanted glare of the Governance Board spotlight, he or she becomes very proactive in seeking ways to overcome difficulties and accelerate.

7. **Project management community peer pressure** — When the PMO begins the portfolio management process, information on the status of projects falls into one of several groups: Green (okay), Orange (caution), or Red (in trouble, help is required).

As the PMO begins operating, bi-weekly project management community meetings should be conducted with project managers. In these bi-weekly meetings, project managers learn which projects are doing well, which projects need investigation, and which projects are in trouble. They will also learn about project acceleration opportunities and threats to project delivery. This means that they will know which projects are under the spotlight of senior management. Peer pressure in this situation can be very motivating. You can bet that the project manager perceived to be in last place among his peers will work his or her hardest to not be in the same position by the next meeting time. This is exactly what the PMO wants. Improving the weakest link makes the chain stronger. The PMO must take great care not to put the project manager into a defensive posture as this could backfire and cause the peer group to choose sides in favor of the victim.

8. **Project work estimates** — Who is managing the work estimate quality of work tasks in the project schedule? How were people asked to estimate their work? What rules or parameters were provided to those who estimated the work tasks in the project schedule?

We have learned that once a schedule becomes public, it tends to become fact whether it is draft or final. Those creating the schedule along with the associated work estimates are held responsible for the estimate expectations. Consider what people are really doing when they estimate their level of effort (LOE) for the work they might do themselves or that might be accomplished by someone else.

In general, work typically expands to meet the estimate. This is known as Parkinson's Law. As we stated earlier, conquering Parkinson's Law is critical to a project manager's ability to deliver a completed project on time.

This topic is covered extensively in Chapter 17, and in the referenced texts. Suffice it to say that the case studies prove it is not unusual to experience savings of up to 50% of the estimated work.

INCREASED TEAM AWARENESS AND PERFORMANCE THROUGH PMO ACTIONS

The main objective of PMO support toward the project team is to help target real or potential delivery bottlenecks. It is incumbent upon the PMO and the project manager to help team members feel accountable, to find ways to accelerate project work related to their work tasks directly and the unfinished project work indirectly.

As various team members uncover and implement improvements for themselves and the team, the critical path or critical chain work focus within the project team will often shift. Awareness for who is in the hot seat is another key ingredient for project team delivery success. Take a hard look at your projects. Who is in the hot seat in each project right now? If you cannot answer that question, or if the answer is "everyone on the project team," this points out a big problem in communications that the PMO must help overcome.

There are many benefits of this awareness. The project manager benefits, with the team awareness bringing help in various forms to the critical path or critical chain tasks. Sometimes, the help is simply ensuring that the team member performing the critical chain task is left alone to get his work done as expediently as possible. At other times, it is helping that team member get answers to issues that are holding him up.

For example, we know of one organization where a red chain is put on a cubicle, signaling everyone not to disturb this individual because he or she is on the critical chain of a project.

ADDRESSING DELIVERY ACCELERATION AND THREATS IN INTERDEPENDENT PROJECT TEAMS

This calls to mind an experience in Chicago where a small telecom equipment manufacturer was working hard to deliver the first-of-its-kind product sub-component to a major local telephone conglomerate. The firm did not schedule development work using basic project management tools such as Microsoft Project to develop project schedules or task lists. It just jumped in and started working. Does this sound familiar?

The major problem was centered around three separate engineering research and development teams. They did not communicate well either intra-project or between project teams.

The critical path to complete the total development effort for this subcomponent kept slipping because of the general lack of information awareness among all three teams. The managers for each team were questioned and each maintained his or her innocence. His or her team was doing just fine. It was the other teams that kept holding them up.

It was recommended that all three teams begin to meet each week, jointly, to report project status. The expected benefit was that the managers would be able to identify where the bottlenecks were among the three teams and take corrective action. All three managers reluctantly agreed but stated that this would be a waste of time for their team.

At the first joint meeting, the teams and their managers gathered (more than 30 people) into a conference room. Each team member was required to state what work he or she had completed, what work he or she expected to complete in the next reporting cycle, what issues he or she had, and where he or she needed help.

As each team member reported, some of the team members were hearing, for the first time, news of certain work tasks that were thought to be completed but were not. Others were hearing news of completed work of which they were unaware. In one case, an engineer learned he could have started his work a week earlier if he had only known that the work output he needed was ready. Upon concluding the meeting, a revised project schedule was handed out to the three teams to help them align their work efforts.

After the meeting was over, a debriefing was conducted with the three managers. One of the managers who had earlier indicated that the problem was not in his team, found out that indeed his team was a major delivery bottleneck and was further embarrassed by the general observation that he did not know about it. In fact, he had been giving some grief to the other two managers about the delays. You can imagine the scene. The first statements in the debriefing were of general amazement that they could be so in the dark.

It is always important to focus on the problem and not on the people. We did manage to solve the bottleneck issues created by non-communication among and within the three teams. The project was successfully delivered — in spite of everything — by conducting the project status meetings weekly in the same format. Since people were expected to discuss their work in front of their peers in these meetings, this had the effect of positive peer pressure. They had to tell the truth, which meant they had to complete their work in order to deliver a positive report.

Once you are aware of bottlenecks, they can be corrected. Just as in baseball, to hit the baseball, the batter must see it first. The questions for most teams are, "Are the project team members looking for the pitch?" "Are they vigilant?" And, more importantly, "Will they score?"

THE BENEFIT TO THE PMO —
GAINING VALUE IN THE EYES OF ITS CUSTOMERS

Any PMO that can help project teams work well together will help project teams overcome issues that would significantly delay projects. Keep in mind, most project teams are very insecure in nature. They are worried about everything and they should be.

Today's project environment is not only challenging, but often threatening as well. Ask yourself this simple question to get a true feel for the insecurity. When you start new project work with a group of people, do you assume they are your friends? When project delivery is threatened, will they be there for you?

This is one way that the PMO can build sustaining value to the community it serves. The PMO should be working alongside the project teams, helping them spot project opportunities and threats to delivery and pointing everyone's finger at the problem, not at each other.

PMOs that are just beginning can find immediate value by providing mentoring services to development project teams. Saving time, saving credibility, and saving people from themselves and each other should be strongly considered as part of the PMO value proposition. PMOs must work at this type of support to determine what works best in the work culture. As PMOs deliver this support, project teams everywhere will realize value.

CREATING THE RIGHT WORK ENVIRONMENT —
GAINING EXCITEMENT IN THE PROJECT TEAM

As the PMO and the project manager teach the project team members to develop their cognitive skills in finding ways to accelerate their work, the PMO and the project manager can help improve the overall team attitude about doing the work — even at a higher speed.

Turn the project team into a "learning team," where the knowledge being learned is how the project progress can be accelerated ahead of the current baseline schedule. The team members become "students" working together in sub-teams to solve project problems with all efforts aimed at "getting there." This approach is like applying the "Kaizen" events that have worked to accomplish major improvements on the shop floor.

Project teams organized in this manner, formally or informally, will find that people work better in a smaller group that is consistently sharing visible information. Team members gain a strong sense of job satisfaction because they see they are contributing to the success of the team and the project, above and beyond the performance of their individual tasks.

SUMMARY

Part of the PMO value proposition is its ability to influence almost every project team to accelerate project delivery. A PMO that delivers this value will become incrementally sustainable over time. Such a PMO becomes an "ROI Engine" for the business it serves.

One powerful tool for delivery management and acceleration is the Deming Workbench, a product of Dr. W. Edwards Deming. The responsibility of creating entrance and exit criteria between hand-offs in a project is given to the project team. The PMO helps break down barriers and coaches the team to view their goal not as completion of a task, but as the final delivery of the project on time and within scope and budget. The entrance and exit criteria then become a vehicle to prevent unnecessary rework.

PMOs also can add tremendous value at project kickoff meetings by coaching team members to help look for delivery acceleration opportunities and threats. Further, the ongoing roles of mentoring projects, improving communications and being a "friend" to whom a troubled project team can turn are all vital to delivery success.

Project teams that have access to PMOs operating in this manner will prosper more and more with each new project they take on. The primary focus on project team and team member attitudes in how they approach their work is one of the most important concepts a PMO can deliver. This is a significant benefit to the bottom line of a business and is mission critical to the survival of a PMO.

CITY OF KANSAS CITY, MISSOURI (KCMO) CASE STUDY

WHAT IS THE CITY OF KANSAS CITY, MISSOURI?

Kansas City, Missouri, which calls itself the "Heart of America," is at the confluence of the Missouri and Kansas rivers and is centrally located within 200 miles of the geographic and population centers of the United States. Kansas City was incorporated in 1850 and played a major role in history as the gateway for pioneers, traders, and missionaries heading west along the Oregon, California, and Santa Fe trails. Railroads,

livestock and grain helped Kansas City establish itself as a major business community in the Midwest in the late 1800s. Today, Kansas City incorporates 317 square miles in parts of four counties and has a population of 442,000, making it the state's largest city. The metropolitan area covers 11 counties in Missouri and Kansas with a total population of 1.8 million.

WHY WAS A PMO ESTABLISHED?

Three years ago, the Y2K project raised the awareness of the City of Kansas City's Information Technology Department (ITD) that a more disciplined approach was needed to manage all city enterprise technology initiatives. Each department, including ITD, had a different approach in addressing technological initiatives. Because of inconsistencies among these departments in planning, estimating, tracking projects, resources and project timelines, it was often a challenge for ITD to provide high quality service to these departments.

Additionally, any attempt to change the business culture within ITD was a politically sensitive process. While many employees within the organization recognized the need for improved project management practices, there was resistance from others who interpreted this process as a loss of power and a threat to their current responsibilities. However, these changes were aligned with the strategic and cross-functional department project initiatives that were in progress. Some of these initiatives included:

Enterprise Resource Planning (ERP) — The ERP project was initiated to identify an enterprise-wide solution to replace and enhance functionality provided by the aging multiple non-integrated systems currently performing the city's core business activities. Phase I of the ERP implementation included financial and accounting systems, human resources, payroll, purchasing, budget, asset management, project and grant accounting, and tax collection. The city intends to replace the current systems with an integrated ERP software package. An RFQ requesting proposals from qualified consulting firms to assist the city in this effort was released in February 2001.

Geographic Information System (GIS) — The demands of constituents, both internal and external, are exceeding the capabilities of the city's current department-oriented, geographic data files and storage structure. The migration to a geospatial data warehouse requires converting the existing data structures and expansion to support new applications. The complexity of the design and implementation requires selecting a consultant with expertise in local government and geospatial warehouses.

Computer-Aided Dispatch System (CAD) — This project studied the different, disparate computer-aided dispatching and records management systems in use in the city. An outside vendor was contracted to do the study and to develop the RFP for an upgraded, enterprise CAD and records management system for the city. The upgrade would provide for the full integration of the public safety communications offices and would provide records management systems that have fully integrated modules that are tightly integrated with CAD. New systems would also provide for a master clock interface that would enable all communications offices to provide the same time information.

Program Project Management (PPM) — This project was a multi-phased effort to improve the processes by which the city handled its Capital Improvement Program (CIP). Phase 1 included an assessment of the city's current project management environment and an inventory of technical systems that maintain project-related data. Phase 2 included a functional requirements definition, a technical environment specification, and an application architecture model. Phase 3 focused on redesigning project lifecycle processes and concepts that were proven through a Model Office. Phase 4 will implement PPM across four departments. The planned deployment includes business process re-engineering and training, and the use of the Project Knowledge System (PKS).

To overcome these challenges and ensure standard processes across departments, Gail Roper, the Department Director, asked an outside consulting organization to conduct an initial assessment of the processes within ITD. The consulting group developed a customized information technology strategy. The plan linked the city's needs with information technology investments necessary to provide improved government functions and enhanced constituent service.

HOW DID ITD ESTABLISH A PMO?

The IT strategic plan spanned more than three years. It included recommendations for the establishment of an Enterprise Program Management Office (EPMO). The primary objectives of the EPMO are to:

- Ensure repeatable, stable project execution within the context of increasing the business value of the city's technology organization's project portfolio.
- Apply project management best practices, focusing on project portfolio creation, assessments, and coaching.
- Address strategic project portfolio management issues.

■   Help ensure alignment of city departments and ITD to the IT strategic plan.

ITD commissioned an outside vendor in April 2001 to implement an EPMO and then transition the management and continued operations to the ITD staff.

This work began with an assessment of the project management maturity levels of the IT organization. The result of the assessment revealed that although the project managers within the IT organization displayed some knowledge about project management, their maturity in exercising this knowledge was not consistent. They were assessed at a maturity level of 0, according to CMM and SEI Standards for project management. This baseline helped to determine the type of EPMO that would be most effective, the skills needed, and what near-term and long-term activities were required. Three months after the EPMO was established, the project managers' maturity level had increased from 0 to 1.

The ITD Director went a step further by recruiting and hiring a seasoned project management professional to manage the EPMO. The manager and the director presented the concept of the EPMO to the City Council members and the department directors, outlining the value of the office.

HOW DID THE PMO EVOLVE?

The introduction of an EPMO in ITD resulted in the following:

■   Establishment of a collaborative project manager community within ITD, where information and ideas about project scope, risks, and costs are exchanged.

■   An increase in the delivery, productivity, and quality of work performed.

■   The EPMO was added to the City's Administrative Regulation (AR 1-16) for all IT enterprise initiatives.

■   Other departments are now tracking some of their projects through the EPMO. There are 12 projects totaling approximately $53M currently being monitored by the EPMO.

■   A critical project for the Revenue Division of the Finance Department, Earnings Tax (E-Tax) was completed on time and within budget. The objectives of the Earnings Tax project are to achieve total compliance of electronic tax processing via banks and the Auto Clearing House (ACH) of employer withholdings, address recommendations to reduce costs and increase efficiencies of processing employer tax withholdings for both the taxpayer and the City of Kansas City, MO, eliminate check processing, reduce median days to post from 29 to 15, and improve deposit posting by Day 1 to Day 0.

■   Projects are now prioritized and completed based on the city's and ITD's strategic plans.

- Structured weekly meetings and weekly project reporting formats provide sufficient information to senior city executive management to ensure that the activities surrounding IT projects support the strategic plan of the city.
- Project managers are more informed of City Council issues and other concerns that may impact their projects.
- The development of standard document templates and methodologies has helped to support a consistent approach to project management throughout ITD.

WHERE IS THE PMO GOING FROM HERE?

According to the IT Strategic Plan, the EPMO was developed to eventually report on all IT initiatives through the City Manager's Office, the highest level within the organization. It is slotted to report to the city's Chief Information Officer, a position that does not yet exist. The EPMO also wants to support the project managers in attaining level 5 in their project management capability maturity within three years.

QUESTIONS

13.1 Discuss the cognitive skills necessary for team members to be successful.

13.2 Explain the "Deming Workbench" and its use in helping to organize workflow in a project team.

13.3 Explain the difference between "Project Management" and "Delivery Management."

13.4 Work attitudes play a large part in team productivity. Explain how "learning teams" can help project teams "get there".

13.5 Discuss how a PMO can assist project teams and become their "friend."

13.6 Identify and discuss the value points the PMO can provide a project team member in relation to delivery.

Web Added Value™

14

PROJECT PORTFOLIO MANAGEMENT

TODAY'S PROJECT PORTFOLIO PROBLEMS

The four biggest universal problems in project portfolios are:

1. Too many active projects (often double what an organization should have)
2. Wrong projects (projects that will not provide value to the organization)
3. Projects not linked to strategic goals
4. Unbalanced portfolio
   - Too much on the supply side, not enough on the market side
   - Too much development, not enough research
   - Too much short term, not enough long term
   - Not reflective of the organization's most important assets
   - Not reflective of the organization's strategic resource value
   - Not reflective of major product revenue opportunities, risks, etc.

Today, one of the reasons that these major problems exist is because many projects have an undefined or unclear ROI. Many organizations have active projects that are not sanctioned by senior management. Further, even if every active project is a positive, sanctioned contribution to ROI, many organizations find their arteries clogged with too many projects. Consequently, projects are forced to compete for resources. With resource competition, project managers and their sponsors face project durations that are far too lengthy to meet the organization's goals.

Many organizations tasked with improving project portfolio performance start with few, if any, formal processes or information. In many organizations, a formal project portfolio is not documented and explicitly managed. Project interrelationships may not be rigorously considered. Further, many projects are simply not linked to the organization's goals. How can a portfolio manager determine if he or she has a healthy portfolio without the basic information?

THE ROLE OF PROJECT PORTFOLIO MANAGEMENT

Portfolio management ensures that the collection of projects chosen and completed meets the goals of the organization. Just as a stock portfolio manager looks for ways to improve the return on investment, so does a project portfolio manager. However, a stock portfolio manager would be embarrassed if he or she could not answer the questions, "What is the value of my portfolio? How has the portfolio value changed since the last reporting period?" In project portfolios, key information to answer these vital questions is often missing. Every PMO and every organization without a PMO should have someone designated in the role of project portfolio manager.

If all of the chosen projects are completed to perfection (on time, on budget, within scope), but they do not even come close to meeting the goals of the organization, then there is something wrong or missing in the portfolio management process. We choose a very broad and important definition of project portfolio management, something well beyond the mechanics of monitoring project progress and changing the project mix. In our terms, project portfolio management has six major responsibilities:

1. Determining a viable project mix, one that is capable of meeting the goals of the organization
2. Balancing the portfolio, to ensure a mix of projects that balances short term vs. long term, risk vs. reward, research vs. development, etc.
3. Monitoring the planning and execution of the chosen projects
4. Analyzing portfolio performance and ways to improve it
5. Evaluating new opportunities against the current portfolio and comparatively to each other, taking into account the organization's project execution capacity
6. Providing information and recommendations to decision makers at all levels

THE 8 STEPS TO SUCCESSFUL PORTFOLIO MANAGEMENT

The following 8 steps, discussed in detail in this chapter, comprise a process to establish and improve any project portfolio:

1. Gather and report the initial portfolio information (see Table 14.4 for an example of the initial information required).
2. Develop the goals, resource and asset portfolios (described in later chapters).
3. Link project, goals, resource and asset portfolios, and perform an initial assessment.
4. Determine the organization's multi-project strategic resource (described in this chapter and in Chapter 17).
5. Prioritize the project portfolio according to accepted criteria and the information currently available.
6. Assess portfolio balance.
7. Develop recommendations for improving ROI.
8. Facilitate the Governance Board meeting and communicate the results.

THE DIFFERENCE BETWEEN PROJECT AND PRODUCT PORTFOLIO MANAGEMENT

Most processes that are used for product portfolio management are focused on new product development. These processes are designed to help an organization choose which new product developments to fund, given limited investment availability and limited resources. There is a direct connection between product portfolio management and project portfolio management.

New product development represents a subset of all of the projects an organization undertakes. It does not include internal improvements, projects undertaken in other functional areas, and often excludes maintenance and other projects applied to already existing products.

It is a mistake for most organizations to conduct product portfolio management without including it in project portfolio management. The reason is simple. In most organizations, the same resources used for new product development are also called upon to perform tasks in other projects. How can an organization set priorities for resources on new products and ignore what might happen in other projects?

In reality, when this is done, resources and their management end up in a huge conflict. The TESSCO case study, discussed previously, highlights this. Resources wonder, "Do you want me to run operations or work on new product development?" Or "Should I work on the new product or solve the emergency on the existing product?"

An organization will have better results with one overall project portfolio and one set of priorities for everyone. This is much simpler and easier to understand. The senior executives will have resolved all the conflicts before resources and managers need to make decisions.

Enterprise Project Management

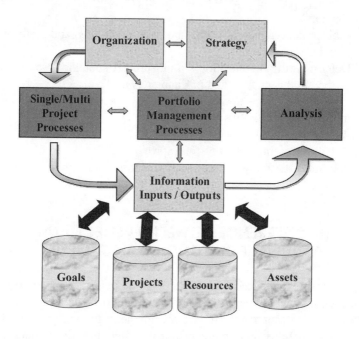

Figure 14.1   Portfolio Management Processes

ENTERPRISE PROJECT MANAGEMENT AND PORTFOLIO MANAGEMENT

These processes are illustrated in Figure 14.1. The organization's strategy is encompassed in a set of goals. To achieve these goals, the company exercises some kind of strategic planning process to determine the ideas it wants to implement to achieve those goals. The project portfolio manager supports the decision-makers by using processes such as prioritization, portfolio balancing, constraint management, and what-if analysis. The outcome of these processes is, hopefully, a viable project mix that every member of the executive team supports.

Once senior management approves the project mix, there are processes (both single and multi-project) to plan and execute the projects through the existing organization. The portfolio manager will be involved in project planning and execution to the extent that it has a significant impact on the portfolio performance.

As data from the planning and execution of projects are analyzed, the portfolio manager uses monitoring and analysis processes to control and improve portfolio results through the organization's management resources.

As a result of analyses, the portfolio manager transforms the data provided into information and recommendations to the portfolio management decision-makers. These decision-makers can be called a Steering Group, Governance Board, etc. As new projects are proposed and current analysis and recommendations are acted upon, the portfolio and criteria for selecting projects are modified.

Throughout this chapter, we explore the data and information needed to perform these functions and why. We explain how to balance a project portfolio based on a variety of factors, with the objective of choosing a project mix that is right for your organization. We also describe how to support the portfolio management process.

DETERMINING THE SIZE OF THE PROJECT PORTFOLIO

Senior management is constantly reviewing ideas to help its organization improve. While there are typically annual processes in line with financial measurements and board of director expectations, the fact is that new opportunities and threats do not wait for the annual planning meeting. They happen every day.

Every organization has two constraints that limit how many projects can be active at any point in time. One is the amount of money the organization has or is willing to invest in change. The other is the organization's strategic resource — the one most in demand across many projects or the most heavily loaded resource across most projects. This determines how many projects can be active at any point in time.

The constraints can become a major problem to an organization. For example, if an organization must complete 20 projects in order to meet its goals, and it has only the capital or staff to complete 15 of those projects, this is a challenge for the project portfolio manager. Often, the executives feel that they have no choice but to shove these projects into their organizations and try to force them through. This is where the daily fights over resources begin to occur.

In this situation, the portfolio manager must find ways to improve project flow (more projects completing more quickly with the same resources) or must look for a better project mix (fewer projects, each achieving a bigger piece of the organization's goals). See Part II of this book for the recommended strategic planning processes, and see Chapter 17 for the recommended project scheduling and execution process.

As budgets are approved annually and modified, all approved project development work is transformed into a project portfolio of investments. The total cost to complete all planned projects that are listed in the project portfolio represents the planned size (and value) of the project portfolio.

If you do not have this information, you may want to apply a rule of thumb to assess your portfolio relative to the organization's goals. For example, standard IT projects average $500,000 in budget (according to reports by the Standish Group and Gartner Group) and 200 calendar days in duration. Using this benchmark, if the new fiscal year budget identifies 100 IT projects, we should expect to spend $50 million in project development costs for the next fiscal year and invest 20,000 calendar days.

This rough information is just a start in determining if you have a healthy portfolio. You need to know the tangible value the combined portfolio is expected to generate, if the portfolio is focused on the right assets, and if it is addressing the real constraint blocking the organization from improving.

DETERMINING AND ACHIEVING PMO VALUE FROM PROJECT PORTFOLIO MANAGEMENT

The PMO can provide "everyday" value to business by simply aggregating the individual project progress information weekly into a report. (See the Arlington, Virginia case study at the end of this chapter, for example). Such a report, when viewed by key stakeholders, provides high visibility to projects. It causes those involved to look for acceleration opportunities and project delay threats.

Without the portfolio management and constant monitoring and visibility of the PMO, chances are good that the existing project will consume this money in one way or another. Parkinson's Law, Student Syndrome and other behaviors illustrate this fact.

Given a project portfolio of $50 million over the course of a fiscal year, the constant search for acceleration opportunities and threats should yield a minimum return of 10% or $5 million. That return should come from a combination of better throughput from existing projects (through acceleration), cost savings (through acceleration and avoiding threats) and flowing more projects through with the same resources. This savings alone is enough to substantiate the implementation of a PMO.

Companies want their projects to be delivered on time. It is a sad reality that many IT projects do not complete or are very late to complete. In many cases, the overage can be double. If we consider the $50 million project portfolio and use conservative estimates for overage of 25%, this means that the business would have to spend another $12.5 million to complete the planned work. New PMOs normally cannot correct the lateness of projects in one action, but over time they can significantly reduce the frequency of late projects every year. Even if the PMO reduced over-spending by 25% in the first year of its existence, it would still result in $3 million in savings.

The actions that the PMO takes to flow more projects through with the same resources are considered key to gaining competitive business advantage. This is one of the sweet spots of the PMO value proposition in helping the business grow beyond its current planned fiscal year work expectations. We will be very conservative here and assume that the organization can achieve only a 4% improvement in the number of additional projects. In the case of our portfolio of 100 projects, this means 4 additional projects. We will take another very conservative figure. We will assume that each project, which is investing an average of $500,000 is worth only $1 million to the company. This means that 4 more projects completed would be worth $4 million to the organization. We assume that these figures are so conservative because, in the Critical Chain case studies that we have documented, the number of additional projects completed ranged from 25 to 300%.

Many businesses fail to recognize the need to cancel projects that are no longer warranted. Thus, the budgeted monies are wasted. Given the visibility of the project portfolio to all pertinent stakeholders, recognizing the need to stop work is a clear opportunity to do work more useful to the business. The earlier the business can make a determination and cancel a project, the better the business will be for it. Instead of spending 80% of a doomed project budget, what if the doomed project had been stopped at 50% sunk costs or even 10%?

The point is that project value propositions are subject to violent changes. It is not abnormal to expect one out of ten projects to be cancelled for some reason over a fiscal year. Standish Group says 74% of all IT projects actually fail every year. We will use the 10% failure rate for our purposes in our value calculation. In a $50 million project portfolio with 100 projects that have an averaged $500,000 project budget, project cancellations would represent 10 projects initially worth $5 million in budget for their fiscal year. Let us assume they have 50% sunk costs for our value opportunity. This would mean that another $2.5 million would be available to spend elsewhere in the business during the course of the fiscal year.

So let us review our thoughts on the portfolio management value in the first 12 months given a $50 million project portfolio:

1. Portfolio visibility savings — $5 million
2. Reduction in overage spending among portfolio projects — $3 million
3. New unplanned projects completed — $4 million
4. Early cancellation of projects — $2.5 million

Total PMO value to the organization in one fiscal year is $14.5 million or 29% of project portfolio total budgeted value. What if your portfolio is only $15 million? These value returns will not necessarily hold true. Due to the complexity relative to how a portfolio "lives" in a fiscal year, the actual returns could be much less. However, the PMO should expect a minimum of 10% every year in hard dollar return. In the $15 million portfolio, that is $1.5 million at a minimum.

DEVELOPING A PORTFOLIO — THE FIRST PASS ANALYSIS

Through a series of simple, but not simplistic, examples, we illustrate what information is important for a portfolio manager to consider. We also use this information to discuss what we mean by a "balanced" portfolio.

Assume you are working for a large communications service provider with some small manufacturing capability. Your company is a public company that has undergone three serious downsizing actions in the past three years. The industry is fiercely competitive, and your company's revenues are shrinking.

Your organization is very excited. For the first time, the organization will have a full-time project portfolio manager — you. Your CIO has given you a list of projects that represent the current portfolio. For simplicity's sake, we will start with the six projects and the information shown in Table 14.1.

The projects were ranked from 1 to 6 by the CIO. Is this the same ranking that you would give to these projects? Try it and see for yourself.

Hopefully, your first reaction is that you do not know how to rank these projects because you are missing some vital information. For example, what is the connection between these projects and the goals of the organization? You know that your company has a serious shortage of sales, based on the downsizing actions. Therefore, a healthy portfolio should be putting its major emphasis on ideas that will generate more sales, and ideas that will, in the meantime, preserve cash. Looking at the third project, for example, it would take a lot of imagination to see how implementing new financial software would help you significantly increase your sales.

We do not have a list of the company goals, so we cannot even begin to connect these projects to the goals. Of course, this example $50 million portfolio does not represent the complete company project portfolio. However, it represents a situation that we see all of the time. Whatever lists of projects exist today, they are probably incomplete. One of your first jobs as portfolio manager is to develop this list and immediately relate each project to the company's goals. You will probably see that some projects have no connection to company goals, so you must ask why the company is doing

Table 14.1   First Pass Project Prioritization List

Project	NPV (mm)	Investment (mm)	Sugg. Rank	Reason
Upgrade the high-speed Web access service	$35.0	$15.0	5	Customers always complaining about slow response time
Distribute hand held Web access products	$7.0	$4.0	6	Marketing says it's a natural for our customers
Implement XYZ Financial Software		$8.0	2	CFO says he has to have it NOW!
Integrate recently acquired cable broadcast company		$4.8	3	It's too hard to support two different systems
Install latest ERP modules and upgrades		$17.5	1	Vendor starts charging support after Jan. 1
Six Sigma for Employee Termination Procedure		$0.7	4	????
TOTAL	**$42.0**	**$50.0**		

those projects. You will also probably see a gross imbalance — too many projects oriented to the supply side of the business (manufacturing and IT systems) and too few projects oriented to the market side (sales, marketing, and the supply chain).

There is other basic information missing. For example, for most of the projects, the net present value (NPV) is missing. This is common in many organizations. With many projects, managers claim that the benefits are intangible, or too difficult to quantify. This is a huge red flag. If we cannot estimate the benefits, then the chances are excellent that upon project completion (if the project completes at all), the benefit to the company's bottom line will be zero or negative.

A lack of definition of the value, in dollar terms or in goal units, means that the sponsor does not understand the cause–effect connection between this project and its impact on the organization. One of the problems in defining NPV is that the benefits are within a range of values. For example, a new product may produce $5 million in revenues or $25 million. Which figure should the portfolio manager assume?

To address this variation, some portfolio managers use a form of graphic display called a "Bubble Diagram." See Figure 14.2 for an example. There is another advantage to a bubble diagram. It can show, through color coding, shapes, and other attributes, multiple variables. The huge disadvantage

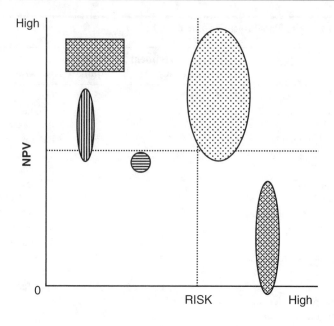

Figure 14.2 Bubble Diagram Showing Four Portfolio Variables — NPV Range, Risk Range, Internal/External Projects, and Originator

is that many executives find these images far too complicated. For more in-depth discussion on diagramming techniques, see the book referenced in the Bibliography called *Portfolio Management for New Products,* by Cooper, Edgett and Kleinschmidt.

For example, in Figure 14.2, there is a project in the lower, right quadrant that has a potential to yield a negative NPV. Part of its range falls below zero. The rectangular shapes denote internal improvements, while the ovals denote projects addressing external factors, such as markets, suppliers, and distribution channels. The fillers denote from which functional area the project originates. For example, bricks are projects sponsored by IT. Dots are from marketing. These kinds of representations are usually brought into play after the executives have had some experience with the basics.

Looking back at Table 14.1, it is obvious that some key information is missing. For example, what percentage of the total NPV does each project represent? What percentage of the total portfolio investment does each project represent? Are these two figures in balance? We would hate to see a situation where we were investing 25% of our total portfolio in a project that would yield only 5% of the value needed to meet our goals.

For a cash-hungry company, we would like to see when these projects will go cash positive — what is the expected cash flow for the first year, the second year, etc. For a cash-desperate company, we might want to see this cash flow by week, month, or quarter.

PROJECT PORTFOLIO — THE SECOND PASS ANALYSIS

Look carefully at Table 14.2. Notice that we still have a $50 million portfolio, but what a difference in its makeup and ranking. We deactivated some projects that are simply not going to help us address this company's constraint. The constraint is in the market, so we deactivated the projects to implement new financial software, to integrate a recently acquired cable company, to install the latest ERP upgrades, and a Six Sigma project.

Deactivating a project does not mean that it will not be implemented at a later time. It simply means that today it will not be on your radar screen for the short term.

We have not only replaced projects, however. We have added some vital information to help us with a suggested ranking. One new column shows us the percentage of the total expected value, in NPV, the project is estimated to bring. The next column shows the percentage of the total portfolio we are investing to gain those benefits. The third added column shows the expected cash flow this year, an important figure to a cash-hungry company.

Immediately, we can see that with one project, called "Market Segmentation," only 2.4% of our investment will deliver over 18% of the estimated total benefits from all projects. And there is something even more wonderful. This project will deliver over $10 million in positive cash flow this year. No wonder we decided to recommend that this project be ranked number one in priority. It is also directly related to the company goal of segmenting markets, not resources. A similar analysis of the other projects leads to a new ranking, one that we feel more comfortable in bringing to our decision-makers.

PROJECT PORTFOLIO — THIRD PASS ANALYSIS

As you can see, the better we understand the key information necessary to analyze each of the project opportunities, the better our decisions will be. In this third pass, we will consider three other vital pieces of information.

We stated earlier that our company's project flow is limited by its strategic resource. This is the one resource that, more than any other resource,

Table 14.2   Project Portfolio Ranking — 2nd Pass

Project	NPV (mm)	Investment (mm)	% NPV	% Port	Cash Flow This Year	Sugg. Rank	Related Goal
Upgrade high-speed Web access service	$35.0	$15.0	23.3	30.0	-$4.5	5	Improve revenue-tied customer service
Distribute hand held Web access products	$14.5	$4.0	9.7	8.0	$7.5	2	Increase throughput by 10%
Launch New Satellite Service	$40.5	$15.3	27.0	30.6	-$5.7	4	Leapfrog the competition
Sales Fulfillment/ Telemarketing System	$22.7	$8.7	15.1	17.4	$11.0	3	Increase throughput by 10%; decrease cost of sales by 5%
Market segmentation	$28.0	$1.2	18.7	2.4	$10.2	1	Segment markets, not resources
Existing product upgrades	$9.3	$5.8	6.2	11.6	-$1.5	6	Increase throughput by 10%
TOTAL	**$150.0**	**$50.0**	**100%**	**100%**	**$17.0**		

Table 14.3 Importance of the Strategic Resource

Project	NPV (mm)	Strategic Resource Utilization (weeks)	NPV per Strategic Resource Week	Risk 0 = low, 100 = high
Upgrade high-speed Web access service	$35.0	12	$2.9	54
Distribute hand held Web access products	$14.5	2	$7.3	18
Launch new satellite service	$40.5	38	$1.1	79
Sales fulfillment/ telemarketing system	$22.7	6	$3.8	1
Market segmentation	$28.0	2	$14.0	43
Existing product upgrades	$9.3	4	$2.3	22

determines how many projects the company can complete. It might signify the place where most projects get stuck for long periods of time, or the one that is fought over the most. See Chapter 17 for a more complete description.

Assume we have two projects, each identical in every respect, except as follows. One project uses 25% of the total capacity of the strategic resource and another project uses 10%. By implication, we could only do 4 of the first type of project per year but we could do 10 of the second type of project per year. This is a significant factor in determining ranking.

Since every project is typically quite different in NPV and utilization of the strategic resource, we convert this data into a comparative form. By dividing a project's NPV by the strategic resource utilization (say in weeks), we obtain how much money we will generate for the company per week, by investing our strategic resource in each project type.

Another significant factor is risk. If two projects are identical in every respect, but one project is riskier than another, we need this information to make valid decisions.

Examine carefully the new data offered in Table 14.3. We can see that the highest risk project, launching the new satellite service, eats up a major portion of our strategic resource. While it returns a high NPV, its return in terms of dollars per week of utilization of the strategic resource is the worst return of the entire set of projects. The data are not sufficient to draw conclusions. However, it should give pause to reflect. It might be that the new satellite service is something worth doing for the long term. However, this might be a sign that other projects are far more important to meet this

Table 14.4 Part I — Important Data Elements of the Project Portfolio

Data Element	Description
Project Name	Description of Program or Project initiative
Status	Describes compliance with planned delivery and cost expectations: Red indicates time or cost trends need management intervention. Yellow indicates time or cost trends need investigation Green indicates time or cost trends are within the realm of common cause variation
Project Force Rank	Prioritization rating assigned by Governance Board. Force rank indicates the order of importance the initiative has relative to the company strategic objectives
Project Manager	The person responsible for this project
Funding Business Unit	The organization that pays for the project budget and normally owns the requirements that the project will develop product or service for.
Primary Strategic Objective	The primary business goal that the initiative is supporting.
Primary Supported Asset	The primary asset that the initiative is supporting.
NPV	Net Present Value figure or range of possibilities for this project
Cash Flow	Projected Cash Flow by year, quarter or month
Strategic Resource Utilization	Utilization, in weeks, of the organization's strategic resource

(continued)

organization's goals. In fact, if we can generate enough cash from other projects, perhaps we can subcontract out part of the satellite project.

Again, the data gives us possible directions, but does not and should not make the decisions for us. With this background, we can now jump into more detail about the data we will want to maintain about the portfolio.

DATA CHARACTERISTICS AND FREQUENCIES OF THE PORTFOLIO

Once a portfolio is established, we need to understand what progress is being made against estimated project schedules. Given that we are reviewing the project level, we need project related tactical data. See Table 14.4.

Project data should be collected minimally on a bi-weekly basis. Anything less frequent means less visibility for project delivery threats and opportunities to accelerate.

Table 14.4   Part 2 — Important Data Elements of the Project Portfolio

Data Element	Description
Opportunity Rating	The score, according to a standard prioritization template (0-100)
Risk Rating	The score, according to a standard risk template (0-100)
Predecessors and Successors	Other portfolio initiatives that are dependent on this project meeting schedule commitments or on which this project is depending
Plan Start Date	The date the initiative is scheduled to start working
Actual Start Date	The date the work actually began
Plan End Date	The date the initiative is scheduled to end work
Actual End Date	The date the initiative actually ended work
Go Live Date	The first day of expected benefit from the initiative.
Plan Budget To Date	The amount of initiative budget that was planned to be spent by this reporting date
Actual Budget To Date	The amount of initiative budget that was spent by this reporting date.
Fiscal Variance to Date	The dollar amount of initiative budget that is over/under spent to date
Related Investments At Risk	The amount of budget from other dependent initiatives that remains to be spent, amount of NPV at risk in other dependent initiatives
Related Investments Current Status	Summary of Red, Yellow, Green statuses of other dependent initiatives based on rules for Red, Yellow and Green definitions

One of the most common problems in establishing an initial project portfolio is how to determine dollars in some of the data elements when the business culture has been very lax in tracking projects in this manner. This problem can be solved by understanding the general nature of project variables and fixed costs.

In most projects, non-labor costs are generally known and easily identified within certain expectations — even at the beginning of the project. These are planned one-time costs and thus can be identified as "project fixed costs." On the other hand, the size of the project team varies over the project life cycle. These labor costs are often more difficult to predict and track.

It would be daunting to try to accurately determine exact labor costs, unless you are from a project company with excellent project management software and accounting methods. Even then, the distortions of many cost accounting systems are readily apparent. However, most organizations do not need such labor estimates when we are talking about their own full-time employees to make the right decisions and to see the right opportunities and threats.

From an accounting point of view, if the project resources are full-time employees, their costs are already reflected in the general ledger salary expenses. What purpose does it serve to take these costs and try to allocate them to two decimal place accuracy to projects? Usually, the answer is, "No purpose whatsoever." If we save a full-time employee's time on a project, we have not saved the company one single dollar, unless that person is fired or overtime is eliminated. However, if we can use that person on another project, now we are beginning to get some real value from finishing a project earlier.

The important question to answer is not "How much of our own organization's employee cost should we allocate to a project?" Rather, the important question is "Given that we have this labor cost already planned, which projects will give us the best leverage using this labor?"

The most important factors to consider when establishing the equations for calculating labor are the speed and consistency of reporting the information. Do not take inordinate amounts of time to make things perfect in the portfolio or the processes developed to support it. It is better to be approximately right than precisely wrong.

RECOGNIZING THE NEED

This real-life event illustrates how important the portfolio management function is to a PMO, and how far astray things can go. The company to which we refer is an insurance business that was delivering $800 million in sales each year prior to this time. The problem began when the PMO implemented a project management tool. The company had finally, after great effort and resistance from the IT project managers, captured all the significant projects for the IT department into the project management tool. The PMO had also requested the most current project schedules for each reporting project. This information was loaded into the project management tool as well.

We modeled this client's current project mix and noticed that 92% of the projects in the IT department were funded by the IT department. This data seemed very strange. Upon investigation, we found that most of the functional areas were finding other ways to meet their IT needs.

We went to the PMO manager and explained our findings. We felt there was a leakage of projects away from IT and that it appeared that IT did not know about this. The PMO manager could not answer why this was happening and thought we should take this information to the CIO.

The following week, we explained our findings to the CIO. At first, he was happy to hear that we were finally collecting project information that would help us "be better." Later in the meeting, he realized the seriousness of the information and what it really meant to him. As we reviewed each project for progress, it seemed that almost every project was being hindered by some dependency "from an internal business partner," according to the CIO.

Over the next week, in conjunction with the PMO manager, we devised a plan to swing the pendulum of project selection and ownership back to the business partners whereby they were required to put themselves on the line for IT project success. Our plan was very simple. It required quick and consistent communication of project progress at various levels of the organization.

We identified three levels of communities that needed delivery information. The first level was the project management community. The second level was the IT management team and the third level was the business partner community. For each community, we had reasons why they needed to be involved in collaboration of the project portfolio.

The project managers needed to understand where other projects stood each reporting period. By knowing this, they could take advantage of projects on which they were dependent whenever those projects accelerated or slipped. As the project managers met once a week for five weeks to reflect and report as well as iron out issues, positive peer pressure from these meetings began to develop and grow. By the third meeting, the project managers were all seeking to know where they stood in delivery progress as measured against their peers. The last thing each manager wanted was to be perceived as the "weakest link."

The PMO provided portfolio status reports to the project managers in red/yellow/green categories. It soon became obvious that no one wanted to become "red." Thus, each week, the trend line for greens, yellows, and reds reversed itself from predominately red to predominately green. After five weeks of meetings with the project managers, the projects in the portfolio had become more than 80% green.

"Red" project managers felt the pressure of being last among peers and they did not like it. In one meeting, one of the consistently "red" project managers questioned the definition of the phrase "project budget." The project manager felt that project budget was different among projects and that he was being unfairly measured. We asked him what he would like to do. He said that he wanted to eliminate the measures. They were simply invalid for him, even though he could not explain why.

We agreed to consider his request. However, we asked him to do several things. First, we wanted him to meet with another project manager who was doing very well on his project and budget, and review the budget and related tracking process being used for application to his project. If he could not make this work for him, with our help, we would grant him a waiver. We further explained that it was necessary to have monetary and time measurements, as this was how the sponsors were measuring IT. Given the role and accountability of project managers, there simply was no other option.

The PMO eventually helped the project manager become successful. As more and more project managers and their teams were assisted by the PMO, the project bottlenecks became more visible to IT management in time to react. The portfolio flow rate increased. Now, the CIO could address one of the issues that had caused the leakage in the first place — poor project performance to plan.

ESTABLISHING THE PROJECT PORTFOLIO REPORT — HOW TO GET STARTED

As the PMO begins the process of establishing the PMO project portfolio report, consider the following framework:

- Portfolio information should separate active initiatives from pending and closed/completed or cancelled initiatives. Also, projects cross fiscal years. The information should indicate in which fiscal year the initiative will be completed. You can further subordinate project information into related business departments if this helps you organize relevant information.
- Initial portfolio can be modeled in a spreadsheet or in project software. If you use project software, you can establish a "task sheet" and a "Gantt" view of the same portfolio data.
- Make sure all financials roll up for all dollar columns, in particular given any logical groupings that reflect ownership such as departments.
- If you want color on your "task sheet," use Microsoft Excel.
- Present the portfolio in force rank order or in suggested rank order. If you are using MS Excel or MS Project, you will be able to sort the columns as needed. Load portfolio data from project status reports (current) and, if necessary, from project schedules (current). Refer to Table 14.4 for the necessary data elements that should be reported in the portfolio.
- Ensure that you are receiving timely project status reports for all projects listed in the portfolio.
- In the beginning update and produce the portfolio reports weekly. The PMO during this period is seeking to populate data gaps that

are unreported in the portfolio. In addition, the PMO is analyzing the project data reflected for anything that may need immediate attention.

MANAGING AND MAINTAINING THE PROJECT PORTFOLIO — PROJECT REPORTING ROLES AND RESPONSIBILITIES

The key to maintaining an active project portfolio is to ensure the reporting chain is in place and that all necessary parties are performing their role and associated responsibility.

Portfolio Manager — As we stated at the beginning of this chapter, this role should be designated to one individual. This individual analyzes all of the current and proposed projects to determine and recommend a viable project mix, one that is capable of meeting the goals of the organization. This individual will then specifically monitor the planning and execution of the chosen projects. He or she is the representative of the Governance Board to ensure timely delivery. But he or she has another important objective to achieve. The portfolio manager should constantly analyze portfolio performance and ways to improve it. This person plays an important role in supporting the overall strategy of the organization and preparing information for Governance Board meetings. The portfolio manager also evaluates new opportunities against the current portfolio and comparatively to each other, taking into account the organization's project execution capacity. As a result, this person is regularly providing information and recommendations to decision-makers at all levels.

Project Manager — Typically this person has the responsibility of reporting project progress.

Team Member — This role normally focuses on the work at hand. The team member should be expected to report the status of his work in a regular manner to the project manager. The information reported should reflect work accomplishments, work in progress, work plans for the next period, current issues, any help needed, work acceleration opportunities, and any work delivery threats.

Project Sponsor — The sponsor considers current and future business impact to the project effort. This person must be informed of project progress on a regular basis by the project manager. Sponsor duties should be well understood by all project members. In most environments, sponsor roles are very ill defined.

Governance Board Member — The executive may be the business unit leader or his tactical delegate. This role is to caucus with other members of the Governance Board on the force ranking of all projects listed in the portfolio as those projects best meet the strategic objective and direction of the business at any particular time in the fiscal year. This includes deactivating projects, considering new opportunities, and activating new projects. The executive is responsible for communicating any sudden delivery opportunity or delivery threat as the business climate changes day-to-day. His value is measured by how well the collection of projects meet their delivery targets and if additional project work can be achieved as a result of exceeding expected delivery targets.

PMO — The primary responsibility of the PMO in reporting the portfolio status is to ensure that the information is communicated in a manner everyone can understand and not misconstrue. Initially, the PMO will need to be sensitive to current projects that are struggling. Remember, it takes time to change behaviors and attitudes that have developed over years of continuous application. Raising the visibility of the portfolio to all key stakeholders may have an unexpected effect. Building relationships with key stakeholders is essential to gaining trust and awareness as the PMO begins to introduce the portfolio process.

ESTABLISHING THE REPORTING CYCLE

This is essentially a three-step process that seeks to standardize the various levels of the business into information groups that will use the portfolio data to calibrate project work order.

EARLY ON — GETTING STARTED

In Step 1, organize the project managers into a group meeting. Meet every week for 3 to 5 weeks until all active projects are reporting project status and providing project schedules in a similar fashion. The PMO may be asked by this group why it must standardize its reporting. The answer is: "To help you, the executives, and the PMO understand and correct variances in project progress."

Step 2 is to meet with the management team that has oversight authority of the reporting project managers. Normally this is the group that is accountable to the sponsors. Its job becomes much easier if most of the news it reports on projects is good to the people who are paying for the work. Plan for a 3- to 5-week interval iterating the portfolio detail through each reporting cycle to help it adjust and learn how to use this new source of progress data.

Step 3 includes executive management and/or its tactical delegate. Their job is to ensure the portfolio is organized in order of what is most important to the organization. The PMO should plan for 3 to 5 meetings with this new Governance Board to help it orient as it adjusts to the new processes.

MAINTENANCE MODE

The PMO will make minor adjustments to this process over time. Most of the changes will occur early in the process implementation. The PMO should be ready to train new members who enter any of the three information groups. The PMO should consider developing an orientation kit to be given to new group members as a means to facilitate an even application of their role in their information group.

HOW DO NEW PROJECTS ENTER AND AFFECT THE PROJECT PORTFOLIO

If a new project is introduced into the portfolio, the Governance Board will schedule discussion time at the Governance Meeting to review the merits of the project. The Governance Board will review the portfolio manager's "what if" analysis, factors, and recommendation. These factors may include implications for existing projects, such as a recommendation to deactivate or even cancel a project. The recommendation from the portfolio manager should also include the activation date of the new project, if accepted, according to resource availability. This will result in a decision by the Governance Board. The decision is either a force-rank for the initiative or a request for further analysis.

DRIVING PROJECT DELIVERY WITH PROJECT PRIORITIZATION

In organizing a portfolio into a prioritized sequence of force-rank order, the primary benefit is in the calibration of what work is important relative to other defined and approved work in the portfolio. This calibration enables productivity improvements through simplifying project progress information that helps people understand what comes next and what contention points to negotiate for with other competing project teams over common resources. Through this calibration of the order of work, time that would be spent contesting some nebulous issue among competing projects can be reconciled easily based on the force rank order. This is assuming there is some degree of significance among competing projects and their force rank.

The value in force ranking projects, resources, assets, and strategic objectives is similar to the value just described above. Given the primary benefit of force ranking to enable project teams to be more effective at completing work, we can clearly see that work conflicts can be reduced to cause project acceleration because they are spending less time fighting for what they need to the job. Thus, the force rank process serves as a catalyst to enhancing the visibility of what is important among all portfolio items that are at risk. Project prioritization actually drives project delivery acceleration. The PMO can enable this process in the first six months of its existence if it has the appropriate sponsorship support to do so.

BALANCING THE PROJECT PORTFOLIO

There are many factors to consider when balancing a project portfolio. Just as an unbalanced stock portfolio can be dangerous or non-productive, so can a project portfolio. Consider the following key factors in balancing.

- Market side vs. supply side
- Research vs. development
- Risk and rewards
- Allocation to assets (maintenance vs. development)

MARKET SIDE VS. SUPPLY SIDE

As in the examples cited earlier in this chapter, if your organization has excess capacity and could deliver more to the market, but it does not have enough customers, the project portfolio should lean toward addressing the market constraint. Similarly, the major constraint of the organization could be internal, but it will not be across every department. It might be in operations, engineering, shipping, etc. Or it might be in another part of the supply chain, e.g., you simply cannot get enough raw materials to produce your products. The portfolio manager must understand where the organization's constraint is, and tilt the portfolio to address it.

RESEARCH VS. DEVELOPMENT

How much pure research is enough to ensure that your organization will stay healthy? This is not a question strictly for business. It applies equally to government and not-for-profit organizations. For example, there is a big question now about how much research the government should have devoted before 9/11.

Market and product research projects must exist in every portfolio. The difference between these and other projects is that it is quite possible that nothing will result from some of these projects. For example, a drug company does a lot of pure research, but only some of the research results in possible drugs. The drugs must be manufactured in small, controlled lots and undergo clinical trials before a drug application to the FDA is submitted. And a drug application is no guarantee that it will be approved.

A balanced portfolio will have pure research, but there is no predetermined answer for what the correct percentage is for either expenditures or number of projects. The portfolio manager must consider the company's position relative to its needs, in order to assess this and recommend an answer to the Governance Board.

RISK AND REWARDS

How many high-risk projects does the company want or is capable of sustaining? This factor must be known by the portfolio manager and taken into account when assessing the portfolio and making recommendations. If the company's cash flow situation suddenly becomes very poor, the portfolio will need to be balanced differently. If the company's shareholders expect huge breakthroughs in product development or new markets, the risk and reward factors in the portfolio need to reflect these expectations.

ALLOCATION TO ASSETS

The asset portfolio reflects the assets of the organization in terms of services and products, as well as in infrastructure to support the sale of those products and services. Assets may include system applications, the hardware to support the software, buildings, or anything that can be legally identified as a taxable asset. It also includes those assets the organization has identified as essential to its business but not necessarily a taxable asset. For example, the organization's Web site and the development effort that goes into the Web site is such an asset.

The Governance Board must ensure that the projects selected for development address assets in a manner that will best help the business grow. Activated projects should help enhance or add to the asset base of the business. If the portfolio manager sees a portfolio where 70% of the investment is going toward declining assets, the portfolio is probably out of balance and needs adjustment. The asset portfolio helps everyone understand what is important in terms of physical or intellectual property.

WORKING WITH THE STRATEGIC OBJECTIVES PORTFOLIO

The strategic objectives of a business can take many forms. Typical strategic objectives are improving profitability, increasing market share, compliance with mandated regulations, improving customer service, and penetrating new markets. The strategic objectives portfolio applies to companies that are non-profit as well. These objectives might include seeking new funding, providing improved security, and decreasing defects.

The Governance Board must ensure that all projects activated are assigned a primary business goal so that the total risk and effort of that goal can be actively considered in the entire portfolio process.

The strategic objectives portfolio helps everyone understand how their work is directly affecting a specific, executive mandated business goal.

SUMMARY

Many organizations are not getting a good return on investment from their project portfolios. Most organizations we visit cannot even show us what their portfolio consists of. Without formally considering, through portfolio management, what collection of projects the organization has the resources to execute, the executives will often push more projects into the organization well beyond its capacity. As a result, projects become slow to execute, and the various parts of the organization are constantly fighting with each other over resources.

The portfolio manager should have a major impact on the organization through five key objectives:

- Determine a viable project mix
- Monitor the planning and execution of all projects in the portfolio
- Analyze portfolio performance and ways to improve the ROI
- Evaluate new project opportunities
- Provide information and recommendations to a Governance Board

In performing these functions, the PMO raises the visibility of the portfolio and its vital importance to all project managers and teams. Such visibility and the help provided by the PMO immediately points out acceleration opportunities and threats. In addition, serious project overages and delays are focused on. Projects that are not right for the portfolio are identified and cancelled much earlier than otherwise. The improvement in effective resource utilization and the reduction of conflict results in more projects being completed by the same resources. An improvement of 10 to 30% in the value of the portfolio should be expected in the first year.

One of the key strategic values of a portfolio manager is to guide the Governance Board to a balanced portfolio. Such a portfolio recognizes where the biggest problems and opportunities of the organization are, and ensures that active projects lean that way. It addresses the need to have ongoing pure research, and to develop the assets of the organization that represent the future, not the past. Balancing also implies a reasonable degree of risk, considering the organization's needs.

Portfolio management is unquestionably at the heart of the PMO success or failure. Everything that a PMO does is somehow linked to driving a better project portfolio through the organization faster and with better results.

CASE STUDY — ARLINGTON COUNTY, VIRGINIA (SUBMITTED BY DENISE HART, PROGRAM MANAGEMENT OFFICER)

Arlington County, Virginia, located directly across the Potomac River from Washington, D.C., is an urban area of approximately 26 square miles in which about 190,000 people reside. The county government consists of 20 departments and elected offices that provide such diverse services as public safety (fire/police/sheriff), human services, parks and recreation, libraries, local courts, public works, tax assessment and collection, recycling and trash collection, economic development and management of the county water supply. The county government, excluding the public school system, employs approximately 3400 workers. This case study relates to the PMO, which assists the county in evaluating, selecting, and monitoring IT projects from an enterprise-wide perspective. The PMO is located in the Department of Technology Services and reports to the Chief Information Officer.

In 2001, the county embarked on an eGovernment Initiative with the goal of enabling county residents, visitors, and businesses to engage in government functions and services over the Internet. The vision is to provide access to Arlington County government "anytime, anywhere, with no wrong door". To achieve the vision, the county seeks to leverage the universality of Web-enabled technologies to transform the delivery of government services. To accomplish this vision would ultimately require significant investment in network infrastructure, data architecture, and Internet-based capabilities that provide eGovernment services.

Faced with the enormity of the task and the inflexibility of the IT capital budget, combined with ongoing operational needs, it was clear that the only means to realize the eGovernment vision would be through careful selection of IT projects and close monitoring of the projects to ensure delivery of expected results. The county also recognized that eGovernment capabilities would result in greater visibility into the delivery of high-quality, user-friendly, and value-added technology solutions.

Historically, government organizations are very operationally focused, which naturally leads to silos building up around each of the disparate service functions the government provides. Further calcifying this situation is that in government, an enterprise-level metric that can be used to drive business goals and rank projects is lacking. Unlike a business where such a metric is readily available (e.g., profitability, market share, stock price), the county measures its contributed value by the quality of services it provides and how those services compare with neighboring jurisdictions. These metrics can be difficult to quantify. The lack of enterprise-level metrics contributes to the county behaving more like a federation of departments fulfilling individual missions, rather than as an enterprise. Since the PMO's role is to take an enterprise view of IT investments and to compare and rank the proposed projects at an enterprise level, a challenge lay in how to overcome an "apples to oranges" comparison of the projects proposed by various departments.

An additional challenge faced by the PMO is that, as with most federal and state government organizations, county government is not primarily a project-based organization. Pockets of project management existed and, without a doubt, some projects were executed quite successfully. However, there was little consistency in techniques or processes. The Gartner Group has coined the phrase "the oral tradition of project management," which is to say that the project management expertise of an organization lies with a handful of individuals who follow a set of practices that have worked in the past, without the benefit of formalized methodology, standard processes, project management knowledge-base, or professional development program. This would aptly describe the situation at the county. The processes in place were seen as insufficient to ensure fulfillment of the eGovernment master plan.

Given the vision of the eGovernment master plan, its directive to tear down the silos and present government services from the resident's viewpoint, and the immaturity of project management practices at the county, the CIO established the PMO with the mission of providing three key functions:

1. Development of a project management methodology appropriate for the county.
2. Provision of an expert project management consultancy.
3. Undertaking a portfolio approach to selecting the "right" information technology projects and monitoring their progress.

Prior to the establishment of the PMO, the county had in place a manner of selecting projects through the Technology Leadership Committee.

However, no monitoring of those projects occurred. The Technology Leadership Committee was a team of department directors and elected officials chaired by the CIO with a mission of taking an enterprise perspective on technology issues facing the county.

The first priority of the PMO and the Technology Leadership Committee was the selection of projects for the following fiscal year. Over 65 projects were proposed from the various departments, each competing for a share of the $3 million capital budget for IT. The list was analyzed and prioritized and ultimately 11 projects were granted capital funding, forming the IT Investment Portfolio for the upcoming fiscal year. See Table 14.5 for the Arlington County Project Evaluation Criteria.

To guide the selection process, the PMO adapted model evaluation criteria published by the United States General Accounting Office. The investment priorities focused on federal mandates, infrastructure investments, evergreening existing capabilities, and improving Web capabilities for the public.

The second priority of the PMO was to monitor the capital projects getting underway in the current fiscal year. These projects could be characterized as "horses already out of the gate" because the standard methodology, which was still under development, had not been applied. Regardless of this issue, the PMO proceeded and adopted the current plan as the baseline and reported on project progress each quarter to the Technology Leadership Committee. In the past, no such formalized, periodic reporting had taken place.

The first quarterly report was met with a visible reaction from the Technology Leadership Committee. They were amazed that such a report could be developed. They recognized a seldom seen level of accountability within its contents, and they adopted a new sense of ownership of the projects they had put forth. By the second issue of the report, they had begun asking the right questions of the project sponsors and the project sponsors were prepared to answer as to how they were planning to address the issues raised in the report. For the first time, the Technology Leadership Committee had the information and common language it needed to fulfill the function of executive oversight.

The third focus of the PMO was the establishment of a very simple project management methodology. The first version of the methodology was a set of templates that addressed project justification, project charter, detailed task plans and spending plans, project control (status reporting), project completion, and a 6-month post-implementation review. In the upcoming fiscal year, the methodology will be applied to all projects in the IT Investment Portfolio. The county looks forward to measuring the contribution that a standard methodology brings to project success.

Table 14.5 Arlington County Project Evaluation Criteria

Mission Effectiveness (8 points) [weight: 20%]

Improves Internal Program Services (0–4 points)

Assess the expected improvement in service to internal customers. Score zero points if the system does not appear to meet a problem defined by an internal customer; little improvement in important customer service criteria such as timeliness, quality, or availability is expected. Score four points if significant improvements are expected or if the system addresses an important problem or area of services defined by the customer.

Improves Service to the Public (0–4 points)

Assess the improvement in service to the public. Score zero points if the system appears to provide little or no direct improvement in service to the public; system may make a small improvement in timeliness, quality, or availability, but there is no documented need for such an improvement. Score four points if the system will improve service to the public in a mission where need is demonstrated or provides a new type of service to meet changing customer demands.

Strategic Alignment (12 points) [weight 20%]

Linkage to County Master Plans (0–4 points)

Assess the extent to which the proposed project fulfills a need outlined in an endorsed County plan or supports a stated, published priority of the County Board and/or County Manager. Score zero points if the project is unrelated to an endorsed County plan. Score four points if the project is specifically referenced in a County plan.

Department Business Model (0–4 points)

Assess the degree of alignment with the department's business model. Score zero points if the system does not support departmental services or processes identified in the business model. Score four points if the proposed system is specifically mentioned in the eGovernment Master Plan and supports products/services or processes identified in the department's business model and the initiative has been coordinated with all departments identified by the model for the respective processes the system supports.

Level of Interest (0–4 points)

Assess the level of interest by senior managers in the department and/or the County Manager and County Board. Score zero points if no interest has been expressed in support for this system. Score four points if system has strong support from department heads and/or the County Board.

Organizational Impact (8 points) [weight 20%]

Inter-Departmental Impact/Cross-Functional (0–4 points)

Evaluate the number of people or organizations that will benefit from the initiative. Score zero points for a limited number of beneficiaries; the system will be used in one department with limited number of users; not a cross-functional system. Score four points if the system is cross-functional and serves a number of departments; system will be used by the public.

Business Process Redesign (0–4 points)

Assess the degree to which this system enables the department to do business in a better way. Score zero points if this system automates an existing business process with little improvement to the process. Score four points if this system enables a significant improvement in the way business is conducted.

Table 14.5 Arlington County Project Evaluation Criteria (continued)

Risk (20 points) [weight 20%]

Schedule Risk (0–4 points)

Evaluate the probability this initiative can be completed on schedule. Score zero points for high risk: acquisition strategy indicates contract may not be awarded in time to meet schedule or obligate budget year dollars; project staff is limited in size and/or experience and initiative is complex; an accelerated schedule was imposed rather than being developed from project planning. Score four points for Low Risk: the above factors are not present.

Cost Sensitivity (0–4 points)

Evaluate the quality of the cost estimates. Score zero points for high risk: initiative is complex and cost estimates appear to require additional refinement; software development is required and represents more than 50% of the predicated cost. Score four points for low risk: cost estimates are well-supported; little software development is required or a software cost estimated technique has been used to produce a reasonably reliable cost estimate.

Technical Risk (0–4 points)

Evaluate the risk to complete the system from a technical point of view. Score zero points for high risk: hardware and/or software solution does not conform to the organization's technical architecture and/or there is little or no experience with this technology in the organization; hardware, software, or support is not commercially available and requires development specifically for the organization; infrastructure/network cannot support the initiative. Score four points for low risk: hardware and software conform to organization's technical architecture and there is successful experience using this technology in the organization; hardware, software, and support are commercially available; little additional demand is placed on the network.

Organizational Risk (0–4 points)

Assess the risk that the proposed system will fail due to organizational disruption. Score zero points for high risk: system implementation requires significant organizational change, process redesign and/or jobs to be done differently and the project team is not proactively seeking to mitigate this risk. Score four points for low risk: system has little impact on the organization or the project team is mitigating this risk through training and/or investment in a business process redesign effort which builds commitment to the system.

Risk of Not Doing It (0–4 points)

Assess the risk to the organization of not proceeding with this initiative. Score zero points for low risk: this initiative is an incremental improvement to an existing system; the impact can be achieved by other means. Score four points for high risk: this initiative is important to provide future opportunities for cost savings and/or much improved customer service. If this system is not built or is delayed a year, the department/County will probably fail to meet customer demands in the near future.

Benefit to Cost Impact (4 points) [weight 20%]

Evaluate the extent to which the benefits of the system implementation exceed the costs to implement. Use the following scale as guidance:

0 points:	*Cost exceeds benefit*
1 point:	*Benefit equals cost*
2 points:	*Benefit slightly exceeds cost*
3 points:	*Benefit moderately exceeds cost*
4 points:	*Benefit greatly exceeds cost*

Lastly, the PMO began undertaking the effort to document the existing asset portfolio. This was felt to be important to provide the Technology Leadership Committee with the background and context they needed to assess the criticality of proposed investments. This portfolio is anticipated to describe over 200 existing systems. Ultimately, it will shed light on which existing assets are reaching the point of declining returns so that a determination can be made if it is within the strategic interest of the county to renew those assets or reinvent those processes. More importantly, the portfolio will contain the department-level IT strategies which will be used by the Technology Leadership Committee to determine if proposed projects are aligned with organizational *and* enterprise strategies. Those will be the projects delivering the most strategic value.

In the first year since the PMO's inception, the county has already seen the impact and reaped the benefits of these efforts. The following two projects demonstrate these results:

■ The PC Replacement Program has shown enormous improvement. During the past fiscal year, the goal of the program was to replace one-third of the PCs throughout the enterprise. The program struggled with unclear definitions of its scope and inadequate processes through which candidates for PC replacement were identified and through which replacement PCs were distributed to departments. During the year, the PC supplier contract expired, resulting in a period of six months for which no contract vehicle was in place for the purchase of PCs. For these reasons, only 61 of the targeted 600 PCs were replaced over the course of the year. This project received "red light" ratings on its status reports. See Table 14.6 for a definition of the county's project rating system.

In a concerted effort to turn the program around in the up-coming fiscal year, the program manager implemented an automated asset management solution to identify candidate PCs for replacement, set standards for minimum PC adequacy levels, drafted a program description defining its scope, and defined operational procedures for replacement of out-dated PCs. The program manager now has the tools to accurately forecast the needs and associated costs for meeting customer demands. Plans are being devised to replace the remainder of the prior year's PC allotment, plus the current fiscal year's allotment within the first four months of the year. This represents a 300% increase in time-to-delivery of program value and a 1600% increase in program performance as measured by the number of PCs replaced.

Table 14.6   Arlington County Project Rating Scheme

Red Light	High-severity risks are currently being realized, substantial over-spending or substantial schedule delay which results in either unrealized benefits or cost overruns, failing to fulfill stated objectives.
Yellow Light	Insufficiently detailed project task plan, insufficiently detailed spending plan, insufficiently detailed risk management plan, significant areas of potential risk, realization of moderate-level risks, unclear statement of objectives, scope, and/or outcomes, or inadequate resources to achieve objectives.
Green Light	Clearly defined objectives and scope, adequate controls in place to monitor progress against the task plan and the spending plan, identified and mitigated risks, substantially on track to deliver the expected results.

■ A project to upgrade the geographic information system's base maps involved contracting with a vendor to take aerial photographs of the county, digitize the images, and "stitch" the images together to result in a new map. The project was proceeding according to plan until significant quality issues were discovered during the digitizing and compilation phases. Resolution of the quality control issues was expected to extend the project completion date by six months. The county project manager was taking the right steps by insisting on quality work products and withholding vendor payment until a satisfactory product was delivered. When the vendor was informed that the Technology Leadership Committee was closely following the progress of the project, they committed to weekly status reports with the county project manager and to apply additional resources, if necessary, to resolve the quality issues and deliver the product in the agreed-upon time fame. The project manager was able to leverage the strong support of the project sponsor and the weight of the Technology Leadership Committee, to impress upon the vendor the need to meet the commitments of the project plan.

Other more indirect, but no less important, changes included the recognition of the value of implementing a PMO at the department level. The county has seen the implementation of mini-PMO's within certain departments to help them prioritize, select, and monitor projects at the department level. Their processes are being aligned and coordinated with the enterprise PMO's processes. Another change is that project managers are starting to employ more mature project management and control techniques. Project sponsors are taking the quarterly status reporting much more seriously and are insisting on timely and accurate information. Most important of all, the seeds of project management values are beginning to sprout and take root across the organization.

The CIO attributes the success of the PMO to the establishment of a project life cycle and the institution of written project plans, schedules, and review procedures. Success in promoting adherence to the project management methodology was achieved by approaching the contents in a pragmatic, flexible, and adaptable manner. But most important, success in the portfolio management aspects stemmed from the fact that the project reviews were conducted in a fair and reasoned manner that built trust with both project sponsors and project managers.

■ ■ ■

A project in need of a PMO. For three years, the county has been slowly implementing an interdepartmental project to reduce the cost of printing payroll and accounts payable checks. Each department that produces checks is expected to implement the tool to produce their own checks. A solution has been acquired which cuts the cost of printing a single check from dollars to cents per check, one order of magnitude of cost reduction, and an enormous return on investment given the number of checks the county writes. The project, however, is challenged by middle managers who have other priorities, time consumed in interdepartmental coordination, and lack of a senior-level project sponsor. The tasks associated with the implementation are straightforward: design the check and advice format, turn them over to the vendor for software development, and review and adjust the results. Sufficient visibility for this project could have potentially reduced the implementation time from years to months.

■ ■ ■

As the PMO-related processes mature and their value becomes better appreciated across the enterprise, demand for project management and project oversight is expected to grow dramatically. As one member of the Technology Leadership Committee states, the PMO has brought a greater awareness of the IT portfolio across the government and created the ability to take an enterprise perspective. Because of a common language and methodology, the county can now compare projects and match them against strategic plans. This allows it to allocate resources to high priority projects.

QUESTIONS

14.1 Discuss the five key objectives of portfolio management.

14.2 Explain how a PMO might bring financial value to an organization through portfolio management.

14.3 Choose any three data elements of a project portfolio report and explain why and for whom they are important.

14.4 Explain net portfolio value.

14.5 Explain how a portfolio ranking would change based on the amount of strategic resource required.

14.6 Why would the Governance Board want to know the current portfolio opportunity?

14.7 Why would the work force want to know the "force rank" order of the portfolio? Explain what the impact would mean to the daily work routine and work productivity of the work force if this data were available.

14.8 Discuss how the project portfolio elevates visibility of project work and the impact of raised awareness.

14.9 Discuss the benefit of the asset portfolio and its relationship to the project portfolio. How is this helpful in project selection?

14.10 Discuss the benefit of the strategic objectives portfolio and its relationship to the project portfolio. How is this helpful in project selection?

14.11 What is the meaning of balancing a portfolio? What types of factors should be taken into account?

14.12 Discuss the reporting roles and responsibilities for portfolio management and why these roles will be self-motivated to perform their reporting duties.

15

RESOURCE PORTFOLIO MANAGEMENT

An excellent project manager who works in the chemical industry described how to plan a maintenance project that includes a plant shutdown. Similar to many industries where there is a huge capital investment, this plant plans the maintenance project using named resources to the hour. One hour lost in this plant could cost the company tens of thousands of dollars. While this approach is correct for the project manager who must manage the details of such a project, this is the antithesis to how a PMO should perform resource portfolio management.

We begin our advice on resource portfolio management by reflecting on the mistakes we have seen in so many organizations. Put simply, it is *not* the role of the PMO to:

■ Ensure that all resources are utilized efficiently
■ Ensure that all resources fill out detailed time sheets
■ Plan at the individual, named resource level
■ Micro-plan

If the PMO is to be the tool for executive leverage in achieving strategy, the PMO must work with resources at a higher level. They must be thinking about the multi-project environment, ensuring that:

1. The organization's most precious strategic resources are giving the best value back to the organization
2. There is enough protective capacity of overall resources to support the organization's project goals and to support the proper use of the strategic resources

3. The organization's precious project resource pool is not wasted on projects that are not the highest priority relative to the organization's goals

In most organizations, the utilization of resources is comprised of peaks and valleys. There are many different types of project resources. The fluctuations in demand on the many resource types should imply how futile it is to try to balance project work across all resources. However, every organization has one (or relatively few) resource type that, more than any other resource, determines how many projects an organization can complete. We call this resource the strategic resource.

THE ORGANIZATION'S STRATEGIC RESOURCE

We are often asked, "How do you identify the organization's strategic resource?" First, look at each collection of projects that uses common resources. For that collection of projects, ask which resource will most determine how many projects the organization can complete. Where do projects get stuck the most or the longest? Which resource, used on at least 50% of the projects, is the most heavily loaded? Which resource do the project managers have to expedite the most? Which resource is most likely to significantly delay a project?

In many organizations, we find that most people can easily agree on one or two resource types. Often, it is in the IT area, front end design (if the company has a highly skilled design group), or at the end of a project when integration work is being done. In any case, if there is more than one candidate, take all the names of the candidates, put them in a bowl and draw a name out of the bowl. Make it as arbitrary as possible, so that no one group feels that there was any bias whatsoever in the selection.

If you have chosen the wrong strategic resource, using the process outlined below and in Chapter 17, you will find out within a few weeks. At that point in time, you can easily switch. Later, we describe how this process works.

Most PMOs with which we have spoken ignore multi-project scheduling at the beginning of the PMO life, thinking it is far too complex. This is a huge mistake, since the opportunity to drive value to the organization from this aspect of resource portfolio management is enormous. However, as Dr. Goldratt states, "the more complex the problem, the simpler the solution must be, or it will not work."

It would be far too complex for the PMO to try to balance the workload of all resources for all projects in the company. For one thing, there is a big difference between workload as it appears in a plan and workload as it is executed. Therefore, you could achieve some degree of balanced workload in a plan, but it would all fall apart during execution.

The approach that we have seen work best is to stagger workload according to the organization's most heavily loaded or strategic resource — the resource that impacts more projects in a significant way than any other resource.

It is critical for the organization to stagger projects according to the capacity of this strategic resource. It is amazing how project flow can be accelerated by only activating projects according to the availability of the strategic resource. The results mean that the same resource pool will handle many more projects. There is more about this topic in Chapter 17.

This approach also has implications for the use (and avoiding overuse or waste) of external consultants. If the PMO can help the organization utilize its internal workforce in a manner that reduces the use of external workers (consultants), this can impact the value proposition of the PMO in a quick, tangible way.

RESOURCE POOLS

At the individual named level, it is impossible to have predictability with resources. People join and leave organizations. Individuals have accidents, get sick, and work at varying and unpredictable levels of productivity. Many individuals are subject to the unpredictable high priority demands of their functional responsibilities.

Further, this is too detailed a level for the PMO to use to get leverage. The level that a PMO needs for planning and control is termed the resource pool. A resource pool is a collection of one or more resources with common skills. These are the skills needed to plan a project. Most organizations have between 25 and 50 resource pools defined. For an example of a subset, see Table 15.1.

With the development of these categories by the PMO, every project manager in the organization benefits. It gives the project manager a more logical way to think about his/her project resources. A high level plan is essential in identifying from where, in the organization, the resources will come. The PMO will also track the overall loading of these resource pools, making sure that the overall project management system stays in control. To do so, the PMO must ensure that there is one major variable to worry about, and only one — the organization's strategic resource. Therefore, the organization must maintain protective (and, perhaps, flexible) capacity on all other resources.

Table 15.1   Example of a Resource Pool

Resource Pool	Qty.	Current Owner	% Utilization and Trend
IT Design	12	IT Director	120 ↑
IT Development	56	IT Director	97 ↑
Financial Analysis	2	VP Finance	76 →
Clerical—Finance and Admin.	10	VP Finance	43 ↓
Engineering Design Electrical	3	Engineering Director	61 ↑
Engineering Design Mechanical	1	Engineering Director	72 ↓
Engineering Drawings	3	Engineering Director	78 ↑
Industrial Engineers	2	Plant Manager	55 →
Production Processes	2	Plant Manager	46 →
Production Management	5	Plant Manager	34 ↑
Purchasing	1	Purchasing Manager	29 ↓
Operations Analysis	3	VP Operations	83 →
Marketing	4	VP Marketing	70 ↑
Sales	3	VP Sales	80 ↑

A RESOURCE POOL OF ONE PERSON

Every organization has some resource pools that have only one person in the pool. What does this tell you about that resource pool? It should be screaming "high risk," especially if the individual is on the critical path or critical chain of a project. What would happen to the projects if that person were hit by a truck, got sick, or left the company? By defining the resource pools and gathering the data about how many people are in each resource pool and to which projects the resource pools are allocated, the PMO can offer invaluable stimulus, advice and help for cross-training. The organization is exposed to failure if such issues are not addressed.

INFORMATION IN THE RESOURCE PORTFOLIO

If I am a resource manager, I want to know what project tasks my resources are working on now, what the status is of those tasks and what new work is coming up. I also want to be able to prioritize tasks when there is a conflict between two or more projects.

If I am a project manager, I want to know that the resources I have scheduled to do work will be available when I need them. I also want to make sure that I will have the number of resources I requested for my project. It would also be very helpful to know what resources are unexpectedly available that could help in my project.

If I am a resource, I want to know to what tasks I am assigned, and whether or not those tasks are on the critical path or critical chain. When will the preceding resource be finished with its work? How much time is allocated on the schedule to complete my work? Who is the next resource that I need to turn my work over to?

If I am an executive sponsor of a project, and the project is in trouble, I want to know if it is a resource issue and what action is being taken to address the problem. I also want to know if there is a resource conflict and, if so, with whom and for which projects.

As you can tell from the nature of these questions, the resource portfolio does not stand alone. It must be connected to the project portfolio, to the portfolio of the organization's goals and to the asset portfolio.

While the definition of the resource pools is fairly static information, the assignment of the resources is totally dynamic, changing at least weekly.

There are other data that belong in the resource portfolio to help project planners. For example, the portfolio should indicate the skills defined by each resource pool. It would also be helpful to know if there are resources in one pool that are cross-trained to work in another pool. However, remember that the more data you decide you want in the portfolio, the longer it takes to gather the data and get the PMO going. We have seen very effective PMOs with only the definitions of the resource pools, their skill sets and the current allocations to projects. This is macro- not micro-management. From this information and its derivatives (e.g., what is the utilization of our strategic resources), key decisions can be made and the organization's resource assets managed to deliver on the executive goals.

INITIAL ROLE OF THE PMO IN RESOURCE PORTFOLIO MANAGEMENT

By examining existing projects, it is a simple process to extract information about resources and make the information generic to all projects. For most existing projects, the PMO will probably find that either there is no project plan at all, or that the project plan does not include resource pools. If resources are included in the project plan, they are probably named individuals. In spite of this, the PMO can look at existing projects and very quickly determine the categories of resources used. By distributing this initial list of resource pools to the project managers, the PMO will gain valuable feedback about its first pass. Usually, in two passes, the resource pool definition is complete.

The next step is to sell the organization's project managers on using these resource pool definitions in their project plans. This requires discipline, and discipline is usually a culture change in an organization. The buy-in can be very easy if three elements are included:

1. The project managers understand how the resource constraint hurts their projects.
2. The project managers believe that the PMO has a viable answer to resolve the resource constraint permanently.
3. No project is authorized or initiated without a resource-based project plan.

In order to resolve the resource constraint permanently, the executives must be party to the solution, and agree to change their behavior relative to projects. Executives must be willing to allow projects to enter the system only in a way that recognizes the capacity of the strategic resources to do the work. This is in contrast to most organizations today, where projects are pushed into the system, irrespective of the capacity of the resources to do the work.

If we want project managers to really believe that the organization is undergoing a fundamental change, then we must have the executives announce this to all project managers. Otherwise, the message will be received with skepticism.

Item 2 above must be bought into by all of the functional executives and their bosses. It is a necessary condition to support a resource-based project management methodology across the entire organization. Once this methodology is in place, the PMO can proceed to the third step — gathering the information about current projects and utilizing the resource pool definitions. From our experience, the fastest way to do this is to have a dedicated team from the PMO go to each functional executive and project manager and establish or redo the project plans.

In every organization with which we work where no centralized project planning exists, we always find active projects that are not recognized by the CEO or even by the functional executives. Therefore, with the support of the functional executives, this step is intended to uncover information that typically does not exist. Simply, what projects are going on in the organization today, and what resources are those projects using from the resource pools?

Once this data is gathered in the first pass, the PMO can load the data into a system and determine loading of the various resource pools. This data can be used to help determine which resource is the organization's strategic resource, if it was not already obvious from intuition.

Assuming that the organization has identified a strategic resource, we have found 100% of all such organizations, at this initial pass, have a situation where the strategic resource appears to be overloaded. The next step, therefore, is to determine which projects to deactivate, and how to stagger the remaining projects according to the capacity of the strategic resource. To do so requires projects to be prioritized — a topic that is covered in Chapter 14.

ONGOING ROLE OF THE PMO IN RESOURCE PORTFOLIO MANAGEMENT

The PMO has a major role to play in modeling, using the capability of most multi-project software to perform what-if analysis with new project proposals. From a resource point of view, there are several important issues that the PMO can deal with, helping the organization to continue to manage resources to produce the best results for the organization.

One question that continually comes up is, if we have a hot new project, and we change priorities to initiate that new project, what will the impact be on our strategic resource and on other resources in the organization?

Another important question is, if a non-strategic resource becomes temporarily overloaded, what options do we have to deal with it? Can we expect some overtime from these resources? Can we hire subcontractors? Is the situation really temporary, or do we need to hire and train some additional resources? Can we do cross-training on a less utilized resource? Can some of the work be deferred? Given that these issues apply to more than one project, the PMO is the logical entity to help the organization find the right answers.

For each new project, the PMO modeling and subsequent questions to project managers (e.g., what are the implications if we delay your project?) become input to a regular pipeline meeting, conducted by the governance board. This group of executives reviews project priorities and officially sanctions a new project. For any new project that is sanctioned, and for any priority changes, the PMO is the communications link to all functional executives, project managers and resource managers impacted by such a decision. The PMO is the official source of this information, playing an important role in maintaining and distributing accurate project management information across the entire organization.

ROLE OF THE PMO IN MULTI-TASKING

Multi-tasking occurs when a project resource splits its time between one task on a project and other tasks (either on a project or related to other duties it must perform). Most executives perceive multi-tasking as good, since it ensures that resources are utilized as much as possible. Some resources consider it good, since it gives them some variety in their work.

From a project manager's point of view, is it good or bad? If the multi-tasking prolongs the project and the due date is important, then it is bad. From the point of view of a PMO, overlooking the entire collection of projects, multi-tasking is bad when it extends the combined cycle time of the collection of projects.

From our experience, in most organizations that share some resources across projects, bad multi-tasking has an enormous impact on the cycle time of many projects. Having projects take two to three times as long with bad multi-tasking is not uncommon.

This topic is discussed further in Chapter 17. The PMO has an important role to play with regard to bad multi-tasking. The PMO can significantly reduce bad multi-tasking by staggering projects according to the capacity of the organization's most heavily loaded resource — the strategic resource. If we only release work into our system according to the capacity of the organization's most heavily loaded resource, what is the immediate implication for all other resources in our system? The implication is that other resources should be able to manage their workload, with only temporary and infrequent exceptions. By managing work this way, the PMO can, overnight, significantly reduce bad multi-tasking, reducing project cycle times by as much as half.*

The identical negative effect of prolonging project duration from bad multi-tasking occurs when resource pools are split between projects. Again, it looks good to the resource managers and executives because the resources are heavily utilized. However, what is the impact on each project's cycle time? Also, the project provides no value to the company until at least some major milestone is achieved and, more likely, not until the project is finished.

The problem of bad multi-tasking must be tackled at the PMO level. It is very difficult for individual project or resource managers to make a significant impact on such a problem.

RESOURCE PORTFOLIO AND
THE ORGANIZATION'S CONSTRAINT

Assume that the organization's constraint is in the market. In other words, if the organization could get more orders, it has the capacity to fill those orders. If the organization has excess internal capacity, and almost all of the organization's project resources are working on projects to improve capacity or internal efficiency or systems, then the PMO should be raising a giant red flag.

---

*See Harold Kerzner Ph.D., *Project Management, A System's Approach, 8th edition,* John Wiley & Sons, New York, 2003, chapter on Critical Chain and case studies.

The PMO must know what the constraint of the organization is, in order to correctly balance the portfolio of projects and help utilize resources correctly. To take another example, assume that the constraint of the organization is within the IT Design Group. The company has several major client opportunities each month, most of which require this IT Design Group. If the Design Group is being drawn into these new projects before it is officially sanctioned, without the proper front end qualifying and requirements definition, a significant portion of that precious IT resource could be wasted.

To understand the organization's constraint, the PMO must be able to view the entire organization holistically, and be in harmony with the executive view. See the earlier description of the 4 × 4 strategic planning process in Section II to achieve this goal.

RESOURCE PORTFOLIO AND ASSET PORTFOLIO

With the information contained in the resource portfolio and project portfolio, executives can answer a very important question. How are the resources allocated relative to the organization's most important assets?

For example, if an IT group has several applications it is supporting, each of the applications would exist in the asset portfolio. The executives might rank an application such as their Web site as being of very high strategic significance. A firm such as Travelocity.com might credit this application with its entire competitive advantage. On the other hand, an application such as order entry for travel agents might be of lower priority. If the IT group looks at the asset ranking and discovers that much more of its resources are being used in order entry, the portfolio analysis might cause it to reexamine its priorities.

The results of the portfolio analysis are distributed to the market and supply-side management teams for their review and appropriate handling. The role of the PMO is to have accurate and complete data available, and to coach executives by turning the data into information in various ways that stimulate questions and analysis.

REDUCING WASTE OF PRECIOUS RESOURCES

The PMO has a major role to play in significantly reducing waste of project resources. There are countless opportunities to do it, but the way not to do it is with detailed time sheet data.

By helping the executive team choose the right projects, and only the right projects, the PMO can eliminate bad projects, one of the biggest wastes of resources. By reducing the number of active projects in the system and staggering projects according to the capacity of the strategic resource, the PMO will significantly reduce bad multi-tasking. Watch the overtime go down significantly. Watch the use of subcontractors start to be reduced. Watch the requests for additional resources being withdrawn or reduced.

The PMO can also play a significant role in making the case for cross-training. For perhaps the first time, there is a global view of the organization's resources. Wherever there are underutilized resources in the organization, the question that should be asked is, "How can we utilize these resources to accelerate projects or take on new projects?"

Finally, the PMO can help through project management training. By applying the practices and methodology outlined in the PMBOK®, significant waste can be reduced. For example, most organizations tell us that they suffer from poor requirements definition. The result is that there is a lot of rework by project teams.

In this area of training, the PMO must be cautious to focus on the biggest reasons for waste. As with projects in the organization, there are endless training programs, but only a few, at any point in time, will yield recognizable value back to the organization.

SUMMARY

The PMO has a major role to play in driving value from the organization's investment in project resources. Its first responsibility is to ensure that resources are providing the best value to the organization's projects. To provide the best value from the project resources available, the PMO must ensure that resources are working on projects that will deliver high value to the organization. It also means ensuring that the resources are balanced correctly — working on the organization's constraint and with an intelligent split according to the organization's most strategic assets.

Further, the PMO's responsibility is to significantly reduce waste. Here, it can play a significant role in bad multi-tasking, bad projects, unnecessary overtime, and unnecessary use of subcontractors. All of this is a natural outcome out of staggering projects according to the capacity of the organization's strategic resource.

A PMO that has the resource focus, approach, executive support and buy-in of all project and resource managers, as described in this chapter, will permanently eliminate resource problems and conflicts, typically within its first few months in operation.

The key to PMO success with resource portfolio management is to take a macro-management view. By focusing on resource pools instead of named individuals, the PMO will begin to understand the leverage points that can drive value. By focusing on one strategic resource, the PMO can quickly implement the initiatives outlined in this chapter, which will show bottom line results to executives within a few weeks or months.

QUESTIONS

15.1   What are the biggest dos and don'ts for the PMO to consider when performing resource portfolio management?

15.2   Why should the resource portfolio contain a minimum of information?

15.3   Why do many PMOs focus on implementing detailed time sheet reporting from resources, especially in IT functions? What is wrong with this focus?

15.4   When starting a new PMO, what are the steps that need to be taken to have a final resource portfolio?

15.5   Describe the connections between the resource portfolio, the project portfolio, the asset portfolio, and the goals and objectives portfolio.

15.6   True or false: Resource portfolios should have named individuals.

15.7   What would make a project manager cooperate with the PMO by using the PMO's resource pool definitions and submitting a resource-based project plan? What value should the project manager expect back?

15.8   Why do the authors suggest that resource pools typically number between 25 to 50 in any organization? Why not 5? Why not 200?

15.9   What do the authors mean by their suggestion that resource portfolio management be done at a macro, rather than a micro, level?

15.10 Describe how a PMO might identify the organization's strategic resource in a multi-project environment and what is meant by the term "staggering projects."

16

ASSET PORTFOLIO MANAGEMENT

WHY FOCUS ON ASSETS

Some PMO directors comment, "We already have enough to worry about. Why should we even think about assets?" Our claim is that the PMO and the portfolio manager must understand the strategic nature of the organization's assets because it will help them and their executives make better choices between projects.

Consider the following analogy. You own an old car. It is really starting to fall apart. You have spent over $3,000 in the past year maintaining it, and you know some major problems are about to blow wide open. Is it wise to continue investing in the old car, or does it make more sense to invest in a newer one? (Of course, many would argue that a car is not an investment at all. They would call it a liability because it generates no income but consumes endless expenses. Nonetheless, even with non-assets, we are forced to make at least spending, if not investment, decisions.)

When we refer to assets, we are talking about tangible, non-human entities. These are things in which the organization has invested money, that are used to generate throughput for the organization. These assets can be the traditional "bricks and mortar" type assets — buildings, equipment, computers, tools, etc. They also can be Web sites, information systems, software, etc.

Every organization has assets that are declining in strategic and real value. This does not mean that they are worth no investment. Rather, when you look at those assets, you do not see them as a major part of the organization's future in 5 or 10 years. There are other assets that are just in their infancy, that are becoming more and more important to the organiza-

253

tion. For example, in many organizations, their Web sites are becoming more strategic for generating and doing business. An ERP system could be an asset, even though in many organizations the executives complain that they have invested tens or hundreds of millions of dollars and not received a positive return on investment.

THE TOP 5 ASSETS

Try to make a list of the top five assets of your organization. We are not referring to its net worth on the books. The top five assets are the ones your executives would consider the most important to your organization. If you have to stop and think about it, this is a red flag. It implies that the organization may be investing disproportionately in assets — spending too much on declining assets and not enough on the future.

Once you have a list of the top five assets, determine the percentage of your total portfolio budget you are spending on those assets vs. the remaining assets. This is very important information for the decision-makers to understand, especially for prioritizing, activating, and deactivating projects.

See, for example, Figure 16.1. This organization has a total of 20 active projects. In this example, the number one asset is receiving only approximately 2% of the total portfolio dollar investment. The asset ranked fourth is receiving more than four times as much investment. The top five assets of the company are receiving 20% of the total dollar portfolio investment. This should also raise a red flag. It does not necessarily mean that the decisions are wrong. There are no hard and fast rules. However, we would normally expect to see a greater percentage invested in the top five.

Another view is provided in Figure 16.2. In this chart, we examine the percentage of the strategic resource time we are investing in each asset. In this chart, we see 34% of the total amount of available strategic resource time being invested in the asset ranked fifth. At the same time, only 3% of the strategic resource is being invested in the top two assets.

As stated above, this may be valid. For example, if the company does not have the internal skills to develop the top two assets, perhaps they have subcontracted the work. The red flag that we would raise is the following. If these are the organization's top two assets, should the organization rely on external resources to develop them?

ASSETS AND GOALS

When executives are formulating the organization's goals and projects, the asset portfolio should be considered. The executives must decide if the ex-

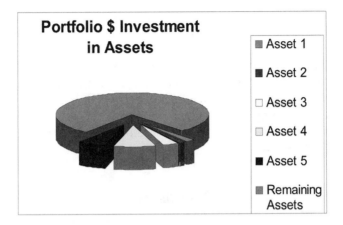

Figure 16.1   Portfolio Dollars Investment in Assets

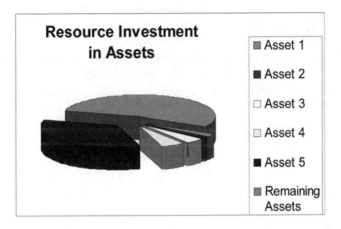

Figure 16.2   Portfolio Strategic Resource Investment in Assets

isting asset portfolio is strong enough to achieve the organization's goals. If not, the project portfolio can be impacted significantly if the executive team decides, for example, to acquire new assets rather than develop existing ones, and vice versa.

If the PMO hones its understanding of what the executive intentions are with respect to assets, this gives the PMO another tool for monitoring the project mix. Further, it allows the PMO to coach the executives on red flags regarding investment decisions.

There are many assets owned by an organization that are not recognized as such. This is because the investment was made not as capital, but rather as labor expenses over a period of years. The organization's computer systems and Web site functionality often fall into this category. Yet this is where a considerable amount of the portfolio investment might be going.

Once the executives understand this, they are more capable of guiding the collection of project teams to work on the right projects, relative to assets. These are the assets that must be developed further to meet goals this year and in the future.

SUMMARY

The asset portfolio represents an organization's investment in the non-human resources needed to generate throughput — to meet the organization's goals. In addition to the traditional financial definition of assets representing capital investment, we also refer to labor investment that was likely expensed over the years. Therefore, organization computer systems, Web sites, engineering drawings, and other such labor-intensive items are also important assets when thinking about projects.

The PMO must help flow projects through the organization more quickly, while having a recognizable impact on the bottom line. This requires a focus on where the portfolio investment is being directed, relative to assets.

The first step for the PMO is to gather the data — to determine the percentage of dollars and strategic resource invested in the top five or ten assets relative to all assets. If the PMO intuition suggests that the investment split is unbalanced, then the PMO must inform and advise the executives. This is an important step in achieving the right project mix and a healthy future for the organization.

QUESTIONS

16.1   True or False: The PMO is responsible for deciding how to allocate project portfolio and resource investment to an organization's assets.

16.2   Why do the author's discuss only the top five assets? Why not the top 50?

16.3   How much information about an asset do you think a PMO needs to develop its asset portfolio?

16.4   How are assets and goals interrelated?

16.5   How are assets and resources interrelated?

16.6   How might an understanding of the priority of assets, relative to executive goals, help the PMO recommend a project to be killed or deactivated?

17

MANAGING THE MULTI-PROJECT ENVIRONMENT — THE CRITICAL CHAIN APPROACH

THE SIGNIFICANCE OF FLOW — DISTINGUISHING SUCCESSFUL FROM STRUGGLING ORGANIZATIONS

When you have the privilege of working with many different organizations, as we do, you notice one characteristic that distinguishes the successful from the struggling. This characteristic is termed "flow" and it characterizes many different aspects of an organization. For example, in a highly successful organization, you can observe an excellent flow of open communications and problem solving dialog between and within functional areas. When a difficult issue occurs that requires the collaboration of multiple functional areas, the good organizations combine forces to work together to solve the problem. The struggling organizations go through at least several rounds of blame, pointing the finger at who is responsible for the problem this time. In bad organizations, the issue often does not get resolved until a higher level executive intervenes.

You can observe the same phenomenon in terms of flow of products and services. In many of the best organizations in terms of earnings, the Deming criteria are met. Products and services flow better than 97.5% of the time, predictably, to meet customer demand. Systems and discipline are in place to keep the flow going, and to deal with problems quickly and effectively. In struggling organizations, customer complaints are rampant. Employees are stressed out and working to the max to try to get orders out the door. Expediting more than 10% of the orders is a way of life. The same observations hold true for project flow, cash flow, engineering flow and so on.

PROJECT FLOW — WHAT DOES IT MEAN?

Even in many highly successful organizations, there is one type of flow that is often observed as dysfunctional — project flow. Good project flow means few resource conflicts occur between projects in execution. It implies a rational, simple, easy to understand prioritization scheme for all projects, fully supported by the senior management team. It also implies that the cycle time of the combination of projects executed is short enough to continually stay competitive, to meet the changing needs of the markets, and to meet the goals of the organization.

In struggling organizations, you can characterize the opposite of the statements in the above paragraph as part of the description of poor project flow. With poor project flow, you can observe executives and managers forcing their projects into the system, regardless of the capacity of the system to handle the work. You also witness fights (except they are called "meetings") to shift resources from someone else's project to "my project."

In poor project flow companies, there often is no overall prioritization scheme that is accepted by all executives. Since each executive is held accountable for the results within his or her silo, the reigning attitude is often, "No one is going to tell me what projects we can do or when we can do them."

We believe there is a strong underlying reason why poor project flow organizations stay the same or even get worse over time. It is not for lack of intelligence among the executive team or the project managers within the organization. And it is often not for lack of trying. In fact, you can often witness more than one attempt to resolve the conflicts.

What we observe is that too often, people overcomplicate the problem. We stress Goldratt's answer to this dilemma — "The more complicated the problem, the simpler the solution must be, or it will not work!"

Poor project flow organizations often make the mistake of attempting to implement planning and scheduling approaches that are far too complicated to ever work. For example, trying to balance the workload of more than a very few resources across all of the projects in an organization is futile. An organization can easily handle a focus on one or two resources. Beyond that, we believe that the difficulty and complexity climb exponentially.

PROJECT FLOW — WHAT BLOCKS IT?

This is an excellent time to read, in Chapter 1, the analogy of multiple projects being scheduled in a hospital. If you look at patients as projects, and you have to identify the biggest constraint, or the most critical resource, in a hospital, what would it be? Some immediate candidates come to mind — the beds, the doctors, and the operating room. To determine what most blocks project flow, you must take away those temporary bottlenecks that cause problems from time to time, and consider, instead, the biggest constraint over the course of, say, six months or a year. Then consider what policies make the constraint even worse.

In a hospital, what prevents a greater flow of projects (patients) in a given year? The number of beds is usually a temporary constraint. In many hospitals that temporarily run out of beds, they take action to move patients through more quickly or to have temporary beds in hallways. They may move more patients into a single room.

Hospitals are unique because of their surgical facilities. While it is true that hospitals often gain a reputation for certain types of surgery, that surgical specialty still represents only a small percentage of the varieties of surgery performed in a typical hospital. Hospitals staff and align with surgeons based on their capacity to support both the types and the volume of surgery in their operating room facilities.

In the ridiculous analogy that we described in Chapter 1, doctors were allowed to initiate projects (schedule patients into surgery) irrespective of the capacity of the critical resource (the operating room). That is when all the problems started — the competition over the critical resource and other supporting resources, the bad multi-tasking and so on.

Simply put, what blocked project flow in the hospital analogy was the practice by doctors of initiating projects to support their own needs (local optima) rather than subordinating themselves to the hospital's decision to exploit the critical resource — the operating rooms.

Note that when a hospital works to exploit its critical resource, by definition it must have protective capacity among all of the other resources to support this approach (i.e., to subordinate to the constraint). It must also have a prioritization system accepted by everyone involved. And there must be one entity responsible for staggering the use of the operating room and communicating across the organization.

This implies that an operating room, the strategic resource of a hospital, should rarely stand idle. There should be enough operating room nurses, surgeons, and anesthesiologists to keep the operating room fully utilized. In some hospitals this is not the case, and we can easily observe poor project flow — patients who spend longer, on average, in that hospital for given ailments than the national average. In some hospitals, they simply have not identified the operating room as the strategic resource, or are not subordinating everything else to help them exploit the operating room. Often, their policies are trying to optimize doctors' time, rather than patients' time. The doctor is not a project. The patient is a project.

In your organization, what is your strategic resource? Which resource, more than any other, determines how many projects you can flow through your organization, and how long those projects will take?

In poor project flow organizations, we find executives or senior managers often do not recognize a strategic resource. They have not identified one. Therefore, the next actions are obvious. They initiate new projects whenever they want to. Then, resource conflicts occur. The resource conflicts are most heated with the organization's strategic resource. However, they often start with other resources. The executives then demand that resources on existing projects be moved to their projects. Other executives are fighting hard to keep the resources where they are.

The longer this kind of situation is allowed to continue, the worse and more frequent are the conflicts over resources. We have seen this deteriorate to a point that, over the course of a year, none of the executive's strategic ideas were implemented.

You might ask, how is this possible? We too, were incredulous, until we met with a CEO who complained bitterly about his ideas not being implemented. What happens is that every senior manager has the perfect excuse for not completing work on any one of the projects. "We were busy doing another project. And you told us (or we told you) that this other project is also important."

THE CRITICAL CHAIN STEPS TO IMPROVE MULTI-PROJECT FLOW

Critical Chain is a methodology to plan and manage projects for greatly increased project flow and significantly reduced cycle time per project. The constraint of an individual project and the Critical Chain solution is described in Kerzner's text, *Project Management, A Systems Approach,* 8th edition, in the chapter on Critical Chain. The overall philosophy of the methodology is described in Goldratt's book, *Critical Chain.*

In the multi-project environment, Goldratt assumes that the constraint is the practice of a "push" system of project management; that is, it is the practice of senior management to push new projects into the system irrespective of the capacity of the strategic or critical resource to do the work. Following Goldratt's process of the five focusing steps, the solution is to move from a "push" system to a "pull" system, based on the organization's constraint:

1. *Identify the constraint.* Identify the strategic resource for the multi-project environment. Identify the resource that, more than any other, determines project flow. Usually, it is the most heavily loaded resource across projects, but not always. Often, it is the resource over which multiple projects fight the most. It is where projects get stuck the longest or the most often. In the previous chapter, we described that if you have several candidates for this strategic resource, we suggest putting all of the names into a hat and picking one as arbitrarily as possible. This was suggested so that no one group would be offended that their suggestion was passed over unfairly, or that bias or favoritism was playing a role here. If you pick the wrong strategic resource, you will usually know within a few weeks. That is because projects will still be clogging up in another area and then it will be obvious to everyone where the strategic resource is located. However, in the meantime, project flow will still improve.

2. *Decide how to exploit the constraint.* To squeeze everything you can out of the strategic resource, you must not overload the strategic resource. You must stagger all projects according to the capacity of the strategic resource, ensuring that it is not overloaded.

   ■ Imagine trying to get an auditorium full of people through a few revolving exit doors. If you try to move 10 people through a revolving door at once, they jam up. You could wait all day for them to move through. On the other hand, if you move one or two through at a time, but get them to move through quickly, the flow improves.

   ■ Often, strategic resources are jammed with too many active projects. As a result, they fall into bad multi-tasking — switching from one project to another to another. (See Chapter 15 for the impact of bad multi-tasking on resources and task times). Each project takes much longer to complete, waiting a long time for the strategic resource to do its part of the project.

   ■ With a reduced number of projects, the strategic resource sees clear priorities and focus. There are no more excuses —work must get done and done quickly. The eyes of the entire organization are on the project. Therefore, to exploit the constraint typically requires the organization to deactivate a significant number of active projects (e.g., Alcan: 50%, TESSCO: 75 to 80%).

3. *Subordinate to the constraint.* Executives must agree that projects can only be initiated according to the capacity of the strategic re-

source. They also subordinate by agreeing to a prioritization scheme or approach that makes it logical for everyone in the organization to know which project should be initiated first, second, third, etc. Further, everyone in the organization subordinates by trying his or her best not to cause the strategic resource to be wasted. For example, at TESSCO Communications, the strategic resource is Technical Services. In order not to waste this precious resource, the functional areas go out of their way to validate specifications before involving this resource.

4. *Elevate the constraint.* Elevate usually means invest. Goldratt claims that in almost all of the multi-project Critical Chain cases in which he was involved, he found that the organization's multi-project strategic resource was not a bottleneck. In fact, he found that when the organization staggered projects according to the strategic resource, there was huge excess capacity for the strategic resource. The message is that most organizations can flow many more projects through if they would only correctly utilize the existing resources. If an organization does need to flow more projects through, they have applied the first three focusing steps above, and still have a constraint, then they must elevate. Either they must hire more resources (usually, more of the critical resource without forgetting to hire more of the supporting resources) or they must do something to improve the productivity of the critical resource, perhaps with better, faster, or more supporting technology.

5. *Go back to Step 1.* In order to have predictability in project flow, it is important to have a constraint — one strategic resource that becomes the focal point for answering the following questions:

- Which projects should we initiate?
- When should we initiate them?
- How many of these projects can we complete in the time period?

In other words, it is good to have and to recognize the organization's critical resource in the multi-project environment. The organization can then expand its project flow at will, knowing the control valves where capacity must be added.

IMPLEMENTING A MULTI-PROJECT SOLUTION — CRITICAL CHAIN OR OTHER

Implementing a new method of flowing projects through an organization is a culture change. To make this happen, some policies must change and the entire executive team must support it. The multi-project Critical Chain solution, outlined briefly above, is a win-win solution. All executives benefit by getting their projects completed sooner. The project managers benefit by having less intra-project conflicts. The quality of life for resource managers improves, having to spend less time worrying about the executives and project managers who will be unhappy, and more time managing their resources consistently.

The biggest mistake we see PMOs make when implementing this kind of approach is an underestimation of the degree of executive education and buy-in required to make this work. Most executives do not want to give up control over important matters that will impact their performance. The idea of sharing control of priorities with a PMO is not easy to sell. Further, many executives fear or distrust the bureaucracy of a centralized organization.

If the benefits are so obvious, why, then, should these multi-project concepts be so difficult to sell and implement correctly? There are two key reasons:

1. The people who are selling the idea are very enthusiastic about the benefits that the new multi-project system will bring to their organization. This enthusiasm leads them to push their solution before the executives even agree with them that a problem exists or what the problem is. As a result, the executive layers of resistance to this new idea end up being cemented permanently in place, instead of being peeled away. The more enthusiastic the advocates, the greater the resistance on the other side. The greater the resistance, the more the PMO advocates push their solution, instead of following a process of dealing with the layers of resistance in sequence.
2. There are some key omissions often missing in the strategy, which the executives recognize as critical to translating the idea into bottom line benefits. This experience encourages them to reject the idea, or put it in limbo.

Therefore, the strategy to successfully sell the multi-project concept to executives is twofold.

1. Presentations must deal with each layer of resistance, in the correct sequence.
2. Executives must be able to raise concerns and be comfortable with how those concerns will be handled.

LAYERS OF RESISTANCE TO IMPLEMENTING A MULTI-PROJECT SOLUTION

LAYER 1 — EXECUTIVES DO NOT AGREE WITH YOU ON THE PROBLEM

Before we can overcome this layer of resistance, we must distinguish between the many symptoms of a problem, and the few root causes. Each executive comes into a presentation with an opinion on the problems of managing multiple projects from his own perspective. To begin to convince executives that they can have their cake and eat it too, we favor using simulations. One of the biggest problems that impacts every executive in the multi-project environment is the project delays caused by bad multi-tasking. Bad multi-tasking, in turn, is caused by jamming the system with too many projects. It is easy to do a simulation demonstrating the devastating effects of bad multi-tasking. This simulation must be backed up by facilitation relating the validity of the simulation to that organization, through pertinent and real examples.

The presentation should show how bad multi-tasking occurs, quite innocently, as a result of projects being pushed into the system without regard to the capacity of the system to do the work. In our simulations, we do not point the finger at the executives, but rather at the measurements that force the executives to initiate new projects immediately.

LAYER 2 — EXECUTIVES MAY NOT AGREE WITH YOU ON THE DIRECTION OF THE SOLUTION

Once you have agreement on the problem (i.e., the practice and the measurements behind it of pushing new projects into the system, irrespective of the capacity of the system to handle the work), the next step is to gain agreement on the direction of the solution.

For example, one executive may suggest that the executive team simply prioritize all projects and just do the most important ones. While that might certainly have a major impact, it does not put in place a permanent mechanism to prevent the situation from occurring every few weeks or months. Therefore, the appropriate response to this kind of suggestion is to agree, but to suggest that more is needed to cure the disease permanently.

Another executive might argue that putting one functional area or one executive in charge of all projects is the best way to go. In fact, most of the PMOs that we have surveyed report to the CIO. However, this also does not cure the problem. The CIO is not the only sponsor of projects, although often the CIO owns the strategic resource of the organization. However, to stagger projects in a way that gives the organization the greatest value for its strategic resource, there must be a mechanism that allows input from all senior management. The decision of how to stagger projects is one of the most important decisions for the executive team to make, in full consensus with one another.

Once again, if the PMO advocates try to sell the PMO solution before overcoming this layer of resistance, the results will most likely be very disappointing.

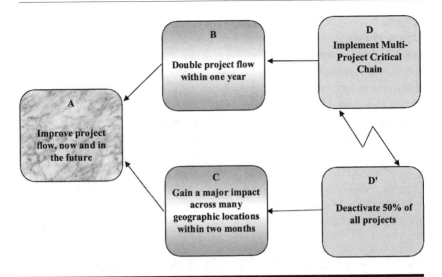

Figure 17.1   Conflict between Implementing Critical Chain and Other Project Management Improvements

There is always more than one way to overcome a problem. Multi-project Critical Chain is just one approach. At this point, what the PMO advocates must determine to overcome this layer of resistance is if there is a conflict between these different directions. The needs of the company to have more projects completed, to reduce cycle times, to have a better track record on each project, are not in conflict. What might be in conflict is the approach advocated to meet these needs.

The Theory of Constraints deals with these conflicts using a diagram called the Conflict Cloud. In five boxes, the diagram shows a very elegant and simple picture of a conflict. By explicitly recognizing the needs of both sides, the diagram brings them together against the problem, rather than against each other. An example of one such conflict is illustrated in Figure 17.1. In this example, assuming the conflict exists between the executives and the people advocating for multi-project Critical Chain, both sides agree that they have a common objective — "Improve project flow now and in the future." In the specific circumstances that exist at this time, there are several necessary conditions to achieve the objective. The executives must have a quick hit. They need things to change within the next two months. The PMO advocates accept that, but have a different need — to double project flow within one year. Based on the number of projects everyone agrees must be completed for the organization to stay healthy, the executives agree with the need to double project flow within the year.

In this example, the conflict arises over how to achieve these necessary conditions highlighted in boxes B and C in Figure 17.1. The executives are demanding that the PMO simply deactivate 50% of all projects according to project priorities. The PMO group sees that as just one of several steps required. They want a full multi-project Critical Chain implementation, which would require training across a wide geographic area. This is a more extensive implementation — and therefore a more time-consuming one.

The Theory of Constraints approach then works on assumptions underlying the conflict, and overcoming one or more assumptions to set a direction that meets both sets of needs, B and C. In other words, it is unacceptable to force anyone to choose between the two needs. It is the D and D' boxes that appear to be in conflict. In fact, the two options are not mutually exclusive and this conflict can be easily resolved. Many conflicts that we encounter in real life are not so easy. However, every one of them has underlying assumptions that can be challenged and good solution can be achieved.

LAYER 3 — PEOPLE DO NOT AGREE WITH YOU THAT THE SOLUTION WILL OVERCOME THE PROBLEMS

If the result of overcoming Layer 2 is that everyone agrees that Critical Chain is the right direction for a solution, then the next stage is "prove it!"

No solution is complete without a set of measurements, policies and training to make it work. Typically, an evaluation team is assembled and trained to develop first and foremost an understanding of the culture change in terms of policies and measurements. They may also investigate other companies that have successfully and unsuccessfully implemented available software alternatives. Feasibility is checked by the evaluation team.

Several years ago, this was a huge issue, since the methodology was new and few organizations had implemented it. There was very little information in the public domain. Today, that has changed and it is easier to "prove it."

LAYER 4 — PEOPLE BELIEVE THAT THE SOLUTION WILL LEAD TO NEGATIVE SIDE EFFECTS

Once you have reached this layer of resistance, you are "home free". Do not lose executive support by ignoring these concerns. In this layer of resistance, the executives are saying that they agree that the proposed multi-project solution will overcome their problems. However, they believe that some new negative consequences will result from the solution.

For example, an executive might argue that if we implement multi-project Critical Chain and one of his or her projects becomes deactivated or falls in priority, he or she will not be able to meet his or her goals for the year. This must not be ignored. With increased project flow, the system should have the capacity to complete more projects sooner than would otherwise have been completed. Either the executive's concern is valid, or through cause–effect logic, the PMO team must prove that it is not. If it is valid, it means that another idea is necessary in order to prevent the negative concern from being realized.

The best person from whom to begin soliciting the ideas is the person who raised the negative concern in the first place. Often, after seeing his or her fears documented precisely using cause–effect logic, he or she is able to make a suggestion to overcome the negative.

LAYER 5 — PEOPLE SEE OBSTACLES TO IMPLEMENTING THE PMO

At this stage, the PMO advocates need only document (rigorously) all of the obstacles the executives see, and give the executives the first shot at how they would like to overcome the obstacle. This is an excellent layer of resistance to arrive at because we can move from this stage directly to an approved project plan and charter to implement the multi-project solution, be it Critical Chain or another approach.

OTHER IMPLEMENTATION ISSUES

As with any significant methodology, multi-project Critical Chain must deal with several implementation issues. For example:

- Who will be responsible for the staggering of projects, the exploitation of the organization's critical resource, the communication of the progress of that resource on various projects, and the tracking of that resource?
- What is the prioritization scheme that will be used for staggering projects?
- How many and which projects should be deactivated?
- Who will make up the implementation team, and what will their duties and responsibilities be?
- Who will gather and help convert all existing project plans to Critical Chain format?
- Do we need multi-project Critical Chain software? If so, which one? Who will implement it and train resources? Who needs to be trained?
- Will we implement all projects at once, or use a phased approach? What about the projects that are more than 50% complete?

We often identify 30 to 50 such issues in every implementation. However, with executive support behind it, the PMO finds that the implementation to multi-project management becomes a triviality by comparison. The executive buy-in must not be ignored.

SUMMARY

Most organizations are struggling to improve their project flow — the number of projects finished within a given time frame and the cycle time of each of those projects. Critical Chain is a relatively new methodology designed to meet these objectives. It deals with both individual and multiple projects as two different issues. In the multi-project environment, Critical Chain requires the identification of the organization's strategic resource — the resource that, more than any other, impacts the combined cycle time of most projects in the organization. The solution requires staggering projects according to the capacity of that strategic resource, being careful not to overload that resource.

Because executives are pushing projects into the system, creating the overloads in the first place, an implementation of Critical Chain requires executive education first. In fact, one of the biggest shortcomings we see with regard to PMO implementations today is the lack of connection to the executives. You must achieve executive buy-in and full support, or the implementation is likely to fail. We advocate the use of simulations to first show executives the nature of the multi-project problem, and gain agreement on the problem, before moving to the alternative solutions and Critical Chain. By dealing with the executive buy-in and issues up front, their commitment becomes the most important factor in driving success.

QUESTIONS

17.1 What does the term "project flow" mean?

17.2 How would you recognize good or bad project flow in an organization?

17.3 How does Critical Chain describe the biggest problem in today's multi-project environments?

17.4 True or False: Executives are to blame for most multi-project problems.

17.5 What are the two major features of multi-project Critical Chain?

17.6 What would make an executive comfortable with relinquishing some control over project priorities to a team?

17.7 Toward the end of this chapter, several other implementation issues were mentioned. Pick two of these and describe how you might approach overcoming these issues.

17.8 Some managers believe that the more work you allocate to a resource, the more work you can get out of that resource. Why does Critical Chain advocate not overloading the strategic resource? How would you respond to an executive who suggests that strategic resources should be overloaded with work, so that the resource is not wasted?

This book has free materials available for download from the Web Added Value™ Resource Center at www.jrosspub.com.

18

REDUCING NEGATIVE HUMAN BEHAVIOR

WE DON'T NEED FIVE YEARS OF PSYCHOANALYSIS

If you do not change some rooted human behavior on projects, you cannot improve anything because humans lie at the heart of any organization and its systems. If you change any aspect of a system (e.g., implement a new methodology), but the people working on that system do not adopt those changes (e.g., use the new methodology), then the situation is actually made worse. The organization has spent money to implement the methodology. Investment has increased with zero return. Further, it took precious human resources away from other things that may have paid off. So the impact on the organization is not neutral — it is very negative.

To impact human behavior, we reiterate Goldratt's adage — "The more complicated the problem, the simpler the solution must be, or it will not work." In science, complexity is defined by how many places we have to touch a system in order to have an impact. The more different points we must touch, the more complicated the system is to control and to change.

By analogy, if we look at an organization and decide that the project managers are weak in many areas of the PMBOK®, how should a PMO seek to improve the situation? If the PMO tries to address all nine knowledge areas at once, it will be like trying to hold nine ping pong balls under water simultaneously in a gigantic swimming pool.

The PMO must consider one other point when deciding where to put its effort. A PMO that influences the cycle time of one project may have an impact that is not visible to the executives. A PMO that can leverage its efforts by changing one thing and impacting many projects will have a much greater chance of achieving visible results and, therefore, surviving and flourishing.

In this chapter, we address those aspects of human behavior that impact the cycle time of most projects. In most organizations, cycle time is the biggest leverage point. Reduce the cycle time significantly without increasing resources, and the impact will be felt on the organization's goals and on the bottom line.

THE MEASUREMENT PROBLEM

If it is so obvious that for most projects, the sooner the project finishes, the sooner the organization benefits, then why do team members take actions that delay the project? Many project managers argue that everyone is working at their peak — most people in organizations are overloaded with too much to do. Murphy exists everywhere. We agree, but this does not negate the previous statement. In spite of everyone working hard, we believe that team members often take actions that delay projects. This behavior is not deliberate or malicious, which makes it that much more insidious to the organization. It is like poison gas — no one is noticing it, but it is killing projects everywhere.

Before jumping to a solution, it is important to have a deeper understanding of the problem. A project is like a chain, containing many links. In fact, a project is like a collection of chains, intersecting at various points, with one final chain at the end of the project representing the integration stage or the final set of events to complete the project. A chain is only as strong as its weakest link. In any chain, there is only one "weakest" link. Within a project, there is a collection of tasks that are connected by dependencies — starting one task depends on another collection of tasks being finished. However, the dependencies are not just logical task dependencies. There are also resource dependencies within the project. For example, Joe cannot start the integration testing yet because he is still working on the complex coding task.

In most projects, the duration of the project is determined by the longest chain of dependent events. Remembering that a dependency can be either task- or resource-related, this longest chain is called the critical chain of the project. In most projects, the critical chain is not even formally recognized. In other words, if you look at the documentation of any project and ask team members, "What is the critical chain of this project?", most of the time the answer will either be a blank stare or the statement, "I don't know."

Therefore, there is no common team focus on the weakest link in the chain of a project. Rather, we observe a behavior better described as "every man and woman for themselves". The attitude is more like, "I got my stuff done on time — why didn't you?" This kind of behavior stems from a predominant measurement common to most project managers and resource managers. Today, the principle measurement in project work is "Finish your task on time, according to the estimate you gave the project manager." By inference, individuals or specific groups are to blame if the project is late. The assumption is that if every individual finishes his or her tasks according to his or her estimates, then the project will finish on time.

On the surface, this looks like a wonderful measurement. However, statistically, the probability of everyone finishing his or her project tasks on time is infinitesimal, even in a small project. We need to look deeper into this measurement to understand its frightening negative consequences.

Project tasks are, by definition, a one-time occurrence. Even if you have performed similar tasks in the past, there is always some uniqueness to each project task. The uniqueness may be because the person on whom you are depending is different from the last time you performed similar work. When people are being measured to finish a task on time, they will try to factor in some kind of safety net.

Consider the earlier statement from many project managers — people are already overloaded with work. This statement implies that when someone is asked to do a project task today, it usually does not mean that they have nothing else to do. Most people that we observe working on projects today have other things to do. Sometimes they are already working on other projects. Many of them also have part-time or full-time work responsibilities. People are constantly telling us that they are juggling several projects and several tasks simultaneously.

So if an individual is being measured to finish tasks to a deadline or to a fixed timeframe and is already juggling different tasks, how will he or she come up with an estimate for a task? If the individual believes, for example, that he or she could finish a task in two non-interrupted days if everything went well, he or she would probably want to allow three to four days for Murphy. If finishing his or her task depends on others also completing their work, the individual might further inflate the task to four to six days. If the individual is juggling other full-time responsibilities and could get called away from this task to do rework on previously completed tasks, the promise date could be two to three weeks.

Of course, project managers try to fight these inflated estimates often by trying to remove other priorities and making their project the top priority. Nonetheless, project managers often are forced to deal with resources with conflicting priorities, other non-project responsibilities and susceptibility to being pulled away for rework or other reasons. Most resources also have compelling arguments and real-life stories about Murphy that force project managers to accept task estimates with some protection embedded.

STUDENT SYNDROME

The bottom line is that most estimates have this kind of reality built in. Do these conflicts and Murphy events occur on every task? Of course not. Sometimes, a conflict or Murphy materializes and is even worse than anticipated. In these cases, the person who did the estimate thinks, "Next time, I'd better put in more protection." When an individual has several things on his or her plate, one type of frequently observed behavior is for the individual to do his own prioritization. If you have something important that your boss is expecting by Friday and something else that is due in two weeks, most people would look at the two week task and leave it until they have completed their more urgent tasks.

Goldratt compares this behavior to "Student Syndrome."* It emulates the behavior of students in a class where the professor announces, "Tomorrow we will have a test on everything we have studied this semester." The students complain that it is unfair. After all, they covered a lot of material in the semester, and they haven't had time to study. If the professor relents and agrees to have the test in two weeks, do the students rush out and start studying that evening? Of course not! The students think, "It's OK. We have lots of time. We'll go to the club tonight. We can work on other things." When do the students begin to study? They start studying the night before the exam.

Goldratt compares this to project work, where people work on the most urgent tasks, and leave other tasks to the latest possible time. Murphy does not usually hit right at the beginning of a task. Murphy often hits more in the later stages of a task. If you start a task at the latest possible time and Murphy hits, it is now too late to adjust and the task is late.

In fact, it may not be Murphy (in the sense of something going wrong with the task work itself) that causes the task to be late. It may be a conflict with another project or rework from another task. If Student Syndrome combines with Murphy or conflicts, it is no wonder that many projects do not finish on time.

PARKINSON'S LAW

However, sometimes, Murphy and conflicts do not materialize. So the individual who was allowed seven days to finish a task, and actually completed it in two days, now has another five days until the due date. What will his behavior be when the measurement is, "Finish the task on time?"

---

*For a full explanation, see Eliyahu M. Goldratt, *Critical Chain*, North River Press, Great Barrington, MA, 1996.

Here, the waters are muddy. Every organization is different, and even within one organization, behaviors will vary from one week to the next, and from one department to another, depending on the visibility of certain priorities.

The Vice President of Production in a shipbuilding company told us that he could get his crews to work twice as fast if there was another ship on the dock waiting to be worked on. Otherwise, the workers have a justifiable fear of layoffs, and set their pace accordingly. Here, Goldratt's other adage comes into play. "If my measurements are unclear, no one can predict how I will behave, not even me."

With unclear measurements, behavior is unpredictable. However, when a project has not identified the critical chain — the focusing point that will drive down cycle time — individuals tend to focus on their own interests or measurements. If an individual finishes a task in 2 days, but it is not due to be completed for several more days, many individuals will exhibit a behavior termed "Parkinson's Law."

Parkinson's Law is "Work expands to fill the time available." People who do creative or complex work often exhibit this behavior. For example, imagine a Web designer who finishes his or her first pass on a new Web design and has several more days until the task is due. Instead of turning the completed task in early, the Web designer thinks, "Let me put a few more bells and whistles into the design."

The next resource, the Web programmer, receives the design documentation and says, "Wow, this is more complicated than I thought it would be." The task that he or she figured would take five days of programming work will now take 10 days because of Parkinson's Law. If the designer had just completed the task and turned it over when it was finished, the project might even have finished early.

Have you heard of many projects finishing early? Have you heard of any projects finishing early? There is ample empirical evidence of Parkinson's Law in action.

Of course, in the above case, the Web programmer had been working on other more urgent tasks, and had left the coding for this Web design to the last minute (Student Syndrome). Now, Student Syndrome and Parkinson's Law combine to guarantee that the project will be delivered late.

WHAT'S WRONG WITH STUDENT SYNDROME AND PARKINSON'S LAW?

If the new Web design is to generate more revenue for the company, then the company is losing money from the delay. The later it is implemented, the greater the loss of revenue to the company.

The Web designer might argue that the additional bells and whistles would bring even more money to the company. This may or may not be true, but this decision to go beyond the strict specifications should go through a change control procedure and be evaluated.

Often, the possibilities for enhancements to any product or service are endless. While it is true that enhancements sometimes have extra value to the market, this is not always the case. Most often, the philosophy of speed-to-market and incremental enhancements brings more revenue in the long run. However, vital decisions that delay a project should not be made by individuals being driven by Parkinson's Law.

The problem with the Student Syndrome behavior described above is that team members do not distinguish correctly between critical chain tasks and other tasks. Remember that the critical chain is part of the weakest link of a project, relative to project duration. The longer it takes to do the critical chain tasks, the longer the project duration will be.

THE BEGINNING OF THE SOLUTION — IDENTIFYING AND EXPLOITING THE CONSTRAINT

The common thread among many great achievements is the focus brought to bear on one or two key aspects needed to reach the goal. Within a single project, the focus is on the critical chain. The project is like a relay race. The faster the critical chain, the better chance we have of winning the race.

In constraint management culture, the job is not just to identify the constraint, but to make everyone involved aware of the constraint, so that they don't waste a single chance to exploit it. Within a project, everyone must be made aware of what tasks comprise the critical chain of that project. Then, everyone who is assigned to a critical chain task must perform that task as if they were in a relay race.

A relay runner tries to run his or her portion of the race as quickly as possible. He or she also passes the baton on as soon as he or she can to the next runner. Relay race runners do not stop in the middle of a race to check e-mail or attend non-relevant meetings. Nor do they take vacations or training programs in the middle of a race, unless it will help them win the race.

The runner who is waiting for a baton to be passed to him or her is not idly standing by. He or she is looking to see if his or her predecessor is coming close, and then he or she runs alongside so that no momentum is lost.

This type of project behavior is what we need to replace Student Syndrome, Parkinson's Law, and other behaviors that unnecessarily inflate project cycle times. The full Critical Chain solution is discussed in depth in Kerzner's text on project management.*

PROCESS OF ONGOING IMPROVEMENT — DEMING, GOLDRATT, AND THE PARETO PRINCIPLE

The critical chain system outlined above and described in the referenced texts is intended to bring drastically shorter project cycle times and predictability to project management, at least in the scheduling attribute. Where should the PMO go from there? Goldratt brings to project management the concept of Buffer Management. He suggests that individual task times are naturally variable. Protection built in to individual tasks breeds Student Syndrome and Parkinson's Law. Instead, he advocates protecting the entire project from variation, where statistics will work in our favor.

Buffers are used to insulate a project from common cause variation. They are also used to insulate the critical chain from variability in the non-critical tasks. However, the more common cause variation that exists in projects, the bigger the buffers must be as insulators.

Goldratt suggests using the Pareto Principle (the 80/20 rule) to help determine where the next improvement effort should be. In other words, 80% of the penetration of the buffers is probably caused by 20% of the different originating causes. The approach is simple and it works. Have each project manager document in a simple spreadsheet the reasons for tasks taking longer than expected. Accumulate those reasons across projects. Take the top one or two reasons and have the PMO do an improvement process on those. If it works, buffers can be shorter across all projects.

For example, assume that the reason for 80% of the problem of tasks taking longer than expected is related to rework. The PMO investigates and finds that most rework occurs because the specifications were not correctly defined to begin with. The PMO further researches and concludes that training and methodology will eliminate most of the problem. While some rework and redefinition will probably be part of projects to eternity, it is of little consequence if you can eliminate most of the problem.

---

*See Harold Kerzner, Ph.D., *Project Management: A Systems Approach to Planning, Scheduling and Controlling*, 8th ed., John Wiley & Sons, New York, 2003, chapter on Critical Chain.

WHAT IF CYCLE TIME IS NOT THE BIGGEST LEVERAGE FOR THE PMO?

Sometimes, a PMO comes into existence because of one or two projects that are in deep trouble. Sometimes, one project could make or break a company. In this case, the constraint management methodology is identical. The first step in any improvement process is to *identify the constraint.* The PMO must recognize at all times that the owners of the organization and the owner's direct representatives (the senior management team) have the sole right to set the goals and determine the priorities of the organization. The PMO must subordinate to those goals. A PMO that has some other agenda, even if it is an admirable one, should reconsider if it hopes to survive.

Some other constraints we have seen within the collection of projects of an organization include:

- Wrong project mix — Too many active projects that do not address the organization's constraint.
- Insufficient project management skills — No one in the organization can create a project plan. The concepts of a Gantt chart and project and task dependencies are over everyone's heads.
- Company-wide measurement systems typically driven by efficiencies or cost accounting — These slant projects toward one part of the organization at the expense of the constraint.
- Impending cash flow problems — Companies that are struggling to stay alive often push more and more new projects into the system, desperate to implement changes to keep the company viable. Desperation often spawns ill-conceived projects and very bad multitasking throughout the company.

Within individual projects, we have witnessed many different reasons for uncontrolled turbulence. These include:

- A major subcontractor not delivering the goods, for a variety of reasons
- Lack of PM skills within the project
- Poor or non-existent change control
- Incredibly poor requirements definition

In the case of a PMO being called in to an individual project in crisis, the onus is on the PMO not only to identify the constraint, but also to obtain consensus from the team and the executives involved on the constraint. The PMO must be very careful, in this case, not to point the finger at the individuals involved, or it may find the finger ultimately pointing right back at the PMO. The root problem is often not a specific individual, but a combination of policies, measurements, or skills that cause the project to be in crisis.

Therefore, using the example from the above list of non-existent change control, the PMO would never point the finger at the PM or any other individual, claiming, "Joe really screwed up. He didn't implement the proper change control procedures."

It is incumbent upon the PMO to dig deeper. If it is a skills problem, the more appropriate statement might be, "Our organization does not have rigorous change control procedures across many projects." Of course, the PMO must also be prepared to answer the question, "Why not?"

SUMMARY

To improve project management results, the PMO must be able to permanently and positively change human behavior. Changing methodology, software, and other aspects of a system are ultimately useless unless the people within the system also change.

While there are valid exceptions, one of the biggest leverage points to improve results across the entire collection of projects is to impact the cycle time. The PMO should be seeking to reduce the cycle time of most projects, not just one or two.

Two human behaviors that have a huge impact on project cycle time are Student Syndrome and Parkinson's Law. Student Syndrome is the tendency to leave tasks to the last possible minute, allowing Murphy and conflicts to cause many tasks to be late. Parkinson's Law — work expands to fill the time available — describes the tendency of creative team members to add bells and whistles to their task work rather than turning the work over earlier to the next resource meeting the minimum specification requirements.

As a result of these behaviors, we rarely, if ever, see a project finish earlier than expected. We also see many projects finish much later than their original due dates.

These behaviors must be replaced by a relay runner work ethic, combined with the Deming Level of predictability. These changes are combined into a system of buffer management that allows drastically reduced cycle times. Buffer management also sets the stage for a process of ongoing project management improvement using the Pareto Principle.

Using these combined techniques, the vast knowledge of the PMBOK® can be successfully harnessed in bite-sized chunks, providing the PMO with a focus during each round of its improvement efforts.

QUESTIONS

18.1   Why do the authors claim that you cannot improve an organizational system without changing human behavior?

18.2   Why is the "critical chain" of tasks considered to be the weakest link in a project?

18.3   Is it possible for something other than the critical chain to be the weakest link in a project? If yes, provide two examples.

18.4   The authors claim that current behavior increases project cycle time, but that this behavior is not deliberate or malicious. Explain.

18.5   How might "Student Syndrome" explain why a person arrives late to work or to a meeting?

18.6   If everyone who worked on the critical chain tasks of a project exhibited Parkinson's Law, how would that explain why it would be impossible for the project to finish early?

18.7   What behavior should replace current project behaviors?

18.8   Why must buffer management be part of a project? Why couldn't you simply get people to turn over their work as early as possible?

18.9   How does the Pareto Principle and Buffer Management help the PMO with its process of ongoing improvement in project management?

19

PMO ORGANIZATION MODELS

EVERY PORTFOLIO IS UNIQUE

Before making any decision on the type of PMO you will establish, we recommend that you do some homework on what your project portfolio currently looks like. You can collect information on all active projects, or just on those that the PMO might be asked to help. This research will help you determine the risks that three out of the four models of PMOs represent.

Consider Figure 19.1. This figure shows one example of how to categorize current projects. In this example, we have plotted three different project types (development, package integration, and maintenance) into the model as data points. We used this IT terminology because in most organizations, IT owns the majority of projects. We also separated programs or projects by small, medium, and large.

Can you already draw some conclusions from this data about what challenges this PMO faces? This "scatter-gram" statistical approach shows some of the bias in this organization. For example, only 5 out of 27 projects shown are not IT. Usually, this means that there is a lot of animosity toward IT, which will be blamed for projects being late and for resource conflicts. It is also a sign that the part of the organization gathering this data is missing some key projects taking place outside of the IT area. There are more projects

	Enterprise			Functional Units			I T		
	D	P/I	M/E	D	P/I	M/E	D	P/I	M/E
Large		1		4			6,7,8 9,10	11,12 13	14,15 16,17
Medium		2,3				5	18,19 20,21 22,23	24	25,26 27
Small									

D = Development Projects; P/I = Package Integration Projects;
M/E = Maintenance or Enhancement Projects

Figure 19.1   Scatter Diagram Showing Breakdown of Enterprise Projects

in this organization. It is a red flag that there might be "leakage" — IT is losing ground to outsourcing.

Another strange characteristic of this data is the total absence of small projects. Of course, they must exist within the organization, but the organization is not accounting for them. This suggests an organization embattled in resource conflicts. The big, long, complex projects keep losing resources to the small, quick, "show results now" projects. Medium and large projects are constantly delayed, but no one in the functional units is willing to do things differently. Why should they? It would only benefit IT, and the functional units do not view IT as their partner.

This is where the PMO can have a great impact. One of the first jobs of the PMO will be to transfer ownership of some of these projects to functional or executive areas, assuming that the projects are worthwhile.

This scatter-gram should be created with several other factors included. For example, plot the projects using level of complexity of each project. If you need to show fast results, are you likely to accomplish this on large, complex projects or on smaller, simpler projects? Some organizations insist on measurable results within six months or else the project is not authorized.

The same plot should be created using the goals of the organization and the asset portfolio. If you are starting out with a lot of projects that are not linked directly to the organization's goals, this also provides a direction.

Table 19.1 Difference between Current PMO Models and Advanced Models

Traditional PMO	Next Generation PMO
Focus mostly on tactical issues	Focus on strategic and cultural issues
Science of project management	Art and craft of project management
Views organization as a "complex machine"	Views organization as a "complex ecology"
Emphasis on monitoring and control	Emphasis on collaboration
Provides tools similar to a precise "map" to follow	Provides tools similar to a "compass" that show the direction
Internal process focused	Focus on end products, customers and outcomes
Process driven	Business driven
Standard (heavy) methods and practices	Adaptable and flexible (agile) methods and practices
Based on rules; follow rules	Based on guiding principles; follow rules and improvise if needed
Defined, repeatable, managed and optimized practices	Adaptive and innovative practices
Focus on efficiency	Focus on effectiveness and innovation
Process leadership	Thought leadership
Heavy management and governance	Balanced management, governance and leadership

Table courtesy of J. Duggal, Projectize Group, www.projectize.com.

PMO MODELS

Early on in PMO history, the Gartner Group identified three PMO models as flourishing. They were the "Project Repository Model", "Project Coach Model", and "Enterprise PMO Model". These models still bring value today. However, much has been learned since their recognition.

There is a fourth model, which we term the "Deliver Value Now Model", that should not be ignored. This model is representative of the throughput, consultative model we have recommended throughout this book. None of the models will yield the "silver bullet" you may be seeking without significant teamwork from key stakeholders within the business to help. Table 19.1 characterizes the conceptual differences between current models and the value model. The value model is strategic, emphasizing results over process.

PROJECT REPOSITORY MODEL

This model PMO serves as a source of information on project methodology and standards. The model assumes the enterprise has embraced a cohesive set of tools for project design, management, and reporting. This model occurs most often in organizations that empower distributed, business-centric project ownership or with weak central-governance.

Benefits from the Project Repository Model include:

- Data gap identification
- Incremental risk management control as projects initiate and mature in the development cycle
- Bottleneck identification for all projects
- "Raising the bar" for delivery "goodness"

PROJECT COACHING MODEL

An extension of the repository model, this model assumes a willingness to share some project management practices across functions and uses the project management office to coordinate the communication. Best practices are documented and shared and project performance is monitored actively. Results are used to raise enterprise performance and train inefficient or new project managers.

Benefits from the Project Coaching Model include:

- Acts as trainer
- Consultant or mentor
- Source of information on project processes
- Often helps in project setup and post-project reviews

ENTERPRISE PMO MODEL

Of the three initial models, the EPMO Model is the most permanent, consolidated, organizational model and concentrates project management within the PMO. The mission of the EPMO implies direct management or oversight of projects. All project managers are staffed within the shared service and consigned to projects as needed. The vision of the EPMO assumes a governance process that involves the EPMO in all projects regardless of size.

The EPMO acts as a contracted project manager, assessing scope, allocating resources and verifying time, budget, risk, and impact assumptions. When this model was first observed, EPMO management style tended to be oriented toward cost containment and oversight and became very rigid and authoritative in nature. This approach brought on resistance in the project management communities. Project teams and functional executives began to shy away from using the EPMO to help them with support and ideas that would enable the project teams to complete their work.

Many firms have since learned that a consultative approach aimed at increasing project throughput and reducing project durations requires teamwork between the EPMO and the project teams. Also, the idea of a PMO owning the project managers, while having some very positive attributes, also has some significant potential negative effects. For example, the project management expertise and standards may not filter through to functional areas, where smaller, self-contained projects are carried out. Also, when significant portions of the projects are part of one functional area, that functional area may not feel as committed.

"DELIVER VALUE NOW" MODEL

This model puts organization goals first. Improvements in PM methodology are viewed as a means to an end, and not the end in itself. It is a holistic approach, embracing methods, skills and strategy that views project management as one piece of a bigger puzzle. It enables consistent motivation for the entire organization to seek out accelerated project deliveries, a stronger, more balanced project portfolio and better project performance.

Benefits from the "Deliver Value Now" Model include:

- A strong, well-balanced project portfolio that identifies up-to-date project workload, sponsorship, tactical progress, health status and current data gaps.
- A monthly "plan and forecast" that identifies portfolio opportunities and threats, top issues and risks, projects over/under budget, portfolio fiscal summary.
- A project prioritization model for all portfolio projects based on ability to form a Governance Board to direct model creation.
- Governance Board setup and/or modification that enables the force-ranking of the portfolio of projects.
- Project management training, coaching, and mentoring to identify audiences based on need.

PMO MANAGEMENT STYLES — STRONG MATRIX VS. WEAK MATRIX

The four PMO models do not always work well with a particular management matrix style. The "Project Coaching" Model may not work well where a strong matrix is required because it relies on voluntary acceptance of the coaching. If some projects are in big trouble and forced cooperation and prioritization from senior management is required, then coaching will simply not be enough to overcome the problems.

The other PMO models will work with either matrix style, but the results to be gained will be significantly less if the wrong choice is made. In choosing the correct PMO style, consideration should be given to the maturity level of the project management community. If rigor and discipline is required, a strong matrix environment will support it best.

If project delivery suffers from late projects and cost overruns, rigor and discipline is initially required with a planned move toward a consultative- and throughput-based PMO model once the PMO model has settled in. It is always better to have PMO buy-in from the work force than to force PMO work on them.

DETERMINING THE PMO MODEL
FOR YOUR ORGANIZATION

As you consider the PMO model that best fits your organization, several questions will need to be answered. Consider this checklist to help you in your initial considerations:

1. Who will initially be the main customers of the PMO? For example, if the main customer is the CIO, and the CIO's top concern is the inexperience of his project managers, the coaching model seems like a good place to start. If the main customer is the senior executive team, and the top concern is with two large multi-functional projects that are bleeding cash heavily, then the EPMO model will bring value initially. In either case, the stage should be set to transition to the "Deliver Value Now" model as the immediate problems are solved.
2. What is the maturity level of the project management community?
3. How well does the Executive Team work together for the good of the enterprise? It will be hard to implement an EPMO model if the executive team does not have its act together. The Coaching and Repository Models will work in this case, but their value is questionable. The "Deliver Value Now" Model has components (e.g., strategy) that are designed to change executive behavior as well as management behavior.
4. Where is the greatest pain? If the organization is suffering from constant conflicts over resources, reprioritization of projects, poor overall company strategy, poor project mix, and similar cross-project symptoms, then the "Deliver Value Now" Model will be much easier to sell to executives. On the other hand, if the greatest pain is in one or two projects or in one or two functional areas, the coaching model or EPMO model may initially bring the required value.

5. Will the PMO be able to deal with the intensity of missed delivery expectations from the executives and all of its implications? This is part of what the "Deliver Value Now" Model delivers. However, it takes a very strong PMO director to pull it off. If your organization is starting a PMO, but does not yet have a strong, executive-oriented leader, then one of the other models may be a better starting point.

6. Will the PMO be able to rescue troubled projects critical to the business? What if it cannot? Assuming that there are no obvious answers to a project in deep trouble, it takes a great deal of skill, experience and executive support to pull off a serious rescue. If these resources are not available to the PMO at the outset, then it would be suicidal to make this part of the PMO mission. This might be a case for starting with the Repository Model and transitioning as experienced staff are recruited. The data gained initially can be very useful as the model evolves toward more value.

7. Will the PMO be funded sufficiently and supported by the executives to meet the value opportunities and threats? A core group of the top project managers, mentors, trainers and a portfolio manager are necessary to launch a "Deliver Value Now" PMO. All of these could be wrapped up in one or two individuals at the outset, but they must be the right individuals. Also, to focus on the value opportunities, such individuals need the data administration and tool support of other experts.

GETTING STARTED

Whichever PMO model is chosen, it will be important to collect, assess and report on progress in meeting customer expectations on program/project delivery. This process is part of the required portfolio management discipline. This process is managed day-to-day through the PMO by collecting project status from participating business units. The portfolio management discipline includes all significant project initiatives — large, medium or small projects that have been identified as mission critical. The portfolio management process force ranks work based on known strategic direction (What do you want to achieve strategically for the current and subsequent fiscal years?).

RECOMMENDATION

The Gartner Group list was an excellent start. In today's economy, more value is needed now. Establishing a PMO that brings recognized value in the first six months of its existence is critical to the PMO's survival. This is why we strongly recommend that you go beyond the original models. As you begin to plan the PMO implementation, seriously consider establishing visible value to senior management from the get-go. Go after the low-hanging fruit that helps everyone win and the PMO will be on its way. Avoid being perceived as sitting in the "Ivory Tower of Project Management Excellence" looking down upon your domain. Build a PMO that will "Deliver Value Now."

SUMMARY

PMO organizations come in four major models. If the PMO model in play in your organization does not consider the needs of the first tier of PMO customers (and their behavior), we claim that this PMO is not likely to survive.

The Project Repository Model emphasizes tools and data. If the PMO becomes perceived as a "tool providing a solution", the need for the "tool" will diminish over time for various reasons and the PMO with it.

The Project Coaching Model provides training, mentoring and other help to project managers. In this model, the PMO is far removed from the executive level, and will eventually be seen as unnecessary overhead.

The Enterprise PMO Model takes over the project management direction and function. The centralized approach usually brings discipline and standardization to project management across the organization. It also brings resistance from functional areas that feel like they have lost control.

The Deliver Value Now Model is the holistic approach recommended in this book. It provides focus on the total project portfolio, linked to the organization's goals and assets. It is launched with full executive support. It takes a consultative approach to win over teams and functional management.

By focusing on the needs of the PMO customers as the primary priority, PMO field demand will begin to rise. This will mark the beginning of the PMO opportunity to help the organization's executives meet the goals.

QUINTILES TRANSNATIONAL CASE STUDY

INTRODUCTION

Quintiles Transnational Corp., incorporated in 1990, employs approximately 18,000 people in 39 countries and provides a full range of integrated product development and

commercial development solutions to the pharmaceutical, biotechnology, and medical device industries. The company also provides strategic services to support healthcare decisions and healthcare policy consulting to governments and other organizations worldwide. Supported by its extensive information technology capabilities, the company provides a broad range of contract services to help its customers reduce the time to market for a new drug or medical device. The company's commercial services focus on helping its customers achieve commercial success for their new product or medical device.

The company manages its operations through three segments: (1) the product development group, (2) the commercial services group, and (3) the informatics group. The product development group is primarily responsible for all phases of pre-clinical and clinical research. The commercial services group is primarily responsible for sales force deployment and strategic marketing services, as well as healthcare policy research and consulting services. The informatics group provides market research and healthcare information to pharmaceutical and healthcare customers.

THE PROJECT MANAGEMENT SUPPORT OFFICE OF THE CLINICAL DEVELOPMENT SERVICES UNIT

This case study focuses on the project office established within the clinical development services unit of the product development group. This unit is a global contract research organization, with project teams simultaneously executing over 1000 pharmaceutical development projects worldwide. In this environment, maintaining a standardized approach to managing projects is difficult. In September 2000, Quintiles' Clinical Development Services Division established Project Management Support Offices (PMSO) at Research Triangle Park, NC, Kansas City, MO, and Bracknell, U.K. to help meet this challenge.

These offices are led by experienced project directors and are staffed with project managers and support personnel. PMSO staff develop, introduce, and teach harmonized global project management procedures, author standard operating procedures, ensure the effective use of project management systems, and serve as project management consultants to operational groups.

The PMSO commitment to mass education is impressive. Quintiles' project managers follow a formal project management orientation program that is scheduled over a 50-week period and includes 21 training modules. As an example, over 600 employees (in the Americas, Europe, and Asia) have completed the 2-day "Managing Projects at Quintiles" course during the past year. This is one of the PMI Registered Education Provider courses that the PMO offers. As of the date of this case study, Quintiles is the only contract research organization that has been granted the distinction of PMI Registered Education Provider.

PMSO FUNCTIONS

By developing and teaching project management best practices, the PMSOs support Quintiles' global project operations by:

- providing project management consulting across the company
- helping select and administer improved project management tools and systems
- developing project metrics, project analysis procedures and risk management techniques
- facilitating project kick-off meetings, project reviews and lessons learned meetings and sharing the information from these sessions with all project teams
- serving as mentors and professional development resources for new project managers
- providing a bridge between the project management groups and operational services and supporting the company's business development efforts

STANDARDIZED METHODOLOGY

The PMO has established a global standardized project management methodology based on the PMI project life-cycle model. This includes well-established best practices, SOPs, work instructions, forms and templates, and other supportive material.

The PMO has recently completed evaluation of enterprise project management software tools and has selected a tool that best fits the company's needs. Senior management has authorized the purchase of this tool to be implemented globally.

Quintiles operates as a strong matrix organization in which project managers are assigned to project management groups and their team members reside in separate operational service groups. Thus, team members are rarely co-located. Therefore, in addition to the training described above, Quintiles Global PMSO took early initiatives to bring these teams functionally closer together. The PMSO introduced a standardized project life cycle that lists all steps from project initiation to project closeout with details of each service group's responsibilities in each phase. This "Project Life Cycle" diagram was organized according to the Project Management Institute's approach of dividing projects into phases based on the five standard processes; i.e., "initiation," "planning," "executing," "controlling," and "close-out."

Well-established best practices for managing projects were added to this life cycle, and "annotated check lists" for all phases of the project were prepared. All of this information was collected in a Lotus Notes database which provides direct/hypertext links to Quintiles' global standard operating procedures, work instructions, and the necessary forms, templates and other support materials needed for teams to conduct projects in an efficient standardized manner.

This "project operations database" was made available to global project team members, and extensive classroom training on proper use of the database was conducted. This database is currently being expanded to include clinical operations procedures and project processes from other service groups, i.e., drug safety, data management, bio-statistics, etc.

Employing a standardized approach to project management allows both Quintiles and project sponsors to have similar expectations for the operational procedures that will be employed during a clinical trial.

CONCLUSIONS

While hard metrics for this PMO are not yet available, it is clear, from the demands and repeat business, that Quintiles PMSO is having a significant, positive impact. The initial approach has improved work performance and communications, using a common language and database, across a broad geography and range of projects.

Contributors: Steve Unwin, Global Business Manager; Douglas Call, Sr. Director, Project Management Support Office

QUESTIONS

19.1   Discuss the four PMO models and their primary benefits.

19.2   Explain what the PMO's first priority should be, regardless of which model is chosen, as it is launched within the work place.

19.3   Compare the model selection for PMOs in a for profit organization vs. a non-profit organization. What are the issues?

19.4   Discuss the primary benefits of a strong and weak management matrix and which PMO model aligns better with certain work place characteristics.

20

PMO ROLES AND RESPONSIBILITIES

As a PMO begins to define its objectives, it needs to consider what services it will provide to meet those objectives. It must also assess when in its implementation schedule it will provide these services. The services that are required dictate the various roles and responsibilities. Table 20.1 outlines the typical services that are part of a comprehensive PMO structure. Each service provided will require some level of staff support.

PMO EXECUTIVE

Role: This person leads the development of the PMO value proposition. He or she leads the PMO strategically and is key to gaining organization-wide support.

Responsibilities: PMO charter development and implementation; ensuring all PMO activities are driving bottom line value; buy-in and involvement of executives; buy-in of all project and resource managers; PMO staffing; approval of monthly forecast and work plan report; PMO staff retention; approval authority on project management contracts for enterprise-wide tools, training, and consulting; PMO annual budget development.

Value: Measured by how much documented value is brought to the organization by applied PMO processes and tools. Normally, this is viewed in comparison to the PMO investment.

Table 20.1   PMO Services

Portfolio Management	Consulting & PMO Services	Training	Admin./ H.R.	Archives
Project portfolio information	Project rescues	Methodology	Project accounting	Information repository
Asset, strategic objectives and resource portfolios	Project acceleration, assessments, threats and opportunities, auditing, risk management	Tools	Operations planning and forecasting	Data integrity and security
Executive reporting and governance	Project management processes, tools, methodologies	Project management basics	Data collection and report distribution	Project document library/ knowledge management
Prioritization techniques	Mentoring	Certification	Asset tracking	Lessons learned
Staggering of projects	Help Desk	Teamwork	Materials and supplies	Closed contracts
Strategic resource management	Web portal/ information management	Advanced project management	Contract and change management	
Analysis	Resource recruiting	Scheduling software	Metrics, bonuses, career path, rewards and recognition	
Customer interface	Customer interface	Customer interface	Customer interface	Customer interface

Required Skills: Executive oriented; project management professional; has the ability to work well with all levels of the organization; should have cross-functional experience with project portfolio management and have a consultative background.

When: This is the first person hired into the PMO.

PROJECT PORTFOLIO MANAGER

Role: This person leads the development of the project, resource, asset and strategic objective portfolios; maintains the project, asset and strategic objective portfolios; reports to the PMO executive; financial and what-if analysis.

Responsibilities: Analyzes the project portfolio and makes recommendations to decision makers; balances the portfolio; evaluates and helps to implement processes to improve project flow and faster delivery; publishes the monthly forecast and work plan report to key stakeholders; manages the development and definition of the prioritization model; can be the backup to the PMO executive; often facilitates the governance meeting.

Value: Same measurement as PMO executive; secondary measurement is improvement in ROI in project portfolio.

Required Skills: Ability to navigate the minefields of executive sensitivity to report bad news; ability to work well with all levels of the business; portfolio management experience required for project portfolios over $25 million.

When: Part of the first group of people hired into the PMO.

Possible Career Path in the PMO: PMO Executive

PROJECT MANAGEMENT MENTOR

Role: Supports project rescues; works in the field assisting project teams to gain delivery speed; trains project managers to overcome the major deficiencies; conducts project assessments; reports to the PMO executive.

Responsibilities: Provides coaching and mentoring services to the project management community on top portfolio-related components; works with project sponsors and project managers to identify project delivery opportunities and threats.

Value: Same measurement as PMO executive; secondary measurement is monetarily identified in overcoming project team threats and opportunities resulting directly from mentoring guidance.

Required Skills: Ability to work well with all levels of business; consultative in nature and duties; should be a certified Project Management Professional (PMP) and have complete grasp of PMI PMBOK® fundamentals; ability to work in high stress situations with business partners of the PMO

When: At least one mentor should be part of the first group of people hired into the PMO.

Possible Career Paths in the PMO: Project Portfolio Manager, PMO Executive

PROJECT MANAGEMENT TOOL MENTOR

Role: Provides technical leadership, coaching and mentoring on all PMO tool utilization. This includes scheduling software application. Reports to the Project Management Mentors.

Responsibilities: Ensures the integrity of all data captured through the supported PMO tools; responsible for the competence of all project managers, resource managers and team members in PMO tools and applications; helps with project rescues in rescheduling work loads and expertise in the scheduling tool.

Value: Same measurement as PMO Executive; secondary measurement is data integrity and completeness.

Required Skills: Expert in scheduling tools; quick learner on software packages; has the ability to work well with all levels of the business; should have complete grasp of PMI PMBOK® fundamentals; ability to work in high stress situations with project team partners.

When: Part of the first group of people hired into the PMO.

Possible Career Paths in the PMO: Project Management Trainer, Project Management Mentor

HELP DESK SPECIALISTS

Role: Customer service; supports the project management community service requests for assistance.

Responsibilities: Answers and tracks field requests for assistance from project management community.

Value: Same measurement as PMO Executive; secondary measurement is responsiveness to customer help desk calls.

Required Skills: The ability to work well with all levels of the business; a complete grasp of PMI PMBOK® fundamentals; trained in all PMO standard tools and methodologies; excellent communication skills, ability to translate technical jargon into simple concepts.

When: Can be part of the first group of people hired into the PMO; should be no later than early in second six months of PMO implementation schedule.

Possible Career Paths in the PMO: Project Management Tool Mentor, Trainer, Project Management Mentor

RESOURCE PORTFOLIO MANAGER

Role: Oversees resource portfolio, including strategic resources; works with Project Portfolio Manager to help balance the portfolios; seeks to implement resource portability among functional units.

Responsibilities: Full and correct utilization of the organization's strategic resources; tracks resource utilization trends in alignment with portfolio objectives; assists project management community in locating just-in-time resources.

Value: Same measurement as PMO Executive; secondary measurement is utilization and throughput per week of the organization's strategic resources; primary PMO executive measurement should motivate this person to reduce delays caused by unavailable non-strategic resources.

Required Skills: Ability to work in high stress situations with project team partners; strong negotiation skills.

When: Should be part of the second group of people hired into the PMO.

Possible Career Paths in the PMO: Project Portfolio Manager

METHODOLOGY SPECIALIST

Role: Works with project teams in the application of the project management methodology.

Responsibilities: Assesses team's methodology usage for method compliance and associative risk management for all key projects. Works with Project Management Mentor to identify and overcome obstacles and resistance.

Value: Same measurement as PMO Executive; secondary measurement is percentage of project management community claiming that methodology is worthwhile.

Required Skills: Should have a strong background in PMI/PMBOK® concepts and their application in the workplace. Ability to teach concepts to work teams. Certified as a Project Management Professional (PMP®); must be able to work with business sponsors and their project teams in project startups.

When: Should be part of the second group of people hired into the PMO. Could be brought in early if the work environment has very low project management maturity.

Possible Career Paths in the PMO: Project Management Mentor, Trainer, Resource Portfolio Manager

PROJECT MANAGEMENT TRAINER

Role: Works with project teams, functional units and other organizations to provide and arrange project management training.

Responsibilities: Teach project management basic and advanced concepts.

Value: Same measurement as PMO Executive; secondary measurement is the agreed upon financial impact of the training, signed off by sponsors or functional executives.

Required Skills: Professional training experience.

When: Should be part of the second group of people hired into the PMO. Could be brought in at the first six months if work environment is low project management maturity.

Possible Career Paths in the PMO: Methodology Specialist, Project Management Mentor

DATA ADMINISTRATOR

Role: Constructs the monthly forecast and work plan report; document librarian; supports all PMO role players; provides primary support for the portfolio manager.

Responsibilities: Ad hoc reporting; PMO data repository processing and integrity; review of portfolio project status reports and schedules for data completion.

Value: Same measurement as PMO Executive; secondary measurement is the customer satisfaction with information (not data) provided.

Required Skills: Ability to work in high stress situations with project team partners.

When: Should be part of the first group of people hired into the PMO.

Possible Career Paths in the PMO: Help Desk Specialist, Methodology Specialist

SUMMARY

Staffing the PMO from the beginning will be dependent upon what the PMO is seeking to accomplish now vs. later. The PMO roles mentioned above were identified from a consultative PMO model that seeks to bring value by gaining project delivery speed (throughput model). This compares to a PMO model that seeks to bring awareness (oversight, cost containment model).

Every role described in this chapter is from a value-based perspective. If the role has value for the PMO and the PMO customers, then the role should be created. If your PMO creates a staff position that is not contributing directly to the throughput of the organization, the executive team will quickly see it as unnecessary overhead.

Every member of the PMO should be measured primarily on achieving the goals of the PMO, which is increasing the measurable value of the project portfolio. Each team member has a secondary measurement, which is linked to achieving the goals of the PMO. This set of common measurements drives the PMO to function as a team, rather than to become bureaucratic process cops.

As the PMO adjusts and fits itself to the business model it serves, the PMO should be adaptive. The PMO should always be on the lookout for new ways to add value to the organization's bottom line.

QUESTIONS

20.1   Discuss the value of the PMO Executive role and the relationships this person must have within the PMO. Where will the challenges be?

20.2   Explain how a Data Administrator could become the PMO Executive someday.

20.3   Discuss how the Project Management Mentor and Portfolio Manager would work together.

20.4   Explain what PMO staff roles you would staff in the first six months and why.

20.5   Discuss who you would call in the PMO first to help with a project rescue and why.

20.6   As a Project Manager, who would you call for help in identifying preferred project management practices and, based on their measurement, what help would you expect to receive?

20.7   The PMO Resource Portfolio Manager would manage the resource portfolio. Explain the relationship with the Project Portfolio Manager in defining overall portfolio opportunities and threats and the impact this awareness could have on resource utilization.

20.8   Explain the value of the Project Management Mentor and list probable value opportunities.

20.9   Why is a PMO Help Desk important to the value proposition of the PMO?

21

INPUTS AND OUTPUTS
TO A PMO

Every PMO produces and receives information in various context, content and form in interaction with the project management community. Most PMOs work with a common set of inputs and outputs. In this chapter we identify common inputs and outputs for the PMO.

INPUTS

PROJECT STATUS REPORTS

Every project listed in the portfolio should have a matching and recent program/project status report. The program/project manager is responsible for producing this document and posting the document within the infrastructure established by the PMO for access by the authorized personnel.

Reporting status should be considered as an absolute tenet of project management discipline. Without consistent project status reporting, project risk increases with the lack of visibility to current progress of that initiative. The Project Sponsor should assume responsibility of ensuring that the project manager is reporting status within the stated reporting requirements. Elements within the program/project status report form should minimally contain the following:

- Program/project name
- Supply side project manager
- Business side project manager
- Planned start date
- Planned end date
- Actual or projected start date
- Actual or projected end date
- Delivery status (red, yellow, green)
- Fiscal status (red, yellow, green)
- Budget costs
- Actual costs
- Project predecessors (dependencies on other projects)
- Project successors (dependencies of other projects on this project)
- Primary strategic objective (in support of)
- Primary asset (in support of)
- Top three issues and status
- Top three risks and status
- Top three opportunities to accelerate project work
- Percentage of critical path/critical chain completed
- Percentage of buffers consumed
- Work accomplishment plans for next reporting cycle
- Requested help (what does the project team need to meet commitments?)
- Program/project manager signature
- Date reported
- Reporting period
- Trend information regarding common vs. special cause variation

PROJECT SCHEDULES

Program and project scheduling should illustrate two levels of delivery methodology. The first level should align to the PMI Project Management Body of Knowledge (PMBOK®) five processes life cycle — project initiation, project planning, project controlling, project execution, and project closing. The second level should align and comply with the PMO sanctioned project management methodology. The rigor and discipline of the PMO project management methodology enables the current work force understanding and language to be applied at the deliverable level of the program/project schedule with which they are technically comfortable.

Every initiative listed in the project portfolio should have a schedule created that contains current delivery targets in alignment with the two delivery methodologies mentioned above. Upon completion of the planning phase (PMBOK®), the schedule should be base-lined.

ISSUES REPORTS

Information in this input reflects some level of change that may jeopardize delivery expectations for one or more work elements in the schedule. Each reported issue should contain the following information:

- Program/project name
- Project manager
- Issue reported
- Person reporting
- Date reported
- Issue description
- Issue impact — description of impact to project and to specific work activities listed in the schedule
- Description of mitigation plans
- Solution priority (urgent, under control, awareness only)
- Expected resolution date

RISK REPORTS

Information in this input reflects change that may jeopardize or already has jeopardized delivery expectations for one or more work elements in the schedule. Each reported risk should contain the following information:

- Program/project name
- Project manager
- Risk reported
- Person reporting
- Date reported
- Risk description
- Risk impact — description of impact to project and to specific work activities listed in the schedule
- Description of mitigation plans
- Solution priority (urgent, under control, awareness only)
- Expected resolution date

TIME SHEET DATA

We urge a great deal of caution in using a PMO to gather detailed time sheet data from every project team member. On the surface, there are good reasons to have data. For one thing, the PMO can learn when employees are not being utilized on one project, and temporarily or permanently help to reassign them elsewhere. For another thing, some data is necessary to determine when certain resource pools are overloaded and could jeopardize project progress.

At the same time, there are two red flags to consider. First, when a central organization gathers detailed time sheet data, team members view this as a measurement. Immediately, they typically play games to ensure that they look busy, even when they are not. The detailed data is often erroneous.

The second red flag concerns the amount of time required to obtain time sheets every week vs. the value provided. Is there a better way to meet the objectives? We believe the answer is "Yes." If we stop measuring people on their utilization and we stop measuring people on their performance to individual task estimates, we can start to obtain valuable information on availability of people. Either the individual or his manager will look for ways to better utilize that individual's contribution to project goals. We want to change the mentality from "this resource belongs to a given silo or functional area" to "this resource belongs to the organization and we need to use this resource where it will do the overall organization the most good."

The better answer is to eliminate the measurements that de-motivate. Instead, educate and track the use of resources for the good of the organization. From a project manager's point of view, he or she should know if a task has started or finished. He or she also needs to know, for any task in progress, how many days are estimated to complete the task. From a resource manager's point of view, he or she needs to know if a resource is likely to finish a task early, to look for other useful work. He or she also needs to know if a resource is likely to finish a task late, to resolve other commitments for that resource. His or her needs can be met by the same data as for a project manager.

If you are still insistent on using time sheets, here is the information that some PMOs are tracking. Information in this input reflects work effort that has been applied to project work and/or non-labor activity such as sick time, vacations, etc. Time is normally reported weekly and contains the following information:

- Employee name
- Employee number
- Employee organization (could be cost center number)
- Date reported
- Period reported
- Work item
  - What day
  - How much time reported
  - If unfinished, how much time left to complete the work item
  - What project or task
  - Task status (complete, need help, etc.)
  - If non-productive time, what type
- Summarized hours reported

PMO HELP DESK CALLS (INCOMING)

Every PMO receives calls for assistance from the work force on how to apply project management techniques and tools. The PMO should study the nature of these requests for improving project management techniques, training, and tools. Data to collect from these incoming calls should include the following elements:

- Caller name
- Caller email address
- Caller department
- Date and time of call
- PMO person taking the call
- Call severity
- Call description
- Was problem resolved
- Follow-up person assigned
- Date follow-up person was assigned
- Description of resolution

TROUBLED PROJECTS

From time to time, the PMO will be approached to rescue a failed or failing project. As these situations occur, it will be very important to the PMO to ensure that it has collected initial data about the project in question. As the PMO is approached to rescue the project in question, all eyes will be on the PMO in how it handles the sensitivity of the situation. Failure to react correctly can cost the PMO significant credibility within the workforce inclusive of the management team. Therefore, the PMO should collect the following minimum data elements:

- Project name
- Current business unit sponsoring troubled project
- Current supply side project manager
- Current business side project manager
- Current project sponsor
- Planned delivery date
- Estimated-to-complete work hours to deliver project
- Description of the problem
- Copy of the project schedule and related artifacts (for review)
- Project portfolio current force rank
- Assets impacted (from asset portfolio if known)
- Primary strategic objective supported
- Sunk project costs

- Remaining project budget
- Project team members and contact information
- Succeeding dependent projects
- Top three to five risks
- Top three to five issues
- Last several project status reports

TRAINING

If your PMO is offering project management training, enrollment information will be necessary. The following minimum enrollment data should be collected for training enrollment:

- Person enrolling (with contact information)
- Course name and code for which person is enrolling
- Cost center of person attending training
- Project management career goal
- Date of course
- Supervisor of person enrolling (you may want to validate authorization)
- Date of training
- Location of training

STRATEGIC OBJECTIVES FOR FISCAL YEAR

This information is critical for the PMO, as this data is key building information for all of the portfolio management processes. Information that the PMO must minimally collect whenever this information is created or modified follows:

- Strategic objective description
- Primary business unit owner of this strategic objective (if known)
- Strategic objective fiscal year budget (development monies for all projects in portfolio)
- Force rank of strategic objective (compared to other strategic objectives)
- Prioritization allocation percentage (based on a total of 100% and comparative to other strategic objectives) (this item is used in the project prioritization template and processes)
- Planned start date for initiating project work for the strategic objective
- Planned end date for completing all development work in the strategic objective

LIST OF BUSINESS ASSETS

Inventorying all known business assets is essential to ensuring the investments in improving assets are correctly directed in the fiscal year. Minimal data to be collected by the PMO includes the following elements:

- Asset name
- Asset functional unit owner and contact data
- Asset manager and contact data
- Date asset created (or date to be created)
- Current asset investment
- Current force rank of asset
- Primary strategic objective the asset supports
- Products and/or services the asset supports directly
- Products and/or services the asset supports indirectly
- Planned budget improvements for asset in fiscal year
- Top three asset risks in fiscal year

OUTPUTS

PROJECT PORTFOLIO

Contained within the project portfolio are the following data elements:

- Program/project description
- Force rank
- Current status (red, yellow, green)
- Sponsoring business unit
- Project sponsor
- Business-side project manager (if this person exists)
- Supply-side project manager
- Project planned start date
- Project planned end date
- Project baselined start date
- Project baselined end date
- Project actual start date
- Project actual end date
- Project planned budget
- Project actual costs (to date)
- Estimated costs to complete
- Project predecessors
- Project successors
- Primary strategic objective supported
- Primary asset supported

RESOURCE PORTFOLIO

This information can be used to spot resources coming available and aggregated to increment resource utilization rates applied to productive work. Contained within the resource portfolio are the following data elements:

- Resource pool name and contact information
- Resource job title
- Resource manager and contact information
- Resource utilization rate to date
- Functional unit assigned
- Force rank (strategic resource identification)
- Primary project assigned
- Primary strategic objective supported
- Primary asset supported
- Current resource status (red, yellow, green)

ASSET PORTFOLIO

Contained within the asset portfolio are the following data elements:

- Asset description
- Force rank
- Status (red, yellow, green)
- Sponsoring business unit
- Asset manager
- Supply-side project manager
- Asset planned budget
- Asset actual costs (to date)
- Current asset value in dollars
- Estimated costs to complete improvements
- Primary strategic objective supported
- Primary projects providing improvements

STRATEGIC OBJECTIVES PORTFOLIO

This process reports current progress of projects completed toward achieving identified strategic objectives. The following data elements are contained within the strategic objectives portfolio:

- Strategic objective description
- Force rank
- Status (red, yellow, green)
- Sponsoring business unit
- Strategic objective sponsor

- Strategic objective planned development start date in fiscal year
- Strategic objective planned development end date in fiscal year
- Strategic objective baselined development start date in fiscal year
- Strategic objective baselined development end date in fiscal year
- Strategic objective actual development start date in fiscal year
- Strategic objective actual development end date in fiscal year
- Estimated costs to complete
- Strategic objective predecessors
- Strategic objective successors
- Primary strategic objective initiative
- Primary asset supported

INTEGRATED PORTFOLIO

This process reports a consolidated view of initiatives from all participating portfolio types. This is a way of grouping projects or strategic objectives that are in support of a broader initiative. Typical data elements are:

- Initiative name
- Consolidated force rank
- Consolidated prioritization score
- Primary strategic objective supported
- Primary asset supported
- Status (red, yellow, green)
- Sponsoring business unit
- Project sponsor
- Business side project manager (if this person exists)
- Supply side project manager
- Project planned start date
- Project planned end date
- Project baselined start date
- Project baselined end date
- Project actual start date
- Project actual end date
- Project planned budget
- Project actual costs (to date)
- Estimated cost to complete
- Project predecessors
- Project successors

OPERATIONS PLANNING AND FORECASTING REPORT (MONTHLY)

This cyclical publication is a collection of various reports that explain the current state of affairs relative to the fiscal year plan. The following components comprise the minimum reporting of this publication (the PMO may not provide some of the portfolio reports and thus these specific portfolio reports are included).

- Executive Summary — Fiscal Year Plan Analysis YTD
- Project Portfolio and Status Report for the Reporting Period
- Asset Portfolio and Status Report for the Reporting Period
- Resource Portfolio and Status Report for the Reporting Period
- Strategic Objectives and Status Report for the Reporting Period
- 30/60/90 Day Project Delivery Outlook — Opportunities and Threats
- Top Issues for the Reporting Period
- Top Risks for the Reporting Period

TRAINING

The PMO should publish a list of offerings (either approved by the PMO and/or offered through the PMO). We are seeing more evidence of learning management systems — an environment to offer, enroll, and track the officially sanctioned training program of an entire organization. These offerings should be designed to improve delivery acceleration within scope and budget and critical PM thinking. They may also be designed to offer a PM career path through the organization. The following training categories are typical of most project management environments. These courses include:

- Project Management Basics — Follows Project Management Institute PMBOK® standards
- Project Management Advanced Techniques — Leading project teams towards successful and accelerated project delivery
- Project Management Tool Training — Learning how to use available tools to accelerate project delivery and avoid delivery threat
- Project Sponsor Training — Teaching a sponsor his or her role and responsibilities in meeting organization goals and supporting and accelerating project work
- Project Manager Training — Helping a PM build a career and accelerate projects
- Project Team Member Training — Critical thinking and communications skills are important
- Portfolio Management — Supporting executive decision-making and improving the ROI on a project portfolio
- PMO — Training for PMO members to help them do a better job, and for prospective PMO members

RESOURCE ASSIGNMENTS REPORT

This report is based on project schedule data contained within the PMO tools. The following minimum data should be reflected in this report:

- Date of report
- Name of resource pool
- Resource department
- Assigned projects (1–n)
- Number of resources available and percentage utilization trend
- Project force rank
  - By month (1–n)
    - Planned hours (days) to be worked
    - Actual hours (days) worked
    - Estimate to complete hours (days)
    - Hours (days) remaining to be worked
    - Total project hours remaining to be worked per resource pool

PRIORITIZATION WORKSHEET

Program and project managers complete this worksheet upon changes that influence prioritization. Typical data requirements in this document include:

- Program/project name
- Name of business side project manager
- Name of supply side project manager
- Summarized prioritization score
- Date prioritization template completed
- Strategic objectives (1–n)
  - Scalable measures per strategic objective (0–5) with defined measures that are quantitative or qualitative
  - Strategic objective weighting from 1 to 100%
- Risk factors (1–n) as above

EPM TOOL MANAGEMENT USER'S GUIDE

This handbook explains the how-to of using the standard Enterprise Project Management tool.

PROJECT MANAGEMENT METHODOLOGY USER'S GUIDE

This handbook explains the project management methodology and its application.

PMO ORGANIZATIONAL WEB SITE

This is the primary reference site for PMO support. Normally various PMO announcements, templates, standards, etc. are available through this output.

SUMMARY

The inputs and outputs of the PMO are normally aligned with the value model of the PMO. Developing the reporting and data collection and using it to provide meaningful information to all stakeholders raises the value proposition of your PMO to its customers.

Many of the inputs and outputs mentioned in this chapter are standard fare for most PMOs. Best practice in portfolio management processes is being defined on a regular basis as new EPM tools and capabilities continue to evolve. Our guidance to the PMO is to develop the input and output processes that it needs now. Ask yourself what is the absolute minimum amount of data with which to start. Remember that providing data, for most people, is viewed as an unnecessary overhead and it is initially resented.

Look closely at the PMO value proposition and develop action plans to implement the necessary processes. The objective of the PMO should always be to help grow the business. The PMO can only achieve its mission if it can incrementally raise the visibility of project progress over the life cycle of project delivery. This is the bread and butter of the PMO. All PMO support should be aligned to achieving this value.

QUESTIONS

21.1   Describe the difference in inputs and outputs between a PMO that is customer-focused vs. a PMO that is oriented to enforcement of standards.

21.2   What outputs will a Governance Board need from the PMO to assess status and why?

21.3   Explain the relationship of strategic objectives information to PMO outputs. Explain how executives might be operating today without this information.

21.4   Based on the inputs and outputs described above, what is your opinion of the most important (top one to five) inputs and outputs of the PMO and why?

22

PMO MEASUREMENT SYSTEM

There are three types of measurements that a PMO must implement to drive correct behavior. One measurement system is required for the PMO organization itself, to keep it focused on those improvements that are good for the organization. The second measurement system is for project teams, to drive behavior that brings drastically improved project results. The third measurement is for the executives, to stop fights over resources and ensure the selection and correct prioritization of the right project mix.

MEASURING THE PMO

"The purpose of a measurement system is to drive the parts to do what is good for the system as a whole." *

This piece of wisdom suggests that we must have clear measurements from the outset for the PMO, or for anyone charged with improving project performance in any organization. When an organization sets its goals for the year, projects are the main vehicle to accomplish those goals. The more

---

*Dr. Eliyahu M. Goldratt, Theory of Constraints Self Paced Learning Program (Goldratt Satellite Program), May 1999. See Bibliography for further information.

projects completed, the better the chances of meeting or exceeding those goals, but they must be the right projects.

When determining measurements, we want to avoid game-playing. It is very easy to implement measurements that will do no good for the organization. For example, if we simply measure how many projects are completed annually, the PMO could take big projects and break them down into multiple smaller projects to meet its measurement. In this case, nothing positive has been accomplished for the organization.

If we measure based on the Net Present Value (NPV) accomplished from projects, there is a large chance of distortion based on the way that NPV is determined today. We see many projects that do not even have an NPV justification. In many other projects, the NPV bears no resemblance to reality. The project NPV is sometimes a fantasy that would not stand up to financial audit.

A PMO provides many separate values to its customers. The values should show up in three major elements of a measurement system:

1. Reduced project cycle times
2. More projects completed during the fiscal year with the same resources
3. More tangible contribution to the organization's goals, in terms of reduced costs, increased goal units (revenues or some other measurement), and better ROI

From these desired values, there are three key measurements for the PMO. The correct approach is driven from the factors and ratios using these factors.

1. **Project Net Goal Units** — If the PMO is successful, the volume of goal units should increase from year to year. This should come from more projects being completed, better management of resources, fewer overruns, etc. Goal units could be net profit dollars, net present value dollars, shareholder value units, or other tangible measurement units.

2. **Project Cycle Time, in Days** — The shorter the combined cycle time of all projects, the more projects the organization can complete. The shorter the cycle times, the faster the investment is returned to the organization. The current project cycle times represent an inventory of time that is being invested in projects. If you can use the same inventory to complete more projects faster, the return on investment increases.

3. **Number of Projects Completed** — If the organization uses a standard definition of a project and does not play games, then the PMO should help the organization perform more projects without increasing resources.

Table 22.1   Project Value Metrics

	2001	**2002**
Goal units	$90,000,000	$120,000,000
Total cycle time	30,000	20,000
Value days	$3000	$6000
Number of projects	30	40
Average cycle time	1000	500

The combination of the first two factors is a ratio we call Project Value Days. It is the total project goal units from all projects expressed as a numeric value, divided by the total number of days duration of project cycle time required to generate those value dollars. It is the value of each day invested in a project. If the PMO is doing its job, this value should increase over time. For example, see Table 22.1. In this sample organization, the company attributed $90,000,000 net increase in goal units to the projects it implemented. Assume that the total days duration of all projects combined was 30,000. Then the Project Value Days works out to $3,000. Every day the organization invested in projects contributed $3,000 to the organization's goals.

If, in the year after the PMO is implemented, the project net goal units increases to $120,000,000 and the total days of project cycle time decreases to 20,000, then the project value days have doubled to $6000. Every day that was invested in a project contributed $6000 to the organization's goals.

This measures the impact that the PMO must have on the organization. Remember that the projects themselves are being managed today without a PMO. To say that the PMO is adding value to the process, we must have this ratio (or something equivalent) improving each year.

It would also make sense to perform an annual audit, and to use planned and actual Project Value Days measurements. Sometimes, the results of a project are not known until several months (or longer) after the project is implemented.

Another measurement is the number of projects completed. The assumption is that most organizations have more valid projects in waiting than they have the resources to complete those projects. Therefore, if current projects can be accelerated, and the PMO can also help to eliminate wasteful practices, then the resources will be freed up earlier to work on other projects. Also, a PMO using the good practices of the PMBOK® should be able to prevent badly chartered projects from being initiated, as well as reduce rework. Therefore, a value-driven PMO should have a significant impact on the number of projects completed.

There is an inherent danger, though, in measuring the number of projects completed. By changing or interpreting the definition of a project, the people being measured could claim that one big project is really two or three intermediate projects. The definition of what comprises a project must be clear and consistent from year to year, to draw benefit from this measurement.

Looking at the last measurement in Table 22.1, we can derive the average cycle time per project. This figure is just one other way of looking at the value a PMO can bring to an organization. The sooner a project completes, the sooner the value is returned to the organization. A PMO could argue that we should not compare this year's projects to last year's projects on cycle time because the projects themselves are different. For example, what if this year's projects are all more complex than last year's projects? Then the PMO might argue that the average cycle time per project could legitimately be longer than last year. However, if the purpose of the PMO is to help complete project work more quickly, then we claim that even if the projects are a little more complex on average, the average cycle time should still decrease. Over an entire portfolio, the averages should be a valid measure.

In Table 22.1, we see that the organization completed an additional 10 projects in the second year (going from 30 to 40 projects completed). At the same time, when you consider the decrease in total cycle time, the average cycle time per project went from 1,000 days (30,000 days total cycle time divided by 30 projects) to 500 days (20,000 days total cycle time divided by 40 projects). Assuming that the figures are audited and not the result of game playing, this is a sign of a PMO doing its job.

With this kind of a measurement in place, the executives will feel much more secure that the PMO will not be just another bureaucracy, but a vibrant entrepreneurial organization that will drive the company forward quickly in its quest for project management excellence and maturity. Further, PMO advocates should consider putting part of their earnings on the line to achieve meaningful results, at least after the PMO's first year of existence.

With this kind of measurement proposed by the PMO advocates, well thought out in advance, the idea of implementing a PMO should be accepted more quickly by executives in search of meaningful ongoing improvement in their organizations.

Once the PMO is operating with the correct driver, the question is how to cause project teams to constantly look for opportunities to accelerate projects and to avoid threats of delays. The rest of this chapter provides an answer to that question.

MEASURING PROJECT TEAMS

In Jim Collins' book, *Good to Great*, he refers to motivation in the companies that sustained three times the average market performance over 15 years. He describes good people as being self-motivated. His research shows that there were no high monetary or other special incentives that were different or in any way superior to those in other organizations. However, he declared that these companies did something different. They removed the demotivators — those measurements and policies that discourage good overall performance.

REMOVING THE MEASUREMENTS
THAT DESTROY MOTIVATION

Within organizations, we observe project measurements that are highly demoralizing and which discourage good team project performance. These measurements should be removed as quickly as possible. For example:

- *Finishing tasks within an allocated or standard time.* By definition, a project task time is variable, subject to many influences. The same work, completed in a physically different environment or on a different computer system, could easily take twice as long or half as long. Therefore, organizations that accumulate data on certain types of tasks, trying to set standards, and using those standards to measure team members, usually end up with Student Syndrome, Parkinson's Law and other distorted behaviors. Standard times also discourage people from thinking about how to do the task faster, better, or with less rework, since all of these distortions are built into the standards. Forcing people to spend time filling out time sheets to try to capture meaningless detailed data is also demoralizing. While this is sometimes mandatory, especially when working on government contracts, the organization should minimize the pain.
- *Utilization.* If you are paying an employee a fixed salary, does it make any difference to the company's bottom line if the employee is utilized 96% or 92%? As soon as an organization starts to measure people and take action based on utilization, we immediately observe utilization percentages that are abnormally high and grossly distorted. Within the multi-project environment, there are two types of resources — strategic and non-strategic. The strategic resource is utilized on most, if not all, projects. The strategic resource determines how many projects the organization can undertake and how

quickly those projects will be completed. Therefore, it is important to utilize those resources properly. For other resources, it is important to not utilize non-strategic resources 100%. You want to have protective capacity in the non-strategic resources to protect your utilization of strategic resources. For a further discussion, see Chapter 17.

■ Any measurements that discourage relay runner work ethic — For example, we have heard many resource managers tell a critical resource, "You're assigned to this project, but you had better not let your regular work slip." The message is clear. The project is second, third, or fourth priority. If a resource is assigned to a critical chain task of a project, those messages must change.

INDIVIDUAL OR TEAM INCENTIVES?

By definition, the benefits of a project are not realized until either a substantial portion or the entire project is complete. By definition, project work is team work. Some of the worst behaviors we observe within projects occur when people within a team point fingers at each other, or become jealous of individual recognition when the project itself is floundering.

While it is certainly true that some people on a team contribute more than others, the first priority is to encourage the team to behave like a team. In sports, if the team does not win most of the games, the major incentives disappear.

Another interesting aspect of teams is the contribution of individuals to the effort. At different times during the project, different team members can have a major impact. For example, in a football game, the defense can be the heroes in one quarter, while the offense might be the key contributors in another quarter. To win the game, each player must contribute.

Because we have seen more disagreement over what any one individual deserves, relative to a project, we encourage the use of team rather than individual incentives for project work. The incentive should be based on completing the project on time, on budget, and within scope. If earlier delivery of the project is meaningful, then there should be a definite incentive for early delivery.

If the organization will be using incentives, there is always a choice in terms of type of incentive. For the PMO, which will have a major impact on all projects across the organization, the executive team should consider stock incentives. For project teams who are often expected to work overtime hours and cope with significant stress, monetary incentives are usually appreciated. Note that incentives are not intended to be a substitute for recognition.

INDIVIDUAL AND TEAM MEASUREMENTS

Before having the right to impose a measurement on anyone, the PMO must ensure that there is a deep, common understanding of the system. The reason for a new measurement is to change behavior. Our experience is that before people will accept a new measurement, they must first agree on what the problem is with the old measurement.

In order to accelerate delivery of a quality project, we want to:

■ Educate the team on the tasks that make up the critical chain of the project
■ Reinforce the relay runner work ethic
■ Identify problems early
■ Reduce or eliminate waste

One of the most effective measurements we have seen in encouraging correct behavior is the weekly project status report, showing the critical chain and progress on the critical chain. This report indicates if the project is in control. If the project is not in control, the buffer management reports indicate which tasks are currently the culprits. The team remains aware of the critical chain and its importance to finishing the project on time. The team also remains aware of problems and is involved in solutions.

Another important tool is the senior management review meeting, using status reports as the measurement vehicle. When team members know that executives will be doing a review, they work hard to ensure that the information about the project is accurate, and that all known problems are being addressed. On the other hand, when team members see executives constantly fighting with each other over priorities or, worse, hear executives declare that their project is more important than what someone is working on, anarchy reigns supreme. If team members do not hear anything from executives, we often see that apathy reigns supreme. Senior management should review status on all major projects once or twice per month.

Finally, if every project has a written, accepted value to the organization, and team members are oriented at the beginning of the project to that value, this is an inherent measurement that can motivate team members significantly. When a team member knows that his project is tied directly to the organization's goals, he understands the cost of a delay as well as the meaning of an early finish.

When teams throughout an organization are working on dozens or hundreds of projects during a year, they often lose sight of what is important. The measurement system should keep the focus clear. Performing work on a project is not important. Finishing a project as quickly as possible is important. Meeting the organization's goals is important. That is what the measurement system must constantly reinforce.

EXECUTIVE MEASUREMENT

Executives have a huge stake and a decisive influence on the success of project management within their organization. They can help projects flow smoothly through the organization, or they can take actions that impede project flow. They can pick and sponsor lame duck projects or pet projects that will not contribute much or they can pick powerful projects that will keep the organization healthy year after year. They can work cooperatively with other executive team members or they can do their own thing, without regard to the dependent processes across the organization.

There are three major executive behaviors that we would like to change or improve:

1. Allow projects to be staggered according to the capacity of the organization's critical resource. In other words, stop pushing projects into the system, irrespective of the human capital available.
2. Perform strategic planning holistically. Ensure that the right projects are chosen with a balance between supply side and market side efforts.
3. Allow the Governance Board to control priorities.

The problem we see with many executive measurement systems is twofold:

1. Many measurements are functionally oriented, not holistically oriented.
2. Many measurements encourage sacrificing the long term for the sake of performance in the short term. When we ask why, we often find answers that should be serious red flags to investors and to the CEO.

A PMO that is forced to operate under such a defective executive measurement system will face constant frustration. It will be in the middle of fights between executives, where no one can ultimately win. This measurement nightmare must not be ignored. Part II of this book and the referenced texts provide some answers.

The Throughput Accounting and Measurement System described in Part II works beautifully to support a PMO and a holistic approach.

INPUT ON METRICS FROM THE WORLD OF PROJECT, PROGRAM, AND PMO MANAGERS

The Project Management Institute (PMI) Metrics Specific Interest Group (MetSIG) makes available its MetSIG Web site to general membership within the Project Management Institute (PMI) and Business Partners/Sponsors. PMI is an association of Project Managers, Project Engineers and people generally associated with Program and Project Management. PMI has a rapidly expanding membership base of approximately 100,000 members.

The MetSIG Web site provides a single repository for knowledge (incrementally growing) on project management metrics, across more than 40 business "Knowledge Categories." PMI MetSIG members pay $20 per year, which gives them access to this information. Content grows each month and membership reaches around the world.

A PMO director who becomes a member will find the following: PMO Project Management Metrics; best practices; latest portfolio management techniques; compelling business case information on the cost of "doing nothing" when selecting an EPM tool; online calculators; templates; benchmarks; CMM processes; PMO case studies; and Project Management Metrics Case Studies for profit and non-profit organizations.

The MetSIG Web site is located at www.metsig.org. If you are interested in a 5-day free trial or for further information, contact the MetSIG Knowledge Chair at Knowledge@MetSIG.org.

SUMMARY

To make a PMO successful, we need three measurement systems — one for the PMO, one for the project teams and associated resources, and one for executives. Each measurement is really just a different window into the organization's goals and how projects are being used to accomplish those goals.

The mission of a PMO is to drive more projects through faster, hopefully at lower cost, while meeting the budget and scope requirements. Table 22.1 illustrates the key measurements and ratios that determine how successful the PMO is, from one reporting period to another.

One key ratio is Project Value Days, an indicator of how much each day spent on a project is worth to the organization. Another key ratio is average duration per project. If the data used to produce these ratios is audited and accurate, and the PMO does not play games fudging the data, then these ratios should drive the PMO to increase the bottom line contribution of all projects.

For project teams and project managers, a PMO can accomplish a great deal by simply eliminating the demoralizing measurements that pervade projects and organizations today. Measurements such as finishing tasks on time or to a standard, or resource utilization percents can drive a lot of negative behavior.

Instead, the PMO should emphasize weekly team status meetings, highlighting the progress on the critical chain of project tasks and any inherent problems. In addition, executive reviews of all projects at least once per month will drive team accountability for meeting project goals. It also reinforces the importance of these projects, a motivator in itself.

Finally, executives must work under a holistic measurement system, one that encourages them to do what makes sense for the organization as a whole. At the same time, measurements that encourage optimizing one functional unit at the expense of another must be eliminated. The throughput accounting and measurement system discussed in Part II is an excellent beginning to the holistic approach.

QUESTIONS

22.1 What are some of the risks inherent in measuring a PMO based solely on the number of projects completed or on the net present value of projects, according to current standards?

22.2 How can the PMO avoid the risks described above?

22.3 How might a measurement drive individuals to accelerate project delivery?

22.4 The ratio of Project Value Days is made up of project goal units as the numerator and total project days duration as the denominator. How should the PMO influence each of these factors?

22.5 Is there a logical meaning to the Project Value Days ratio, or is it simply a numeric value that changes over time?

22.6 Many project managers might argue that trying to reduce average cycle time per project over time is meaningless. Why would they appear to have valid arguments? What assumptions are you attacking when you use this ratio?

22.7 If executives are operating with functionally oriented measurements and not holistic measurements, what problems should a PMO expect to encounter?

22.8 A team member is working on a critical chain task of a very important project. The executives will be reviewing this project next week. The team member is currently behind schedule on that task. How should the team member act, given the executive review next week?

22.9 When a PMO first comes into existence, much of the data required to determine Project Value Days and average cycle time does not exist. What is the PMO's role at startup, with regard to all of the measurements discussed in this chapter?

22.10 What are the three executive behaviors that a measurement system aligned with a PMO should drive?

22.11 True or false: Executives have only a minor influence on project team behavior and performance.

EPM TOOLS AND THEIR VALUE ON PROJECT DELIVERY

Many organizations are looking for better control over their project management environment. Executives have increasing concern about projects being completed in time to achieve their quarterly and annual goals. These premises help to create a developing market for project management tools that enables any organization to measure, control and manage the project data for which they are responsible. Most businesses want to apply this concept to all projects they perform. This is known as Enterprise Project Management (EPM).

THE COST OF "DOING NOTHING" OR THE VALUE OF EPM TOOLS

Consider the following business case information, which examines a company that does not use EPM tools and the growth opportunities lost by "doing nothing".

ASSUMPTIONS

1. 1000 work force members available to work on project teams
2. 100 program/project managers available

3. Expected completed projects over the next 12 months — 200
4. Average program/project development budget — $.5 million
5. Total fiscal year (12-month period) program/project portfolio size equals $100 million (200 × $.5 million)

JUSTIFICATION #1 — SUPPORT THE IMPLEMENTATION OF CORPORATE PROJECT MANAGEMENT STANDARDS

According to the Gartner Group (August 1, 2000), projects following a standard lifecycle are more often completed on time, on budget, and within scope.

Estimated Savings: 25% of 200 Projects (50 projects) × 5 People (per team) × $60/hour (labor rate) × 40 hours/week × 4 weeks = $2.4 million. Assumes time to market will be reduced by four weeks for 25% of all projects.

Verification: Baseline scheduling and cost estimates along with scope definition will be tracked and reported on a monthly basis through an EPM tool that aligns to standard project management rigor and discipline.

JUSTIFICATION #2 — IDENTIFY PROJECT RISKS AND (RESOURCE) CONSTRAINTS

PMO tools require project managers to examine their projects for risks, dependencies, constraints, and impacts on the business. Using rigorous standards to move projects from the planning to execution phase will reduce organizational costs.

Estimated Savings: 20% × 200 projects × 5 people × $60/hour × 40 hours/week × time remaining = $5.3 million. The Gartner Group estimates that proper risk identification will result in the cancellation of 20% of projects before the execution phase. Our savings assumes 40 projects (or 20% of current project portfolio) will be cancelled before execution begins.

Verification: The PMO will use the EPM tool to track the number of projects in the project portfolio that were cancelled because of risk and impact on the organization.

JUSTIFICATION #3 — PORTFOLIO REPORTING WILL ASSIST IN THE PRIORITIZATION AND DEPLOYMENT OF RESOURCES AND CAPITAL

Within 2 years, the enterprise should go from tracking less than half of the portfolio projects to more than 75%. Payback will occur from having better information to make decisions on the deployment and use of resources and capital. It is also driven by the visibility of key portfolio information to all decision-makers. The effect of this information should enable the portfolio of projects to accelerate their delivery.

Estimated Savings: Average aggregated budget of (200 active projects) projects in portfolio annualized equals $100 million. A 5% annual delivery improvement in time and budget for the projects in the portfolio brought on by raised visibility equals $5 million.

Verification: The Executive Team will recognize delivery improvements as reported in the PMO portfolio reports. Much of the information is available through EPM tools online. The executives can also view actuals to budget information.

JUSTIFICATION #4 — CANCELING PROJECTS NO LONGER VIABLE

The portfolio along with the PMO phase review will answer the question: "Where do category leading priority projects stand?" This information will at times lead to the canceling of the project due to changing conditions in the business and project. According to the Gartner Group, "project delivery rates directly impact customer satisfaction, IT's value to the business, the enterprise's competitive edge, market share and profitability. A project portfolio management capability includes a set of organization-specific metrics pertinent to project delivery."

Estimated Savings: Average cost of a cancelled project = $500,000 or annualized at 10 projects minus 50% sunk project costs cancelled for a total expected savings of $2.5 million. This assumes that the project portfolio along with the PMO phase review process assist management in making the decision not to implement a portfolio project based on organizational priorities.

Verification: The PMO will use the portfolio management process to review and identify the number of projects that actively follow the lifecycle and use the EPM project control tools in the everyday management of the projects.

JUSTIFICATION #5 — IMPROVING RESOURCE UTILIZATION

The progress reporting of all projects contained in an EPM tool along with resource assignments will enable the business to effectively predict resource assignment order of work and availability from the improved visibility of progress of all project initiatives competing for similar resources.

Estimated Savings: Average annual cost of a 1000 resources = 1000 user $\times$ 2080 hours $\times$ $60/hour = $124 million. Implementing project management rigor and discipline with tools should bring a minimum of 2% resource utilization return in first year after project management rigor and discipline with tools are implemented. Thus, $124 million × .02% = $2.5 million applied labor effort gained towards project portfolio work. This assumes that the resources must be paid for 12 months and that the 2% utilization gain will come from more projects completed and accelerated ROI from existing projects.

Verification: Project teams will use the resource project management and tools to review and identify the project data in alignment with the project portfolio.

"DOING NOTHING" OR VALUE OF THE EPM TOOL SUMMARY

In a $100 million portfolio, the combined benefit of an EPM tool and a PMO is difficult to separate. The tool alone will not result in the benefit because it takes effort to implement it and also to change people's behavior to use the tool and the information. However, in combination, the following summarizes the expected benefits in an average implementation:

1. Support the implementation of corporate project management standards = $ 2.4 million
2. Identify project risks and (resource) constraints = $ 5.3 million
3. Portfolio reporting will assist in the prioritization and deployment of resources and capital = $ 5.0 million
4. Eliminate projects no longer viable = $ 2.5 million
5. Resource Productivity Improvement = $ 2.5 million

Total annual opportunity, based on stated assumptions = **$17.7 million**

Change the parameters to fit your business and re-calculate the lost opportunity. Whatever result is calculated, the final tally will still be very compelling. Thus, the key question to answer is "How soon will you implement an EPM Tool?" Be ready to answer this question because the executives who must approve the recommendation will want to know.

CHOOSING AN EPM TOOL

We have given considerable attention to the PMO defining its value proposition to the organization. As the PMO determines which EPM tool vendor to select, the final decision should be driven by how well the tool supports the PMO value proposition.

Many issues will have to be considered in selecting the EPM tool solution for your organization. A common dilemma for organizations is determining whether to choose an EPM tool that complies with their IT infrastructure requirements or choosing an EPM tool that will best help the business grow. There are so many different EPM tool options in the market place today that choosing the right EPM tool fit can easily outweigh the IT infrastructure requirements. The question can be a political hot potato. Do you comply with the supply side business model or do you enable the business to take advantage of new capabilities that encourage faster growth? Consider the following 10 EPM tool requirements for your organization (in no particular order) to help you answer these questions:

1. **Easy to use** — Has an intuitive look and feel that enables anyone to find his way around as he applies the tool features. Tool should have strong online help features. Is the EPM tool as "easy to use" as common applications such as Microsoft Word?

2. **Implementation and conversion** — Consider how long the conversion period might be which includes actual end-user utilization. If you expect it to take longer than 90 calendar days to include your top projects, this is a major red flag. The EPM tool may be far too complex and you should consider looking for another product. Integration with your project management software files is a big plus.

3. **Organization project management maturity** — If the work force maturity level is low, you probably want a project management tool that matches the degree of user sophistication. In a low project management maturity work environment, a complicated tool will be met with major resistance. If your environment requires earned value functionality, the EPM tool you buy should have a working earned value feature function. Ensure that the earned value feature works or can be customized to work according to your organization's requirements.

4. **Cost of training** — Consider if you can conduct training yourself, or if outside vendors must constantly be called in. We suggest that the more flexibility you have in training, the better it will be for your organization in the long run.

5. **Portfolio management features** — Any product you are considering must have the ability to aggregate data for projects and resources. Resource data must have functionality that allows for multiple resource skills, job codes, and related cost rates.

6. **System connectivity** — The EPM tool must have the ability to easily interface with other systems such as Human Resources and Accounting, especially general ledger and time entry systems.

7. **Customer service** — Talk with the EPM tool users in several other customer sites to determine if the support levels are sufficient for your organization. Timely vendor support is essential, especially when the organization is relying on live information to run the project management business. In this case, it is much better if the vendor gives you a comprehensive customer list, where you can pick and

choose the reference checks, rather than receiving one or two customer names.

8. **Vendor financial status** — Check out the vendor's financial strength. In 2002, the EPM tool market was approximately $200 million. Competition among EPM tool vendors is extremely fierce. Some of these vendors may be experiencing cash flow or other financial difficulties. As an EPM tool is selected, consider if you want to own the source code if the vendor ceases operations.

9. **Web enabled** — This is an absolute must. Most EPM tool vendors have this ability. Having the ability to access project data from anywhere or to simply enter project time will help the project manager sooner understand project opportunities and threats. Some projects today require daily updating of task information. In virtual teams, this is practical with Web-based capability.

10. **Document Library** — Another absolute "must-have" requirement. Most EPM tools are built around a "single repository" database model that enables all project documentation to be aligned by project and with assignable security rights. Containing all the project intellectual property work products and associated deliverables adds significant value to the business. Where would you rather have project data, in someone's briefcase, a team member's hard drive, or scattered ad hoc on the LAN/WAN?

MICROSOFT PROJECT, WHY OR WHY NOT?

Microsoft Project is a powerful product, with extensive capabilities for both the single and multi-project environment. We are big fans of Microsoft Project as a project manager's tool. However, we have some reservations about its use as an EPM tool, based on the capability we have seen as it exists at the time of writing. Microsoft products are constantly changing and being enhanced. Therefore, we recommend that you validate current product features and capabilities to determine if our concerns are still valid.

If the PMO needs to manage project delivery data across the project management spectrum, for the benefit of a large group, we believe that there are some shortcomings. While Microsoft Project works well as input to an EPM tool, several PMO issues exist with using Microsoft Project as the EPM tool of choice for your work force.

1. **End-to-End Support:** Microsoft Project has traditionally lacked all the necessary components to enable end-to-end management of a project. An example of this is the Risk Component. The PMO will

have to buy licenses of software compatible plug-ins such as "Risk+" to help provide the tool with some of the necessary and basic features that the core software is missing. Another missing component is the systemic connectivity required to pass data to downstream systems. A third element where Microsoft seems to rely on third-party solutions is in the PMO dashboard and executive level reporting, especially in the portfolio management arena.

2. **System Connectivity:** Microsoft Project does not easily enable data flow from the point of entry into the project schedule to the final resting point of data in the general ledger. To our knowledge, Microsoft is not currently working on providing this capability internal to Microsoft Project. This means additional development, risk and costs to enable system connectivity through Microsoft Project. From a PMO perspective, this does not make good sense, given all of the other tools that will easily accept a direct and indirect data exchange from Microsoft Project.

3. **Tool Integration Within the Workforce:** Microsoft Project is designed for program and project managers to help them manage their assignments. While multiple programs and projects can be aggregated in one MS Project file, this is not the primary intent of the tool. However it is important to note that MS Project normally interfaces very well with most EPM tools.

While we have these reservations, it is also important to note that Microsoft does not have the financial risk that other tool vendors have. Microsoft also has sufficient resources to address these issues, if they decide to change their priorities. The real question is where will Microsoft decide to place its priority, relative to PMO requirements.

CURRENT EPM TOOLS

We are very grateful to Forrester Research Inc. for allowing us to reproduce their evaluation of the most popular EPM tools. Based on their comparison published in the May 2002, "Apps for Adaptive IT" report by Forrester researcher Tom Pohlmann, EPM tools were rated in the following categories:

- **Project Portfolio Management** — prioritization, business linkage, and organization budgeting
- **Resource Management** — skills matching, scheduling and measurement
- **Project Support** — project planning, management, and accounting

- **Workflow Support** — demand management and project collaboration
- **Service Procurement** — purchase of external, project-based services and contingent staff
- **Intangibles** — market viability, clients, reporting usability, non-project support

Table 23.1 is derived from Figure 7 in Forrester's report. Since this data is subject to change, we recommend that you visit Forrester's Web site at www.forrester.com or contact the Forrester customer research staff for current information.

VENDOR WEB SITES AND BRIEF PRODUCT DESCRIPTIONS

ARTEMIS (WWW.ARTEMISINTL.COM)

Artemis International Solutions Corporation provides enterprise-based portfolio, project and resource management software solutions, using Web-enabled technology.

CHANGEPOINT (WWW.CHANGEPOINT.COM)

Changepoint enables fee for service organizations (internal and external) to improve financial performance by maximizing operational efficiency, enabling total operational visibility and improving the performance and productivity of individual employees.

EVOLVE (WWW.EVOLVE.COM)

Evolve provides enterprise software for optimizing people and projects for IT and professional services organizations worldwide.

KINTANA (WWW.KINTANA.COM)

Kintana is an enterprise software company focused on enabling CIOs to execute their top three issues: cost reduction, business/IT alignment, and service delivery.

NIKU (WWW.NIKU.COM)

Niku builds enterprise application software for Services Relationship Management (SRM), software that helps companies align peoples' work with strategic priorities more efficiently.

Table 23.1   EPM Vendor Landscape

Vendor	Portfolio Management	Resource Management	Project Execution	Workflow	Service Procurement	Intangibles
PeopleSoft	○	●	◑	○	◑	●
Evolve	●	●	◑	◑	○	⊗
Systemcorp	◑	●	●	◑	○	○
PlanView	◑	◑	●	○	⊗	◑
Niku	◑	○	●	●	⊗	◑
Tenrox	○	◑	◑	●	○	◑
Changepoint	○	○	◑	●	⊗	●
Oracle	○	○	◑	○	⊗	●
Kintana	○	○	◑	○	⊗	●
Artemis	○	○	○	●	⊗	◑
Business Engine	○	○	●	○	○	○
Lawson	○	○	◑	◑	⊗	○
Primavera	○	○	●	○	⊗	○
Elance	⊗	○	○	◑	●	◑
NeoIT	⊗	⊗	○	◑	◑	○
Novient	⊗	●	○	○	⊗	◑
Pacific Edge	○	○	○	○	⊗	○
ProSight	◑	⊗	⊗	⊗	⊗	◑

Relative strength of functionality: ⊗ = Absent; ○ = Okay; ◑ = Strong; ● = Category leading.
Source: Forrester Research, Inc.

PACIFIC EDGE (WWW.PACIFICEDGE.COM)

Pacific Edge offers broad solutions that cover all levels of an organization. With Pacific Edge, project and portfolio managers can drill deep for project details while executives can step back and get a view of how all the organization's business initiatives are working together as a whole.

PLANVIEW (WWW.PLANVIEW.COM)

PlanView offers a solution that uses the Web to optimize value from an organization's staff and other investments. PlanView provides the integrated tools and process models to help improve performance on projects and other work and optimize the value from resources.

PRIMAVERA (WWW.PRIMAVERA.COM)

Primavera brings together the disciplines of strategic planning and project management, and provides a framework for effectively managing both the resources and the tactical plans for completing projects within its varied software options.

PROSIGHT (WWW.PROSIGHT.COM)

ProSight offers a flexible portfolio management software application, accompanied by related services that are designed to implement — and automate — the portfolio management process for today's extended, and sometimes fragmented, companies.

SYSTEMCORP (WWW.SYSTEMCORP.COM)

Systemcorp's PMOffice™ is an EPM solution that automates projects, people, and methodologies across an entire organization. Companies can organize all projects into portfolios, and instantly track all project deliverables, budgets, tasks, changes, risks, and issues from one central location.

SUMMARY

In choosing the EPM tool solution for an organization, evaluators should give significant consideration to how well the tool will deliver the value proposition discussed in this text. Many choices exist on the market today. Our general recommendation is that you choose an EPM tool solution that provides you with the most complete end-to-end solution possible. This implies a tool that will integrate all of the data in the organization's total project portfolio. By doing so, it will raise the visibility of project delivery opportunities and threats throughout your organization. Such a tool must be easy to use and have significant functionality in total portfolio management, resource management, and project tracking.

Understand the political culture and project management maturity level of your organization and take this insight into strong consideration as you recommend the favored vendor. The vendor's projected longevity is also vital. It is much easier for vendors to respond when their cash flow is strong and when they have customers. It is also much easier for a PMO to deliver more value when it has customers that are willing to use a tool. Make sure that the tool will deliver value to all users and not just to the PMO.

QUESTIONS

23.1 Discuss the value of an EPM tool.

23.2 Explain the five justifications for buying an EPM tool.

23.3 Discuss the 10 requirements to consider when choosing an EPM tool. Which of the 10 requirements are most important to your organization and why?

23.4 Explain why a "single repository" EPM tool is important for bottleneck identification.

23.5 Why might an organization choose "system connectivity" as a key requirement in selecting an EPM tool?

23.6 Discuss how work force project management maturity could effect the selection of an EPM tool.

23.7 Explain how important it is to consider selecting an EPM tool that complies with IT infrastructure policy vs. meeting current and future project management needs of the organization.

PMO, PMI, AND THE PMBOK®

THE PMI EFFECT

The Project Management Institute has spent a great deal of time in developing project management standards while supporting project management excellence everywhere. One of the major values of the PMI effort has been to standardize what is expected in project management applications and environments. As professionals, we are in our infancy in establishing guidelines for excellence in supporting the entire project management organization, from executives through all organizational levels. The concepts of what a PMO should do, how portfolio management should be performed, and other multi-project considerations need to be extensively developed. Because of the gap, project managers lack models and support mechanisms to meet their critical needs within the organization.

THE OPPORTUNITY

Membership in the PMI today numbers almost 100,000. PMI is organized into 200+ local chapter components, 35+ specific interest groups (SIGs), and a few knowledge area colleges.

More and more members and non-members are surfacing who must establish standards for PMOs. They are wondering how to best provide the inside support value for the program and project managers who follow PMI standards. The opportunity for improvement is very visible to those who work in the PMO. Already, the PMO SIGs within PMI are growing and becoming more visible.

THE NEED

The current state of affairs in the project management profession, brought on by the declining worldwide economy, is contributing to a significant loss of project management jobs. Many project managers who had no one to go to for help when they needed it most are losing their battle. In 2001, more than 1,000,000 people lost their jobs through no fault of their own in most cases. What if a "Deliver Value Now" PMO had been in place within their organization? Would businesses be eliminating these same jobs? PMI now has an outstanding opportunity to show organizations the opportunity they are missing.

WHY PMI CAN

The project management profession is in high demand in other areas of the world, such as China, India, Japan, and Europe. Many projects today span continents. Currently, PMI is embryonic in its presence outside of North America. Watch out when the PMI influence becomes stronger. The globalization of the world economy is an important contributing factor to PMI future value. More people will be united within PMI for the common cause and good and this will mean more resources to tackle common problems and issues.

There are other reasons why PMI can become the true standard bearer in the PMO world. They include:

1. Largest project management association worldwide
2. Recognized standard in the Project Management Body of Knowledge (PMBOK®)
3. Organization PMOs and software vendors are aligning project delivery within the PMBOK® guidelines
4. Growing trend in business hiring requirements to hire project managers that are PMI Project Management Professional certified (PMP®). If you don't have your credential today and you expect to be a project manager throughout your career, this credential is in-

creasing in importance. Your organization may require this in the future.

5. Significant volunteer leadership team around the world
6. Strong communication infrastructure to membership
7. PMI reflects changing trends in project management. People from around the world attend PMI conferences to find out what is new and emerging in project management.

IS PMBOK® SUFFICIENT FOR THE PMO?

PMBOK® is the generally accepted standard for project management practices. Defined within the PMBOK® are nine knowledge areas. They are:

1. Project Integration Management
2. Project Scope Management
3. Project Time Management
4. Project Cost Management
5. Project Quality Management
6. Project Human Resource Management
7. Project Communications Management
8. Project Risk Management
9. Project Procurement Management

The nine project management knowledge areas are well defined. Senior Management Oversight, PMO Management, and Portfolio Management need to be added and developed extensively. If an organization simply follows the nine knowledge areas and the guidelines conveyed, project delivery will definitely improve over time. How fast gains are made becomes the question.

Without considering the three additional areas, it is likely that functional unit isolation will remain. The need for the PMO to have more of a presence in PMI's genre is critically important, now more than ever.

PMI, PMBOK®, AND THE PMO — SEEKING ALIGNMENT

Many PMOs have established company-based intranet Web sites that have PMI/PMBOK® related tools and templates to take advantage of pre-existing PMI knowledge among the user community and thereby saving training costs.

PMOs seeking to build value and internal customer acceptance would do well to place PMI/PMBOK® alignment and support in their value model. Over time, even in a low maturity situation, workforce alignment with the PMO will become more and more consultative in nature rather than just oversight. Increasing demand for PMO services by a PMI centric user community is a contributing factor to sustaining the PMO year after year.

SUMMARY

It is important that PMOs have an international public champion to model after. PMOs today are still awaiting the emergence of the PMO champion so they can replicate the model. The best opportunity for a PMO champion to emerge will be from within the PMI standards community. Various PMI components exist today that are working to develop and identify PMO standards such as the PMO SIG (www.pmi-pmosig.org) and the Metrics SIG (www.metsig.org). These two groups are staffed completely with volunteers. The objectives of these two components will bring incremental improvements, but more PMI involvement is required.

It is our recommendation that PMOs everywhere endorse a central project management association. PMI is the largest project management association of its kind with the best chance of making a difference for the PMO community. The need exists today. Alignment and recognition of that need by both sides will be critical to fulfillment. We hope that PMI will find ways to bring out the value proposition of a PMO so PMOs can replicate at will. PMOs want to know if what they are delivering is correct. PMOs have no central source on PMO standards to the degree of influence that PMI now has. We hope that books such as this one, with further debate and discussion, will help PMI to close the gap in knowledge.

QUESTIONS

24.1   What are the needs for PMI to help PMOs?

24.2   What value does the PMBOK® bring to a PMO?

24.3   What kind of help do the PMO and Metrics Special Interest Groups provide to PMOs?

24.4   What is the significance to a PMO of having certified project management professionals?

PART IV:
IMPLEMENTING A PMO

25

THE EXECUTIVE PROPOSAL IN DETAIL

The following information is a general proposal template for implementing a PMO in your business. The assumption behind this proposal is that the PMO advocates have done their homework. They have prepared and presented a powerful buy-in presentation, utilizing the concepts covered in Chapter 26 and elsewhere in this book. Chapter 26 describes the executive presentation content. This proposal then becomes the formal written document for chartering the implementation of the PMO as a project.

EXECUTIVE SUMMARY/COMMITMENT LETTER

This proposal addresses enterprise support needed to improve the Return on Investment (ROI) in the projects activated to achieve the organization's goals. This is a multi-million dollar opportunity for your organization. Getting the right projects completed far more quickly is key to meeting executive and stakeholder goals. This capability will be accomplished by deploying a PMO with the following key objectives:

1. **Produce an executive-sanctioned, prioritized enterprise project portfolio.** This portfolio would be governed and visibly supported by the executive team. It would be utilized by all project and re-

source managers to ensure that decisions are made and resources are allocated according to executive mandate. Data in this portfolio would emanate from all business units. All executives and managers would receive reports to guide decision-making and actions from a common base of data.

2. **Build knowledge and skills to improve delivery performance.** The PMO structure and executive support increases management's ability to meet executive goals through faster and more effective project execution. Managers will effectively utilize progress data within the portfolio and PMO tools to improve delivery performance and manage the constantly changing composition of the portfolio.

3. **Track, report, analyze, and improve project portfolio performance.** This step provides quick-starting tool utilization to collect, track, and perform project management activities on key project investments while providing strategic and tactical progress data to all stakeholders.

4. **Replace deficient project management processes with standard and best practice tools, methods, and processes.** In order to drive best practices across the organization, and be able to share information meaningfully, the organization needs a common language and methodology.

5. **Drive higher value from project management training and skills development.** This step improves project management delivery capability by mapping current skills of the project management community, analyzing the collected data, and creating effective project management training curriculums which focus on key project management weaknesses.

6. **Implement PM help desk.** To obtain consistent, needed executive information on a timely basis, users will need help with the computer-based tools. The PMO tool and usability help desk will help users with readily available documented procedures and support when required.

SECTION I: BUSINESS CASE

PROJECT OVERVIEW

Implement a PMO to improve return on investment in the $xx million project portfolio by a minimum of xx% (input numbers applicable to your project).

BACKGROUND

The business is seeking to improve its capabilities to deliver projects that are strategic to the vitality of the business. The need for this improvement has been demonstrated by the following:

- Lack of capability across top strategic initiatives to effectively collaborate to avoid project delivery delays
- Frequent priority changes, with constant disruption across the organization
- Inability to complete sufficient projects to counter competitive and economic threats
- Constant schedule and cost overruns

OBJECTIVES

1. Deliver the capability of creating a balanced project portfolio that the executives believe will meet the organization's goals
2. Put in place processes for managing projects and priorities in the portfolio, data gathering, reporting, tracking, analyzing and improvement
3. Improve delivery of projects in both speed and quality
4. Allow more projects to be completed with the same resources
5. Provide the information needed to support excellent executive decision-making in project selection and management

STRATEGIC CORPORATE ALIGNMENT

- Internal Perspective: Effective management of capital
- Operational Excellence: Improve organizational process productivity and leverage strategic technology capabilities
- Learning and Growth: Results-oriented leadership and decision making and communicate and share knowledge across the organization

OPPORTUNITY TYPE

Select the appropriate box to demonstrate the type of opportunity this project provides:

☒ Increased revenue   ☒ Decreased cost   ☐ Regulatory compliance
☒ Increased productivity ☒ Decreased risk   ☐ Maintenance

SECTION II: SCOPE

PROJECT SCOPE

- Identify minimum data requirements for project scheduling.
- Develop and document best practices, in an easily accessible Web-based tool.

- Determine minimum data requirements needed for the project port-folio.
- Gather, report, and analyze initial project portfolio data.
- Establish and facilitate first governance meeting.
- Deliver a library of easily accessible user guides for project managers, resource managers, team members, sponsors, and executives.
- Develop and implement processes to enable all project managers to deliver on minimum criteria.
- Add/hire staff to take on roles that provide effective enterprise support.
- Implement necessary training/education/development processes.

IMPACT ANALYSIS

See Table 25.1 for a description of the impact of the PMO on each stakeholder.

CRITICAL SUCCESS FACTORS

- Executive and project office support across the organization
- Project management training and skills development at every level of the organization
- Quality marketing of the PMO, its tools, and support
- Acquisition/development of quality products to support excellence in portfolio management and project management
- Effective tool training
- Executive ownership of the portfolio

SECTION III: APPROACH

PROPOSED SOLUTION

A project team consisting of five senior project managers will assemble initial data and select and implement all initial tools and data structures. This will allow the project team to focus on the hard and soft tools needed to further develop project management delivery rigor and discipline throughout the organization.

ALTERNATIVES CONSIDERED

- Continue to manage projects as we do now (lack of common structure and procedures). This alternative was eliminated because the

Table 25.1 Impact of the PMO

Stakeholder	Impact
Executives including CEO, CIO, CFO	Executives will have a real-time view of how their project capital and resources are allocated. This enables more informed decision making, and what-if scenario planning. Executives will have improved information on the implications of timeline constraints and scope changes. All projects will be prioritized by the executives.
Project Offices	Project Offices will have access to processes, a portfolio view of their collection of projects, and detailed analysis of how their project resources are being deployed.
Project Managers	Improved project management competencies, standardized life cycle, planning and scheduling methodologies, help with resource issues, issue tracking, and collaboration will help reduce project overruns. Most project managers will need training to leverage the capabilities of tools provided. Sponsor support will be significantly enhanced. Cross-functional executive support will be more visible.
Team Members	Team members will be called on to help improve delivery. They will better understand the link between their work and the organization's goals. Team members will not make decisions on task priorities. Cross-functional barriers between team members will be broken down to improve work flow and quality.
Resource Managers	Project priorities will be clear. Conflicts between project and resource managers will be significantly reduced.

opportunity represents over $xx million to our organization's bottom line.

- Minimum infrastructure. Begin with one senior project manager, no formal PMO and no tools. This alternative was eliminated because an optimistic estimate of the amount of work required is several person years. Our organization cannot afford to wait that long for the results. Also, three members of the executive committee were involved in the assessment of capital investment for tools. They concluded that such tools are 100% vital to linking project progress to the achievement of enterprise goals.
- Temporary infrastructure. Build a PMO and disband it once the initial objectives are accomplished. This alternative was eliminated because we believe that the PMO will prove that it will continue to

provide outstanding ROI from improvement in project execution. In fact, this is one of the metrics that the executive team will use to continually evaluate PMO performance.

ASSUMPTIONS

1. Deficient project managers will need to attend project management concept course.
2. All project managers who are managing portfolio projects will buy-in to the PMO project guidelines, including using a standard PMO tool suite as the project management tool.
3. All organization units will ultimately use this tool to report status of their top projects.
4. PMO tools and other training will be provided for all users at every level. Executives will be vocal and positive in support of this training.
5. PMO tool functionality will drive certain project processes.
6. PMO staff will take an executive view of the business, driving project improvements to meet organization goals.

OBSTACLES

- Finding qualified resources to support the PMO project.
- Defining the best way to incorporate every functional unit's need without sacrificing the need for a common structure.
- Buy-in of functional units to move approach to project management and utilizing the tools made available.

STAKEHOLDER EXPECTATIONS

See Table 25.2 for the stakeholder group expectations.

PROJECT ORGANIZATION

An organization chart for the project is located in Appendix I (include chart for your organization). Core team members and time commitments are identified in the Project Resource Plan in Appendix II (include list of team members and planned commitments).

PROCUREMENT PLAN

Jane Doe and John Smith have been our primary negotiators from Corporate Purchasing. We have negotiated a purchase price for PMO software, and have surrounding agreements for maintenance, training, and consult-

Table 25.2 Stakeholder Expectations

Stakeholder	Expectations
Executives including CEO, CIO, CFO	Reports, views, and project portfolios will provide timely, accurate, and relevant information for improved decision making and strategic objective realization. In addition, there must be minimal impact to budgets.
Project Offices	Improved ability to view resource allocations, environment to further develop project managers' skill sets, and the capability of leveraging learning from past projects. They will also look for corporate support.
Project Managers	More stable, more advanced tools and processes to assist in planning and actively managing their projects. They must be able to efficiently and effectively control their projects, while maintaining a collaborative environment. There will be much less resource contention.
Team Members	An easier method of tracking their project participation. There will be much less conflict between projects and between project work and operational duties. (Automating their time reporting may initially be a burden, but increased task clarity and reasonable personal accountability for completing work will balance this.)

ing. In addition, we have a master consulting agreement in place with XYZ Supply Company to provide implementation consulting, training development, and project manager mentoring. We continue to evaluate alternatives in acquiring implementation expertise from external providers as opportunities arise.

COMMUNICATION PLAN

Upon executive authorization, the team will:

- Develop a welcome packet for PMO participants — include background, expectations, schedule, key contacts, overview of the PMO, etc.
- Develop training materials and presentation for project management training in the new tools, reporting and delivery acceleration strategies
- Conduct training for pilot participants
- Provide weekly communications to pilot participants — status, results, recommendations for improvement and request for feedback

- Provide one-on-one project mentoring to discuss experiences and concerns
- Provide project status updates, portfolio analysis and recommendations to executive management at critical junctures
- Hold regular meetings with participants to discuss experiences, concerns, and successes
- Provide a pilot summary report for all key audiences
- Create content for the PMO Web site regarding the team's activities and project managers' testimonials as they use the PMO (including FAQs, issues, etc.)
- Adapt pilot welcome packet to meet the needs of each new group of users; distribute prior to communication
- Conduct awareness sessions during business unit rollouts
- Coordinate with business unit contacts to promote the PMO within their business unit
- Present PMO results/findings and future outlook at a project management network meeting
- Provide a conclusive rollout summary to all key audiences at the end of the PMO implementation

CHANGE CONTROL PLAN

As potential changes to the project base-lined scope, time and budget are identified, they will be documented by the PMO Implementation Manager, logged, distributed to the Change Control Committee and core team, and reviewed weekly (unless urgent). For urgent change matters, an emergency teleconference or meeting will be convened. The Change Control Committee consists of the PMO Director, the CIO, and the CEO.

The core team will first review changes and escalate questions and recommendations to the project executive sponsor and business unit contacts as appropriate. Once the change has been accepted or denied, the request resolution is documented and the appropriate project documents are also updated to reflect any changes. The PMO Implementation Manager will be responsible for managing this process.

SECTION IV: RISK

RISK IDENTIFICATION MATRIX

See Table 25.3 for a description of the key risks of this project, and the approach that the PMO implementation team is planning to take.

Table 25.3   Risk Identification Matrix

Description of the Risk	Quantification of the Risk	Risk Response
May have difficulty acquiring the appropriate core team, business unit and external consultant resources needed for the project. Too much delay in acquiring or assigning resources could result in a delay in critical path activities.	This is considered a high impact risk.	Work closely with resource manager to assess and respond to resource needs. Identify staff needs as far in advance as possible to allow enough lead-time for acquisition. Keep sponsor updated on resource issues and escalate as needed.
Project Team needs to coordinate with multiple departments/ business units. This could result in communication breakdowns and spreading core team support too thin during pilot and rollout. We can also be at risk that the PMO tools might not be in alignment with some existing functional unit processes.	This is considered a high probability and high impact risk.	Detailed marketing and communication plan for how to handle cross-functional unit communication. Align core team members to focus some efforts on specific business units. Investigate staffing a position to specifically work with business unit configurations and implementations.
Lack of buy-in for the PMO Implementation Project at the senior management level will reduce or eliminate the enterprise level benefits we are targeting to achieve from implementation. Lack of agreement over project priorities and resource assignments will also significantly reduce benefits. Users may also resist cultural changes that would result from tool implementation.	This is considered a high probability and high impact risk.	Leverage functional unit contacts to uncover concerns/issues and develop a plan to address those at the functional unit level. Leverage executive owner and sponsor to uncover senior management concerns/issues and develop a buy-in presentation. We will not proceed with implementation until we have secured majority executive team support. Work with functional units to uncover cultural change issues and incorporate a plan to address those during the functional unit rollout.

Table 25.4   PMO Cost Summary

	Costs			
Cost Category	Year 1	Year 2	Year 3	Year 4
Project Costs:				
Internal Resources	$459,701			
External Resources	$855,795			
Equipment & Software	$780,000			
Other Project Impacts (Training)	$100,000			
Total Project Cash Outlay	**$2,195,496**			
Ongoing Costs:				
Internal Resources				
Equipment (Maintenance)				
Total Ongoing Cash Outlay				
Total Costs	**$2,195,496**			

SECTION V: COSTS AND BENEFITS (SEE APPENDIX FOR DETAILED COST BENEFIT ANALYSIS)

PROJECT COSTS BREAKDOWN

See Table 25.4 for the cost breakdown summary.

PROJECT RESOURCE COSTS SUMMARY FOR EXECUTING/CONTROLLING PHASE

1. Project Manager — Project Executing/Control Phase 17 weeks — 100% (External) $102,000
2. PMO Tool Strategist Lead — Executing/Controlling Phase 17 weeks — 50% (Internal) $34,000
3. Project Management Integration Project Leads (2) — Executing/Controlling Phase 17 weeks — 50% each (Internal) $34,000 each
4. Systems Connectivity Lead — Executing/Controlling Phase 17 weeks — 100% (Internal) $68,000
5. Training/Education Coordinator Lead — Executing/Controlling Phase 17 weeks — 100% (External) $74,800
6. PMO Tool Help Desk Lead — Executing/Controlling Phase 17 weeks — 50% (Internal) $34,000
7. PMO Tool Support Analyst — Executing/Controlling Phase 17 weeks — 100% (Internal) $34,000

Table 25.5   PMO Benefits Summary

Benefit Category	Benefits			
	Year 1	Year 2	Year 3	Year 4
Tangibles:				
Support the implementation of project management standards		$1,920,000	$1,920,000	$1,920,000
Identify project risks and (resource) constraints		$1,584,000	$1,584,000	$1,584,000
Development cost improvements for 60 projects		$7,500,000	$7,500,000	$7,500,000
Portfolio management		$12,000,000	$12,000,000	$12,000,000
Intangibles				
Total Benefits		$23,004,000	$23,004,000	$23,004,000

8. Portfolio Management Lead — Executing/Controlling Phase 17 weeks — 100% (External) $51,000
9. Portfolio Management Analyst — Executing/Controlling Phase 17 weeks — 50% (Internal) $34,000
10. PMO Tool Trainer/Mentor — Executing/Controlling Phase 17 weeks — 100% (External) $74,800
11. HR and Admin/Support — Executing/Controlling Phase 17 weeks — 50% (Internal) $34,000
12. Facility, Training and Equipment Support — $100,000 (estimated)

PROJECT BENEFITS

See Table 25.5 for a project benefits summary. Benefits can be verified using the following measures.

Support the implementation of corporate project management standards. According to the Gartner Group (August 1, 2000), projects following a standard lifecycle are more often completed on time, on budget, and within scope.
Estimated Savings:

# of projects × # of people × average hourly rate × hours saved

Example:

20 Projects × 10 People × $60/hour × 40 hours/week × 4 weeks = $1,920,000

This example assumes time to market will be reduced by four weeks for 20 projects. Of course, the additional revenue that can come from new products delivered to market more quickly can make these benefits pale by comparison.

Verification: Baseline scheduling and cost estimates along with scope definition will be tracked and reported on a monthly basis.

Identify project risks and (resource) constraints. PMO tools will require project managers to examine their projects for risks, dependencies, constraints and impacts on the business. Using rigorous standards to move projects from the planning to execution phase will reduce organizational costs.

Estimated Savings:

$$\text{\# of projects} \times \text{\# of people} \times \text{hourly rate} \times \text{hours}$$

Example:

$$6 \text{ Projects} \times 10 \text{ People} \times \$60/\text{hour} \times 40 \text{ hours/week} \times 11 \text{ weeks} = \$1,584,000$$

The Gartner Group estimates that proper risk identification will result in the cancellation of 20% of projects before the execution phase. In the example above, savings assumes 6 projects will be cancelled before execution begins. The time savings are the average for the execution and subsequent phases.

The benefits are actually much greater than portrayed. These resources can be used to execute other projects, which bring far greater value than the cost savings alone.

Verification: The PMO will track the number of projects in the project portfolio that were cancelled because of risk and impact on the organization.

Development Cost Improvement. By the end of 200X, the enterprise will go from tracking less than half of the portfolio projects to more than 75%. Payback will occur from having better information to make decisions on the deployment and use of resources and capital. In addition, the significant increase in visibility, cross-functional executive support and tracking of these projects will enable the portfolio of projects to accelerate delivery.

Estimated Savings:

Average aggregated budget of (60 active projects)
projects in portfolio annualized = $150,000,000

A 5% annual delivery improvement in time and
budget for the projects in the portfolio = $7,500,000.

Verification: The executive team will recognize delivery improvements as reported in the PMO portfolio reports. These reports will illustrate comparable difference between baseline delivery forecasts and current progress at a summary level to enable management decision action.

Portfolio Prioritization. The portfolio along with the PMO phase review will answer the question: "Where do high-priority projects stand?" According to the Gartner Group, "project delivery rates directly impact customer satisfaction, IT's value to the business, the enterprise's competitive edge, market share and profitability. A project portfolio management capability includes a set of organization-specific metrics pertinent to project delivery."

Estimated Savings:

> Elimination of 10 projects, at an average cost of $1,200,000
> or annualized for a total expected savings of $12,000,000.

This assumes that the project portfolio along with the PMO phase review process assist management in making the decision not to implement a portfolio project based on organizational priorities.

Verification: The PMO will use the portfolio management process to review and identify the number of projects that actively follow the lifecycle and use the project control tools in the everyday management of the projects.

SECTION VI: TIMELINE

PROJECT DELIVERY TIMELINE SUMMARY

1. Project Planning Phase completed by 6/3/200X
2. Project Executing/Controlling Phase completed by 11/6/200X
3. Project Closing Phase commenced by 12/3/200X
4. Project completed by 12/31/200X

SUMMARY

The Business Case for implementing a PMO should define the benefits, time, costs, and feature functionality. Once the costs have been identified, the summary cost of the implementation effort (which includes operation expenses for the remainder of the fiscal year) becomes the baseline number against which the PMO will be evaluated for value added to the organization.

QUESTIONS

25.1   Explain how a PMO might bring financial value to any organization through a PMO and portfolio management.

25.2 The executive proposal makes assumptions about why and how the expected benefits would occur. How could you substantiate those assumptions in a real organization?

25.3 Suppose an executive is willing to accept the proposal, but insists that you start with one resource, rather than five resources. How should you respond?

25.4 The example timeline shown is 6 months. Why is this type of timeline attractive to executives?

25.5 Explain the impact that you would expect a PMO to have on executives, project managers, and resource managers.

25.6 What negative impacts from implementing a PMO might a project manager be concerned with? How could a PMO change the project manager's perception?

26

OBTAINING
EXECUTIVE BUY-IN

INTRODUCTION

A PMO must be launched with comprehensive top executive buy-in in order to be successful. Otherwise, your PMO will languish into obscurity. This buy-in must be obtained because:

- Executives are at the root of the multi-project nightmare. Without their full understanding and support, you will never solve the constant fights over resources and reprioritizations.
- Cross-functional executive support is an absolute must to make the PMO work in every aspect of what it does.
- There can be no meaningful governance without top executive participation.

This does not mean that a successful PMO cannot be launched by a functional unit. However, we must be clear on what we mean by a functional unit. Such a unit has full P&L responsibility for at least a division of the organization. It has the finance, sales, marketing, IT, engineering, and operations responsibility for a given subset of the business. Without these functional areas supporting the PMO, the multi-project nightmare and fighting over resources will continue to exist.

The top executives will compare a PMO proposal to all other ways and means of using money and resources to improve their organization. Therefore, the PMO proposal must speak their language. It must be a better opportunity than other choices they have for investment.

Executives typically do not get excited about standardized methodology, better PM practices, certification or other professionalism issues, unless they see a connection between these issues and their goals. So what is in it for the executives to support an improved project management practice? According to recent case studies, the following potential holds true:

- 20 to 30% improvement in time to market*
- 25 to 300% improvement in number of projects completed with the same resources**
- Average project duration cut by 25 to 50%***
- Over 90% project success rate, with double the profit margin****
- 50% improvement in R&D productivity*****

All of these are tangible results easily translatable to the bottom line of any organization, including not-for-profits. However, quoting these kinds of facts and figures will not be enough to convince executives. Just because some other organization did it does not mean that executives will buy-in to your organization doing it.

In fact, starting a presentation to executives quoting these results will likely have the opposite effect. If you are not prepared, as soon as you quote these kinds of figures, you will hear comments like, "Yes, but they are different than us," "Those figures were probably fabricated — no one can possibly improve that much."

Do not be disheartened by these comments. All this means is that you must not begin any presentation to executives with how wonderful life will be after they invest in a PMO. This is a great way to kill a proposal.

THE CURRENT ENVIRONMENT — ASSESSMENT

The first step to successfully gain executive buy-in is to spend an hour with each functional executive, exploring a few simple questions.

---

*See Performance Measurement Group, LLC, Web site (www.pmgbenchmarking.com) with several articles about over 1000 development projects that they have analyzed. Data is from "Better Project Management Practices Drop Time-to-Market 20-30%", *Signals of Performance,* 2(1).
**See case studies in Harold Kerzner, Ph.D., *Project Management, A Systems Approach,* 8th edition, John Wiley & Sons, New York, 2003, chapter on Critical Chain.
***Performance Measurement Group, see case studies
****Performance Measurement Group, "Pipeline/Portfolio Best Practices Yield Higher Profits", *Signals of Performance,* 3(1).
*******Insight Magazine,* Summer/Fall 2001, "How to Boost R&D Productivity by 50%".

Table 26.1 Typical Executive Complaints About Projects

1. Most projects finish later than their original target date.
2. Projects take too long to complete.
3. Project priorities change frequently without our control.
4. We are constantly fighting over resources.
5. Project information is misleading or non-existent.
6. We are working on the wrong projects.
7. Some projects get shelved or terminated after substantial investment.
8. There is too much rework.
9. Project ROI is poor.
10. Our people have too much to do.

1. What are the biggest problems you see with projects in your organization? What blocks the three goals of every project — delivering on time, on budget, and within scope? A list of complaints will quickly develop. It will probably be similar to the sample list illustrated in Table 26.1. You should also ask how long these problems have been around. What you will discover is that the executive team has a lot in common relative to these types of problems.
2. What is the cost of these problems to your organization, or what is the value of fixing these problems? This is the financial justification for the PMO. Look for tangible, bottom-line dollars.
3. Why do you think these problems have never been fixed? Much executive speculation will be heard. You may even hear them express, with great frustration, a root problem. This information is very important to your proposal and presentation back to the executives. What you should sense is that these problems are deeply rooted. You should also sense that behind all of these problems is the lack of an effective holistic approach. Most likely, several of the executives have attempted to resolve these issues, but ultimately gave in to them. They assumed that there was no lasting solution — perhaps that it was just human nature for people to perform badly on projects.

Now that you have the raw data, you need to develop an executive presentation — one that will grab their attention from the outset and create excitement and enthusiasm for your PMO proposal.

THE EXECUTIVE PRESENTATION

A compelling introduction and a well-rehearsed presentation, timed to allow for executive questions, is needed. We suggest that you demand a 3-hour time slot from the executive team. They should understand that this presentation is about a major change in how the organization conducts all of its projects. The implications are far reaching.

These are the main items that must be covered:

1. The problems in managing projects — Show the executive team that they have much in common. Every one of them is experiencing at least some of the problems that they have described. Do not point fingers at anyone.

2. The cost of the problems — You should have obtained tangible information, provided by each executive, about the cost or value of each problem they described to you. If you are not sure how to develop these costs, go to the Performance Measurement Group Web site referenced earlier and read some of the articles. Give the executives the cumulative opportunity — what you get by adding all of the figures together. This should be a figure that is more significant than most, if not all, other opportunities they have in front of them.

   Note that this figure is not an idle claim about improvement in some other organization. It is a simple statement of what the current project management problems are costing the organization.

3. The connections between the root problem and the executive problems — Explain that each of the problems the executives described does not exist randomly. You must now show how each problem is connected to some underlying problems. You must also be very careful not to point fingers at any executive for the existence of any of these problems. Rather, the tone here should be that the organization has a very smart group of executives and a very smart group of people. Why, then, have these problems lingered so long? What has prevented us from solving these problems in the past? Our approach is to take two or three of the executive problems and show how each one is a huge conflict that cannot be solved without a holistic approach. Figure 26.1 and Figure 26.2 provide two examples.

   Resource conflict: See Figure 26.1. The resource conflict begins with everyone committed to meeting the company goals. To meet the company goals, each executive initiates new projects and/or requires existing projects to complete on time. Each executive, in other words, has totally valid project needs. These needs drive each executive to demand resources. Since some of these resources are scarce, the conflict arises over to which projects to allocate the resources. You must be prepared to give some tangible examples of this conflict within your organization. Show how it happens over and over again.

   Rework conflict: See Figure 26.2. To meet the company goals, we have to accomplish two things. First, we must stop shooting our-

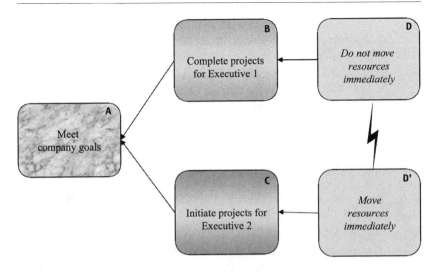

Figure 26.1   Resource Conflict between Projects

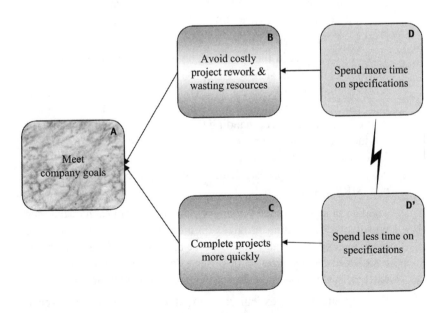

Figure 26.2   Conflict Over How Much Time To Spend on Specifications vs. Rework

selves in the foot in every project with costly rework — mistakes that waste precious resource time and money. At the same time, almost every project is in a rush. To meet the company goals, we must try to finish the projects faster. The fight is not over the needs shown in boxes B and C in Figure 26.2. Rather, the fight is over how much time to spend on the specifications. If we want to avoid rework, our own professional employees constantly tell us to do a better job up front by defining the specifications. That requires much more time. Yet the executives say, and rightly so, "We don't have time. Do it now. Show me progress now."

By explaining these problems in this way, we are showing how no one is to blame. It is the system that must be fixed. But what is at the root of all of these problems?

The root problem is the current organization's practice of managing each project as a separate entity. The connection between this practice and all of the resulting problems are really the subject of the first part of this book. However, a more concise explanation is offered below.

4. Simulate one of the problems to show the executives the impact. One of our favorite simulations for executives uses three projects to simulate the multi-project environment. We simulate just one aspect of allowing each project to be managed as a separate entity. That aspect is something that we term bad multi-tasking.

Looking at Figure 26.1, put yourself in the shoes of a resource manager, for example, in the IT area. You have a critical resource, one that is in demand for several vital projects. You could use 10 of that resource, but you only have 1 or 2. The vice president of finance has that resource deployed on a new financial system. The vice president of engineering is demanding that resource to meet his goals for productivity improvement in engineering — implementing a new CAD hardware and software. The vice president of manufacturing has also initiated a project demanding that scarce IT resource for a new MRP system.

The IT manager is receiving angry calls daily from each of the vice presidents, demanding progress on their project. So what does the IT manager do? He takes the resource and splits its time three ways. Each vice president sees some progress on his or her project, but it is extremely slow — much slower than each project planned.

We simulate this for executives using three bowls of beads — each bowl representing a project. We get five resources that are shared between the three projects and are multitasked, moving from one project to the other after completing a part of a task. Since every organizational culture is different, we will have executives as direct participants in some cases. In other cases, they are the project managers, and in other cases, they are simply observers.

Each project is timed. This first simulation with bad multi-tasking takes approximately 30 minutes to explain and execute. After the first simulation is complete, we explain the impact of bad multi-tasking. We ask the executives to provide an estimate of how much improvement they expect. Since most executives believe that multi-tasking is good because it keeps all resources busy, they typically estimate about 10% improvement.

The second simulation is run, replacing bad multi-tasking with good multi-tasking. The result is much better than 10% improvement. In fact, this simulation causes many executives to rethink their whole approach to performing and assigning work.

5. The PMO Solution: The multi-tasking simulation provides an excellent entrée into the need for and opportunity with a centralized approach to managing the multi-project environment. Here, the solution must allude back to each of the problems raised by each of the executives. You must show them how the solution will address their problems without significant negative consequences to them. Further, it is imperative at this point to discuss some PMO targets in the first 6 months and how the PMO will be self-sustaining. The proposed measurement system for the PMO is another topic that will interest executives, if the PMO metrics are properly aligned with the executive metrics.

6. Discussion: You should allow one third of the presentation time for discussion. During discussion, you may hear alternative suggestions for a solution to the problems. Do not ignore these suggestions and do not be fearful of them. Often, the suggestions appear to be alternatives but are actually ideas that can and should be implemented by a PMO.

7. Conclusion: Remind the executive team of the opportunity that is on the table. Leave them with a written proposal, copies of relevant articles, and ask them for a time frame for a decision. Make an appointment to sit down with each executive and discuss their individual concerns, preferably before the meeting breaks up or immediately afterwards.

THE CONNECTIONS BETWEEN THE CURRENT PRACTICE AND PM PROBLEMS

Look at Figure 26.3 and Figure 26.4. These cause–effect diagrams can be read from the bottom up, simply by using the words IF and THEN between the boxes. The diagrams are greatly simplified, but are very powerful in their explanation of why the current practice leads to the problems.

In Figure 26.3, we start with the current practice of managing each project as a separate entity. As a result, each project is initiated without regard to whether or not the organization's resources can handle the work. Since you have already established that the organization has some very critical resources whose capacity is severely limited, the next effect is obvious. We do not have enough of these critical resources to go around to all active projects.

The chart should read like a story, explaining what actually happens in your organization. You may need to add some logic to this chart to explain it more fully. For example, to explain the bad multi-tasking (box 3), you need to show how resource managers are put in a box with their critical resources. Customers are making demands. Vice presidents are making demands. The resource manager of the critical resources believes he must satisfy all of these demands, so he multitasks his resources.

The effects of bad multi-tasking are universal in every organization we visit. There is constant fighting over resources. Tasks take much longer to complete than planned. Now projects are late and priorities start to change. When priorities change, tasks take even longer to complete. The chart now shows a negative loop. The situation is not bad enough. The loop suggests that in some organizations, it gets worse. Tasks are even later. Projects are delayed even further.

Figure 26.4 begins with the same root problem, but shows how more of the executive problems occur, stemming from the same root problem. If the PMO team has done its homework, this chart should accurately reflect what its intuition tells it is going on in the organization, and what the executive team has already confirmed in the interviews. The big difference is that now all of these seemingly disconnected problems are linked to the current practice of "every project is an island."

DEMAND A DELIVERABLE FROM THE EXECUTIVES

Your proposal must make one thing clear. Assuming that the executives buy in to the problems, the root cause, and the solution, you must educate them on governance, choosing the right project mix, and prioritization.

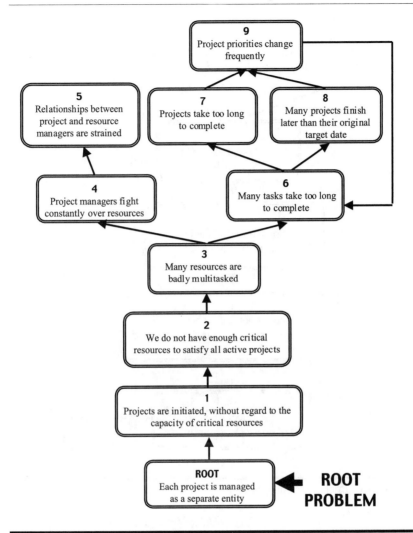

Figure 26.3   Root Cause Analysis Part I

You may not be able to do all of that in the proposal. After all, your primary objective is to get executive sanction for the PMO. However, you must make clear that for a PMO to work, the executives must be willing to devote several hours per month to it. Some environments need more executive time, where the industry is moving faster or where the company is a project company in a highly volatile environment.

When the executives fully understand and accept the impact that a properly sanctioned PMO will have on the bottom line, this is not asking for too much. You can make some reasonable demands to ensure that this concept will work.

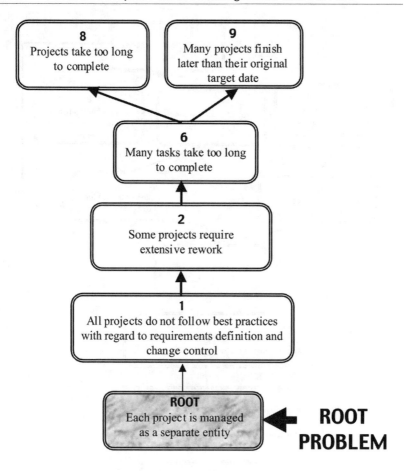

Figure 26.4   Root Cause Analysis Part II

SUMMARY

The PMO will have little or no impact, and will not survive long term without executive buy-in. For executives to enthusiastically support the PMO, they must believe that it will solve some of their biggest project management problems.

The PMO must do its homework, interviewing the executive team to assess what their biggest project management problems are, and what the value of solving these problems is to the organization. This information will be crucial in delivering a buy-in presentation and financially justifying the effort.

The buy-in presentation consists of seven parts. Each part must be delivered in sequence to logically build the excitement for the solution. To begin, the PMO team must not start with the solution (a fatal sales mistake) but rather with the problems. The seven parts of this 3-hour presentation are:

1. Present the problems that the organization has in getting project results, as stated by the executives during the assessment interviews.
2. Using the executive's own claims, show what the problems are costing the organization.
3. Show how the root problem, the current practice of leaving every project as an island unto itself, leads to all of the executive problems highlighted. Use compelling cause–effect logic to prove the connections.
4. Use a before and after simulation of one of the problems to prove the value of the PMO.
5. Explain how the PMO solution will overcome the problems the executives raised.
6. Discussion. Steel yourself for skepticism. Welcome the predictable comments and challenges. Answer them logically. Do not be defensive.
7. Conclusion. Review the opportunity in dollars and leave the executives with a detailed proposal and supporting articles. Determine their time frame for a decision.

There are cases, referenced in the chapter, that document what good project management practices are worth. One major benefit is 30 to 50% improvements in average project duration, with many more projects completed during the year. The PMO team must demand executive participation in the governance process to make sure that the PMO works and is successful in the long term.

QUESTIONS

26.1   Why is executive buy-in absolutely critical to a PMO's success?

26.2   What is the biggest mistake that many PMO teams make when presenting their proposal to the executives? Why?

26.3   What are the financial justifications for a PMO?

26.4   Suppose that your company has an R&D budget of $100 million. Based on the articles, how would you justify a PMO investment, first year, of $2 million? Use one method of justification which is cost cutting, and use another as more products are developed.

26.5   What are some typical complaints you have heard from executives, or that you think executives might have about their projects?

26.6   If you are interviewing a vice president of marketing to assess that area's project management problems, what are the three important questions to ask, and what answers might you expect from this executive?

26.7   How do the authors recommend that you use the assessment interview data in a buy-in presentation?

26.8   Why do you think the authors recommend using a simulation in the executive presentation instead of just using overheads and data?

26.9   If the PMO team uses the 7-step presentation outlined in this chapter, why might they still fail to get buy-in, at least initially? What should the team do about it?

26.10   What commitment does the PMO team have the right to demand from the executive team, in order to make the PMO work?

27

THE PMO VALUE PROPOSITION MATURITY MODEL — WHERE IS YOUR PMO?

Many PMOs continue to struggle with the measurement process of PMO value. Implementing and improving PMOs are also projects. A PMO must know if it is progressing in maturity on the value curve. Much of the confusion is caused from the lack of a well-defined value model. Such a model should have been well thought out at the beginning of PMO development. In this chapter, we focus on measuring the PMO value and how to measure that value in a reasonable and easy to apply method through a PMO Maturity Model (see Appendix A).

ASSESSING THE PMO MATURITY LEVEL

The PMO model is comprised of eight levels of maturity and is measured across nine knowledge areas of the project management body of knowledge (PMBOK®) defined by the Project Management Institute (PMI). In applying the PMO maturity model, the PMO must clearly identify the top ten strategic initiatives that reached completion in the last 12 months. This excludes any cancelled projects. Each of these top ten projects are reviewed and compared to the specifications within each knowledge area outlined in Appendix A, to see how well the projects complied.

The delivery speed of each of the ten projects is also assessed in the same manner of "high," "average," and "low." If a project completed (deployed) ahead of schedule by more than 5% of planned project duration, then this project should be rated "high" in delivery speed. If a project completed (deployed) behind schedule by more than 5% of planned duration, then this project should be rated "low." Projects that fall in between should be rated "average."

We suggest that the final scope of the delivered project not be measured against the initial scope of the project. Rather, we suggest that you include this assessment with the final project delivery speed assessment. Give the project a "high" rating if and only if the speed of delivery did not take away substantial benefits based on what was planned. The delivery speed for each project is summarized and averaged into a final project delivery maturity level rating of "high," "average," or "low."

The review process should also assign a "high," "average," or "low" rating for each knowledge area per project. As each project is assessed against the nine knowledge areas, the overall assessment knowledge area for each project is derived as the overall knowledge maturity level. This value should equal the summation of the knowledge area ratings from each project by knowledge area and then by averaging the summation to derive the overall knowledge area rating. Thus, if scope management was rated "average" for seven of the ten projects, then the rating for the ten projects in scope management should be "average." In this manner, the remaining eight knowledge areas should be measured. People who feel so compelled are welcome to develop sophisticated mathematical formulas. Our belief is that simplicity is more helpful.

Overall assessments that fall below the overall "average" rating for five or more knowledge areas indicate that the overall PMO maturity level is below average (once the PMO has achieved Level II). Also, PMO maturity levels that are assessed at Level VI and higher should not have a project delivery maturity level that is less than "high." Otherwise, we believe that the PMO maturity is less than Level VI. The same is true for PMO maturity levels that are assessed at Level IV and V. These should not have a project delivery maturity level less than "average." Otherwise, the PMO maturity level is less than Level IV.

Consistency in how the PMO maturity is measured from year to year is dependent upon the acceptance of the criteria requirements from each of the PMBOK® knowledge areas. Normally, the criteria in these areas of knowledge will not change over time.

Measuring PMO maturity is straightforward and easy to apply. This process should be conducted at least once every 12 to 18 months by the PMO, with some audit from outside the PMO. The PMO can certainly help itself by making this information available to the project management community so that the project teams can understand what is necessary and sufficient relative to project delivery expectations.

LEVELS OF PMO MATURITY

Level I — PMO defining value
Level II — PMO organized
Level III — Searching for delivery value
Level IV — Portfolio management
Level V — Community buy-in
Level VI — Project teams delivering on schedule
Level VII — Project teams calibrated w/portfolios; more projects in fiscal year
Level VIII — Organization delivering

KNOWLEDGE AREAS OF THE PMBOK®

Scope Management
Time Management
Resource Management
Communications Management
Risk Management
Quality Management
Cost Management
Procurement Management
Project Integration

PMO MATURITY MODEL OVERVIEW

LEVEL I — PMO DEFINING VALUE

In this stage, the PMO is identifying what the current situation is as it begins to develop the PMO value proposition. Common characteristics include the following. Poor definition of in-scope or out-of-scope items. Project teams are in silos and not aware of team member utilization rates and trends. Resources are allowed to work at their own pace. Resources are sought as tasks begin instead of preplanned. Projects start late and most finish late because of the late start. Project and resource managers are constantly fighting over resources, not fully comprehending which project is more critical to the business. Standard reporting processes for project delivery status are not implemented. Risks are not considered outside of the project manager's informal thought process because they are so isolated from availability of external project information. Project teams do not understand their customers' needs and do not understand who their customers are and in what circumstances their customer status changes. Project costs are not estimated or tracked. Project managers do not give or receive project reports. Vendors and contractors are not considered part of the project team. No standard project definitions, terminology, scheduling or methodology are used.

HOW TO MOVE TO LEVEL II

Focus on the behavior needed to affect work expectations at the project team level. Key information will germinate the motivation needed to cause others to pick up the pace. Provide clear information on the Critical Path/ Critical Chain and focus on work tasks to step up the pace on the critical path tasks for key projects. The PMO must bring consistency to project status reporting that best reflects delivery progress to date. Begin a public relations campaign from within the PMO which places focus on the fiscal year strategic objectives in relation to key projects. The PMO should begin identifying predecessors and successors within the project portfolio for all to see and understand. Organize the project management community into regular portfolio review meetings.

PITFALLS TO AVOID

Stay away from anything that makes the PMO be perceived as too authoritative. The PMO should be selling itself as a consultant who is there to assist the project manager and project team with their success. The PMO should never force the issue to gain compliance. Use group peer pressure techniques to obtain the information required. Work confidentially, not combatively, with project managers to help them do better.

LEVEL II — PMO ORGANIZED

Level II initially focuses on identifying the "As Is" of project delivery. Common characteristics include a scope statement developed by supply-side project manager, often with IT emphasis. Business partner participation is very limited and weak. Functional requirements are poor and not aligned in value to the business. Project managers understand their project's position among all strategic projects at a high level of understanding but do not have sufficient information to anticipate external dependencies with other projects. A high-level resource portfolio is established but normally is not aligned to the force rank order of strategic projects as determined by the business partners. Project team members' work assignments are not sufficiently calibrated in a manner so that each resource can predict his or her future work load beyond two calendar weeks with a high degree of certainty. Periodic status meetings are just that — periodic.

Top risks for major projects have been identified and are known to the PMO. PMO mentors are available to help project managers determine customer needs and are assigned to the most important strategic projects as a project management subject matter expert. The project portfolio budget has been identified for fiscal year at the project level and baselined. Vendors/contractors are managed to end dates only by project managers. Projects are managed on milestone reporting, and predecessor/successor dependencies are not well known.

HOW TO MOVE TO NEXT LEVEL

Project status reports and project schedules are consistent with business side initiatives and expectations. The PMO must focus on leveling this process so the business side can contribute. The PMO should begin to receive notice from the business side at this level. Portfolio reporting should bring more visibility to strategic objective run rates to dates and related accomplishments so bottlenecks are be identified by people who are more aware.

PITFALLS TO AVOID

Do not get bogged down in complex methodologies, forced tools and templates or complex software implementations. Standards are good, but keep it simple at the outset. Minimize the number of forms and the amount of work required for reporting.

LEVEL III — SEARCHING FOR DELIVERY VALUE

Level III brings awareness for the potential for project delivery speed improvements. Common characteristics include the following. Functional requirements are better defined and easier translated for development purposes. In-scope and out-of-scope items are identified and planned for. Project work delays that cause rework are documented. Project managers are using the PMO as an information source to learn and develop their own project level strategy for project delivery acceleration opportunities and/or delivery delay threat avoidance. Resource pool utilization rates are known for planned and actual for 80% of resources for more than 30 calendar days in the future. Strategic resource is identified.

Regular PM community status meetings raise delivery visibility within the group. The top project delivery acceleration opportunities and delivery threats are known within the project management community at the project manager level. Project team members are focused on meeting customer needs that affect organization goals. The workforce is aware of the organization fiscal year strategic objectives and the primary relationship of the top 10 projects to a primary strategic objective. Project financials (plan vs. actual) are tracked monthly at the project level by the project team. Total project portfolio baseline and fiscal year-to-date financial data are available. The overall fiscal health of the project portfolio is known to date. Contractors are reporting progress at least monthly to the project teams in a standard format. Earlier delivery is beginning to occur for critical path items. Project management delivery metrics are inducing project teams to accelerate while avoiding project work delay. Project team members are learning and developing their new attitudes in considering their personal work delivery speed and attempting to stay off the critical path of the project on which they are working.

HOW TO MOVE TO THE NEXT LEVEL

Implement asset and strategic portfolio management and use these tools to help balance overall portfolio management. Force rank assets by organization value now and expected by end of fiscal year. Organize all strategic projects by their primary strategic objective and identify visible positive and negative bottlenecks.

PITFALLS TO AVOID

Do not worry too much about becoming perfect in collecting project cost data. Use the 80/20 rule for tolerance when calculating project resource costs. Use standard labor resource rates that include overhead when calculating estimate to complete effort and related estimates. Using a common denominator in all cost projections will enable management decision making to cycle in shorter intervals.

LEVEL IV — PORTFOLIO MANAGEMENT

Level IV brings more focus on working on the right projects, reducing the number of active projects in the system, and having greater senior management involvement in the process. Common characteristics include the following. Scope interdependencies between projects are understood among project managers so that when the lead project accelerates in delivery, the other dependent projects can as well. All important projects are being tracked within the project portfolio. Projected scheduling delays are identified and projects are strategically re-ranked within the project portfolio. The resource portfolio is applied to help plan project delivery dates. Resource portability is beginning to emerge as a key PMO value point. Resource progress by project is electronically entered by resource by reporting period (at least weekly). Project managers understand the status of other projects in the portfolio and how they relate to their project. Project team calibration is enhanced and predictive. The project portfolio and related project artifacts and information are available online to project managers. Contingency plans include consideration for external projects and are developed for project risks that can be mitigated. Project managers know the impact of their project on the end customer and the market and have improved vision in predicting project delivery achievement throughout the life cycle. Project managers understand how project acceleration and delay can impact the budget and the aggregate portfolio management processes, and take responsibility for their project's impact on the total fiscal year work plan relative to related projects. Problem vendors/contractors across projects are identified and dealt with. Procedures are developed to manage inter-project changes particularly in force ranking, track performance against plan, and report on all projects, affected assets, and strategic objective compliance within the portfolios.

HOW TO MOVE TO THE NEXT LEVEL

Project mentoring is in full swing for all key strategic projects. The PMO mentors are instructed to coach team member cognitive skills and techniques to assist teams in developing faster delivery solutions ahead of delivery expectations. The PMO drives the quality of delivery data through the portfolio processes in a manner that begins to identify real business growth in the form of less realized project costs. Project sponsor training is being provided.

PITFALLS TO AVOID

Focus on top project risks. The PMO should deal with the critical path/ critical chain items identified in each of the portfolios and work to reduce their potential effect.

The PMO should give more attention to troubled projects and toward improving delivery prediction visibility through the portfolios. Pay close attention to what is on the executive radar screen. Do not overcomplicate project prioritization with sophisticated templates and scoring models. Keep it simple. Do not rely totally on financial data to prioritize projects. Look at strategic value, long term vs. short term, and other balancing factors.

LEVEL V — COMMUNITY BUY-IN

A change in work force attitude has emerged within the culture. Project teams have an air about them that is fostering positive events. Common characteristics include the following. Executive buy-in and project management community buy-in exists for combined scope of all projects for the planned fiscal year. Force ranked project calibration is understood and accepted. The Governance Board is operational and responsible for project portfolio delivery results and order. Some projects are deactivated because they are no longer viable. Projects are staggered according to availability of strategic resource. The entire customer community is educated about the strategic resource, and does their best not to waste it. Operations plans are published to the Governance Board from the PMO. Sponsors, teams, functional executives, and other stakeholders have accurate delivery information regarding status and acceleration opportunities and delivery threats. Risk management is a normal part of status reporting at the project level. Risk mitigation is supported by the Governance Board, sponsors, and functional management. Project management metrics are established which support quality goals. Boundaries between functional disciplines are torn down. Project vendors, team members, and functional executives understand their impact on project financial objectives. Vendors/contractors have incentives to seek delivery acceleration on critical items. There is an increased number of PMP®s. A PMIS is being used throughout the project lifecycle. The community is beginning to feel safe in reporting "bad" news as problems are seen as opportunities to make a difference.

HOW TO MOVE TO NEXT LEVEL

The PMO begins reporting within the project management community meetings, the supply side business units leadership meetings, and the Governance Board meetings new delivery accomplishments that are fostering business cost avoidance and early delivery news. The PMO should begin to measure, in six-month increments, its value to the organization and be able to plan PMO-based action derived from these results for the next six months.

PITFALLS TO AVOID

The PMO should be aware that everyone will not be successful. The behavioral processes implemented to date will raise the cloak of cover for poor performers wherever they may be. The PMO should help project managers deal with this dysfunction through mentoring and through standardizing project status reporting and status meetings. Do not overlook the extensive communication required to keep all stakeholders informed of what the PMO is doing and why. The PMO must market itself to stay alive.

LEVEL VI — PROJECT TEAMS DELIVERING ON SCHEDULE

Level VI brings about improved vision in project delivery predictability. Common characteristics include the following. Projects are completing within scope most of the time. Some projects are completing early. Resource assignments are calibrated to the project portfolio through the re-source portfolio. Resource needs are manageable without excessive peaks and valleys, across all disciplines. Functional partners are actively engaged in the overall process through their delegates at the project level and through the meaningful PMO regular communications and reporting. All project managers and teams have information in time to take preventative action on project threats and to take advantage of acceleration opportunities. Project teams are seizing delivery opportunities and have become adaptive in their attitudes toward acceleration of project work. Quality issues preventing on-time delivery are documented and addressed. Project teams are collectively managing their project budget within 10% of budget plan. Subcontractors manage projects using the same system as the company. The planning pro-cess always balances scope, schedule, and resources without overloading the system.

HOW TO MOVE TO THE NEXT LEVEL

PMIS tools are implemented and well utilized. Workers can see at a glance where their time must be applied. Management aligns the new projects with confidence on project estimates based on recent delivery successes. Project communication is taking place more and more without formality, as people have realized the need for urgency is related to staying informed about project opportunities and threats. People are no longer waiting to discuss project information at status meetings and thereby delaying action.

PITFALLS TO AVOID

The PMO should be careful not to overlook delivery successes everywhere, as more and more success will occur. Marketing of the successes is vital to keep motivating all project teams and functional managers. Send a positive message back to the workforce. The worst thing the PMO can do at this level is to not campaign for project delivery brilliance.

LEVEL VII — PROJECT TEAMS CALIBRATED WITH PORTFOLIOS, MORE PROJECTS IN FISCAL YEAR

In Level VII, the organization begins to see quantifiable payback in terms of unexpected budget money left over from projects completed earlier than expected. Common characteristics include the following. Project teams are using their delivery knowledge of scope interdependencies between projects to meet or optimize scope requirements. Everyone understands his or her workload and how it relates to project priorities. Strategic resources are no longer causing project delays. Team-based performance process has been implemented. All resources look for acceleration opportunities and threats in project work assignments. Resource utilization rates are improving and are in alignment with the portfolios. Bad multitasking is visibly reduced. Portfolios are integrated to allow changes in one project or resource area to be proactively addressed when they impact other projects, resources, assets, and strategic objectives. Metrics, procedures, and training are used to raise visibility of delivery acceleration opportunities and to decrease delivery threats. The Governance Board is taking a global view of all portfolio costs and opportunities. The Governance Board is balancing the portfolios by investing more in marketing and strategic assets. The supply side business leaders are becoming more aligned within their skill set and less directive in project selection. Business side leaders are taking more responsibility for project delivery speed and work within the Governance Board to communicate opportunity and threats. Vendors are integrated into project planning process and use the same procedures and methodology. Project selection is a formal process performed at speed. This process is adhered to and respected by all functional leaders and has become a "way of life". The Governance Board demands and supports project management methodology from all functional areas.

HOW TO MOVE TO THE NEXT LEVEL

Quantifiable ROI is found in project delivery, resource utilization improvements, and the order of asset improvement and strategic objectives are balanced with all portfolios. Resource portability is in full swing. The value of each day invested in projects has measurably increased, and these measurements are known to everyone and accepted by everyone.

PITFALLS TO AVOID

The work environment should be as safe as it can be to report bad news. The PMO should continue to find ways to improve the culture and to prevent a return to the carnivorous work culture.

LEVEL VIII — ORGANIZATION DELIVERING

Level VIII is nirvana for the PMO. By this time, there is no question about the PMO value to the business and to each individual in the workforce. Common characteristics include the following. All strategic objectives of the organization are achieved in the fiscal year. Over 95% of projects are completing on-time worst case. Approximately 10% of projects are completing early. Resource utilization rates are stable yet improving in productivity. The organization is delivering more projects without needing to add resources. Every stakeholder understands and supports the connections between organization goals, projects, resources, and assets. Suggestions for acceleration and better project mix are available without solicitation. The combined portfolios are balanced so that even several disasters do not affect meeting organization goals. A process of ongoing improvement is in place, with statistical controls and identification of biggest leverage points for improved quality. The Governance Board actively reallocates excess project budget to other project work. Vendors/contractors cannot be differentiated from organization staff.

PM maturity is integrated with all other processes and is continually reviewed for improvement. PMO maturity is enabling more than a 10% return on investment, making it even better than plan.

PITFALLS TO AVOID

Most PMOs are funded at a 50 to 80% level of what they actually need to operate. PMOs need to research methods to bring problem resolution in terms of timeliness that will continue to enhance the PMO value to the business. Identifying and establishing key vendor support agreements over 2- to 3-year periods are essential to the lifeblood of the PMO.

WHERE IS YOUR PMO?

In this chapter we have reviewed the PMO maturity model and what should normally occur. Consider the resources and assets available to the PMO and use this information to craft the PMO maturity improvement plan. If you are just beginning the PMO, consider organizing an approach in six-month increments that can be measured every 12 to 18 months. The key to PMO success is not so much in process and methodology but more in how safe people feel in using the PMO.

SUMMARY

The PMO maturity model supports for-profit and not-for-profit entities alike. Each stage of maturity indicates more value, more alignment between functional areas, more executive awareness and support, and greater synchronization between projects, project managers, and project teams. Further, the maturity model lays out a measurable road map that PMO directors can use to self-evaluate their progress in building a healthy project management environment.

QUESTIONS

27.1   Discuss the PMO maturity model and its overall value to an organization.

27.2   Explain what is more important: PMO process, tools, or project delivery acceleration.

27.3   How long might it take a PMO with a $20M portfolio of projects to achieve Level IV when they are at Level II now? Why? How might you accelerate the maturity progression?

27.4   Discuss the possible pitfalls of each maturity level. In general, why do these pitfalls exist?

27.5   Explain Level I PMO maturity level and how a PMO would improve to Level II.

27.6   Discuss how to assess the PMO maturity level.

27.7   Explain the consequences to a Level VI PMO maturity that has less than average knowledge area ratings.

27.8   Should a PMO assess itself? What might be a better alternative?

27.9   Where would a PMO seek to grow its value if it is at Level VIII? Discuss three possible opportunities and their value to a PMO.

27.10 True or False: Level I PMO maturity should be considered an embarrassment to any organization.

28

THE ROAD MAP TO IMPLEMENTING A PMO EXECUTIVES WILL EMBRACE

In this chapter, we identify the essential steps to implement a healthy PMO. The basics involve the following critical success factors:

1. Continuous pursuit of project delivery value, in the eyes of the key stakeholders, especially the senior management team.
2. Acceptance of the discipline of consistent, timely, and useful project portfolio and progress information, reporting, and feedback.
3. Encouraging project teams to embrace and seek help from the PMO.
4. PMO capability to capitalize on project delivery opportunities and help avoid threats.
5. Full senior management support for the PMO establishment.

If you are just beginning to develop the PMO for your organization, you should plan a 24- to 30-month interval that is staged into 6-month increments. The plan should focus on implementing measurable PMO benefits in each 6-month stage.

If you already have the full support and high interest of the entire senior management team, the plan will appear quite different than if you are beginning with only one functional executive. For example, part of the assessment work in Stage 1 below, which normally requires 3 months time, was actually done over several days with the CEO direction.

It is much more typical for this initial work to be done on a part time basis, with resources that are already stretched too thin. Therefore, this initial work takes longer than what we would call ideal. It can also take substantially longer because trust must be built. Sometimes, it is easier to establish trust by going a little slower on the front end. Otherwise, people may have the impression that they have just been run over by a steamroller.

The length of time to implement is also greatly dependent on the scope of the PMO, the size of the organization and its geographic dispersion. Other factors, such as the project management maturity level, play a major role in determining length of implementation and degree of buy-in effort required.

The plan outlined below is an extension of the plan introduced in Chapter 3. The first 5 stages might look something like this:

Stage 1   Assessment, buy-in to the problems and solution, charter
Stage 2   Start-up of the PMO, identifying the "As Is" available information on project delivery and "What should be"
Stage 3   Raising the visibility of project delivery progress
Stage 4   EPM tool identification, selection, implementation and conversion
Stage 5   Becoming an "ROI engine" and implementing system connectivity

STAGE 1: ASSESSMENT, BUY-IN TO THE PROBLEMS AND SOLUTION, CHARTER

Here are some quick Dos and Don'ts:
Do:

- Collect the initial project portfolio data, including the real status on all key projects
- Meet with key stakeholders and project managers
- Determine which projects are on the executive radar screen, based on organization goals

Don't:

- Force methodology down everyone's throats
- Make a lot of rules that project managers must follow
- Gather detailed time sheet information

In Stage 1, you need to understand some important aspects of the current situation. Therefore, a PMO assessment is performed that reviews current project delivery practice, issues progress reports, conducts interviews with key stakeholders, identifies organizational strategic objectives, and determines the extent of alignment with the Project Management Institute's Project Management Body of Knowledge (PMBOK®). Any data gathering should be applied against a statistical sampling of at least 20% of the project management work to ensure statistical validity results.

Within the first month, you should have a PMO assessment report that includes findings and recommendations. This report is reviewed with the team that is constructing the PMO. The "Recommendations" portion of the assessment report becomes input to a PMO improvement plan that identifies the work breakdown structure (WBS) for the remaining time in this stage and for the following stages.

The sooner this assessment is complete, the sooner the senior management team and all functional teams will stop viewing this new organization as "unnecessary overhead." The WBS for this first stage should appear similar to the following:

1. Meet with PMO and executive leadership and set expectations for the assessment process.
2. Schedule assessment interviews with key stakeholders.
3. Schedule survey sessions with a 20% sampling of the project management community that minimally includes project sponsors, project managers, and team members.
4. Collect and review progress information on strategic projects.
5. Review current project management methodology and discipline.
6. Conduct assessment interviews with key stakeholders.
7. Conduct survey sessions.
8. Compile PMO assessment "Findings and Recommendations" draft report.
9. Conduct initial review with PMO executive of the PMO assessment draft report.
10. Update and prepare final PMO assessment report.
11. Present PMO assessment report with a proposed PMO charter (value proposition)
12. PMO executive identifies assessment recommendations to act on and sequence priorities.
13. Construct PMO improvement plan based on selected assessment recommendations.

STAGE 1 DELIVERABLES

1. PMO Assessment Report
   a. Findings and Recommendations
   b. Interview Notes
   c. Completed PMO Surveys
   d. Power Point Summation Presentation

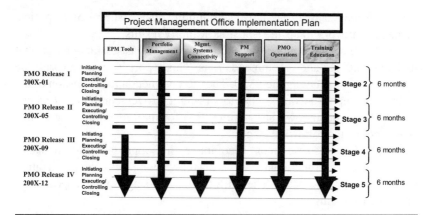

Figure 28.1 Plan for Incremental Deployment of a PMO

2. PMO Improvement Plan
3. PMO Value Proposition Charter

Figure 28.1 provides an overview of the incremental deployment of the PMO value proposition. Observing how the work force reacts to the "staged" deployment of "releases" will definitely add punch to the PMO deliverables as they are developed and deployed. As in all projects recommended throughout, the PMO effort to raise the value bar for the PMO is delivered through the process lifecycle of the PMBOK® five-phase model that consists of the following phases: initiating, planning, controlling, executing, and closing.

Figure 28.2 summarizes the tasks and deliverables in a typical Stage 1 deployment of a PMO. The term "MARCOM" refers to the extremely important task of marketing and communications — connecting the PMO activities to the needs of the PMO customers, and reporting back to the customers on PMO achievements that helped customers meet their goals.

STAGE 1 SYNOPSIS

As PMO improvements are considered, it will be important to perform an assessment of the current situation. Management and sponsors may already agree that numerous and compelling reasons exist which are sufficient to proceed with the PMO improvement plan. Making these improvements may be very vital to the business mission of the enterprise.

Several questions are worth considering during this phase:

1. How important is it that project cost data such as labor time is processed through the enterprise systems to the general ledger? Is system connectivity a critical success factor now or later?

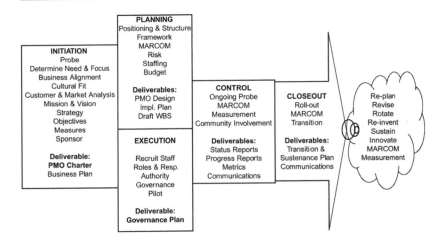

Figure 28.2   Building the PMO: Sample Project Lifecycle (Courtesy of J. Duggal, Projectize Group, www.projectize.com)

2. How well do the current PM tools meet the needs of the project teams and their sponsors?
3. Has the project management community "bought in" to the PMO?
4. What are some of the immediate needs of the PMO customers?
5. What types of project management skills need to be enhanced for the supply side and business side work force?
6. What is the maturity level of project management within the enterprise? What opportunities are available now to improve project management maturity?

STAGE 2: IDENTIFYING THE "AS IS" AVAILABLE INFORMATION ON PROJECT DELIVERY AND THE TACTICAL "WHAT SHOULD BE"

In this stage, the PMO is launched over a 6-month interval. Early on, identifying and communicating the project environment in terms of project delivery opportunities and threats is an absolute must for the new PMO. The PMO seeks to deliver on project delivery opportunities that may have been hidden from view. However, when all the project data is collected and aggregated, inter-project relationships become clearer and thus raise the visibility of possible opportunities and threats to the current work.

In Stage 2, continuous improvement of the data quality derived from the project status reports and project schedules is sought by the PMO. Aggregating this data into project- and project manager-oriented reporting will

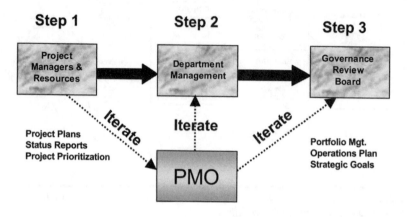

Figure 28.3   Stage 2 — Implementing a Value-Add PMO

generate the awareness sought by management to effectively navigate the fiscal year work plan of projects.

Some projects will complete early, some will complete on time, some will complete late, and some will be cancelled. The key to optimizing project delivery can be seen in Figure 28.3. This three-step iterative model yields improved understanding of project delivery expectations for all key stakeholders at each of the three steps.

In implementing this three-step model, consider using a relatively rapid approach, where the project management community meets each week in Step 1 over a period of five to seven weeks until the project portfolio data content and quality achieves the expected level. During this time, the PMO may wish to declare a period of "amnesty" if needed so as to place a positive focus on receiving accurate information from the project teams. The data still needs to be collected frequently, but without formal meetings. After all, project managers and team members are compensated to deliver their work assignments. This means they must report progress in an effective manner so that their managers (Step 2) can manage and report any opportunities or threats to their customers. Step 2 participants may only need 3 to 5 weekly meetings with the PMO to align themselves with the process before the PMO is then ready to involve Step 3 participants — the Governance Board.

The Step 3 participants may need only a few meetings to organize and take ownership on the force ranking of the projects within the project portfolio. It is in this manner that each of the participant groups from Step 1 and Step 2 become calibrated with the senior management in Step 3. These three steps clearly move the pure decision-making leadership to the Governance Board and moves project and functional managers toward the correct strategic order of work.

As each group of participants are brought into the communication flow of progress reporting information, the PMO should place emphasis on tuning participant expectations directly through motivation created by inter-project/inter-dependencies among and within each group level rather than directly from the PMO. This overall approach will help ensure the consultative approach of the PMO for PMO customers.

The WBS for Stage 2 should appear similar to the following elements:

1. Month 1
   a. Week 1
      i. Staff portfolio management function of the PMO
      ii. Staff project management mentoring function of the PMO
      iii. Collect project schedules and project status reports for projects listed in project portfolio
      iv. High level fiscal year strategic objectives collected
   b. Week 2
      i. Update project portfolio
      ii. Publish project portfolio
      iii. Review project portfolio for data collection process potential improvements and take action
      iv. Assign PMO mentors to key strategic projects
      v. PMO mentors establish mentoring schedule for as signed projects with their customers
   c. Week 3
      i. Collect project schedules and project status reports for projects listed in project portfolio
      ii. Ongoing PMO mentoring
   d. Week 4
      i. Update project portfolio
      ii. Publish project portfolio
      iii. Ongoing PMO mentoring
2. Month 2 (Same as Month 1 plus):
   a. Week 1
      i. Draft initial operations forecasting and planning report
   b. Week 2
      i. Publish initial operations forecasting and planning report

    c.   Week 3
- i. Draft reporting period operations forecasting and planning report
- ii. Conduct initial project manager portfolio review meeting

    d.   Week 4
- i. Publish operations forecasting and planning report

3.   Month 3 (Same as Months 1 and 2 plus):
    a.   Week 2
- i. Conduct initial senior project management leadership/ portfolio review meeting.

4.   Month 4 (Same as above plus):
    a.   Week 1
- i. Staff the PMO help desk

    b.   Week 2
- i. Conduct Supply side leadership/portfolio review meeting
- ii. PMO help desk setup process

    c.   Week 3
- i. PMO help desk setup process

    d.   Week 4
- i. PMO help desk online and open for business

5.   Month 5 (Same as above plus):
    a.   Week 2
- i. Initiate Governance Review Board membership and schedule first meeting

6.   Month 6
    a.   Week 2
- i. Conduct initial functional unit leadership/portfolio review meeting
- ii. Assess PMO ROI for first six months in quantitative terms

    b.   Week 3
- i. Support and facilitate initial Governance Review Board Meeting — establish process and begin effort to force rank strategic project work order

STAGE 2 PROCESS DELIVERABLES

1.   Portfolio management support
    a.   Operations forecasting and planning report (normally monthly)

      b.   Project portfolio management process implementation
2.   PMO data administration
      a.   Project status and scheduling collection processes
      b.   Single data repository of project information
3.   PMO help desk
      a.   Call center staffed from within PMO
      b.   Project management mentoring
4.   Communication
      a.   Project manager portfolio review meetings
      b.   Supply side leadership portfolio review meetings
      c.   Governance Review Board portfolio review meetings
5.   Project management methodology support

STAGE 2 SYNOPSIS

If the number of strategic projects in the business is 100 or less, a project portfolio process should be constructed in the first calendar month using reported data from each project. If the number of projects is greater than 100, another 15 to 20 work days may be required to complete the initial "As Is" project portfolio.

Inputs from each project are imported into a basic spreadsheet tool such as Microsoft Excel or Microsoft Project (Task Sheet View). Data from these inputs will tell the story as to where in the delivery lifecycle the project has progressed.

It is during this time that "data gaps" will appear because the reporting project manager may not have provided the information required to construct a project view in the project portfolio. This is normal and represents the "As Is." Once all strategic projects have been loaded into the initial project portfolio, all of the data gaps will be visible.

This data enables the PMO to evaluate project delivery opportunities and threats to the business fiscal year work plan regarding the grouping of these projects. This work can be completed in the first calendar month and it is important that this occurs.

The second month activity is oriented toward updating the project portfolio, ensuring that the data integrity is strong and that the reporting project teams are becoming consistent in their reporting.

In addition, as the "As Is" project portfolio becomes more robust in information, the PMO will identify basic status values that indicate project health. This might include color-coding such as "Red, Yellow, Green" for statuses that reflect "trouble, caution, normal."

STAGE 3: RAISING THE VISIBILITY OF PROJECT DELIVERY PROGRESS

In Stage 3, the focus is on improving progress visibility of currently active projects. In addition, the PMO mentors increase their activity with these same project teams, coaching the project managers on delivery acceleration techniques and delivery threat avoidance.

New training is developed for project managers and project team members within the PMO. The processes for publishing the operations forecasting and planning report are augmented with new processes for the asset portfolio and the strategic objectives portfolio. The entire emphasis of this stage is to strengthen useful communication on delivery bottlenecks and acceleration opportunities. In this stage, the PMO reporting, analysis, and control mechanisms should be so strong that the entire user community relies on the PMO for the information status and alerts.

In Stage 3 (Months 7 to 12), regular monthly and weekly PMO activities should include the following standard tasks:

    a.   Week 1
-     i.   Collect project schedules and project status reports for projects listed in project portfolio
-     ii.   Draft operations forecasting and planning report
-     iii.   Ongoing PMO mentoring
-     iv.   Ongoing PMO help desk support

    b.   Week 2
-     i.   Update project portfolio
-     ii.   Publish project portfolio
-     iii.   Publish operations forecasting and planning report
-     iv.   Conduct project manager portfolio review meeting
-     v.   Conduct supply side leadership/portfolio review meeting
-     vi.   Ongoing PMO mentoring
-     vii.   Ongoing PMO help desk support

    c.   Week 3
-     i.   Collect project schedules and project status reports for projects listed in project portfolio
-     ii.   Support and possibly facilitate Governance Review Board Meeting — validate and organize force rank strategic project work order
-     iii.   Ongoing PMO mentoring
-     iv.   Ongoing PMO help desk support

    d.   Week 4
-     i.   Update project portfolio
-     ii.   Publish project portfolio

        iii. Ongoing PMO mentoring

        iv. Ongoing PMO help desk support

The following new activities are recommended for the Stage 3:

1. Month 7
    a. Week 1
        i. Collect asset information and current status for projects specified in project portfolio
        ii. Draft strategic objectives portfolio report
        iii. Draft asset portfolio report
    b. Week 2
        i. Publish asset portfolio report
        ii. Publish strategic objectives portfolio report
        iii. Commence development of project manager basic training
    c. Week 3
        i. Commence development of project team member training
    d. Week 4
        i. Commence development of advanced project manager training
2. Month 8
    a. Week 1
        i. Collect asset information and current status for projects specified in project portfolio
        ii. Draft strategic objectives portfolio report
        iii. Draft asset portfolio report
    b. Week 2
        i. Publish asset portfolio report
        ii. Publish strategic objectives portfolio report
    c. Week 3
        i. Complete development of project manager basic training course
        ii. Complete development of project team member training course
    d. Week 4
        i. Complete development of the advanced project manager training course
        ii. Organize cross functional team to develop project prioritization process for enterprise
3. Month 9
    a. Week 1
        i. Collect asset status reports

   ii. Draft strategic objectives portfolio report

   iii. Draft asset portfolio report

   iv. Conduct first prioritization development team meeting

  b. Week 2

   i. Publish asset portfolio report

   ii. Publish strategic objectives portfolio report

   iii. Conduct second prioritization development team meeting

  c. Week 3

   i. Conduct third prioritization development team meeting

  d. Week 4

   i. Conduct fourth prioritization development team meeting

4. Month 10

  a. Week 1

   i. Collect asset status reports

   ii. Conduct fifth prioritization development team meeting

   iii. Draft strategic objectives portfolio report

   iv. Draft asset portfolio report

  b. Week 2

   i. Publish asset portfolio report

   ii. Publish strategic objectives portfolio report

  c. Week 3

   i. Present prioritization process and obtain approval from Governance Review Board to deploy

  d. Week 4

   i. Deploy prioritization process to project teams listed in project portfolio

5. Month 11

  a. Week 1

   i. Collect asset status reports

   ii. Draft strategic objectives portfolio report

   iii. Draft asset portfolio report

  b. Week 2

   i. Publish asset portfolio report

   ii. Publish strategic objectives portfolio report

6. Month 12

  a. Week 1

   i. Collect asset status reports

   ii. Draft strategic objectives portfolio report

   iii. Draft asset portfolio report

  b. Week 2

   i. Publish asset portfolio report

   ii. Publish strategic objectives portfolio report

STAGE 3 NEW DELIVERABLES

1. Portfolio Management Support
   a. Asset Portfolio Management Process Implementation
   b. Strategic Objective Portfolio Process Implementation
2. PMO Data Administration
   a. Ad hoc Portfolio and PMO Report Generation
3. Project Management Methodology Support
4. Project Portfolio Prioritization processes developed and deployed
5. Project Management Training Support
   a. Basic Project Manager Training with Materials
   b. Advanced Project Manager Training with Materials
   c. Project Team Member Training with Materials

STAGE 3 SYNOPSIS

The asset and strategic portfolio processes are developed and implemented. The global prioritization process for projects in the project portfolio is developed, approved and deployed. Initial project manager and team member training courses are developed and implemented. Monthly communication meetings are conducted with the project managers, departmental management, and the Governance Review Board. The operation forecasting and planning report is augmented with information from the asset and strategic portfolio processes. Project management methodology support is implemented within the PMO and PMO help desk. Project manager mentoring is provided to all projects listed in the portfolio. Every project manager of every project listed in the project portfolio has met a PMO mentor to determine if PMO assistance is required.

STAGE 4: EPM TOOL IDENTIFICATION, SELECTION, IMPLEMENTATION AND CONVERSION

In Stage 4, current project management tools are upgraded with a more comprehensive and end-to-end solution that improves data collection, data storage, data access, and project management rigor and discipline. Regular monthly and weekly PMO activities should include the following standard support efforts in Months 13 through 18.

1. Week 1
   a. Collect project schedules and project status reports for projects listed in project portfolio
   b. Collect asset status reports
   c. Draft strategic objectives portfolio report

    d.   Draft asset portfolio report

    e.   Draft operations forecasting and planning report

    f.   Ongoing PMO mentoring

    g.   Ongoing PMO help desk support

2. Week 2

    a.   Update project portfolio

    b.   Publish project portfolio

    c.   Publish asset portfolio report

    d.   Publish strategic objectives portfolio report

    e.   Publish operations forecasting and planning report

    f.   Conduct project manager portfolio review meeting

    g.   Conduct supply side leadership/portfolio review meeting

    h.   Ongoing PMO mentoring

    i.   Ongoing PMO help desk support

3. Week 3

    a.   Collect project schedules and project status reports for projects listed in project portfolio

    b.   Support and possibly facilitate Governance Review Board meeting — validate and organize force rank strategic project work order

    c.   Ongoing PMO mentoring

    d.   Ongoing PMO help desk support

4. Week 4

    a.   Update project portfolio

    b.   Publish project portfolio

    c.   Ongoing PMO mentoring

    d.   Ongoing PMO help desk support

The following new activities are recommended for the Stage 4:

1. Month 13

    a.   Week 1

        i.   Form EPM tool core team

    b.   Week 2

        i.   Initial EPM tool core team meeting

    c.   Week 3

        i.   Weekly EPM tool core team meeting — determine enterprise and PMO requirements of an EPM tool

    d.   Week 4

        i.   Weekly EPM tool core team meeting — caucus and concur on EPM tool requirements

        ii.   Complete business case for EPM tool initiative

2. Month 14

   a. Week 1
  - i. Weekly EPM tool core team meeting — approve RFI to send to EPM tool vendors

   b. Week 2
  - i. Weekly EPM tool core team meeting — identify EPM tool vendors to whom RFI should be sent

   c. Week 3
  - i. Weekly EPM tool core team meeting — review RFI status and begin reviewing vendor information
  - ii. Complete development of project team member training course

   d. Week 4
  - i. Weekly EPM tool core team meeting – complete RFI process
  - ii. Schedule selected EPM tool vendors to come in for a product demonstration

3. Month 15

   a. Week 1
  - i. Weekly EPM tool core team meeting – EPM tool vendor product demonstrations

   b. Week 2
  - i. Weekly EPM tool core team meeting — EPM tool vendor product demonstrations completed
  - ii. Create EPM vendor short list of 3 to 5 vendors and request final pricing

   c. Week 3
  - i. Weekly EPM tool core team meeting — determine final two vendor choices and validate final vendor pricing

   d. Week 4
  - i. Weekly EPM tool core team meeting — present to executive team final EPM tool vendor recommendations
  - ii. Vendor notified
  - iii. EPM tool monthly pilot started

4. Month 16

   a. Week 1 through Week 3
  - i. Weekly EPM tool core team meeting — EPM tool vendor pilot status report

   b. Week 4
  - i. Weekly EPM tool core team meeting — EPM tool vendor pilot status report — final acceptance decision

5. Month 17

   a. Week 1

       i.   Begin conversion process to new EPM tool for selected project teams

      ii.   Conduct EPM tool training for affected project teams

     iii.   Convert PMO processes to new EPM tool

  b.   Week 2 through Week 4

       i.   Continue conversion process to new EPM tool for affected project teams

      ii.   Conduct EPM tool training for affected project teams

6. Month 18

  a.   Week 1 through Week 4

       i.   Continue conversion process to new EPM tool for affected project teams

      ii.   Conduct EPM tool training for affected project teams

STAGE 4 NEW DELIVERABLES

1. EPM Tool Identification and Review Process
   a. Requirements specification
   b. Core team formed for EPM tool selection process and meeting minutes
   c. Vendor demonstrations conducted
   d. Vendor financials collected
2. EPM Tool Selection Process
   a. EPM tool business case
   b. Management approval to proceed with purchase
3. EPM Tool Implementation
   a. PMO staff trained
   b. Software installed
   c. Pilot testing
   d. Software acceptance
4. EPM Tool Conversion
   a. Top force ranked projects converted to new EPM Tool
   b. Top force ranked project managers trained on EPM Tool
   c. Basic PMO standards reports converted to new EPM Tool
5. Project Management Methodology Support
6. Project Management Training Support
   a. EPM tool training for project managers (upgraded)
   b. EPM tool training for project coordinators (upgraded)
   c. EPM tool training for project sponsors (upgraded)
7. Portfolio Management Support
   a. Project portfolio management process implementation
      i. Process conversion to EPM tool

    b.   Asset portfolio management process implementation

        i.   Process conversion to EPM tool

    c.   Strategic objective portfolio process implementation

        i.   Process conversion to EPM tool

8. PMO Data Administration

    a.   Ad hoc portfolio and PMO report generation

    b.   EPM tool training for PMO data administration staff

9. PMO Help Desk

    a.   EPM tool training for PMO help desk staff

10. Communication

    a.   Some data and reports available online, Web-based

    b.   Some updates are more timely, up to the day

STAGE 4 SYNOPSIS

The PMO can save itself a great deal of time if the PMO value proposition and supporting PMO charter are current by identifying EPM tool vendors who are determined to meet most of the PMO EPM tool requirements (based on the PMO charter). We strongly recommend that the tool evaluation team take their time to map EPM tool requirements to the PMO value model.

STAGE 5: BECOMING AN "ROI ENGINE" AND IMPLEMENTING SYSTEM CONNECTIVITY

In addition to the activities described previously, these new tasks should be completed by the PMO in Months 19 through 24.

    a.   Week 1

        i.   Project schedules and project status reports for projects electronically filed by project teams in EPM tool

        ii.   Asset status reports electronically in EPM tool

        iii.   Draft strategic objectives portfolio report from EPM tool

        iv.   Draft asset portfolio report from EPM tool

        v.   Draft operations forecasting and planning report from data in EPM tool

        vi.   Ongoing PMO mentoring

        vii.   Ongoing PMO help desk support

        viii.   Ongoing PM training conducted for workforce

    b.   Week 2

        i.   Publish project portfolio

        ii.   Publish asset portfolio report

     iii. Publish resource portfolio report
     iv. Publish strategic objectives portfolio report
     v. Publish operations forecasting and planning report
     vi. Conduct project manager portfolio review meeting
     vii. Conduct supply side leadership/portfolio review meeting
     viii. Ongoing PMO mentoring
     ix. Ongoing PMO help desk support
     x. Ongoing PM training conducted for workforce

c. Week 3
     i. Project schedules and project status reports for projects
     ii. Electronically filed in EPM tool by project teams
     iii. Support and possibly facilitate Governance Review Board meeting — validate and organize force rank strategic project work order
     iv. Ongoing PMO mentoring
     v. Ongoing PMO help desk support
     vi. Ongoing PM training conducted for workforce

d. Week 4
     i. Ongoing PMO mentoring
     ii. Ongoing PMO help desk support
     iii. Ongoing PM training conducted for workforce

The following new activities are recommended for the Stage 4:

1. Month 19

    a. Week 1
       i. Form system connectivity core team

    b. Week 2
       i. Weekly system connectivity core team meeting — review objectives and establish draft schedule and assignments

    c. Week 3
       i. Weekly system connectivity core team meeting — finalize objectives and establish baseline schedule and assignments

    d. Week 4
       i. Weekly system connectivity core team meeting — complete and approve system connectivity initiative business case
       ii. Commence project work

2. Month 20

    a. Week 1 through Week 4
       i. Weekly system connectivity core team meeting — status report (4 to 8 weeks of estimated effort to establish system test bed per legacy system and complete testing and

    acceptance for HRIS, G/L, Labor Distribution, and Time
    Entry Systems)
3. Month 21
    a. Week 1 through Week 4
        i. Weekly system connectivity core team meeting — status
           report (4 to 8 weeks of estimated effort to establish system
           test bed per Legacy System and complete testing and ac-
           ceptance for HRIS, G/L, Labor Distribution, and Time
           Entry Systems)
        ii. Conversion processes testing completed for all legacy
            systems affected
        iii. Acceptance testing completed for all legacy systems affected
4. Month 22
    a. Week 1
        i. Resource portfolio management processes implemented
        ii. System connectivity turned on selected application (HRIS)
5. Month 23
    a. Week 1
        i. System connectivity turned on for selected application
           (G/L)
        ii. System connectivity turned on for selected application
            (Labor Distribution)
6. Month 24
    a. Week 1
        i. System connectivity turned on for selected application
           (Time Entry per Project Team)

STAGE 5 NEW DELIVERABLES

1. Portfolio Management Support
    a. Resource portfolio management process implementation
    b. Process conversion to EPM tool
2. Project Management Training Support
    a. Basic project manager training with materials (upgraded)
    b. Advanced project manager training with materials (upgraded)
    c. Project team member training with materials (upgraded)
3. System Connectivity
    a. Existing time entry systems migrated to EPM tool
    b. Business legacy systems integration, i.e., G/L/Labor, HRIS

STAGE 5 SYNOPSIS

In this stage, the recently implemented EPM tool is connected to business
legacy systems in order to improve the flow of information in a more timely

and efficient manner. This might include legacy systems such as HRIS, G/L, Labor Collection, and others as deemed necessary by management.

Additionally, the resource portfolio management processes are enabled in this stage. This portfolio is typically the last of the portfolio processes to be brought online. This is due to the complex nature of the data content and logical relationships, both internal to the data and external to legacy system files.

SUMMARY

Each implementation of a PMO is unique. However, it is of utmost importance to have a roadmap and to customize it to your requirements. We stress that in customizing the roadmap, it is absolutely critical that the PMO understand its value proposition. These PMO requirements must be defined as part of the plan for building the PMO. Without this, the PMO will not be able to detect or react quickly to potential changes in the delivery climate during the 2-year PMO deployment plan.

As the PMO completes each stage in the roadmap, the PMO should re-evaluate the tangible and intangible value that has been provided to that point in time. This is a good time to adjust the next stage of the roadmap accordingly to accelerate or avoid threats to the PMO deployment plan.

In conclusion, the focus of the PMO roadmap is centered on the PMO providing portfolio management support in a manner that raises awareness on project progress. It is mission critical that the PMO maintain the image of a consultative nature in order to obtain accurate information and be in a position to facilitate bottleneck visibility from the data reported by various project teams.

QUESTIONS

28.1 Discuss the stages of the PMO roadmap and their relationship to each other.

28.2 Explain Stage 1 and its relationship to defining the PMO value proposition.

28.3 Explain how Stage 2 can establish consistent project delivery expectations from the three key work groups of project managers, their management, and the business partners.

28.4   Discuss Stage 3 and its dependency on Stage 2 task completion.

28.5   Selecting an EPM tool is important to the PMO. Explain under what other types of circumstances this selection, implementation, and conversion could take place in other "releases" of the PMO deployment plan.

28.6   Why is implementation of resource portfolio management recommended in the last stage? Explain.

28.7   List some of the likely value opportunities from each stage that support the need for a PMO.

28.8   Why would the Governance Board want to know the status of the resource portfolio?

28.9   What should be the consequences endured by a non-reporting project team if it misses reporting the following: project status, resource labor, project schedule.

28.10   Explain the EPM tool identification/selection/implementation processes.

29

SUSTAINING THE PMO VALUE — MOVING FROM THE SUPPLY SIDE TO THE MARKET SIDE

WHAT NEXT AFTER THE LOW-HANGING FRUIT

Usually, PMOs arise out of some kind of crisis. It requires some very compelling arguments to convince an executive team to forfeit investment in "exciting ventures" and invest money in some internal infrastructure. Often, we see a PMO born out of some highly visible project that is failing or out of product development cycles that have fallen deeply behind the competition. Sometimes, it is simply because executives are tired of hearing all of the excuses for why every project is late, over budget, or not within scope.

With a crisis, there is always low-hanging fruit. We are not suggesting, by any means, that this low-hanging fruit can be picked by just anyone. Assuming that most people are not downright stupid, we can conclude that crises occur because of things that are not obvious to the people involved. It takes someone with significant experience and leadership skills to get an organization out of a crisis.

Nonetheless, as Peter Senge points out in his book *The Fifth Discipline,* organizations do tend to pull themselves out of a crisis. The big question a PMO must answer is, "What next?"

We suggested in Part II that, following Dr. Deming's philosophy, it is wise to bring the project management system and other delivery systems within the supply chain under control before attempting to improve. To bring the project management system under control, we suggested that the PMO needed to implement a combination of PMBOK® practices and Critical Chain methodology (or equivalents). Some implementations of Six Sigma may also help to reduce variability in some areas. This combination will move the organization toward the system goal of 95% or more of all projects finishing on time, on budget, and within scope.

Part II discussed the other systems within the supply chain that also need to meet Deming's goal of predictability. When organizations continue to allow bad practices (ones that negatively affect customers) to continue throughout the organization, it is like digging a deeper hole that will eventually bury the organization. As Dr. Goldratt intimated, "if you find yourself in a hole, the first thing to do is to stop digging!"

The next step must be to ensure that the organization will have increasing and sustainable long-term demand for its current and future products and services. This implies that the PMO must initiate some projects of its own and have these projects approved by the Governance Board. Further, the PMO must have or develop the ability to influence the project mix of the entire organization.

CHANGING THE PROJECT MIX

Often at start-up a PMO recruits project management, support, and technical skills. These skills are usually sufficient to get the organization started. However, to sustain the organization, the PMO must be able to influence which projects are chosen by the Governance Board.

We recall working with a process improvement team (performing the functions of a PMO), which correctly identified the constraint of the company to be in the market. The company, over the previous two years, saw a decline in demand for some of their products. This decline put the company in a position of having excess capacity, especially in the form of employees.

The process improvement team also saw the company executives dealing with a constant crisis in sales, leading to short-term initiatives to find quick sales. However, this effort was happening at the expense of a sustainable, longer-term strategy. Every resource was commandeered to work on the short-term crisis, at the expense of the longer-term marketing effort.

While the process improvement team, reporting to one of the senior executives, continually pointed out that the marketing projects were not being worked on, the executive team continued to use precious resources to work on short-term sales.

The outcome is almost 100% predictable. Without some amazing luck, these organizations always revert to layoffs when the economy or the demand for their particular products decreases.

In hindsight, we believe that one of the big shortcomings of this team was in its composition. This team lacked experienced marketing resources from the outset. At the same time, we commend this team for having the courage to point out the shortcoming to senior executives. It is unfortunate, in this case, that the executives did not heed the message.

There is another reason to examine and change the project mix. There is always a lot of change occurring within an industry. Yet the organization cannot digest or endure massive constant change. In fact, most changes (see comments in Part II) do not bring any improvement to the organization. Therefore, every organization must have some research projects that will constantly examine change and identify which changes will be good for the organization. Some percentage of every organization's overall project budget must be devoted to R&D.

To sustain PMO value, we advise the PMO to promote a project mix that:

1. Moves the organization to true marketing — identifying those market needs and opportunities that can make the organization number one in its industry, even in a not-for-profit organization. This effort must be combined with finding ways, after product development, to bring the customers to prefer the organization instead of its competitors.

2. Researches better practices in project management. If you want to be eons ahead of the competition, you must be prepared to adopt practices that, by definition, most of the world is not using today. Therefore, you need people to be looking for these practices, researching and finding ways to pilot and adopt these with low risk to your organization.

3. Researches better practices in all aspects of the supply chain. As Collins points out in Good to Great, a company does not need to be the first to adopt a new technology. However, the company needs to identify that this new technology is a useful or necessary tool to support what customers want. Pioneers have arrows in their backs, but some pioneers staked out some valuable real estate that sustained them for a lifetime. A healthy organization can survive a few arrows. Being too late to market could mean wasting valuable energy just trying to stay alive.

TWO PERMANENT MARKETING
PROJECTS NEED PMO SUPPORT

The two necessary marketing projects are described in Chapter 9 and Chapter 10. In brief, one of these projects looks for the one factor or single focus that will make your organization number one in the industry.

This idea of focus is not new. We have seen the concept promoted by marketing guru Jay Abraham, who describes the need to have a "Unique Selling Proposition." What distinguishes your company from every competitor in your industry? For example, a small, family-owned ice cream chain describes their product as delicious; their unique selling proposition is that they only sell what they don't eat. Similarly, Collins describes the "Hedgehog Concept" in his book *Good to Great* and Goldratt describes the search for the single factor that should be developed to be exponentially better than the competition.

The reason we claim that this ongoing project must have the focus of the PMO is that it requires multiple, cross-functional projects to be timed and coordinated in order to have a successful conclusion. Imagine, for example, that you have the fiasco that AOL created several years ago, when they developed enormous demand for their product (a successful marketing project), but did not develop sufficient capacity to deliver (a necessary operations project to support the marketing project). Customers abandoned AOL due to the constant busy signals and poor service.

The marketing department must have the cooperation of other functional areas and multiple projects to achieve their goals. Who better than the PMO to bring the necessary coordination, assurance and value to this effort?

The second marketing project is the compelling marketing offer — the achievement of competitive edge with existing products and services, by identifying industry-rooted policies that drive customers crazy. This goes beyond the stand-alone efforts that go on in engineering departments, developing and enhancing products. These efforts are admirable. However, we continually see that the better mousetrap or product often does not win a competitive battle. As above, this project often requires collaboration and cooperation from operations, finance, and sales to make it work. Other functional areas may also be involved.

This collection of projects is not like the typical "program management" that you see in high technology organizations. Most organizations that do program management have a program manager who coordinates multiple projects related to the development of a product line. Often, they have influence over engineering and manufacturing relationships.

What we are describing is different. It requires much broader coordination across more functional areas. It requires significant research and work outside of the product development.

The PMO value is to use its influence, trust, and multi-project coordination ability to drive down the cycle time of these vital marketing projects. In addition, by using the good principals of portfolio management, the investment in multiple projects must be managed to ensure early and sufficient return. The PMO contributes by bringing the Governance Board the correct vision of these projects working together in alignment, not isolation, to secure the future of the organization both short and long term.

RESEARCHING BETTER PRACTICES IN PROJECT MANAGEMENT

The PMO needs to constantly look for practices that are better than "best." Most so-called best practices have received that tag because they are already accepted and being used by many of the large organizations. For at least several years, these "best practices" have been promoted at conferences, have been the subject of several books, and are in the mainstream.

To be better than your competition, your organization must actively seek the non-traditional — the breakthroughs. This does not mean inventing something from scratch. As Marshall McLuhan, the great Canadian philosopher and oracle of the communications age, said, "You can see the future, because the future is now." Any exciting new methods are already being tried, but only by a small percentage of organizations.

When we talk about new practices at conferences and in training programs, we often hear the response "It makes sense. It is what we should do, but our company will never implement it." This reaction is common because most people recognize that implementing a breakthrough practice will require some senior executives to approve new policies and measurements. This kind of culture change is beyond the periscope of most people working within a functional silo. Further, so many bright people have seen their organizations practice common nonsense, and reject common sense, that they have given up on trying to change their organization.

The PMO must be the opposite of the naysayers. Therefore, the PMO needs some people who are not afraid to push the envelope on project management, to proactively seek out those tools that will support drastically shorter project cycle times with even greater predictability.

When looking for these better than best practices, you will hear about some of them at conferences. However, PMO people should be looking beyond their national confines. We must stop keeping our heads in the sand and look at what other countries are doing. Attend conferences in other countries. Read books. Seek to meet people from other countries and other industries. Get out of the box.

RESEARCHING BETTER PRACTICES IN THE SUPPLY CHAIN

Pure research often has no immediate ROI. However, it is absolutely necessary for survival. One of the big problems we have witnessed with some

R&D organizations is their tendency to research without regard to the needs of the market. Another big problem is the tendency for most R&D dollars to be spent in product research, with very few dollars invested in process research.

Today, we are witnessing increasing evidence of supply chains competing with each other, more so than companies or products. For example, it is not Wal-Mart competing against other superstores. It is Wal-Mart, linked electronically from the individual store's cash registers right back to the manufacturers supplying the goods, competing against other superstores that do not have such links. We worked with a T-shirt manufacturer who prepares its Wal-Mart orders with customized pricing and sales tags, shipping directly to each store in time to meet customer demand.

Another example is Amazon. Amazon and Borders teamed together to provide a combination of online and retail offerings. Further, Amazon teamed with electronics and other manufacturers to provide an online superstore.

The PMO added value is to proactively drive the Governance Board to be aware of deficiencies and imbalances in research. The PMO can also add value by proactively driving research across multiple disciplines in the supply chain. It is important to have marketing, engineering, and production working together with suppliers, distributors, and retailers to find new ways to satisfy the markets.

SUMMARY

The PMO must initiate its own projects to ensure it remains on its own process of ongoing improvement. This is a necessity in order for the PMO to continue to add value to the rest of the organization, after it has picked the low-hanging fruit. To sustain value, the PMO needs to concentrate its efforts in three areas:

1. Marketing — especially to coordinate the multidisciplinary breakthroughs that involve projects in different functional areas. Also, the PMO has a major contribution to make in driving down cycle times across functional areas in the two vital marketing projects described in Part II.
2. Project Management Practices – The PMO must look for better than "best practices". The goal of the PMO should be to find whatever the "best practices" will be in the next generation and implement them before the competition does. To find these great ideas, the PMO staff should be looking outside of their own country and industry.
3. Supply Chain Improvements — It is no longer sufficient to improve just your own organization. You must also pay attention to the com-

petitiveness of your supply chain. The PMO can add value here by ensuring that some pure research is done by multidisciplinary teams to proactively seek future directions and improvements that will leverage the existing company resources.

QUESTIONS

29.1   Why must the PMO be concerned with marketing? Why not just leave marketing to the marketing department?

29.2   What unique contribution can the PMO make to marketing projects, which will significantly help the marketing department?

29.3   How should the PMO interact with the Governance Board to help achieve the right project mix?

29.4   True or False: The best project management practices can always be found in your own industry.

29.5   True or False: You do not need to spend the extra money to look outside your country for the best project management practices.

29.6   If someone suggests a change to another project management practice, how can you quickly determine if it is worth evaluating?

29.7   What value does the PMO have to contribute to an improved supply chain? What might a PMO have that an individual project manager from a functional area might not have?

29.8   Is it possible for a PMO to outlive its usefulness? State your assumptions and reasoning behind your answer.

This book has free materials available for download from the Web Added Value™ Resource Center at www.jrosspub.com.

30

CONCLUSIONS

THE NEXT STEPS

There are many opportunities to bring value in the work place through a PMO. The question is where to start. Business case approval will be important. Therefore, this activity is worth consideration as a first step. Also important is having executive sponsorships identified and agreed to.

Remember, when the PMO is first deployed, the PMO will be entering the work culture where the current is the swiftest. Be steady and sure as you go forward with deployment. The current has many pushes and pulls that are unseen. Because it is natural for people to resist change, do not rush at full speed to directly force changes. We have been strongly recommending that you must correctly and in sequence overcome the various layers of resistance to change. This requires more subtle and indirect approaches in the face of a workplace culture fraught with high stress and anxiety. Once the PMO becomes perceived as an authority figure or "Process Cop," the deployment effort will become more difficult to gain work force buy-in.

Identify the segments of the workplace that will be most likely to accept the PMO and set the PMO deployment plan to include these groups early on. This might include functional units, divisions, or programs. Let the success of the PMO for these participants develop the positive peer pressure that isolates the functional units that resist. This will take time, but the PMO needs at least 2 years to incrementally mature. Those functional units that may have initially been unable to jump on the PMO bandwagon will do so as time permits. Remember, you are building a "customer-focused" PMO. You want people in the workplace to seek you out for assistance in project delivery. This is how the PMO builds sustaining value and helps the organization grow in value and competitively within its industry.

As the PMO begins deployment, several key themes of the PMO must remain in the forefront. These are:

- Keep looking for ways to improve project delivery speed.
- Be vigilant of workplace behavior for opportunities and threats.
- Quantify and qualify PMO value every six months.
- Seek to implement common tools and processes that support portfolio management in a single data repository manner.

ANALYZING THE WORKPLACE

What is the personality of the workplace that the PMO will be serving? The PMO must be able to distinguish what it is today and where it needs to be over time. This information is used in constructing the PMO deployment plan regarding value and speed. High anxiety work cultures require careful execution early on to set the PMO framework in place. The choice sometimes requires a slower initial implementation, to be sure of gaining the buy-in before mandating standards and methodologies.

HITTING THE "SWEET SPOT"

The PMO implementation focus should be clearly aimed at the major development oriented project teams that are vital to achieving organization goals. It is here that the PMO can instill the cognitive skills the project teams need to recognize and meet project delivery acceleration opportunities and delivery threats.

The more the environment encourages people to come to the PMO, rather than the PMO forcing or enforcing, the better and faster the change will take place. As one team begins to understand the value of these new PMO provided skills, tools and information, other project teams will see and learn as well. The natural competitiveness among project teams, team members, and functional units will help to proliferate the new techniques that successful project teams have discovered. They will "own" this discovery. Thus, the PMO can sit outside the team peer group to simply provide assistance as requested.

Team members on successful project teams will be perceived as good people to work with because they will have learned how to collaborate to beat the project estimate for delivery. This is the sweet spot for the PMO. When projects complete early, business grows because the cost of development was less than predicted. The remaining monies left over can be reallocated to other projects needing funds.

If your PMO is to have any hope of sustaining itself, the PMO must accomplish this feat of delivery acceleration. In collecting and aggregating project delivery data, the PMO can make this happen by raising project progress visibility for everyone involved.

ROI FROM IMPLEMENTING A PMO

Implementing portfolio management with the simplest of approaches will bring value to the organization because of the visibility of progress the portfolio processes will bring about. Organizations should expect to see a minimum 10% return against the fiscal year budget for planned development project work on the PMO investment (ROI).

The key to achieving the PMO ROI in the first year is identifying the difference between the current organization project culture and what it should be. These gaps can immediately be reduced and eventually eliminated over time. As project management process improvements are achieved, delivery value will follow. But the PMO must perform an excellent job of communicating progress and issues through portfolio management processes to the workforce and senior executives. This must be a closed-loop communication cycle that communicates to all levels of the workforce to achieve the ROI.

THE VALUE OF PROJECT MANAGEMENT REALIZED

As the PMO becomes recognized by executives as a vital tool to help them achieve their goals, its influence and positive outcomes can also significantly increase. The area of portfolio management holds great potential. Organizations must do more than correctly perform projects. They must choose the correct projects. While many PMOs begin their life focused on PM methodology, with significant results, we believe that the role of portfolio management holds even greater value.

FINDING OUTSIDE SUPPORT

PMO support is available commercially through many consulting firms and non-profit project management businesses. The Project Management Institute (PMI®) should become the centerpiece of outside information for any PMO. PMI® represents the largest association of people seeking project management value anywhere. This organization is already driving many project managers to become experts, as noted by the PMI® certification of Project Management Professional (PMP®).

CONCLUSIONS

We hope we have provided sufficient information in "blueprint" fashion to help you be more successful in implementing a high value PMO.

The information provided in this book has been a labor of love, passion, and intrigue. We have demonstrated that implementing a PMO is vital to sustaining any organization, yet not rocket science. The critical success factors of implementing a PMO involve dealing with people, changing workforce behavior dynamics, and raising progress visibility.

In 2001, more than 1,000,000 people lost their jobs. In 2002, many businesses failed or lost significant shareholder value where the shareholder was eventually left holding the bag. Ignoring the cases of executive fraud, what was the common element that led to these job losses? In our opinion, their organizations could not execute the correct portfolio of projects quickly enough to meet opportunities and threats. Too many people in these organizations were working on the wrong projects, or moving those projects to completion too slowly.

If you choose to implement a PMO, you have many choices on where to focus the PMO team's efforts. We beseech you to clearly define the PMO value proposition as a starting point. Remember that your customers include the executives, project managers, resource managers and team members. Check your customer satisfaction frequently, and adjust accordingly. After all, if you cannot define and measure the value of the PMO, then of what value is it?

We invite you to comment and share your stories for future revisions of this book. Please send e-mail to Gerryikendall@cs.com or Steve@pmousa.com.

THE PMO
MATURITY MODEL

	Level I	Level II	Level III
	PMO Defining Value	**PMO Organized**	**Searching for Delivery Value**
Scope Management	Poor definition of in-scope or out-of-scope items.	Scope statement developed by supply-side project manager, often with IT emphasis. Functional requirements are poor.	Functional requirements are better defined/in-scope and out-of-scope items are identified, causes of rework are documented.
Time Management	Project teams are in silos. Not aware of team member utilization.	Project managers understand their project's position among all strategic projects.	Project managers are using PMO for info source for delivery acceleration. Opportunities and/or delivery delay threats among strategic projects.
Resource Management	Resources are sought as tasks begin. Projects start late and most finish late. Project and resource managers are constantly fighting over resources.	Resource portfolio established.	Resource utilization rates known for planned, ETC and actual for 80% of resources. Strategic resource is identified.

	Level I	Level II	Level III
	PMO Defining Value	**PMO Organized**	**Searching for Delivery Value**
Communications Management	Standard reporting process for project delivery status is not implemented.	Periodic status meetings; reports as requested by management.	Regular PM community status meetings to raise delivery visibility.
Risk Management	Risks are not considered outside of PM's informal thought process.	Top risks for major projects have been identified.	Top project delivery acceleration opportunities and delivery threats are known.
Quality Management	Project teams do not understand their customers' needs.	PMO mentors are available to help PM's determine customer needs.	Project team members are focused on meeting customer needs that affect organization goals.
Cost Management	Costs not estimated or tracked. PM does not receive project reports.	Project portfolio budget identified for fiscal year.	Project financials (plan vs. actual) are tracked monthly. Total project portfolio cost is available.
Procurement Management	Vendors and contractors are not considered part of the project team.	Vendors/contractors are managed to end dates only.	Contractors are reporting progress monthly. Earlier delivery is sought for critical path items.
Project Integration	No standard project definitions, terminology, scheduling or methodology is used.	Projects managed on milestone reporting.	Standards are applied in group meetings of project managers to seek delivery acceleration opportunities and threats.

	Level IV	Level V	Level VI
	Portfolio Management	Community Buy-In	Project Teams Delivering on Schedule
Scope Management	Scope interdependencies between projects are understood.	Executive buy-in and PM community buy-in exists for combined scope of all projects.	Projects are completing within scope most of the time.
Time Management	All important projects are being tracked. Projected scheduling delays are identified.	Governance Board is operational and responsible for project portfolio delivery results. Some projects are deactivated.	Some projects are completing early.
Resource Management	Resource portfolio applied to plan project delivery dates. Resource labor is electronically entered by resource.	Projects are staggered according to availability of strategic resource(s). The entire customer community is educated about the strategic resource, and does their best not to waste it.	Resource assignments are calibrated to project portfolio through resource portfolio. Resource needs are manageable without excessive peaks and valleys, across all disciplines.
Communications Management	Project managers understand the status of other projects in the portfolio and how they relate to their project. Information is available to PMs online.	Operations plans are published to the Governance Board from the PMO. Sponsors, teams, functional executives and other stakeholders have accurate information that they need.	All project managers and teams have information in time to take preventative action on project threats, and to take advantage of acceleration opportunities.
Risk Management	Contingency plans are developed for delivery that can be mitigated.	Risk management is normal part of status reporting. Risk mitigation is supported by Governance Board, sponsors and functional management.	Project teams are risks seizing opportunities.

	Level IV	Level V	Level VI
	Portfolio Management	**Community Buy-In**	**Project Teams Delivering on Schedule**
Quality Management	Project managers know the impact of their project on the end customer and the market.	Metrics are established that support quality goals. Boundaries between functional disciplines are torn down.	Quality issues preventing on-time delivery are documented and being addressed.
Cost Management	Project managers understand how project acceleration and delay can impact the budget, and take responsibility for it.	Project vendors, team members and functional executives understand their impact on project financial objectives.	Project teams are collectively managing their project budget within 10% of budget plan.
Procurement Management	Problem vendors/ contractors across projects are identified.	Vendors/contractors have incentives to seek delivery acceleration on critical items.	Subcontractors manage projects using same system as company.
Project Integration	Procedures developed to manage changes, track performance against planned, report on all projects in the portfolio.	Increased number of PMPs. A PMIS is being used throughout life-cycle.	Planning process always balances scope, schedule, and resources without overloading the system.

	Level VII	Level VIII
	Project Teams Calibrated with Portfolios More Projects in FY	**Organization Delivering**
Scope Management	Project teams are using their delivery knowledge of scope interdependencies between projects to meet scope requirements.	All strategic objectives of the organization are achieved in the FY.
Time Management	Everyone understands his or her workload and how it relates to project priorities. Strategic resources are no longer causing project delays.	Over 95% of projects are completing on time worst case. 10% of projects are completing early.

	Level VII **Project Teams Calibrated with Portfolios More Projects in FY**	Level VIII **Organization Delivering**
Resource Management	Team-based performance process has been implemented. All resources look for acceleration opportunities and threats.	Resource utilization rates are stable. Organization is delivering more projects without needing to add resources.
Communications Management	Resource utilization rates are improving and in alignment with Project Portfolios. Bad multitasking is visibly reduced.	Every stakeholder under-stands and supports the connections between organization goals, projects, resources and assets. Suggestions for acceleration and better project mix are available without solicitation.
Risk Management	Portfolios are integrated to allow changes in one project or resource area to be proactively addressed when they impact other projects or resources.	The combined project portfolio is balanced so that even several disasters do not affect meeting organization goals.
Quality Management	Metrics, procedures and training are used to accelerate delivery opportunities and decrease delivery threats.	A process of ongoing improvement is in place, with statistical controls and identification of biggest leverage points for improved quality.
Cost Management	The Governance Board is taking a global view of all project portfolio costs. Governance Board is balancing the portfolio by investing more in marketing and in strategic assets.	Governance Board actively reallocates excess project budget to other project work.
Procurement Management	Vendors are integrated into project planning process and use same procedures and methodology.	Vendors/contractors cannot be differentiated from organization staff.
Project Integration	Project selection is a formal process, adhered to and respected by all functional leaders. Governance Board demands and supports project management methodology from all functional areas.	PM maturity is integrated with all other processes and is continually reviewed for improvement.

BIBLIOGRAPHY

Larry Bossidy and Ram Charan, *Execution: The Discipline of Getting Things Done,* Random House, New York, 2002.

Oded Cohen and Domenico Lepore, *Deming and Goldratt,* North River Press, Great Barrington, MA, 1999.

Jim Collins, *Good to Great,* Harper Collins, New York, 2001.

Robert G. Cooper, Scott J. Edgett, and Elko J. Kleinschmidt, *Portfolio Management for New Products,* 2nd ed., Perseus Publishing, Cambridge, 2001.

Thomas Corbett, *Throughput Accounting,* North River Press, Great Barrington, MA, 1998.

Eliyahu M. Goldratt, *The Goal,* North River Press, Great Barrington, MA, 1984.

Eliyahu M. Goldratt, *It's Not Luck,* North River Press, Great Barrington, MA, 1994.

Eliyahu M. Goldratt, *Critical Chain,* North River Press, Great Barrington, MA, 1996.

Eliyahu M. Goldratt, *Necessary But Not Sufficient,* North River Press, Great Barrington, MA, 2000.

Eliyahu M. Goldratt, Theory of Constraints Self-Paced Learning Program, in CD format. For further information, see www.tocinternational.com:

Operations
Finance and Measurements
Project Management
Distribution
Marketing
Sales and Buy-in
Managing People
Strategy

Mikel Harry and Richard Schroeder, *Six Sigma,* Doubleday, New York, 2000.

Institute of Management Accountants and Arthur Andersen, Theory of Constraints (TOC) Management System Fundamentals Statement Number 4HH, IMA, 1999.

Gerald I. Kendall, *Securing the Future: Strategies for Exponential Growth Using the Theory of Constraints,* St. Lucie Press, Boca Raton, FL, 1997.

Gerald I. Kendall, *Choosing the Right Project Mix,* White Paper available at www.iil.com, 2001.

Gerald I. Kendall and Steve Rollins, *How to Get Value Out of a PMO,* White Paper available at www.iil.com, 2002.

Gerald I. Kendall, George Pitagorsky, and David Hulett, *Integrating Critical Chain and the PMBOK®,* White Paper available at www.iil.com, 2001.

Harold Kerzner, Ph.D., *Project Management — A Systems Approach to Planning, Scheduling and Managing,* 8th ed., John Wiley & Sons, New York, 2003.

Victoria Mabin and Steven Balderstone, *The World of the Theory of Constraints,* St. Lucie Press, Boca Raton, FL, 2000.

Neil Rackham, *Spin Selling,* McGraw Hill, New York, 1988.

Donald J. Wheeler, *Understanding Variation, The Key to Managing Chaos,* 2nd ed., SPC Press, Knoxville, TN, 2000.

INDEX